Writing in a Speaking World

The Pragmatics of Literacy in Anglo-Saxon Inscriptions and Old English Poetry

MEDIEVAL AND RENAISSANCE
TEXTS AND STUDIES

VOLUME 445

Writing in a Speaking World

The Pragmatics of Literacy in Anglo-Saxon Inscriptions and Old English Poetry

Peter Orton

ARIZONA CENTER FOR MEDIEVAL
AND RENAISSANCE STUDIES

Tempe, Arizona
2014

THE ARIZONA CENTER FOR
MEDIEVAL &
RENAISSANCE
STUDIES

Published by ACMRS (Arizona Center for Medieval and Renaissance Studies)
Tempe, Arizona
© 2014 Arizona Board of Regents for Arizona State University.
All Rights Reserved.

Library of Congress Cataloging-in-Publication Data

Orton, Peter (Peter R.)
 Writing in a Speaking World : the Pragmatics of Literacy in Anglo-Saxon
Inscriptions and Old English Poetry / Peter Orton.
    pages cm. -- (Medieval and Renaissance Texts and Studies ; Volume 445)
 Includes bibliographical references.
 ISBN 978-0-86698-493-5 (alk. paper)
 1. English literature--Old English, ca. 450-1100--Criticism, Textual. 2.
Literacy--England--History--To 1500. 3. Inscriptions--England--Early works
to 1800. 4. Literature and society--England--History--To 1500. I. Title.
 PR179.L57O78 2014
 829'.09--dc23

2014003679

Cover Art:
Sculpture of Pythagoras within the tympanum at the right bay of the royal portal of
Chartres Cathedral, situated on top of the middle column of the right jamb. Image is
in the public domain.

∞
This book is made to last. It is set in Adobe Caslon Pro,
smyth-sewn and printed on acid-free paper to library specifications.
Printed in the United States of America

For F. J. R.

Table of Contents

Preface and Acknowledgments	xi
Abbreviations	xiii
CHAPTER 1: INTRODUCTION	1
CHAPTER 2: DEIXIS AND INCIPIENT LITERACY	37
§1. The 'speaking' text	37
§2. Speech, writing and incipient literacy	38
§3. Coding time and receiving time	42
§4. The inscribed medium as surrogate 'speaker' and 'hearer'	43
§5. The book as first-person speaker: Anglo-Saxon scribal colophons	46
§6. Deixis	48
§7. The deictic gap in literacy	50
§8. Closing the deictic gap	51
§9. Medium-deixis in Anglo-Saxon inscriptions	52
§10. The written 'speech'	53
§11. Summary	55
CHAPTER 3: ANGLO-SAXON INSCRIPTIONS	59
§1. The beginnings of literacy in Anglo-Saxon England: The runic and roman alphabets	59
§2. The inscriptions	61
§3. The forms of inscriptions	63
§4. Runes or roman	85
§5. Old English or Latin	88
§6. Language and script	88
§7. The content of Anglo-Saxon inscriptions	89
§8. The deictic forms of Anglo-Saxon inscriptions	90
§9. Medium deixis	90

§10. Place deixis	93
§11. Person deixis	94
§12. Absence of deixis	94
§13. Summary	94

Chapter 4: From Inscription to Manuscript Text — 97

§1. Artifacts and books	97
§2. The speaking text and the speaking work	98
§3. The name of the poet	112
§4. Cynewulf	115
§5. Cynewulf's runic signatures	121
§6. The reception of Cynewulf's poems	127
§7. Runic and roman in Cynewulf's poems	130
§8. The Ruthwell Cross inscription and *The Dream of the Rood*	132
§9. Summary	135

Chapter 5: Experiments in Literacy: The Old English *Riddles* — 139

§1. The Old English *Riddles*	139
§2. Speaker or observer? Two forms of *Riddle*	144
§3. The homodiegetic *Riddles*	146
§4. The runic *Riddles*	149
§5. *Riddle* 42, 'Cock and Hen': form, orality, and literacy	162
§6. *Riddle* 47, 'Bookmoth' and *Riddle* 60, 'Pen': The materiality of writing	165
§7. *The Husband's Message*	172
§8. Summary	183

Chapter 6: The Disembodied Speaker — 187

§1. The speaker *in propria persona*	187
§2. The Old English lyrics, the *Riddles*, and wisdom poetry	188
§3. Genre and form in the lyrics: autodiegetic narratives, explicitly autobiographical	190
§4. The content of the lyrics: the speaker in space and time; past happiness, present misery; separation and absence	191
§5. The problem of identification	192
§6. Narratological issues: speaker, narrator, poet	194
§7. The solitary writer	201
§8. The Old English lyrics: history or fiction?	212

Table of Contents ix

CHAPTER 7: CONCLUSIONS 231
  §1. Runes versus roman in inscriptions 231
  §2. Runes versus roman in manuscripts 232
  §3. Concurrent orality and literacy; thinking through form 235
  §4. Inscriptions and the deictic gap 238
  §5. Inscriptions and manuscript writings: distinctions and intersections 239
  §6. The transcription of oral utterances in the roman alphabet 241
  §7. Literacy, psychology, and fiction 244
  §8. Other directions 246
  §9. 'Incipient' literacy? 249

Bibliography 253

Preface and Acknowledgments

Preliterate societies know language only in its spoken and heard form. Under these conditions, the formulation and reception of utterances inevitably coincide in space and time, or (to put it in less abstract terms) the hearer hears what the speaker says where and when he or she says it. When literacy arrives, this unity remains undisturbed in spoken exchanges, but written communication dissolves it: having written, the writer may move on or die, leaving the text to await the attentions of a reader, or may send it elsewhere; in either case, the writer is usually absent when his or her work is read. Writing thus splits linguistic communication into two moments: 'coding time' and 'receiving time' respectively. The chief purpose of this book is to consider some of the manifestations of this split in Old English writings.

The Anglo-Saxons acquired literacy in the roman alphabet at the time of their conversion to Christianity in the seventh century; but there was some literacy in runes before this. Inscriptions on hard surfaces, initially only in runes but later, after the conversion, in the roman alphabet too, must therefore be considered among the very earliest manifestations of English writing. An examination of the whole corpus of Anglo-Saxon inscriptions in both runic and roman scripts and in both Old English and Latin reveals, not only a heavy preponderance of 'deictic' forms—utterances, that is, depending for their understanding at least partly on an awareness by the reader of the nature and position of the inscribed vehicle—but also assertions of a kind which would scarcely have been possible prior to literacy. These inscriptions, and some elaborations of the forms they exemplify in manuscripts, are examined here as illustrations of certain emergent and intrinsically literary forms and genres in the period. Other debts owed by manuscript literature—chiefly the works of the Old English poet Cynewulf, the Old English *Riddles*, and the poem *The Husband's Message*—to the epigraphical legacy are also discussed, and some Anglo-Saxon attitudes to both spoken and written language, for which they offer important evidence, are considered. Finally, a chapter is devoted to a group of lyric poems in the tenth-century Exeter Book. Here an attempt is made to bring out some of the processes and difficulties involved in 'reclaiming' the deictic first person pronoun from the various impersonal uses to which it was put in inscriptions and in many of the other poetic texts I have mentioned, so that it could fulfil the same familiar function in writing as it had continued to do in speech: that of pointing directly to the human source of utterance. The difficulties lay chiefly in the fact that writing had some rather profound consequences for deictic reference: paradoxically, writing made it more 'natural' to use the first-person pronoun as a reference to non-human or even material 'speakers' than for human beings *in propria persona*. First-person lyric poetry was not, it seems, achieved in the Old English alliterative tradition without a struggle with some very fundamental problems arising from the individual's expression of his or her interior experiences. The lyrics also have some peculiarities which give them a special interest and significance for the emergence and development of the human subject in the early period of English literacy. Finally, the concluding chapter tries to address some basic issues of literary history and theory on which the texts examined here have a bearing.

My interest in Anglo-Saxon literacy and its manifestations in Old English poetry goes back many years, though the actual writing of this book was much advanced by a period of sabbatical leave in 2002, funded partly by Queen Mary, The University of London, and partly by the British Arts and Humanities Research Council (as it then was). I am grateful to these bodies for their financial support. Papers read to various research seminars and other scholarly assemblies, including Queen Mary's Language Research Seminar, the London Medieval Society, the London University Old and Middle English Research Seminar, the English Departments of the Universities of Leeds and Dundee, and Queen's University Belfast, enabled me to test some of the ideas developed here on scholarly audiences, and I thank all of them for their comments and criticisms. Numerous friends and academic colleagues (the categories happily overlap) have also been kind enough to read and discuss with me earlier drafts of the book or parts of it, or have answered my queries; here I should mention in particular Ruth Evans, Tom Shippey, Rory McTurk, Jane Roberts, Katie Wales, Jenny Cheshire, Paul Hamilton, Julia Boffey, Tony Edwards, and my brother Robin Orton for sharing their expertise and giving of their time. I also owe a large debt to the publisher's anonymous readers, who commented on the entire book in draft; but although the version which here appears has benefited considerably from their astute criticisms, I must of course accept full responsibility for the final product and for any uncorrected errors. I want to thank Professor Robert E. Bjork, Director of the Arizona Center for Medieval and Renaissance Studies, for his interest in the project at an early stage; Roy Rukkila, Managing Editor of the Medieval and Renaissance Texts and Studies series, published under the auspices of the Center, for an unfailing supply of helpfulness and support during the longish period when the book was being made ready for publication; Leslie MacCoull who coped magnificently with the copy-editing and provided a number of useful additional references; and Todd Halvorsen, who dealt patiently and efficiently with several lists of proof-corrections, most of them arising from my own negligence, that I sent him. My partner Felicity, to whom *Writing in a Speaking World* is dedicated, herself an academic and so used to the normal hazards of research work—accidie, anxiety, absent-mindedness, in fact a very wide range of socially dysfunctional behaviour—has responded to these side-effects with just the right kind of tolerance and sympathy during the book's gestation.

Abbreviations

acc.	accusative
ASE	*Anglo-Saxon England*
c.	century, circa
Cambs.	Cambridgeshire
BL	British Library
cf.	compare
dat.	dative
ER	East Riding
f.	feminine
fol./fols.	folio(s)
Fates	*The Fates of the Apostles*
gen.	genitive
Gloucs.	Gloucestershire
Gmc.	Germanic
Hants.	Hampshire
JEGP	*Journal of English and Germanic Philology*
masc.	masculine
MLN	*Modern Language Notes*
MLR	*Modern Language Review*
MP	*Modern Philology*
MPD	*The Metrical Preface to Wærferth's Translation of Gregory's Dialogues*
MS(S)	Manuscript(s)
N.	North
NM	*Neuphilologische Mitteilungen*
Northants.	Northamptonshire
no(s).	number(s)
nom.	nominative
NR	North Riding

N.S.	New Series
OE	Old English
ON	Old Norse
PCP	*The Metrical Preface to the Pastoral Care*
pl.	plural
PMLA	*Publications of the Modern Language Association of America*
PQ	*Philological Quarterly*
RES	*Review of English Studies*
sg.	singular
SN	*Studia Neophilologica*
W.	West
Wilts.	Wiltshire
Yorks.	Yorkshire
WR	West Riding

Chapter 1
Introduction

This book is a study of some of the earliest known writings in England, its theme the contribution made by the advent of literacy to the development of new forms of linguistic and literary expression in English. The texts that form the book's subject-matter were produced in England during the Old English period, which extended from the mid-fifth century to the mid-twelfth. The beginning of this period is defined with reasonable precision by the arrival and settlement in Britain of the first Anglo-Saxons, an assortment of Germanic tribes who migrated from southern Scandinavia and the low countries. Old English is the name given to the variety of Germanic language that they spoke. The end of the Old English period is not so definitely marked. There was no sudden historical change affecting the language in the mid-twelfth century, though the choice of this date for the end of Old English and the beginning of Middle English is defensible on the grounds that certain structural developments that had been gradually changing the language over the preceding centuries culminated around that time. For instance, Old English made much use of inflexions to indicate the relationships between words in the sentence. By about 1150 the simplification of the inflexional system had reached a point where we are justified in speaking of a new phase in the history of English. Other important changes in the language were a consequence of the Norman Conquest of 1066, which introduced French as the language of government and other central institutions in England; but these need not concern us here.[1]

Much of this book is about texts in Old English preserved in parchment manuscripts and written in the roman alphabet. The Anglo-Saxons learned both the use of parchment and the roman alphabet from missionaries who began to convert them to Christianity at the end of the sixth century and continued with the task during the seventh. By this time, however, some Anglo-Saxons already knew and used the runic *fuþorc*, a system of twig-like symbols distinct from the alphabet (though certainly derived, at least in part, from some version of it) and widely used for hard-surface inscriptions in the continental Germanic

---

[1] On Old and Middle English generally, see Albert C. Baugh and Thomas Cable, *A History of the English Language*, 3rd ed. (London: Routledge & Kegan Paul, 1978), Chapters 3 and 7.

language-area from the second century A.D. onwards.² Before the conversion, and the method of writing on parchment with pen and ink that came with it, the Anglo-Saxons appear to have used runes in very much the same way as their European ancestors had done, incising letters, words, or longer sequences in their mother-tongue on durable surfaces such as bone, clay, or metal. Runes were not lost with the conversion; the Anglo-Saxons continued to use them for inscriptions, though the runic *fuþorc* now acquired other functions as well. The most important of these, in retrospect, was its use as a source of extra letters to supplement the roman alphabet. The latter was not perfectly adapted to the task of representing the Old English phonemic system in a straightforward way, so two runic letters were introduced into it and used to denote the sounds that they already represented in the *fuþorc*. These borrowed runes were 'thorn' (þ, as in the word *fuþorc*), representing the two dental consonants (voiced and unvoiced) that are indicated in modern English spelling by the combination *th* (as in 'then' and 'thick'), and 'wynn', a symbol somewhat resembling an angular modern *p* in shape but used for the consonant represented in modern English spelling by the letter *w*. These transfers were complete by the second half of the eighth century at the latest,³ and thereafter both runic letters were used very consistently by Anglo-Saxon scribes. This means that any text of Old English written in the Anglo-Saxons' version of the roman alphabet will normally contain examples of these two runes as a matter of course; but some manuscript texts of Old English, though written largely and basically in this runically augmented roman alphabet, include other runic letters too for special purposes. Several of the most interesting examples of this mixing of scripts will be discussed in Chapters 4 and 5 of this book. In most of the societies in which the impact of literacy has been studied, reading and writing were brought in from outside in a single wave; but as we have already seen, Anglo-Saxon literacy came in two stages. The later of these, the arrival of the roman alphabet, coincides with the conversion in the seventh century. We cannot be so precise about the date of the earlier acquisition of runic literacy by the continental ancestors of the Anglo-Saxons, though it must lie sometime between the second century A.D., to which the earliest continental runic inscriptions have been dated, and the fifth century, when evidence of runically literate Anglo-Saxons in Britain first appears.

 A brief account of the way this book is organized may be helpful at this point. Most of the present chapter is taken up with a general but very selective in-

---

 ² It is reasonably certain that the Anglo-Saxons already knew runes when they first came to Britain, for the earliest known runic inscriptions have been dated to the fifth century. The alternative, of course, is that they learnt about runes very soon after their arrival, though there is no positive evidence pointing in this direction. On the very earliest runic inscriptions in England and the origins of the script, see R. I. Page, *An Introduction to English Runes*, 2nd ed. (Woodbridge: Boydell Press, 1999), 16–21.
 ³ See A. Campbell, *Old English Grammar* (Oxford: Clarendon Press, 1959), §§57(6), 60.

troduction to previous scholarly work on the impact of literacy on those linguistic communities that have acquired it. It concludes with an indication of what is distinctive about the specific approaches to the beginnings of literacy in England that are adopted in this book. Chapter 2, "Deixis and Incipient Literacy," describes the main theoretical ideas that govern the book's scope and perspective on primary sources. Chapter 3, "Anglo-Saxon Inscriptions," is an account of the numerous epigraphical inscriptions that survive from the period, written in either Old English or Latin, and using either the roman alphabet or runes, or (in a few cases) both. The inscriptions of Anglo-Saxon England, their relationship with manuscript texts, and the uses, both separate and combined, of the runic and the roman alphabets are some of the book's main concerns; this chapter prepares the way for later arguments relating to these topics and questions. Chapter 4, "From Inscription to Manuscript Text," looks for signs of the pragmatic, formal, stylistic, or textual influence of inscriptions on Old English poetic texts preserved in manuscripts. The poems discussed here are four verse-prefaces to other works, the runic signatures of the poet Cynewulf, and *The Dream of the Rood*. Chapter 5 is chiefly devoted to the Old English *Riddles*, but also embraces *The Husband's Message*, a poem closely allied with the *Riddles* both formally and in its manuscript context. The few *Riddles* that incorporate runes as part of the puzzle are given particular attention here, because of their relevance to questions about the continuity of the epigraphic tradition of runic writing in manuscript literature; but the non-runic *Riddles* 47 ('Bookmoth') and 60 ('Pen'), both of which seem to exploit some of the paradoxical implications of literacy for riddling purposes, are also considered in some detail. Chapter 6 is taken up with a discussion of five of the Old English lyrics (or 'elegies', as they used to be called by critics): *The Wanderer*, *The Seafarer*, *Deor*, *The Wife's Lament*, and *Wulf and Eadwacer*. The main argument here is that these texts were all composed, if not by literate poets, at least by poets working in a cultural context affected by literacy, and that the combined evidence of their form, pragmatics, and content marks the introduction into English writing of strains of psychological introspection and fictionality that are scarcely conceivable prior to literacy. The concluding chapter draws together the various threads of my argument and attempts to derive some general conclusions from them about the earliest period of literacy in England. Chapters 2-5 all conclude with a summary of their arguments.

 Students of both language and literature are now showing a rapidly increasing interest in literacy, and some attempt must be made here to define this whole area of study (which I shall term 'literacy-studies') and trace its history to date. Though still quite short chronologically, this history is already very complicated, mainly because of the multi-disciplinary character of literacy-studies, but also because the study of literacy as a social phenomenon has inevitably become closely bound up with the study of pre-literate orality in societies that have subsequently become literate. All that will be attempted here is a very partial account of those areas of research, and influential scholarly initiatives, that seem to me to provide either essential background, or some more specific point of contact or contrast with what I want to say here about the earliest period of literacy in English. Unfortunately, this narrow focus will involve giving very short shrift to many complex, detailed, and important works, and even omitting any mention at all of many significant contributions to the general field. For this I can only apologize, though readers who would like to see a much more comprehensive account of scholarship on every kind of relationship between spoken and written language may consult (for example) Jahandarie's recent survey, to which I shall often refer.[4]

Literacy-studies began somewhere near the middle of the twentieth century. It is difficult to be more exact, partly because the various concerns that have contributed to its development emerged only gradually, and partly because literacy-studies is still not really a single, well-defined area of work; there are several strands. These have tended, at least until very recently, to run parallel, though there are now clear signs of a greater integration of effort, as scholars occupied in their separate areas become increasingly aware of the need to take account of advances elsewhere.

Something of the variety of preoccupations that have been brought to the study of literacy is reflected in the various usages of the terms 'literacy' and 'literate' in this field. Developmental psychologists and educationalists use these terms in their discussions of the teaching and learning of reading and writing to children, where the aim is to induce literacy and so produce literate individuals; but competence in reading and writing varies, not only at different stages of an educational career, but also from person to person and from society to society. This is one of the contexts, then, in which 'literacy' and 'literate' can scarcely be used as absolute terms; there are degrees of literacy. These terms are more likely to be used in an absolute sense in reference to the historical acquisition of reading and writing by particular social classes, language-communities, or peoples. All human societies use spoken language, but a society may or may not acquire literacy in the course of its history.[5] If it does, it is natural enough to label it a 'literate' society, though here too, as recent writers on literacy are increasingly

---

[4] Khosrow Jahandarie, *Spoken and Written Discourse: A Multi-disciplinary Perspective*, Contemporary Studies in International Political Communication 1 (Stamford, CT: Ablex, 1999).

[5] It has been calculated that of the total number of languages that have ever existed, which probably runs into tens of thousands, "only some 106 have ever had a literature, and that of the some 3000 or more languages spoken today, only some 78 as yet have a literature" (Walter J. Ong, "Orality, Literacy, and Medieval Textualization," *New Literary History* 16 [1984–1985]: 1–12, at 5). Literacy is thus the exception rather than the rule. On some of the difficulties involved in achieving a generally acceptable definition of literacy, see William V. Harris, *Ancient Literacy* (Cambridge, MA: Harvard University Press, 1989), Chapter 1.

concerned to point out, there will be great variation, not only in the degree of literacy achieved by different social formations at different periods (whatever measure of general literacy one may choose to apply), but also in the type of literacy they adopt. Literacy may come to a society in the form of some version of the alphabet, or in other forms of visual linguistic representation, for example ideograms, hieroglyphs, or syllabaries. The medium used for writing will vary; some are hard and relatively durable (for example clay, bone, stone), others soft and easily destroyed (papyrus, parchment, paper). The quality of these various surfaces affects the kind of writing that can be imposed on them, and the availability, portability, and durability of the medium may also have a bearing on the uses to which writing is put. The ability to write may be confined to a small elite, whether or not reading is a more general accomplishment. In multilingual societies, literacy in one language may be more widespread than in another. The relationship between the spoken and written modes is particularly complicated in diglossic communities, where one form of a language is generally used for writing and another (or several others) for speech.[6] Literacy-levels, and the distribution of literate individuals, may be related to social organization, or to the specialized production and use of certain types of document which serve particular social or political requirements; and there may be distinctive sub-literacies within a culture based on the use of different orthographies or writing systems.

Some of these complexities are illustrated by the situation in early England already sketched. Literacy in the runic *fuþorc*, used initially only for inscriptions in Old English on hard surfaces, came first, though the scarcity of surviving runic inscriptions, even from the earliest part of the Old English period (before c. 650 A.D.),[7] suggests that it may have been restricted to a small minority. Book-literacy in the roman alphabet, used for Latin originally but soon afterwards for Old English as well, came, as we have seen, with Christianity; but this was a literacy already embodied in an extensive manuscript literature in Latin. Latin books were brought to England by the early leaders of the church, and subsequently imported, copied, and sometimes translated into Old English. Runic literacy survived the conversion and there was a period during which both scripts were available for some purposes, though roman soon came to dominate, even in inscriptions, and there is little evidence for the continuation of the original, epigraphic use of runes beyond the tenth century. The extent of literacy in the roman alphabet during the Anglo-Saxon period is a controversial question, as we shall

---

[6] See, for example, Felicity Rash, *The German Language in Switzerland: Multilingualism, Diglossia and Variation*, German Linguistic and Cultural Studies 3 (Bern: Peter Lang, 1998), 17. The diglossia in German-speaking Switzerland was originally 'medial', i.e. standard Swiss German for writing, dialect for speech, but has since become 'functional', so that the standard form is now used not only in writing but also in formal speech, and dialect is occasionally used in informal writing, chiefly between familiars.

[7] See Page, *An Introduction to English Runes*, esp. 21–29.

see. For the moment, these observations are enough to warn us against using or understanding the terms 'literacy' and 'literate' as necessarily denoting a single, uniform, universal phenomenon. A cautious relativism must inform any discussion of literacy and the literate.

For these and other reasons, one would not expect the early effects of literacy to be the same on all societies and groups that acquire it; existing social, political, and linguistic differences among the receiving communities will affect the way literacy is accommodated and cultivated, as will the system of writing adopted, its origin, its dissemination, and the nature of the inscribed medium or media. This book aims to explore some of the linguistic and literary evidence from England, though whether the conclusions I shall reach have any broader application remains to be seen: the primary historical transition from orality to literacy in different linguistic and social groups is still rather thinly represented within literacy-studies, with intensive work concentrated on ancient Greece between the eighth century B.C., when (according to one view) the first alphabet originated, and the fifth century B.C., by which time literacy had become more widespread in Greek society.

One might expect that new literacy would have no immediate impact on the fundamental structure of a spoken language, except, of course, in the form of lexical and semantic developments to accommodate the expression of ideas and concepts related to reading, writing, and all the material equipment of literacy—in the case of England, engraving tools, pens, ink, parchment, books, texts, and so on;[8] and with the roman alphabet, of course, came also the need for new words taken from Latin, or the creation of new meanings for existing Old English words, to express the myriad conceptual innovations of Christian culture. There is no obvious reason to expect radical structural changes in grammar, though the difficulties involved in identifying and interpreting possible evidence of this kind of change are formidable. An example will illustrate the problem. Unlike modern English, Old English had dual first- and second-person pronouns which enabled a speaker or writer to address two persons in particular (Old English *git*, 'you two', genitive *incer*, 'your' in the sense of 'of you two', etc.), or refer to himself or herself jointly with one other person—either the person addressed, or a third party (*wit*, 'we two', genitive *uncer*, 'our', 'of us two', etc).[9] These distinctive dual

---

[8] Recent work by Christine Fell on the vocabulary of literacy in the Old English period is published posthumously in *'Lastworda Betst': Essays in Memory of Christine E. Fell with her Unpublished Writings*, ed. Carole Hough and Kathryn A. Lowe, foreword by R. I. Page (Donington: Shaun Tyas, 2002); see particularly "Wax Tablets of Stone," "Runes and Riddles in Anglo-Saxon England," and "Introduction to *Anglo-Saxon Letters and Letter-Writers*" (249–63, 264–77, and 278–87 respectively).

[9] For the forms, see Campbell, *Old English Grammar*, §703. The two usages of the first-person dual are exemplified in Joseph Bosworth and T. Northcote Toller, *An Anglo-Saxon Dictionary* (Oxford: Oxford University Press, 1898), s.v. *wit*.

pronouns finally disappeared from written records of (Middle) English in the early thirteenth century;[10] but when did they disappear from speech? The question has a bearing on the reasons for the dual's general disappearance. It seems possible, on the face of it, that literacy itself was a causative influence, at least on its extinction in written records. There may be occasions when a writer wants to speak of himself or herself in conjunction with one other person; but writing is an essentially individual and solitary activity, and circumstances requiring the dual first-person pronoun would no doubt be rarer for a writer than for a speaker. Similarly, although it is conceivable that a writer would want to direct an utterance towards two readers in particular (in a letter aimed at a couple, for example), it again seems likely that the circumstances would be uncommon and hence that the second-person dual pronoun would not be needed very often. These considerations might suggest that the extinction of dual pronouns in written English is connected with the most basic conditions of writing and written communication. The alternative possibility is that the dual's disappearance is a straightforward sociolinguistic phenomenon. It certainly originated in the spoken language and must have been a useful feature of the grammar at some stage in the development of English society; but its disappearance from written English might have been simply a manifestation of its disappearance from the spoken language as a result of social changes, specifically the decline of speech-situations in which an individual needed to speak as one of a pair, or to address a pair, thus rendering the dual forms redundant. The general point here is that although fairly fundamental changes in the English language might be related to the acquisition of literacy, cases are difficult to identify because of our necessary reliance on written records for evidence of the form of English in the early medieval period. In order to attribute a change to literacy with any confidence, we would need to have a clear idea of what was happening in the spoken language at the same time; and this we cannot know when we are studying earlier historical stages in the language, or at least those that predate the invention of electronic recording equipment.

The general problem which the dual's disappearance illustrates is one of immediate concern here: without direct access to the spoken language in the Old English period, how can we pinpoint any of the effects of literacy on the language or its usage in the written texts that are our only sources of evidence? Confidence in any attempt to investigate the original impact of literacy on English or English expression is further undermined when we remember the founding principles of the discipline of linguistics. In the last century, de Saussure established the orthodoxy that the spoken language is the primary object of linguistic research, the written language merely a secondary representation of it.[11] Spoken language

---

[10] See Fernand Mossé, *A Handbook of Middle English*, trans. James A. Walker (Baltimore: Johns Hopkins University Press, 1952), §64 (55).

[11] Ferdinand de Saussure, *Course in General Linguistics*, ed. Charles Bally, Albert Sechehaye, and Albert Riedlinger, trans. Wade Baskin (New York: McGraw-Hill,

thus became the centre of interest in the study, not only of language as a human phenomenon, but also of individual languages. One of the consequences of this development was, of course, that it tended to discourage the linguistic study, not only of dead languages, but also of superseded versions of living ones, because linguists could gain no direct access to them. The historical study of literacy in any language where it was already well established, such as English, was doubly marginalized by this emphasis within linguistics; for if writing is no more than a reflection of speech, it might seem to follow that literacy has no impact at all on a language when it arrives.

This is probably the best point to mention the work of the Canadian psychologist David Olson, most of whose ideas about literacy are to be found assembled in *The World on Paper*, published in 1994.[12] Olson constructs an ambitious and extensive theory of literacy and its impact which cannot be adequately summarized here, though I shall refer to particular aspects of it at various points in this book. I bring in Olson here, however, because of his challenge to Saussure's blunt assertion that writing is merely secondary to speech as an object of study. At the core of Olson's theorizing is the idea that writing, when a society acquires it, does not express the existing structure of the spoken language, but provides a 'model' for it, the nature of the model being determined by the kind of writing system adopted. Thus in languages such as English, which employs an alphabetic script, the concept of the phoneme (for example) can arise only when literacy has made its mark. Phonemes are not "available to consciousness" in the oral phase, prior to the coming of literacy; the alphabetical script itself, the purpose of which is to represent the discrete sounds of speech within individual words, is "responsible for *bringing them into consciousness.*"[13] The same principle applies to larger units of language as perceived in the western tradition, such as words. Olson sees writing as giving birth to new concepts, in particular to conceptions of language, its

---

1966). It should be said that Saussure is quite positive about the possibilities of studying superseded forms of languages, or dead languages, by a careful and scientific evaluation of written evidence for them; see esp. Chapter VI, "The Graphic Representation of Language"; but the implications for the practising linguist of several remarks about the relationship between writing and speech are clear enough: "Language and writing are two distinct systems of signs; the second exists for the sole purpose of representing the first. The linguistic object is not both the written and the spoken forms of words; the spoken forms alone constitute the object" (23–24). For an account of how literacy is still generally ignored as a factor contributing to the general linguistic competence of the individual, see Robert J. Scholes and Brenda J. Willis, "Linguists, Literacy, and the Intensionality of Marshall McLuhan's Western Man," in *Literacy and Orality*, ed. David R. Olson and Nancy Torrance (Cambridge: Cambridge University Press, 1991), 215–35.

[12] David R. Olson, *The World on Paper: The Conceptual and Cognitive Implications of Writing and Reading* (Cambridge: Cambridge University Press, 1994), identified by Jahandarie (*Discourse*, 113) as "the most complete formulation of Olson's position."

[13] Olson, *The World on Paper*, 263 (Olson's italics).

nature and its constituent parts; and this, he believes, is the justification for Derrida's well-known claim that writing is prior to speech.[14]

Olson's work is all relatively recent; but as early as the nineteen-twenties there were researchers outside linguistics who compared spoken and written usage synchronically from a fairly traditional point of view, and found statistical differences between the two in (for example) grammar, sentence-structure, frequency of parts of speech, and lexical variety.[15] This research does not seem to have revealed any rigid structural divisions between the two modes of expression. Empirical research in this area within linguistics did not really get under way until the last quarter of the twentieth century, when it was accompanied by considerable experimentation in methods of approach. A recent development that might become important for future research is the growing awareness that some, at least, of the differences that have been noticed between speaking and writing are to be explained by reference to "differences in the formality and purpose or register of the discourse rather than true differences between spoken and written language;"[16] it is easy to assume that the mode itself is the primary source of differences which may in fact have other origins connected with the distinct uses to which speech and writing are generally put. Goody, reviewing in 1987 some recent work in literacy-studies, points to a study of language-use among the Vai people of West Africa suggesting that literacy affects individuals' internalization of language "in ways that feed back to the structure of speech and of perception."[17] If literate individuals use spoken language differently from illiterate ones, this obviously complicates the question of whether any clear general distinctions may be drawn between written and oral language-use. For present purposes, however, a more encouraging line of inquiry is represented by a survey by Chafe and Tannen, published, like Goody's, in 1987, in which they summarise work supporting the view that many of the differences in the use of the two modes may be a function of "the very different conditions under which conversation and literary production typically take place."[18] This suggests that more work on the consequences of the different pragmatics of spoken and written utterances might help to explain observable differences in the use of the two channels. Chafe and Tannen also suggest that closer attention might be given to spoken conversation as "the prototypical form of language, the baseline against which all other genres, spoken or written, should be compared."[19] Both of these

---

[14] Olson, *The World on Paper*, 68.

[15] See Wallace Chafe and Deborah Tannen, "The Relation between Written and Spoken Language," *Annual Review of Anthropology* 16 (1987): 383–407 (at 383–91).

[16] Chafe and Tannen, "Relation," 389.

[17] Jack Goody, *The Interface Between the Written and the Oral*, Studies in Literacy, Family, Culture and the State (Cambridge: Cambridge University Press, 1987), 269.

[18] Chafe and Tannen, "Relation," 390.

[19] Chafe and Tannen, "Relation," 390–91.

suggestions raise important historical possibilities: the different pragmatics of spoken and written language, and their consequences for some kinds of linguistic usage, is a theme that will be taken up here in Chapter 2 and developed further in later parts of the book.

Early developments in the science of linguistics, then, originally tended, if not to inhibit, at least to delay any confrontation with the consequences of literacy for languages and language-use. Some other more recent developments in literacy-studies, important and promising though they are, must be passed over rather quickly here. The different ways in which speech and writing are mentally processed is now being studied intensively by cognitive psychologists, but no consensus has yet emerged even on basic questions, such as whether readers mentally convert the letters of the words they see into sounds so that each word can be processed by the 'mental lexicon', and supplied with meaning, in just the same way as if it had been heard rather than read. Jahandarie's review of work in this area concludes that we still know very little about "the exact processes and mechanisms that determine the cognitive handling of spoken and written discourse."[20] Similarly, in spite of a good deal of work in this area, no clear answer has yet been found to the question of whether the acquisition of literacy by societies and groups leads inexorably to more general cognitive changes, and what those changes are exactly.[21] Chapter 6 of this book, on the Old English lyrics, has some bearing on this enormous question.

For the literary and linguistic historian, research into literacy finds a natural focus in the transition from an oral society to one in which orality and literacy coexist, whenever and however this takes place. A powerful impetus to work in this area came in the 1920s from literary studies, as represented by the classicist Milman Parry. Addressing the 'Homeric Question' (arising from narrative inconsistencies in the *The Iliad* and *The Odyssey*, taken by some as indications of multiple authorship), Parry suggested that the Homeric texts were not composed in writing, but represented an accumulation of work by several generations of oral Greek epic singers, assembled by Homer, himself an oral poet within this tradition, and transcribed at his recitation. The structural feature of this poetry which revealed its oral origins was the repeated use of standard, traditional verbal collocations or 'formulas', the use of which relieved oral poets of some of the burden of extemporization as they performed. A formula, the correct definition of which has much preoccupied Parry's successors in their attempts to construct a generally applicable oral theory, was "a group of words which is regularly employed under the same metrical conditions to express a given essential idea." The extensive use of formulas in a work, even when it survives only in written form, was taken by Parry as a sure sign of its originally oral composition. No two oral performances of a story were ever exactly alike, because poets made different

---

[20] Jahandarie, *Discourse*, 196.
[21] See Jahandarie, *Discourse*, 263–78.

choices among the formulas at their disposal, even at points where they were dealing with the same theme; but there is little room for the development of an individual style in this form of composition: the tradition and the formulas that embody it set a style that is broadly similar for all practitioners. Although new formulas may develop in response to the needs of singers, the process is slow, and oral poets tend, in extemporization, to rely on the tradition, generally composing poems on subjects with which their predecessors have dealt. This leads, for obvious reasons, to certain limitations in the scope of orally composed poems: the themes, as well as the formulas, are passed down through generations of poets and the result is a highly conservative tradition.

This, in very brief outline, is the 'oral theory', otherwise known as the 'oral-formulaic theory'. Its application to Old English poetry will be described in more detail later on in this chapter. In the 1930s, Parry set out to support his hypotheses by reference to the work of living oral epic singers in Yugoslavia. On his death in 1935, Parry's assistant, Albert Lord, went on to refine and elaborate upon Parry's work, eventually (in 1960) publishing *The Singer of Tales*, a book generally recognized as a milestone in the articulation of oral-formulaic theory.[22] The theory itself has now been applied to a large number of poetic corpora in various languages, among them Old and Middle English alliterative verse.[23] Modifications of the theory have been proposed, among the most influential being the recognition (by Lord himself) of the possibility of 'transitional' texts lying somewhere between orality and literacy, which Parry had rejected.[24]

In hindsight, the work of Parry and Lord stands out for its recognition, very important for later work on medieval literacy, of the existence of an identifiable oral (i.e. pre-literate poetic) 'literature' which could be channeled into writing when literacy arrived, and yet still remain essentially oral in style and theme. The search for 'oral' texts preserved historically in writing in languages other than Greek could begin on this basis. Parry and Lord's theory also stimulated interest in the historical transition from oral to literate cultures, because it implied the

---

[22] Albert B. Lord, *The Singer of Tales*, Harvard Studies in Comparative Literature 24 (Cambridge, MA: Harvard University Press, 1960). I have relied heavily on this work in my summary above of the beginnings of oral-formulaic theory. For Parry's work on Homer, see *The Making of Homer's Verse: The Collected Papers of Milman Parry*, ed. Adam Parry (1971; repr. Oxford University Press, 1987).

[23] See further below, 25–33.

[24] See Albert B. Lord, *The Singer Resumes the Tale*, ed. Mary Louise Lord (Ithaca: Cornell University Press, 1995), 212–37, and John Miles Foley, "Orality, Textuality, and Interpretation," in *Vox Intexta: Orality and Textuality in the Middle Ages*, ed. A. N. Doane and Carol Braun Pasternack (Madison: University of Wisconsin Press, 1991), 34–45 (at 36). Franz H. Bäuml, "Medieval Texts and the Two Theories of Oral-Formulaic Composition: A Proposal for a Third Theory," *New Literary History* 16 (1984–1985): 31–49, questions the use of the concept of the transitional text in oral-formulaic research.

abandonment of a formula-bound, thematically conservative poetic tradition in favour of something more innovative and individualistic, once literacy had undermined, or at least set itself up as a rival to, the oral tradition that preceded it. If Homer's work, which was transcribed, is essentially oral, why did Greek literature change subsequently? Presumably literacy itself was an influential factor. Scholars could now also ask how other oral 'literatures' preserved in writing have been affected by the transition from orality to literacy, and begin to consider the possible consequences of literacy itself for work produced under its own conditions. Finally, the identification of a stylistic index of orality set a precedent for an emphasis that we find in most subsequent work on the historical orality-literacy continuum: it is the style of spoken as opposed to written utterances (or vice-versa) that has emerged as the main centre of interest, rather than structural, abstract linguistic differences between speech and writing during any period of their coexistence. *Parole*, rather than *langue* (to borrow De Saussure's terms), has become the favoured object of study across the oral-literate divide, and this is partly due to the influence of the oral-formulaic theory.

Eric A. Havelock's work on the transition from oral to written language in Greece was influenced by oral-formulaic theory,[25] though he criticized some aspects of it. For Havelock, Plato is a crucial figure in the development of Greek literacy. When he wrote *The Republic* in the fifth century B.C., alphabetic literacy, though established in Greece three hundred years earlier, remained limited to what Havelock calls "craft literacy":[26] inscriptions were being produced, and poets were composing their work in writing, but not with readers in mind: oral recitation was still the norm. The scarcity of readers was attributable, Havelock argues, to a heavy reliance in education on oral poetry and oral methods of instruction. The traditional forms of knowledge, even practical knowledge, were preserved and transmitted in metrical form because such knowledge was most easily memorized and absorbed as verse. Havelock opposes standard oral-formulaic theory in his assertion that formulaic composition "came into existence as a device of memorisation and of record; the element of improvisation is wholly secondary."[27] The kind of heroic narrative in which traditional knowledge was embodied in Greece was only (for the audience, at least) the sugaring on the pill: it ensured that a body of vital but prosaic information could be conveyed

---

[25] The earliest full statement of Havelock's theories is to be found in Eric A. Havelock, *Preface to Plato* (Cambridge, MA: Harvard University Press, 1963). Havelock died in 1988. For a late statement of his views on some of the questions he originally raised in *Preface to Plato*, and a useful summary of the explosion of work on orality and literacy in the early nineteen-sixties, see Eric Havelock, "The Oral-Literate Equation: A Formula for the Modern Mind," in *Literacy and Orality*, ed. Olson and Torrance, 11–27. See also Jahandarie, *Discourse*, 11–28.

[26] Havelock, *Preface to Plato*, 39.

[27] Havelock, *Preface to Plato*, 93.

in a palatable form. But Plato was suspicious of the emotive effect of poetry, which made it in his view a poor vehicle for philosophical reflection. According to Havelock, Plato wanted to replace poetry with "a conceptual language in which to describe phenomena whether human or natural." The concrete will be rejected in favour of the abstract; society will no longer be dominated by "the poetised tradition with its habit of passionate emotional identification with persons and stories of heroes, and with the play of action and episode."[28] Only when the oral tradition is rejected can abstract thinking begin.

Although there is no doubt that Havelock's work, which he developed up to the later 1980s, represents a very important model for much that came later in literacy-studies, his interpretations of Plato in particular have been criticized, and there are some obvious loose ends in his discussion. For example, Havelock's whole argument in *Preface to Plato* seems to depend on the idea that Homer's epics represent purely oral compositions; but even here, in the earliest publication of his views, Havelock allows that Homer's work as preserved may have "benefited from some reorganization made possible by alphabetic transcription."[29] One is bound to wonder how fundamental this reorganization might have been, and therefore whether it is helpful to describe Homer's works, in the form in which they have survived, as 'oral'.[30] At any rate, the chief general value of Havelock's work lies in the possible complexities in the effects of literacy that it suggests — the delay, for example, by several centuries of the full impact of literacy on Greek thought and writing, or the connection between literacy and new ways of interpreting and organizing experience, the study of which Havelock did much to promote.

Harold Innis, a Canadian political economist, became interested in the media of communication, especially linguistic communication, as an index (rather than a determining factor) of social organization, with particular reference to

---

[28] Havelock, *Preface to Plato*, 282–83.

[29] Havelock, *Preface to Plato*, 46. The same general point about the transcription of oral compositions is made by Goody, *Interface*, 80.

[30] Havelock's view that the Greeks devised the first true (i.e. phonetic) alphabet by adding vowel symbols to Phoenician script has also been questioned; a more recent theory is that the Old Canaanite writing system, which was either syllabic or alphabetic, was the ancestor of the Greek alphabet. The date of the earliest alphabet may be several hundred years earlier than was once thought, though the question depends partly on the criteria one uses to decide whether a writing system should be called alphabetic or syllabic. The Greek version of the alphabet may also be older than the eighth century B.C.; one authority suggests c. 1100 B.C. as a possible date; see Goody, *Interface*, 40–48, 61. These questions about the origins of the alphabet assume importance because Havelock attributes the unique linguistic and literary richness of Homer to the superior opportunities for close verbatim transcription offered by the alphabet proper (as opposed to the syllabaries that he supposed preceded it), though in the absence of any opportunity to compare oral with literary versions of the epic works in question, the case for this view must remain uncertain.

administration and the exercise of political power. The spectacular extension of his interests was revealed in his most influential book, *Empire and Communications*, first published in 1950.[31] This is a complex, demanding and rather eccentrically expressed work, impossible to summarise briefly; but one of its most basic and suggestive hypotheses is a correlation between the historical development and promotion of various literary supports—clay, stone, papyrus, parchment, paper (made first from fabric but then, in the nineteenth century, from wood-pulp)[32]—and the kinds of social organization whose interests they are made to serve. The theory is based on the physical nature of the inscribed medium: durable materials such as clay, stone and parchment "emphasize time" and so "favour decentralization and hierarchical types of institutions"[33] that possess a strong sense of continuity, history, and community,[34] whereas media that are less durable and lighter, chiefly papyrus and paper (though Innis is ambiguous about paper, as well as radio),[35] "emphasize space" and so serve the needs of trade and of centralizing governments that are always more preoccupied with the present than the past. Empires, like all large-scale political organizations, tend to combine both time- and space-centred media: they "persist by overcoming the bias of media which over-emphasize either dimension."[36] Linked with these contrasts is a homological opposition between religion and power: religion, with its concern for tradition, is time-bound, states (especially governments with territorial ambitions) are space-bound.[37]

It has been noticed that Innis is not entirely consistent in applying these homological sets to particular periods or social formations;[38] but it is tempting to speculate about how an analysis by Innis of Anglo-Saxon literacy might have proceeded. Following the conversion to Christianity in the seventh century, stone (a typical time-binding medium in Innis's scheme) was used by the church (a time-binding institution) for inscriptions in both runic and roman script. Parchment, another time-binding medium according to Innis, was actually introduced into Anglo-Saxon society by the church. On the other hand, the missionary activities of the church, both in Britain and elsewhere in the Germanic area of Europe, demonstrate its space-binding ambitions. It is also interesting to observe that, previous to the conversion, the only media for writing (in runes) in England were

---

[31] Harold A. Innis, *Empire and Communications*, rev. Mary Q. Innis, foreword by Marshall McLuhan (Toronto and Buffalo: University of Toronto Press, 1972).

[32] Innis, *Empire and Communications*, 159.

[33] Innis, *Empire and Communications*, 7.

[34] See Jahandarie, *Discourse*, 31. Parchment is space-bound because its production cannot be centralized.

[35] See Jahandarie, *Discourse*, 44–45.

[36] Innis, *Empire and Communications*, 7.

[37] See Jahandarie, *Discourse*, 31–32.

[38] Jahandarie, *Discourse*, 44–45.

metal, bone, and clay, all durable media which might be associated, like stone, with time-binding, according to Innis's scheme; whereas it seems to be generally agreed that the original medium for runes on the European continent was wood, perishable, recyclable, and portable, a fairly obvious example of a space-binding medium. A more detailed application of Innis's ideas to the earliest period of English and Germanic literacy, with due attention paid to the political and institutional history of the period, might produce some provocative conclusions.

Marshall McLuhan, in the "Prologue" to *The Gutenberg Galaxy* (1962), defines his own book as "in many respects complementary" to Lord's *The Singer of Tales*, and describes his own concerns in terms of Parry's: McLuhan intends to "trace the ways in which the *forms* of experience and of mental outlook and expression have been modified, first by the phonetic alphabet and then by printing," supplementing Parry's work on "the contrasted *forms* of oral and written poetry."[39] McLuhan's chief focus is the continuing development and impact of the electronic media, and the earlier effects of the introduction of printing; but his interests extend back as far as the original, primary transition from orality to literacy that began the whole process of the transformation of language from an aural to a visual mode. This process was, in McLuhan's view, going into reverse in the English-speaking world in the early sixties, when he was writing. Parry and Lord, according to McLuhan's reading of them, "studied the poetic organism when the auditory function was suppressed by literacy;"[40] McLuhan means to extend their investigations to "the effect on the organism when the visual function of languages was given extraordinary extension and power by literacy."[41] 'Sense-extension' is a key idea of McLuhan's: "all man-made material things can be treated as extensions of what man once did with his body or some specialized part of his body;"[42] and all media, including speech, are extensions of this kind; but they are (or have been, until the electronic age) 'closed' extensions;[43] they have not interacted with each other in the way that the basic human senses interacted, "endlessly translated into each other," in preliterate societies.[44] Now, in the electronic age, these extensions "demand an interplay and ratio that makes *rational* co-existence possible;" their separation is no longer "psychically supportable," now that "sight and sound and movement are simultaneous and global in extent."[45] McLuhan thus heralds the dawn of a new oral age.

---

[39] Marshall McLuhan, *The Gutenberg Galaxy: The Making of Typographic Man* (London: Routledge & Kegan Paul, 1962), 1.
[40] McLuhan, *Gutenberg*, 3.
[41] McLuhan, *Gutenberg*, 3.
[42] McLuhan, *Gutenberg*, 4.
[43] McLuhan, *Gutenberg*, 5.
[44] McLuhan, *Gutenberg*, 5.
[45] McLuhan, *Gutenberg*, 5.

McLuhan offers a hypothesis about the effect of the alphabet on cultures that acquire it. He argues that the 'opening' of traditional 'closed' societies (such as Greek society before Homer) was due to the phonetic alphabet; now, at the opening of the electronic age, we are on the verge of a new, global closing, a "sealing of the entire human family into a single global tribe." In order to explain how the introduction of *alphabetical* literacy in particular achieved this first detribalization, or opening, of human society, McLuhan argues that in closed societies, spoken words were "resonant, live, active, natural forces;"[46] language was action and the very act of utterance was an exercise of magical power. Literacy puts an end to this by "shifting habits of perception from the auditory to visual stress."[47] Written words are visible and static; they lose the "dynamism" and also the "personal element" they had under orality, because writing is not normally directed towards individuals. Written language makes possible "verbal thought"; language becomes "separable from action," it can be "ineffective and contained within the man." Here McLuhan is quoting the psychiatrist J. C. Carothers, who based his ideas on work with nonliterate rural populations in Africa. McLuhan then narrows Carothers's ideas (which he quotes at great length) to alphabetic ('phonetic') writing in particular: "Mere writing" does not "detribalize" man; only the phonetic alphabet can achieve this social and psychological change, because it involves the "abstraction of meaning from sound and the translation of sound into a visual code."[48]

McLuhan also adds that the the phonetic alphabet "makes a break between eye and ear, between semantic meaning and visual code."[49] Here one might comment that even though alphabetical writing is usually regarded as superimposing an additional symbolic layer on linguistic meaning, and hence as separating words from their originally more direct relationship with their meanings in the way McLuhan describes, it is by no means clear why this gap between word and meaning should not be created just as well by other, non-alphabetic writing systems, for example syllabaries.[50] An even more crucial question, perhaps, is whether the gap is necessarily permanent. The general neglect of cognitive considerations by most writers on literacy means that we seldom find any distinction drawn between the original role of writing in a society, which it might seem reasonable to regard as the representation in visual terms of what could only be heard previously (as De Saussure seems to imply), and the cognitive perception of meaning via the written word once writing has had a chance to assume parity with speech as a mode of linguistic expression. McLuhan's argument implies that writing always retains its secondary status and can never offer a genuine

---

[46] McLuhan, *Gutenberg*, 19.
[47] McLuhan, *Gutenberg*, 20.
[48] McLuhan, *Gutenberg*, 22.
[49] McLuhan, *Gutenberg*, 27.
[50] See Goody, *Interface*, 62.

1. Introduction

alternative to speech, though this is by no means self-evident.[51] However reasonable it may be to regard writing as the servant of speech at its inception, in English at least, as we shall see later in this book, the use of writing certainly enables people to produce utterances which could not possibly have originated in speech. The evidence of Anglo-Saxon inscriptions, considered in detail in my Chapter 3, also challenges McLuhan's generalizations about the loss of magical power in words that literacy involves: inscriptions, as we shall see, exemplify uses of language that strongly suggest a belief in the power of written words to enhance the practical effectiveness of the artifacts on which they are inscribed.

The idea of writing as essentially and eternally secondary to speech is also accepted by Walter J. Ong, whose wide-ranging scholarship includes a valuable and influential general introduction to literacy-studies: *Orality and Literacy: The Technologizing of the Word*, published in 1982.[52] Ong covers both orality and literacy, but he is more interested, in this book at least, in "primary orality, that of persons totally unfamiliar with writing,"[53] than in the secondary orality of the electronic age greeted so enthusiastically by McLuhan. The idea that spoken language is "paramount" in human communication, more important even than non-linguistic signals such as gesture,[54] is a mainstay of Ong's theorizing. He refers, for example, to the "natural, oral habitat" of words which, when spoken, are "part of a real, existential present,"[55] and supports the primacy of orality over literacy with evidence of the persistence of oral habits of mind and expression long after literacy is established.[56] Ong identifies nine distinctive sorts of thinking and expression that are typical of primary oral linguistic productions, and these have been used by other scholars to assay the 'orality' of particular texts that they are interested in.[57] A well-known example is Edward B. Irving's application of Ong's orality-criteria to the Old English poem *Beowulf*.[58]

The advent of writing is, for Ong, revolutionary. The aural sense which perceives oral utterances is passive and unselective, whereas the eye, which perceives writing, selects a focus from the world in view. "Dynamic sound" is reduced by

---

[51] On the history of the idea that writing is nothing more than a representation of speech, see Roy Harris, *The Origin of Writing* (London: Duckworth, 1986), 26–27.

[52] Ong's ideas are cited here from Walter J. Ong, *Orality and Literacy: The Technologizing of the Word* (London: Methuen, 1982; repr. London: Routledge, 1988).

[53] Ong, *Orality and Literacy*, 6.

[54] Ong, *Orality and Literacy*, 7.

[55] Ong, *Orality and Literacy*, 101.

[56] Ong, *Orality and Literacy*, 115–16.

[57] Ong, *Orality and Literacy*, 37–49.

[58] Edward B. Irving, Jr., *Rereading Beowulf* (Philadelphia: University of Pennsylvania Press, 1989), 16–30. See also Lois Bragg, *The Lyric Speakers of Old English Poetry* (London: Associated University Presses, 1991), 25–26.

writing to "quiescent space."⁵⁹ Hearing and orality are non-analytical, whereas the selection involved in seeing and looking encourages a more critical, abstracting interpretation of the eye's perceptions by the mind. Ong builds an elaborate theory of the new thought-processes made possible by literacy on the basis of these observations. Sound has a specially close connection with what Ong calls "interiority;"⁶⁰ an individual may be "immersed" in sound but not in sight. Writing undermines the sense, created by an individual's experience of sound, that he is at the existential centre of the universe. Sight disturbs the inner harmony of man which the world of sound had maintained, and encourages a more objective conception of the universe as "something laid out" before our eyes, open to physical exploration.⁶¹ The removal of some features of extralinguistic context that writing involves also has important consequences: the writer, alone at his work, is engaged in "a solipsistic operation,"⁶² and the writer is a fiction for the reader just as much as the reader is for the writer. Ong defines the fictionalization of readers as "the underside of literary history, of which the topside is the history of genres and the handling of character and plot."⁶³ "By separating the knower from the known,"⁶⁴ furthermore, writing encourages "increasingly articulate introspectivity."⁶⁵ An attempt will be made in Chapter 6 of this book to document this last point of Ong's; and I shall also have something to say about fictionality in writing, though I shall base my own theorizing on a rather narrower definition of the fictional than Ong permits himself.

In "The Consequences of Literacy," a highly influential article first published in 1963, Jack Goody and Ian Watt reinvigorated an existing but by then etiolated anthropological strain in literacy-studies.⁶⁶ Historically, the primary interest of anthropologists had been in 'primitive man' living in purely oral cultures; 'civilised man' in his literate societies was left to sociologists. Now, according to Goody and Watt, the pendulum has swung too far the other way: reactions to earlier approaches now perceived as ethnocentric have effectively obscured differences between literate and non-literate societies. Oral societies constantly revise traditional knowledge and narratives over time in accordance with current social relations, and so achieve social homeostasis.⁶⁷ "Myth and history merge into one;"

---

⁵⁹ Ong, *Orality and Literacy*, 82.
⁶⁰ Ong, *Orality and Literacy*, 71.
⁶¹ Ong, *Orality and Literacy*, 73.
⁶² Ong, *Orality and Literacy*, 101.
⁶³ Ong, *Orality and Literacy*, 103.
⁶⁴ Ong, *Orality and Literacy*, 105.
⁶⁵ Ong, *Orality and Literacy*, 105.
⁶⁶ Jack Goody and Ian Watt, "The Consequences of Literacy," *Comparative Studies in Society and History* 5 (1963): 304–45; repr. in *Literacy in Traditional Societies*, ed. Jack Goody (Cambridge: Cambridge University Press, 1968), 27–68.
⁶⁷ Goody and Watt, "Consequences," 33.

traditions change, but oral societies remain unaware of any inconsistency between past and present beliefs or ideas. When writing arrives, it creates a new awareness of the 'pastness' of the past.[68] The alphabet, first adopted by the Greeks according to Goody and Watt in this article, contrasts with all earlier systems of writing in its 'phonetic' aspirations: ideally, each phoneme in a language is represented by a distinct letter. The alphabet, more easily learnt and used than its predecessors, led to the first-ever popular literacy in Greece. Previously and elsewhere, literacy had been the preserve of elites who used it to "reify only those items in the cultural repertoire which the literate specialists have selected for written expression," whereas the alphabet enables anyone who memorizes its characters to "write easily and read unambiguously about anything which the society can talk about."[69] Classical Greece thus provides "the prime historical example of the transition to a really literate society;"[70] all other cultures that adopted the alphabet subsequently — Roman society, for example — received "other cultural features . . . inevitably imported from the loan country along with the writing system."[71] Ancient Greece is the only field in which it is possible to isolate the consequences of alphabetic literacy in particular.[72] Here we are reminded of our frustrating uncertainties about the cultural background of runic writing in the Germanic world. If we knew more, we might be able to put this claim to the test.

Oral communication, according to Goody and Watt, involves a close relationship between symbol and referent;[73] but writing establishes "a relationship that is more general and more abstract, and less closely connected with the particularities of person, place and time, than obtains in oral communication."[74] The authors here draw attention to the different pragmatics of speech and writing. By the fifth century B.C., writing had encouraged a more sceptical attitude to religion and ethics in Greece. Plato himself is taken, on the basis of *Phaedrus* and the *Seventh Letter*, to be anti-writing,[75] though the ideas in *Phaedrus* about how to arrive at the truth of any matter by orderly, structured intellectual procedures show the effects of literacy.[76] Goody and Watt are uncertain about the importance of

---

[68] Goody and Watt, "Consequences," 34.
[69] Goody and Watt, "Consequences," 39.
[70] Goody and Watt, "Consequences," 42.
[71] Goody and Watt, "Consequences," 42. This last point is taken up in Chapter 7 of the present work in relation to the original introduction into Anglo-Saxon society of the roman alphabet as a system of representation for Latin rather than English.
[72] Goody and Watt, "Consequences," 42.
[73] Goody and Watt, "Consequences," 29.
[74] Goody and Watt, "Consequences," 44.
[75] Goody and Watt, "Consequences," 56, n. 1. Havelock's *Preface to Plato*, published in the same year as their article, ignores the *Phaedrus* and argues in exactly the opposite direction; see Jahandarie, *Discourse*, 25.
[76] Goody and Watt, "Consequences," 53.

the alphabet itself "as the cause or as the necessary condition of the seminal intellectual innovations that occurred in the Greek world during the centuries that followed the diffusion of writing,"[77] though they suspect that

> the overwhelming debt of the whole of contemporary civilization to classical Greece must be regarded as in some measure the result, not so much of the Greek genius, as of the intrinsic differences between non-literate (or protoliterate) and literate societies — the latter being mainly represented by those societies using the Greek alphabet and its derivatives.[78]

In the "Introduction" to the 1968 anthology in which his and Watt's article was reprinted,[79] Goody is at pains to remove any impression their article might have created that advances in Greek thought and expression after the advent of literacy were actually due to the special qualities of alphabetical writing: the alphabet was a "liberating" technology, not a determining one; and Goody would now prefer to speak of the "implications" of literacy instead of its "consequences."[80] This represents a measure of retreat from the position he and Watt had taken up originally, but a sensible one: we have seen that several scholars of literacy have stressed the unique consequences of alphabetic writing as opposed to other systems, without offering any conclusive arguments in support of their position. Goody reaffirms his revised view on this question in his 1987 book *The Interface Between the Written and the Oral*,[81] which represents perhaps the fullest statement he has produced of his views on orality and literacy; but he still regards the primary transition from orality to literacy in ancient Greece as a special case on the grounds that in Greece the use of the alphabet was "unrestricted by centralized religious, political or scribal interests," and so "penetrated into most areas of culture."[82]

Goody's *Interface* includes a list of "non-oral" uses of writing "which incorporate literacy and are not simply straightforward adaptations of the new channel to the oral mode."[83] It includes lists of names (of Olympic victors, for example) written for public display; legal texts; records of temple business; "monuments ... inscribed with the names of the dead;" and "personal property ... marked linguistically" in "the form of 'I am X's', i.e. the object speaks, a use parallel to that of 'X wrote me';"[84] and finally, "lists of the alphabet ... in the form of that widespread learning device, the abecedary." We shall see later in this book (Chapter 3)

---

[77] Good and Watt, "Consequences," 55.
[78] Goody and Watt, "Consequences," 55.
[79] Goody, "Introduction" to *Literacy in Traditional Societies*, 1–26.
[80] Goody, "Introduction," 4.
[81] Goody, *Interface*, 61–64.
[82] Goody, *Interface*, 70.
[83] Goody, *Interface*, 107–8.
[84] Olson, *The World on Paper*, 183, also mentions early Greek inscriptions of this type in the context of a discussion of how early writing "tried to emulate speech."

how closely the latter part of this list corresponds with the main uses of inscriptions in Anglo-Saxon England.

One of Goody's severest critics is his fellow anthropologist Brian Street, whose most influential work in this area is *Literacy in Theory and Practice*, first published in 1984 and reprinted in 1995.[85] For Street, reading and writing in any society are "embedded in an ideology and cannot be isolated or treated as 'neutral' or merely 'technical'."[86] The "skills and concepts that accompany literacy acquisition, in whatever form, do not stem in some automatic way from the inherent qualities of literacy . . . but are aspects of a specific ideology."[87] Street thus sets up a clear opposition between two models of literacy-acquisition: the 'autonomous' and the 'ideological', to the second of which Street is himself committed. Goody, in Street's view, cleaves to the autonomous model. The dividing line between oral and literate societies is never clear-cut, according to Street: "Every society represents some 'mix' of oral and literate modes of communication."[88] Any attempt to generalize about differences between the two kinds of society cannot, therefore, be tested because conditions for a proper assessment of the problem nowhere exist. Street thinks that the shift from orality to literacy "involves changes in conventions for which social explanations have to be offered, rather than a change in 'cognitive' processes or at the radical, absolute level that Goody implies."[89] The 'literate mentality' is an ideology, something "constructed; it is not something imposed by the form of literacy itself as though the 'technology of the intellect', as Goody terms it, were determinate."[90]

Jahandarie criticizes Street for exaggerating the differences between his own views and Goody's:[91] the technological differences between oral and literate societies (with which my Chapter 2 is partly concerned) are matters of fact, not opinion as Street seems to imply; and Street's 'ideological model' seems to be a way of defining out of existence the possibility of any regularities in the relationship between orality and literacy in different societies.[92] It boils down to an assertion of the superiority of cultural relativism over more universalising approaches to literacy-studies.

A paragon of the 'ideological' approach to literacy is, in Street's view, Michael Clanchy, whose much-admired book *From Memory to Written Record: England*

---

[85] Brian V. Street, *Literacy in Theory and Practice*, Cambridge Studies in Oral and Literate Culture 9 (Cambridge: Cambridge University Press, 1984; repr. 1995).
[86] Street, *Literacy*, 1.
[87] Street, *Literacy*, 1.
[88] Street, *Literacy*, 46.
[89] Street, *Literacy*, 46.
[90] Street, *Literacy*, 47.
[91] Jahandarie, *Discourse*, 287–93.
[92] Jahandarie, *Discourse*, 291.

1066–1307 appeared in its first edition in 1979, and has since been revised.[93] The first part of Clanchy's book, "The Making of Records," deals with the production and preservation of written documents intended for practical and business use (Clanchy generally excludes non-functional literature and concentrates on texts in Latin, not English), the political, administrative, and legal uses to which these documents were put, and the 'technology' of document-production. The second part of the book, "The Literate Mentality," analyses in depth the various attitudes and ways of thinking connected with, and perhaps consequent on, literacy, for example the implications of the use of different languages in early medieval English documents, the relative authority invested in the spoken and the written word, and other forms of authority that rivalled writing, such as oral traditions, seals, and symbolic objects of various kinds. One of the broad arguments of Clanchy's book is that oral attitudes to language changed only slowly up to the end of the thirteenth century: it was a long time before writing was regarded as an autonomous mode of linguistic expression, rather than just a record of something that had been said;[94] but Clanchy does present clear evidence that the written word did eventually achieve a genuine rivalry with speech in this regard.

From Memory to Written Record is the first extended study of the relationship between orality and literacy in medieval England;[95] but its period begins with the Norman Conquest, by which time the Anglo-Saxons had been literate in the roman alphabet for over four hundred years. Runic literacy, though probably defunct by the eleventh century except in areas of strong Scandinavian influence, was even older among the English. Clanchy justified his choice of period by the fewness of charters and writs surviving from Anglo-Saxon England compared with thirteenth-century England: his rough estimate is two thousand and "tens of thousands" respectively. With this growth in production went a "spread of literate modes both territorially and socially" which Clanchy documents extensively and uses as the basis of his generalizations about attitudes to speech on the one hand and the written word on the other.

Mainstream historical research on Anglo-Saxon literacy had already begun when the first edition of Clanchy's book appeared, but only just, and it was slow to develop subsequently. Two years before, in 1977, C. P. Wormald's article "The

---

[93] M. T. Clanchy, *From Memory to Written Record: England 1066–1307*, 2nd ed. (Oxford: Blackwell, 1993).

[94] On this distinction, see also Jeffrey Kittay, "Utterance Unmoored: The Changing Interpretations of the Act of Writing in the European Middle Ages," *Language in Society* 17 (1988): 209–30.

[95] Clanchy acknowledges H. J. Chaytor, *From Script to Print: An Introduction to Medieval Literature* (Cambridge: Cambridge University Press, 1945) as an inspiration. Chaytor also influenced several of the scholars already mentioned, particularly McLuhan; see *The Gutenberg Galaxy*, 86–89, 92–93.

Uses of Literacy in Anglo-Saxon England and its Neighbours"[96] was published and has since established itself as one of the main points of departure for subsequent work on Anglo-Saxon literacy. In spite of its title, Wormald's article concentrates on the extent of lay literacy in Anglo-Saxon England; and the type of literacy he looks for in the period—"cultured literacy," the symptoms of which are anything between "reading free prose in the vernacular to composing Latin in the classical tradition"—is *a priori* unlikely to have been achieved in the initial period of English literacy except, perhaps, in a few individuals. Wormald argues that the survival of inscriptions and documents in the vernacular are not in themselves sufficient evidence for the sort of *"civilisation de l'écrit"* that he is looking for; the existence of "schools catering for laymen, books owned and written by laymen, and a significant role for writing in government"[97] needs to be proved as well. Wormald also makes the point that in most areas of the Germanic barbarian world, Christianity successfully promoted literacy in Latin at the expense of the local vernacular languages, and so "actually contributed towards the restriction of literacy."[98] King Alfred's educational programme, as set out in his *Prose Preface* to the translation of Pope Gregory's *Pastoral Care*, implies that there were few readers even of English in Alfred's time, let alone of Latin; but Alfred would not have "considered the vernacular any long-term substitute for the Latin scholarship which alone could bring true wisdom."[99] After Alfred, Latin retained its status as the language of learning. Alfred's promotion of the use of the vernacular in writing did not necessarily extend lay literacy. There is evidence of literate laymen in the tenth century, especially among royalty, and "the later Anglo-Saxons do seem to have had some appreciation, like the Carolingians, of the value of documentation";[100] but the level of "cultured literacy" among the Anglo-Saxon laity was low. Literacy was, in fact, largely "a clerical monopoly," and Wormald's often-quoted conclusion is that "the traditional view of restricted literacy is substantially valid for the whole early English period."[101]

These negative conclusions are perhaps to be expected in view of the very stringent criteria imposed by Wormald as tests for literacy in the period, though an article by Simon Keynes, appearing in 1990 in a collection of essays on early European literacy, was in some respects a reply to Wormald.[102] Keynes explores

---

[96] C. P. Wormald, "The Uses of Literacy in Anglo-Saxon England and its Neighbours," *Transactions of the Royal Historical Society*, 5th ser., 27 (1977): 95–114. Jahandarie, *Discourse*, surprisingly does not refer to this article.

[97] Wormald, "Uses of Literacy," 96.

[98] Wormald, "Uses of Literacy," 100.

[99] Wormald, "Uses of Literacy," 106.

[100] Wormald, "Uses of Literacy," 111.

[101] Wormald, "Uses of Literacy," 113.

[102] Simon Keynes, "Royal Government and the Written Word in Late Anglo-Saxon England," in *The Uses of Literacy in Early Medieval Europe*, ed. Rosamond McKitterick

the practical use of texts in various processes of royal government (administration of the law, verbal communication between the king and his officials, for example) in the later part of the period, and finds plentiful evidence that in the tenth and eleventh centuries royal government "depended to a very considerable extent on the use of the written word."

An article in the same collection by Susan Kelly, covering some of the same ground as Wormald's paper, contrasts with Keynes's in emphasising a distinction between literacy in Latin and in English.[103] Kelly begins, unusually, with runes, which historians generally are inclined to dismiss or ignore, partly, no doubt, because the evidence of their use is relatively meagre, but also, one suspects, because runic writing finds no very obvious place in the history of individuals and institutions that mainstream medievalist historians have (until rather recently) been accustomed to pursue. Kelly notes that the borrowing of two letters of the runic *fuþorc* into the roman alphabet "suggests that some Anglo-Saxon clerics were literate in runes"—a point which may be supported (as we shall see in my Chapter 3) by reference to the production of runic inscriptions in ecclesiastical contexts in Anglo-Saxon England. Kelly mentions the runic legends on coins from the seventh and eighth centuries, which show that moneyers were also literate in runes in this period. The main body of Kelly's article consists of a methodical analysis of the use of Latin and English in documents relating to secular life. The diploma, the origins of which Kelly pushes back to the mid-seventh century, earlier than might be suggested by the period (late seventh century) to which the earliest surviving examples refer, probably functioned more "as a potent symbol of ownership"[104] than as a linguistic communication, for there is little evidence of their being understood in any detail. Laymen are increasingly mentioned as beneficiaries in land-charters as the period progresses, sometimes in cases where no benefit to the church seems calculated to arise from the terms of the charter; so here, perhaps, are signs of an increase in the use of documents in lay society, influenced initially by ecclesiastical example and (perhaps) the active encouragement of clerics. From the early ninth century, English is more and more used in charters and related documents as a supplement to Latin, and the majority of English wills from the period are wholly in English. Chirographs, used for ecclesiastical leases and other similar purposes, may have been a way of "involving illiterate laymen in the documentary process."[105] Many of these leases are in English, and most of those which use Latin also contain some English too, often in the form of summaries of the Latin. All this points to a more widespread ability to read English than Latin. In the tenth and eleventh centuries, "English had

---

(Cambridge: Cambridge University Press, 1990), 226–57.

[103] Susan Kelly, "Anglo-Saxon Lay Society and the Written Word," in *The Uses of Literacy in Early Medieval Europe*, ed. McKitterick, 36–62.

[104] Kelly, "Lay Society," 44.

[105] Kelly, "Lay Society," 50.

a respected place as an alternative literary and documentary language,"[106] a statement that marks a distinction between Kelly's findings and Wormald's. King Alfred's educational plans, which included the laity, and the translation programme he initiated to support it, probably contributed to the status of English; but Kelly is able to show that vernacular literacy was already well established in Alfred's time:[107] vernacular poetry and the *Anglo-Saxon Chronicle* "were secular literature and . . . probably imply a secular audience,"[108] irrespective of the fact that the clergy appreciated the first and may have actually compiled the second. However, the case for widespread lay literacy "in the modern sense" in the early part of the period "must remain unproven."

This research by historians like Wormald, Keynes, and Kelly into literacy in the Anglo-Saxon period is fairly recent. Within Old English literary studies, questions connected with the advent of literacy in the period had been raised much earlier (though incidentally) by the application of the oral-formulaic theory to Old English poetry in the 1950s. The American scholar Francis P. Magoun, Jr. published three articles in 1953 and 1955 that introduced the theory to Anglo-Saxonists, illustrated how it might be applied to Old English verse-texts, and measured the level of use of formulas in selected passages from the corpus.[109] Magoun concluded on the basis of these analyses that all Old English verse is formulaic, and must therefore (according to oral-formulaic theory as it then stood) have been composed by oral singers. The existence of recurring verses (*Parallelstellen*) within the Old English poetic corpus had long been recognized, and they were usually explained as signs of the direct influence of one particular poem on the author of another. Now, however, a more satisfactory explanation of *Parallelstellen* became available: they are manifestations of a common oral poetic stock drawn upon by all Old English poets.

The implications of Cynewulf's runic signatures in the four poems of his that are known to us are briefly considered by Magoun. He accepts that Cynewulf was "a lettered person" on the basis of his signatures; but if (as Magoun already had reason to suspect) Cynewulf's verse is formulaic in the "narrative parts" of his poems, the implication is "that those parts at least he composed in the traditional

---

[106] Kelly, "Lay Society," 50.
[107] Kelly, "Lay Society," 54.
[108] Kelly, "Lay Society," 61.
[109] Francis P. Magoun, Jr., "The Oral-formulaic Character of Anglo-Saxon Narrative Poetry," *Speculum* 28 (1953): 446–67, repr. in *An Anthology of Beowulf Criticism*, ed. Lewis E. Nicholson (Notre Dame: University of Notre Dame Press, 1963), 189–221 (to which reference is made here); idem, "Bede's Story of Cædmon: The Case History of an Anglo-Saxon Oral Singer," *Speculum* 30 (1955): 49–63; and idem, "The Theme of the Beasts of Battle in Anglo-Saxon Poetry," *NM* 56 (1955): 81–90. Another seminal article contemporary with these is Stanley B. Greenfield, "The Formulaic Expression of the Theme of 'Exile' in Anglo-Saxon Poetry," *Speculum* 30 (1955): 200–6.

way," and that he later "got them written down," either "dictating to himself, as it were," or reciting them to a scribe. "In any event there would be no conflict with, or contradiction to, tradition."[110]

Oral-formulaic approaches to Old English poetry have been transformed since Magoun's pioneering work in the 1950s.[111] One early but significant moment was the reaction to Magoun's work represented by Larry Benson's influential 1966 article on "The Literary Character of Anglo-Saxon Formulaic Poetry."[112] Benson does not challenge Magoun's judgement that all Old English alliterative poetry is highly formulaic,[113] but rejects the positive correlation made by oral-formulaic theory between a high incidence of formulas and oral composition, at least where Old English poetry is concerned. Benson bases his case on evidence of literacy on the part of several Old English poets whose work has survived. In the case of Cynewulf, Benson argues, ". . . we have Cynewulf's own word for the fact that he was literate and used written sources;" and "the visual punning of the runic signatures shows that he wrote for readers."[114] Having demonstrated that literate poets could compose in a formulaic style,[115] Benson defines a "literate composition" as a work composed pen-in-hand, and "with the leisure and forethought that literary composition allows."[116]

Benson's arguments expose a number of hitherto underappreciated general problems. One is that the conditions and effects of what he calls "written composition" are not easy to define with precision in any given case. Furthermore, although there were no doubt Old English poets who could read and even some who could write (Cynewulf being the likeliest instance of a poet who could do both),[117] it is difficult to establish the impact the possession of these skills had on

---

[110] Magoun, "Oral-formulaic Character," 212.

[111] Developments up to the late 1980s may be traced via Alexandra Hennessey Olsen, "Oral-Formulaic Research in Old English Studies: I," *Oral Tradition* 1 (1986): 548–606, and eadem, "Oral-Formulaic Research in Old English Studies: II," *Oral Tradition* 3 (1988): 138–90. See also Mark C. Amodio, *Writing the Oral Tradition: Oral Poetics and Literate Culture in Medieval England* (Notre Dame: University of Notre Dame Press, 2004).

[112] Larry D. Benson, "The Literary Character of Anglo-Saxon Formulaic Poetry," *PMLA* 81 (1966): 334–41.

[113] As perhaps he might have done; see John Miles Foley, *Immanent Art: From Structure to Meaning in Traditional Oral Epic* (Bloomington and Indianapolis: Indiana University Press, 1991), 14, n. 30.

[114] Benson, "Literary Character," 335.

[115] Benson, "Literary Character," 336.

[116] Benson, "Literary Character," 336.

[117] On Cynewulf's composition methods, see John D. Niles, *Homo Narrans: The Poetics and Anthropology of Oral Literature* (Philadelphia: University of Pennsylvania Press, 1999), 92–93: Cynewulf's dictation of his poems to a scribe is in Niles's view unlikely, though "He might still, in a sense, have 'dictated' his poems to himself" (93). Cynewulf's literacy is also discussed below, Chapter 4.

the processes of composition, except what we might deduce *a priori*. A poet who wrote his own work down as he composed, or had someone else write it down, would have had to work more slowly than an oral poet composing and delivering his work to an audience in the traditional way; but what effect did this reduced pace have on the finished product?[118] How dependent was a literate poet on the oral tradition, compared with an oral poet? Would the relative slowness of composition pen-in-hand or for dictation have made poets more reflective, more original, less dependent on the common oral stock? Not necessarily: the extra time might have been used to make more judicious selections of traditional elements than was possible for the oral poet composing as he performed.

These uncertainties, and others connected with them, have been confronted more productively in recent work in oral-formulaic theory and practical analysis. Here, instead of attempting the impossible task of doing justice to the vigour, extent, and sophistication of scholarly work on orality and oral traditional literature over the last half-century, I offer here only a sketch of some of the basic ideas contained in three recent and substantial contributions to research in this area. All three of these books include discussions of the Old English poetic tradition; and taken together, they probably give a fair indication of the directions in which the study of oral traditional literature has moved since Magoun and Benson wrote. These are John Miles Foley's *Traditional Oral Epic*,[119] the same author's *Immanent Art*, and John D. Niles's *Homo Narrans*. All three works are comparative, dealing with several distinct oral traditions in different languages, cultures, and historical periods, and both writers are concerned with identifying the distinguishing features of traditional literature generally.

In *Traditional Oral Epic*, Foley's main project is to clear the way for the development of a poetics appropriate to the appreciation of 'traditional' literature.[120] He uses ancient Greek (i.e. Homeric) poetry, modern Serbo-Croatian oral poetry, and Old English poetry, all representing traditions that are either oral or have clear oral backgrounds, as the basis for constructing a 'reading programme' for traditional texts generally. The study of works from the same and different traditions should observe certain methodological principles. One is 'text-dependence': for example, an oral-derived work surviving (like *Beowulf*) only in a manuscript may, for all we know, represent just one stage in a lengthy textual history

---

[118] See Niles, *Homo Narrans*, 111–12. In Serbo-Croatian oral tradition, the poet Avdo Medjedović composed a lengthy poem of particularly high poetic quality (*The Wedding Song of Smailagić Meho*) after hearing a printed record of the story by another poet read out to him several times. Here, at least, is evidence that oral poets sometimes produce more polished performances when freed from the pressures exerted by a living, traditional audience.

[119] John Miles Foley, *Traditional Oral Epic: The Odyssey, Beowulf, and the Serbo-Croatian Return Song* (Berkeley: University of California Press, 1990).

[120] On the meaning of 'traditional' in Foley's usage, see further below.

during which traditional elements have been modified by written transmission in ways now undiscoverable; so *Beowulf* should not be compared uncritically with (for example) an audio record of an actual oral performance by a traditional poet in another tradition. The investigator must always keep in mind the possibility that the conditions of transmission or preservation have affected the traditional poems in which he is interested. Furthermore, oral poetry proper, such as some of the Serbo-Croatian poems recorded electronically in live performance by Parry and Lord, must be distinguished from 'oral-derived' poetry such as *Beowulf* which, though plainly drawing heavily on oral tradition, bears an uncertain relationship to any actual oral performance in which it may or may not have originated.[121] The term 'traditional literature' is used by Foley (and others) to cover both these kinds of work.

Foley's *Immanent Art*, written as a companion volume to *Traditional Oral Epic*, attempts to reach a general understanding of how traditional literature conveys meaning. Foley sets out to redeem such works from the negative judgements on their poetic value that often result when they are read and interpreted as if they were the work of fully literate authors. Putting aside much modern literary theorizing as inadequate for uncovering and defining the poetics of traditional literature, Foley develops a concept of "traditional referentiality", the essential point of which is that traditional elements "reach out of the immediate instance in which they appear to the fecund totality of the entire tradition;" they "bear meanings as wide and deep as the tradition they encode."[122]

Both these books by Foley are much taken up with the proper identification of traditional elements in oral and oral-derived works, and with understanding and appreciating such works in their own terms. John D. Niles's *Homo Narrans*, though in very close accord with Foley's theoretical positions, is an anthropological study of traditional oral storytelling, emphasising the circumstances of its composition and delivery in relation to its social functions. Niles places oral storytelling at the very centre of human culture: oral narrative "is and for a long time has been the chief basis of culture itself,"[123] and even "defines the human species."[124] When an Old English poem was recorded in writing, "its orality is likely to have remained latent, ready to be reactivated through the voicings of people who were competent performers."[125] Again, some traditional texts recorded in writing "may have been a secondary phenomenon, essential for the preservation of the work in fixed form but intended more as an aid to public performance than as documents to be filed away for safekeeping or private perusal."[126] Niles, as a

---

[121] See Foley, *Traditional Oral Epic*, 3–8.
[122] Foley, *Immanent Art*, 7.
[123] Niles, *Homo Narrans*, 2.
[124] Niles, *Homo Narrans*, 3.
[125] Niles, *Homo Narrans*, 19.
[126] Niles, *Homo Narrans*, 23 (also 28, where a similar point is made).

practising folklorist, returns repeatedly to this point: an oral story may pass into textual form and then be returned via recitation of the text to the world of oral performance. It is therefore inappropriate to speak of a "great divide between the oral and the literate"; there is only a "continuum between 'orality' and 'orality plus a full deployment of the resources of literacy and mass communication'."[127] Niles's position here is in some ways analogous with that of the anthropologist Brian Street, discussed earlier:[128] Street, as we saw, played down the importance of the technological innovations that accompany new literacy; in his view, as in Niles's, there is no "great divide" between orality and literacy. Although it is not at all difficult to accept a theory of 'transitional' stages between oral and written poetry—indeed, in some matters, for example metre, it is difficult to see how any other view could be maintained—or O'Keeffe's related idea of 'residual orality' as a factor in the process of written transmission of traditional verse (on which see further below), one of the most basic points that will be made in the main body of this book is that there is a very important divide between oral and literate communication and composition arising from the different pragmatics of speech and writing—not, perhaps, necessarily a 'great' divide, but certainly a *radical* divide in the pragmatics of the two modes of linguistic expression, and one, furthermore, with an observable history and observable consequences.[129]

On the question of the origins of *Beowulf*, Niles favours the view that we owe the poem's preservation on parchment to an "outsider"—a person somewhat removed from the oral tradition but in touch with it.[130] But this was no simple transcription by a literate individual of a particular oral performance of the story: the preserver of *Beowulf* in written form was responsible for some, at least, of the "artistic excellence"[131] that characterizes the text as we have it. *Beowulf* is neither "a literate island in a sea of much inferior oral poetry," nor "the unmediated gift of an oral poet's inspiration,"[132] but "a unique hybrid that comes into being at the interface of orality and literacy through an unknown person's prompting."

Both Foley and Niles are committed, in their different ways and amongst other objectives, to rescuing Old English poetry from the negative judgements of critics in thrall to theories of interpretation and standards of evaluation developed on the basis of literature produced later under the conditions of advanced literacy. Niles, for example, writes of those "whose lives are deeply invested in Western

---

[127] Niles, *Homo Narrans*, 48.
[128] See above, 21.
[129] See especially Chapter 2 below.
[130] Niles, *Homo Narrans*, 91.
[131] Niles, *Homo Narrans*, 102: ". . . the artistic excellence of *Beowulf* is one factor that leads to the conclusion that intervention by an outsider—the example of the monks and Cædmon, transposed to a secular key—is a plausible way of accounting for the fact that his poem is written down on parchment."
[132] Niles, *Homo Narrans*, 104.

educational institutions" who "naturally tend to understand illiteracy as nothing but deprivation."[133] Both scholars express very clear views on what constitutes traditional literature. It may be worth remarking here that to attempt what I am attempting in this book—to work, so to speak, in the opposite direction and look for the marks of authorial literacy in poetic works some of which both Foley and Niles would call 'oral-derived'—is in no way opposed to their critical enterprises. In fact, the distinction drawn by Foley between oral performances and 'oral-derived' texts implies the need for a programme of research on what distinguishes the two forms of work, both from each other and from works produced in a more thoroughly literate milieu, when traditional features such as the poetic mechanisms he describes in *Immanent Art* are beginning to atrophy.[134]

The publication of Foley's *Traditional Oral Epic* and *Immanent Art* more or less coincided with that of Katherine O'Brien O'Keeffe's 1990 book *Visible Song*,[135] a significant landmark in the study of Anglo-Saxon literacy. O'Keeffe makes some use of oral-formulaic theory as it impinges on the composition of Old English verse, but her real interest in this book is in reception and textual transmission. O'Keeffe looks to the manuscripts of Old English poetry for evidence of developing literacy in the period. She accepts the possibility of "one or more transitional states" on a continuum between the theoretical extremes of pure orality and pure literacy.[136] A key term (borrowed from Ong) in *Visible Song* is 'residual orality' (closely related to Foley's 'oral-derived' category of text), a

---

[133] Niles, *Homo Narrans*, 127.

[134] On the general nature of oral-derived works, see Albert B. Lord, "Oral Composition and 'Oral Residue' in the Middle Ages," in *Oral Tradition in the Middle Ages*, ed. W. F. H. Nicolaisen (Binghamton: Center for Medieval and Early Renaissance Studies, State University of New York at Binghamton, 1995), 7–29. The term 'oral residue' is borrowed by Lord from Ong, *Orality and Literacy*. On the distinctive poetics of oral-derived themes and motifs in Middle English literature, see Mark C. Amodio, "Old-English Oral-Formulaic Tradition and Middle-English Verse," in *De Gustibus: Essays for Alain Renoir*, ed. John Miles Foley (New York and London: Garland Publishing, Inc., 1992), 1–20.

[135] Katherine O'Brien O'Keeffe, *Visible Song: Transitional Literacy in Old English Verse*, Cambridge Studies in Anglo-Saxon England 4 (Cambridge: Cambridge University Press, 1990).

[136] For a later project, comparable with O'Keeffe's in its spectrum-based emphasis, see Nancy Mason Bradbury, *Writing Aloud: Storytelling in Late Medieval England* (Urbana and Chicago: University of Illinois Press, 1998). Using several different internal and external criteria, Bradbury seeks to position a selection of medieval English metrical romances along a spectrum extending from pure 'voiceness' at one extreme ("the assumption or the pretext that the audience has gathered to listen to the teller's voice" [97]) to pure 'bookness' at the other ("the competing assumption that a story is a fixed set of symbols on a page awaiting visual decoding." The terminology is borrowed from Donald Howard, *The Idea of the Canterbury Tales* [Berkeley: University of California Press, 1976]).

phenomenon O'Keeffe infers from two kinds of evidence: the use of 'meaningful space' in copying verse, and 'variance' (mainly formulaic variation) in their literary transmission.[137] The broad argument is that the increase over time in the use by scribes of spatial and graphic conventions of presentation ('cues') indicates a progressively more literate reading community,[138] though one less in touch with the oral poetic tradition, whereas a high degree of 'variance' (lexical or formulaic variation) between the extant texts of verse, which she associates with oral transmission, points in the opposite direction along the continuum towards orality, suggesting "the continuance of oral techniques of reception in the reading of verse" until the tenth century.[139] O'Keeffe's book includes (in Chapter 2) an account of the textual development of the Old English poem *Cædmon's Hymn* in fourteen manuscripts written between the eighth and the twelfth centuries. When the presentation of the vernacular poem is compared with that of Latin verse in Bede's *Historia*, the latter contains relatively plentiful visual cues (formatting, pointing, capitalization), suggesting "awareness that Latin required extralinguistic cues to help the reader work through the verse."[140] Readers of Old English poetry did not require these cues: in the two earliest Old English texts of *Cædmon's Hymn*, graphic cues are few, in O'Keeffe's view because "graphic marking was perceived as redundant."[141] Texts of the poem attached to later manuscripts of the Latin Bede (all belonging to the textual groups distinguished by the *ylda* and *eorðe* variants in line 5) reveal a relatively static text, whereas the variants among the versions (the *eorðan* group) of the text in the *Old English Bede* show "a dynamic of transmission where the message is not embellished but where change within the formula is allowed."[142] The explanation offered for the difference is connected with the different linguistic environments: the *Old English Bede* is a vernacular text, and the vernacular, though written, "was still heavily influenced by its earlier, purely oral condition."[143] The 'variance' in its texts of *Cædmon's Hymn* is 'formula-dependent' and arises from "suggestion, by 'guess' triggered by key-words in formulae." Oral tradition is here still "at an early stage in its adaptation to the possibilities of writing";[144] indeed, "reading and copying have actually become conflated with composing."[145] These texts of the poem in the *Old English*

---

[137] O'Keeffe, *Visible Song*, x.
[138] On O'Keeffe's interpretation of scribal pointing of Old English verse, see the review of *Visible Song* by Peter J. Lucas, *RES* 44 (1993): 401–3.
[139] O'Keeffe, *Visible Song*, x.
[140] O'Keeffe, *Visible Song*, 32.
[141] O'Keeffe, *Visible Song*, 35.
[142] O'Keeffe, *Visible Song*, 39.
[143] O'Keeffe, *Visible Song*, 40.
[144] O'Keeffe, *Visible Song*, 40.
[145] O'Keeffe, *Visible Song*, 41.

Bede show that "under certain conditions the 'literate' reception of Old English verse retained a substantial element of oral process."[146]

The following year, 1991, saw the publication of Seth Lerer's *Literacy and Power in Anglo-Saxon Literature*,[147] an intellectually demanding work that aims to reveal certain 'mythologies' of reading and writing embedded in literary works of the period. Lerer assembles a group of scenes of "inscription and decipherment," written narratives "reflecting on themselves, as they become allegories of the making and reception of a literary tradition."[148] Each scene is a microcosm of the whole work in which it is embedded, and they function "more as tropes than as unmediated versions of historical reality."[149] The conventions of runic writing, in which Lerer shows a particular interest, are used to evoke the past and contrast it with a Christian present. Runes "contributed to the mythology of writing for a literate vernacular poetics"; they represented the "alterity" of the past to Anglo-Saxon writers,[150] and could "provide a later, literate community with a mythology of writing and a foil for the depiction of their own authorial and hermeneutic skills."[151]

Two of Lerer's scenes involve runic writing, and these are of particular interest in the present context. One of Lerer's key points about runes is that they were regarded, from the perspective of the Christian period, as having derived their power under paganism from "their own inscription";[152] runes were seen as representing a magic of the word, in contrast with roman writing, which was symbolic of the power and will of God.[153] Lerer illustrates this last point in his analysis of Bede's story of Imma in Book 4, Chapter 20 of the *Ecclesiastical History*, which Lerer reads as "a kind of parable of the mythologies of writing in a newly Christian Anglo-Saxon England." Imma represents a paradox, a prisoner who cannot be restrained; the bonds in which he is placed fall away as if by magic. His puzzled captor asks him if he carries "releasing letters" (*litteras solutorias*) on his

---

[146] O'Keeffe, *Visible Song*, 46. For some reservations about O'Keeffe's concept of 'formulaic reading' in relation to *Cædmon's Hymn* in particular, see Peter Orton, "The Transmission of the West Saxon Versions of Cædmon's Hymn: A Reappraisal," *SN* 70 (1998): 153–64 (at 161–62), and Daniel Paul O'Donnell, *Cædmon's Hymn: A Multimedia Study, Archive and Edition* (Cambridge: D. S. Brewer, in association with SEENET and The Medieval Academy, 2005), 187–90. On O'Keeffe's evaluation of the variants in *Solomon and Saturn*, see also Peter Orton, *The Transmission of Old English Poetry*, Westfield Publications in Medieval and Renaissance Studies 12 (Turnhout: Brepols, 2000), 201–6.

[147] Seth Lerer, *Literacy and Power in Anglo-Saxon Literature*, Regents Studies in Medieval Culture (Lincoln and London: University of Nebraska Press, 1991).

[148] Lerer, *Literacy and Power*, 3.
[149] Lerer, *Literacy and Power*, 4.
[150] Lerer, *Literacy and Power*, 12.
[151] Lerer, *Literacy and Power*, 15.
[152] Lerer, *Literacy and Power*, 16.
[153] Lerer, *Literacy and Power*, 17.

person. The question reflects the new English church's concern "to perpetuate a notion that its converts once believed in a nonsymbolic magic of the letter."[154] Lerer contrasts Bede's *Historia* as a history with the fables about rune-magic that Imma's captor has heard:

> By relegating a knowledge of the releasing letters to the realm of oral lore, Bede privileges his written narrative, garnering for it an *auctoritas* similar to those texts that form the basis of a monastic education.[155]

The second of Lerer's runic scenes is the one in *Beowulf* where Hrothgar examines the runically inscribed hilt of a sword that the hero has found in Grendel's lair and used to kill Grendel's mother and decapitate the body of her son.[156] Lerer takes the hilt as "a figure for the poem as a whole."[157] The length of the account of Hrothgar's examination of the hilt mimics the time the reading itself will have taken;[158] Hrothgar and the reader encounter the inscription together.[159] The hilt represents "the nature of all writing,"[160] and the scene's significance is the "move from listening to reading."[161] *Beowulf*, Lerer argues, "presents two versions of itself," one oral, communal, and involving the presence of the poet, the other showing us "what mythic narrative can become when written down and read long after both its makers and its audience have died." The poet "imaginatively anticipates" the debate over whether *Beowulf* is oral or literate in origin.[162] We read the poem; but the poet enables us to imagine what it would be like to hear it as well.

Any general survey of 'literacy-studies' is bound to carry its own biases and underlying ideological preoccupations. The emphasis in this survey on work relevant (directly or indirectly) to English medieval literacy in its infancy was pointed out earlier, and perhaps needs no special defence in the introduction to a book whose main centre of interest is the primary transition from orality to literacy in Anglo-Saxon England. Some might, however, challenge the very existence of 'literacy-studies' on the basis that there is not one literacy but as many literacies as there are literate societies.[163] Obviously there is some truth in this; but only

---

[154] Lerer, *Literacy and Power*, 32.
[155] Lerer, *Literacy and Power*, 32–33.
[156] *Beowulf* 1687–99; Lerer, *Literacy and Power*, Chapter 5, "Hrothgar's Hilt and the Reader in *Beowulf*," 158–94.
[157] Lerer, *Literacy and Power*, 160.
[158] Lerer, *Literacy and Power*, 165.
[159] Lerer, *Literacy and Power*, 165.
[160] Lerer, *Literacy and Power*, 182.
[161] Lerer, *Literacy and Power*, 182.
[162] Lerer, *Literacy and Power*, 194.
[163] As Street argues (see above). This also seems to be the view taken by Kathryn A. Lowe, "Lay Literacy in Anglo-Saxon England and the Development of the Chirograph,"

comparative study will tell us how much. We are certainly not yet in a position to assume that the advent of literacy affects each society that acquires it in ways that are absolutely distinct. This book will not take a comparative approach to the advent of English literacy; the English evidence is itself quite complex and engrossing enough for several books, let alone one. But enough has been said in my summary of earlier work to suggest that not all manifestations of new literacy are confined to single cultures. There is much scope for more research into the extent of such correspondences and their significance. Meanwhile, we are not in a position to write off the 'autonomous' model of literacy-acquisition espoused by (for example) Goody and Olson. For the moment, what is most needed is more, and perhaps more varied, approaches to particular societies and their literacies.

This brings me back to the subject of this book. At the beginning of this chapter I described how the primary texts examined are organized from chapter to chapter. I must now try to describe my interest in these texts and the approaches to them that I intend to adopt. There are, perhaps, three main aspects of Anglo-Saxon literacy that are given close attention in this book, though they often combine because of the nature and generic groupings of the texts that are relevant to their investigation. The first of them may be described quite briefly. As we have seen, Anglo-Saxon literacy is distinctive for its staggered start: runic literacy came first, held the field until the roman alphabet arrived, coexisted with it in some uses for a time, and went into decline in the later part of the period. R. I. Page and other runologists have already opened up this area of investigation, though I hope to supplement their conclusions about the relationship between the two scripts, based on my own analysis of their respective or combined employment in both inscriptions and those manuscript texts on which I shall concentrate.

The easiest way of describing the second aspect of the advent of literacy with which this book is concerned—the distinctive pragmatics of literacy and its consequences in terms of new forms of expression and new meanings—is to consider two very brief examples of texts which are dealt with more systematically later on. The first of these has the Old English form *hring ic hattæ*, which means "I am called 'ring'." A conception of writing that regards it simply as a visual channel for utterances that were originally spoken, or might be spoken, cannot easily cope with a text like this. Was there a person named, or nicknamed, 'ring'? If so, why and to whom is he revealing his name? One reason (though not the only one) why such questions are unanswerable is that I have presented the text out of context: it is in fact a runic inscription on a silver-gilt finger-ring recently discovered at Wheatley Hill in Durham, dating perhaps from the later eighth century.[164] Although an oral origin for such an utterance is not, perhaps, completely out of the question—there just *might* have been someone calling himself 'Ring' who

---

in *Anglo-Saxon Manuscripts and their Heritage*, ed. Phillip Pulsiano and Elaine M. Treharne (Aldershot: Ashgate, 1998), 161–204.

[164] On the inscription and its preservation, see Page, *Introduction to English Runes*, 169.

proclaimed his identity to someone or other in these terms—there can be little doubt that the text was written for, and intended to be understood in relation to, the medium that preserves it, the ring upon which it is inscribed. A puzzle still remains, which is why the inscriber made the ring declare its own nature in this apparently redundant way; but I leave this question aside for the moment because it will be easier to address it in the context of the broader study of Anglo-Saxon inscriptions which constitutes Chapter 3 of this book.

My second exemplary text, also in Old English, is *Wulfwi me wrat*, "Wulfwi wrote me." This would be even less likely than *hring ic hatta* as a spoken utterance by a human being, for the obvious reason that no person can be "written". Here too it is the circumstances of the text's preservation that makes its significance clear: it is a scribal colophon attached to a manuscript text of an Old English version of the Gospels; "Wulfwi" is the scribe who copied the translation, and *me* is the copy of the text that he is claiming the credit for producing.

In this latter case a text, and in the former an inscribed medium, are made to 'speak' for themselves; but paradoxically, in the circumstances, it is most unlikely that either utterance ever has been, or ever could be, oral. The form and meaning of each utterance combines with its pragmatics—the circumstances under which it was 'uttered' (in these cases written), and was intended to be received—to identify it as an essentially literate production lacking any specific oral prehistory or precedent. I hope to show that the analysis of the forms and effects of such texts can tell us much about how the Anglo-Saxons conceptualized literacy. Both of my examples contain the first-person pronoun (*ic*, 'I', and *me*, 'me', respectively) used in an unexpected and unfamiliar way. The leitmotiv that recurs with the greatest regularity throughout this book is the use and the implications of the first-person pronoun in Old English, and in particular the impact of literacy on the way the pronoun came to be used by Old English writers.

The third aspect of literacy that is given close attention here is exemplified chiefly in Chapters 5 and 6. Here the typical pragmatics of two Old English poetic genres, the *Riddles* and the lyrics respectively, are analysed to illustrate not only the problems but also the opportunities created by reading and writing for Old English poets working in a period of early literacy. Chapter 6, on the Old English lyrics, will argue further that literacy was instrumental in provoking what one critic has called (with reference to the eighteenth century) the "inward turn of narrative"[165]—what amounts, in effect, to the beginnings of psychological analysis, as writers, with the aid of literacy, begin to examine their own mental and emotional experiences from within. I shall also raise, in this final chapter, the question of whether it is possible or useful to distinguish between historical and fictional writing in this, the earliest period of English literacy.

---

[165] Erich Kahler, *The Inward Turn of Narrative*, trans. Richard and Clara Winston, intro. Joseph Frank, Bollingen Series 83 (Princeton: Princeton University Press, 1973).

Chapter 2
Deixis and Incipient Literacy

§1. The 'speaking' text

Native speakers of a language seldom have reason to reflect on the usages and idioms they employ. Unless we take an academic interest in them, it takes special circumstances to draw these things to our attention as objects of critical interest—an inquiry into the origin of some word, say, or a question from a foreign learner puzzled by an opaque expression encountered for the first time. No doubt all languages involve usages which, if subjected to even the most superficial analysis, would appear strange and illogical. An example in modern English is the verb 'to say' with a book or other written document as subject. Although 'say' normally denotes speech, utterances of the type: "The book says . . ." or "The notice on the board says . . .", or "What does it [i.e. a book, a letter] say?", which appear to attribute speech to a written or printed document, are familiar enough. The usage seems to represent a sort of smudge on the boundary between two fields of expression. The fact that we may, if we choose, bypass the document or text as subject and replace it with the author, as for example in: "The author of this book says . . .", does not make it any less striking.

The *Oxford English Dictionary* recognizes this usage (s.v. **Say**, v^1), though it does not categorize it as involving a distinct meaning of 'say': the relevant quotations are mixed in with others illustrating the common usage of the verb with a human speaker as subject. The *OED* does, however, show some awareness of its peculiarity, for it includes a note on its signification:[1]

> In English, as in other Teutonic languages, *say* is an approximate synonym of *speak*, from which it differs in having normally as its object a particular word or series of words, or a sentence representing the meaning of a particular series of words. Cf. Latin *dicere* and its representatives in Romanic (which, however, have also senses that are now expressed in English by *tell*), and Latin *aio, inquam*.

---

[1] In quoting the *OED* I expand some of the standard abbreviations.

As the word designates not the action of speaking itself, but its relation to the object, its use with reference to written expression does not ordinarily, like the similar use of *speak*, involve any consciousness of metaphor.

These comments describe modern usage clearly enough, but they rather discourage any attempt to understand its history. To assert that 'say' designates the "relation" of the action of speaking to its object seems almost to deny that it is a verb at all, and obscures the direct denotation of vocal utterance which most people would want to claim for it. The semantic description seems inappropriately abstract. And although it is true that 'say' always takes the same kind of object—a piece of direct or indirect speech, or a noun denoting a speech of some kind—this aspect of its usage does not seal the verb off from variations in meaning arising from differences in the nature of the subject: it is clear that a book cannot 'say' something vocally as a human being can, as in a sentence like "Mary said that she was happy," where actual speech is indicated. From the point of view of this latter usage, which most native speakers of English would probably recognize as the basic one for this verb, it is anomalous, not to say illogical, to refer to a book, which is, after all, a material manifestation of language, in a context which seems to imply that it is the actual origin of an utterance. How did the verb 'say' come to be used like this? Or (to ask a slightly different question), how did books and documents come to be spoken of as if they were capable of speech?[2]

§2. Speech, writing and incipient literacy

Is there, perhaps, or has there been in the past, some deficiency in the vocabulary of linguistic ideas which this usage of 'say' was designed to remedy? After more than a millennium of literacy one would expect the English language to possess an adequate range of terms for distinguishing the spoken from the written word, as well as the expression from the reception of language. In fact, the system according to which we say that a speaker says something which a hearer hears and a writer writes something which a reader reads seems both symmetrical and complete. But the usage under discussion points to an awareness at some stage in the history of English that communication by speech and writing are not the perfectly homologous processes this system might imply. Analysis leads to a recognition that only written language interposes a material medium—a book or other document—between the originator of an utterance and its recipient.[3] Spoken communication is direct; no medium but air intervenes between communicator

---

[2] Ong, "Orality, Literacy, and Medieval Textualization," makes the point in passing that "a text does not say anything of itself" (2).

[3] I use the term 'utterance' here and in what follows to cover both spoken and written verbal productions.

2. Deixis and Incipient Literacy

and recipient. An expression like "The book says . . ." illustrates the transposition of 'say', a verb which must have applied only to speech before the English became literate, into the semantic field of written linguistic expression. The extension in meaning must clearly be connected with this special requirement of writing, for it is the inscribed medium itself, not the writer, that replaces the speaker as the verb's subject.[4]

The usage is an old one. Although the *OED*'s examples do not include any from the Old English period, many instances could be cited of forms of the Old English verb *secgan* (infinitive), the direct ancestor of our verb 'say', in this sense.[5] They occur in Old English poetry, where expressions such as *þæs þe secgað bec* ("as books say"), or *Us secgað bec* ("Books tell us"), abound.[6] As we have already seen in Chapter 1, it was the Anglo-Saxon period that saw the production of the very first English books, written in Old English or Latin following the conversion; and a period of early literacy offers a satisfactory historical background for the origin of our usage of 'say'. The semantic extension of the verb into the field of written language was in all probability caused by an idea in the minds of newly literate Anglo-Saxons of an analogy between books as sources (in a sense) of utterances and the human speakers who were the only sources of utterances before literacy arrived.

Perhaps we can achieve a more precise formulation of this supposed sense of analogy, and a fuller appreciation of the processes involved, which are important for my general argument in this book. What were the consequences of the historical supplementation of speech by writing as a new form of linguistic communication in Anglo-Saxon England? Today, as members of a fully literate society that takes the differences between speech and writing for granted, we are not in an ideal position to recreate imaginatively the sense of novelty that must have attached to reading and writing (and all the paraphernalia and activities connected with them) when the Anglo-Saxons became literate. There is no contemporary account in Anglo-Saxon sources of the advent of literacy and it would be astonishing if there were; but in the oral phase, any general Anglo-Saxon assumptions

---

[4] Another kind of extension is observable in the usage exemplified by "Mary said in her letter that . . .", but here there is no substitution of the inscribed medium (or the text) for the human originator of the utterance it bears, so this latter usage represents a less radical departure from the standard than "Books say . . . ."

[5] I follow the usual practice of reserving the term 'Anglo-Saxon' for the historical period and 'Old English' for the language, for the period it represents in the history of English, and for its literature.

[6] Examples of these and similar expressions from Old English poetry include *Lord's Prayer II* 20, *Genesis* 227, 1723, *Battle of Brunanburh* 68, *Christ* 785, *Guðlac* 878. Unless otherwise stated, all references here to Old English poems are to George Philip Krapp and Elliott Van Kirk Dobbie, eds., *The Anglo-Saxon Poetic Records: A Collective Edition*, 6 vols. (New York: Columbia University Press, 1931–1953).

about language must obviously have been based on the spoken language alone. The arrival of literacy would have required a revision of these assumptions—or, more likely, forced the Anglo-Saxons to address the phenomenon of language itself, both written and spoken, squarely for the first time. This historical confrontation with language in Anglo-Saxon England, provoked by the advent of literacy, is one of the main subjects of this book.[7]

The most obvious difference between speech and writing lies in the faculties and senses used in their production and reception: speech is made with the voice and perceived through the ear, writing made by the hand and perceived through the eye.[8] A second, connected difference is that whereas speech is evanescent, writing achieves a stable physical form. No vocal utterance is remembered verbatim for long unless the hearer makes a deliberate attempt to memorize it, or it is fixed in his mind by repetition, as for example in the case of proverbs or spells. Writing, on the other hand, because it relies on a material medium rather than human memory, preserves utterances infallibly and indefinitely in their original verbal form. Books and manuscripts can, of course, fade, decay, or be destroyed, but that does not alter the basic principle of writing's permanence: barring accidents or deliberate destruction, written documents can last for hundreds of years, and are renewable by copying. Thirdly (as mentioned in Chapter 1), the chronological relationship between spoken and written language is the same in all human societies: speech is always the precursor of writing, never the other way round. Every human community, past and present, uses speech; literacy comes later, if it comes at all.

A fourth distinction, the most important one for my argument, lies in the temporal and spatial limitations imposed on spoken linguistic communication but removed when language is written. The moment of speaking and the place of utterance must obviously be the same as those of its reception; unless speaker and hearer coincide in time and space (the human voice carrying over only a short distance), there can be no communication.[9] A broad model of spoken communication, presented schematically, is as simple as this:

---

[7] For some suggestions about connections between the particular system of written representation adopted by a society when it becomes literate and the way language itself is conceptualized in that society, see Olson, *The World on Paper*, 65–90 (Chapter 4, "What Writing Represents").

[8] For accessible general discussions of these differences, see John Lyons, *Introduction to Theoretical Linguistics* (Cambridge: Cambridge University Press, 1968), 63, and Jahandarie, *Discourse*, 131–49.

[9] See Ursula Schaefer, "From an Aesthetic Point of View . . . : Receptional Aspects of Old English Poetry," in *De Gustibus*, ed. Foley, 494–541 (at 499): ". . . textuality . . . makes verbal discourse more and more independent of the actual situation. As to oral discourse, production and reception coincide, making the actual extra-linguistic context a frame of reference both the producer and the recipient may rely on."

2. Deixis and Incipient Literacy

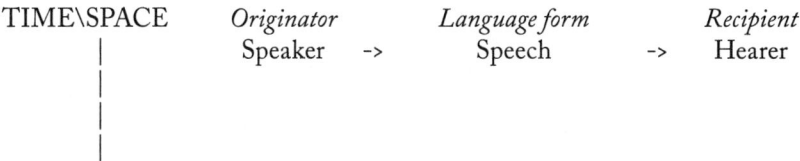

FIGURE 1.

When language is written, on the other hand, the moment of communication is normally delayed, and whatever the writer writes may be read at any future time by anyone competent in the language and form of representation used. Although speakers may be overheard, they normally have full control over who hears what they have to say. Writers, by contrast, cannot so easily calculate or limit their readerships. They may direct a communication to a particular individual as a personal letter, or write with readers of a particular type or background in mind and steer their words towards them in various ways; but unless they take the exceptional step of ensuring that their writings are destroyed once they have been assimilated ("Now burn this letter"), writers cannot be certain how wide a circulation their works will achieve in the end. For example, King Alfred of Wessex would no doubt have been sceptical of a prediction that his circular letter to the Anglo-Saxon bishops of his day, prefixed to manuscript copies of his English translation of Pope Gregory's *Cura Pastoralis*, would be reproduced in countless copies of Old English 'Readers' and would find a large, non-episcopal readership a thousand years later.[10] The case simply illustrates how writers communicate 'blind' unless they make careful arrangements to restrict their readerships.

These considerations suggest the following as a broad schematic model of written communication, constructed out of the same elements as my earlier model of spoken communication:

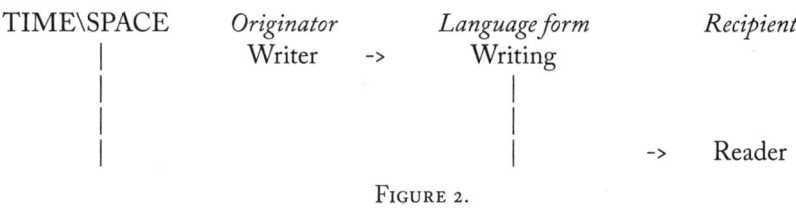

FIGURE 2.

---

[10] For a modern English translation of the text and a useful commentary on it, see Simon Keynes and Michael Lapidge, *Alfred the Great: Asser's Life of King Alfred and Other Contemporary Sources* (Harmondsworth: Penguin, 1983), 124–26, 293–96.

§3. Coding time and receiving time

The difference between the two models has important historical implications. Figure 1 represents not just a general model for all spoken communication, but also the oral phase in the history of any language, before the arrival of literacy.[11] The branch of linguistics known as pragmatics, which is concerned with the relationship between utterances and the entire range of contexts and circumstances in which they are produced, distinguishes between two moments in the process of linguistic communication: 'coding time' is the moment when a linguistic utterance is formulated and uttered, and 'receiving time' is the moment when the utterance reaches a recipient.[12] In speech, and in the historical oral phase, the two moments must always coincide; but when literacy arrives, the production of language and its reception no longer necessarily coincide in space and time—would not normally do so, in fact, in the case of writing, because much of the value of literacy resides in the possibilities it creates for linguistic communication across space and time.[13]

Although the difference between the two models is simple enough, it is open to alternative analyses depending on which temporal point of reference one adopts—coding time or receiving time. Coding time finds speaker and writer in a structurally identical position in both space and time in relation to their utterances; but spoken and written communications differ in the presence or absence of the recipient: the hearer is present when a speaker speaks because his presence is always necessary if communication is to be achieved in speech; but the reader is absent when communication is initiated by a writer. He appears later, either in the same place or elsewhere, to receive the written communication, read it, and so complete the linguistic transaction. The key feature of a coding-time-based analysis of written communication is thus the absent reader. If, on the other hand, we take receiving time as our reference-point, it is the hearer and the reader who are in the same position in relation to the linguistic message. The speaker is present too at this moment, as he must be, whereas the writer is absent. He

---

[11] There are, admittedly, some exceptional cases and situations. An oral message might be relayed verbatim by messenger to a third party, in which case a distinction arises between the originator of the utterance, who is absent when his message is received, and his spokesman, who is present. There are also situations in which human beings speak even though there is no one else to hear them. Later we shall see evidence in Anglo-Saxon writings of a significant interest in some of these marginal circumstances in which speech and writing draw close together. On the general fuzziness of the boundaries between speech and writing, see Jahandarie, *Discourse*, 131–33.

[12] See Stephen C. Levinson, *Pragmatics* (Cambridge: Cambridge University Press, 1983), 62. When the two stages coincide, as in spoken communication, we may speak of 'deictic simultaneity' (73).

[13] Again, there are exceptional cases—the passing of notes, for example.

2. Deixis and Incipient Literacy 43

may have moved on, or died, or (in the case of letters) remained where he is and sent his message to its recipient elsewhere; but whatever his position in space and time, he is not normally present when the communication he has initiated is fulfilled. The essence of a receiving-time-based analysis of written communication is thus the absence of the writer. These alternative analyses might seem pedantic, though they are, as we shall see shortly, both useful for an understanding of the formal innovations that literacy brought in its wake in Anglo-Saxon England.

§4. The inscribed medium as surrogate 'speaker' and 'hearer'

We are now, perhaps, in a position to return to our original problem. It is only, it seems to me, by reference to a theory of a historical attempt to 'map' writing and reading as concepts and activities on to the model of speaking and hearing that it is possible to offer an explanation of the peculiar usage of 'say' which provoked this discussion. I suggest that newly-literate individuals in Anglo-Saxon society, accustomed, like members of any society that has hitherto been oral, to the invariable presence of the originator of an utterance (in most conditions identical with its speaker), and consequently very aware of the absence of the writer whenever they encountered the written word, sometimes tried to supply what was missing. In effect they attempted (unconsciously, of course) to construct a homology with the familiar model of spoken communication by casting the medium of writing, the book or manuscript — an 'extra' element, with no place in the model of spoken communication — in the role of a surrogate 'speaker' of the language it contains. In the Old English sentence: *þæs þe secgað bec*, "as books say", the book is conceived as a 'presence', comparable with the presence of a human being, which fills the structural slot left empty by the absent writer.

If this reasoning is accepted, it follows that the receiving-time-based analysis of linguistic communication is the appropriate one so far as the conceptualization of language reflected in such expressions as "The book says . . ." is concerned. The usage suggests that, for Anglo-Saxon readers, the moment when the message actually reached its destination was the important one, rather than the moment when a writer set pen to parchment or other surface. This is only to be expected, of course: from a reader's standpoint, a written document might just as well not exist until it is seen and read. The foundations for communication are laid when a writer finishes his work; but the communication remains dormant until a reader appears on the scene to complete it. "The book says . . ." and the Old English equivalents quoted earlier are clearly and essentially readers' expressions (for the obvious reason that they refer to or introduce ideas taken from books).[14]

---

[14] See below, Table 3, for a schematization of the interrelation between coding and receiving time on the one hand and the writer and the reader on the other.

Later we shall consider examples of Old English utterances which are in some ways the writer's equivalent of them.

Meanwhile, a question that arises here is the attitude to the writer's role in written communication implied by such expressions as "Books say . . .". In using them, readers effectively remove the writer from the picture. His absence at receiving time works against him in that his identity as the originator of his own work is forgotten in the way the communication is conceptualized and expressed in language. Such, it seems, is the implication of "Books say. . .". How significant is this implicit dismissal (if one may use so dramatic a term) of the writer? Is it no more than a consequence of the workings of the structural mapping process I have described, or might it also reflect some more general feeling about the relative unimportance of writers? Is the weakened sense of authorial identity partly a result of his or her absorption by what he or she has written? Or is our problem here simply that the world in which we now live raises the profile of authors in relation to their work far higher than was the case in the medieval period? It is difficult to know in what terms exactly the question should be framed; but the general issue raised here is plainly the status and conception of writers and (to draw a distinction I have so far avoided) of authors in Anglo-Saxon England. Having formulated these questions, I put them to one side because nothing more can be done with them for the moment; but they will arise again in a more pressing way later in this book when we come to consider records of the names of authors and the notion of authorship in Anglo-Saxon England.[15]

The idea that books may 'say' things to those who read them has far-reaching implications. It suggests the possibility, which may seem absurd at first sight, that writers may 'say' things to the books they write. If the book may speak, perhaps it may also, in a sense, be addressed, even 'hear'. The logic of this analogy would suggest that if a book hears, what it hears will be the words which are written into it; the book will represent itself as the audience of its own text, 'spoken' to it by its author. There is, as we shall see later in Chapter 5, some evidence for this curious and distinctive conception of writing as something heard by the medium that preserves it in the Old English poem *The Husband's Message*. It appears, however, that we must look to later medieval English literature for an example of an author 'speaking' *in propria persona* to a book he has written. This is in the epilogue to *Troilus and Criseyde*, where Chaucer worries about the accuracy of the future transmission of his poem:

> Go, litel bok, go, litel myn tragedye,
> Ther God thi makere yet, er that he dye,
> So sende myght to make in som comedye!
> But litel book, no makyng thow n'envie,
> But subgit be to alle poesye;

---

[15] See Chapters 4 and 6 below.

> And kis the steppes where as thow seest pace
> Virgile, Ovide, Omer, Lucan, and Stace.
>
> And for ther is so gret diversite
> In Englissh and in writyng of oure tonge,
> So prey I God that non myswrite the,
> Ne the mysmetre for defaute of tonge;
> And red wherso thow be, or elles songe,
> That thow be understonde, God I biseche![16]

As in our usage of 'say' (*secgan*), Chaucer's book as a work seems to be regarded as an active agent, here a traveller in time and space. But there is a notable difference too: Chaucer's *litel bok* is a surrogate of the absent reader, not of the author. The poet's rhetorical flourish reflects a coding-time-based analysis of written communication, not a receiving-time-based one. The point of reference in time and space is the moment and place of utterance, in this case the moment and place of writing. One consequence of this is that Chaucer does not efface himself as author of his own work; it is the reader who is pushed into the background. As in the case of "The book says . . .", the process of written communication is implicitly truncated, but with the difference that here it is the role not of the writer but of the reader which is 'cut' from the drama of linguistic communication.[17]

I know of no comparable direct addresses by writers to manuscripts or texts in the Anglo-Saxon period; but this is not surprising in a period when literacy was still very young. We saw earlier how writing lies dormant until a reader arrives to activate it as a communicative utterance. It is, perhaps, to be expected

---

[16] *Troilus and Criseyde*, 1786–98; see *The Riverside Chaucer*, ed. Larry D. Benson, 3rd ed. (Oxford: Oxford University Press, 1988), 584. See also 1056, note to line 1786: the motif derives from Ovid, though Chaucer probably took it from the envoi to Boccaccio's *Filocolo*.

[17] An effect in some ways complementary to this is detected in *The Canterbury Tales* by Barry Sanders, "Lie it as it Plays," in *Literacy and Orality*, ed. Olson and Torrance, 111–28. The "General Prologue" to the *Tales* begins with a complex sentence in which two substantial subordinate clauses precede the independent clause (*thanne longen folk to goon on pilgrimages*) — a "difficult syntactic form for a nonliterate to grasp" (114–15). This would have alerted the audience (to whom Chaucer is envisaged as reciting his work) to the fact that "a text precedes [the recitation], and that meaning lies locked in *it*, not in the author — and certainly not in them" (115). Sanders argues from this that even as he recites his own work, Chaucer as author "has in some ways rendered himself superfluous" (115); that "the text has now assumed its own, independent authority, one that Chaucer has in effect authorized" (p. 115). The text's receivers are not pushed into the background, as in the *Troilus* passage quoted above; but in the course of establishing the work as a text, Chaucer here seems to find a way of drawing attention to his authorship of the work while paradoxically (if we agree with Sanders's analysis) drawing a line under his authorial responsibilities to what he has written. What the two works have in common, of course, is the emphasis they place on the text as an independent entity.

that the Anglo-Saxons, accustomed to taking language for granted during the oral phase as a means of *immediate* communication, would have been more acutely aware than we are today of this element of suspension in writing—the 'sleeping beauty' factor, as we might call it. That would help to account for their focus on receiving time as the vital moment in the process of written communication, when the reader's kiss awakens the slumbering text.

§5. The book as first-person speaker: Anglo-Saxon scribal colophons

The corpus of Anglo-Saxon writings yields other forms of utterance which suggest a similar sense of analogy between a human speaker and the written medium. In one highly distinctive formula, found among the scribal colophons that are occasionally added to longer texts in Anglo-Saxon manuscripts, the scribes create the vivid illusion that the manuscripts they are writing are indeed able to speak, just as expressions of the type: "Books say. . ." would imply. The formula consists of a scribal attribution denoting by a first-person pronoun the text to which it is added. A plain example is the one mentioned briefly earlier, towards the end of Chapter 1, *Wulfwi me wrat*, "Wulfwi wrote me", which comes after the text of an Old English prose translation of the Gospels in MS. BL, Cotton Otho C.i, vol. I.[18]

Colophons of this type are of great interest for an investigation of early conceptions of writing among literate Anglo-Saxons, even though they present some difficulties of interpretation. One is whether *Wulfwi me wrat* and similar utterances reflect a receiving-time-based or a coding-time-based analysis of linguistic communication. It all depends on how we interpret the past tense of the verb, in our example *wrat*, "wrote." The tense is probably best taken as a sign that these utterances anticipate the reader's perspective, looking back, so to speak, to the moment when they and the texts to which they refer were written. The writer has envisaged his future readers and is encouraging them to think about him in their own present (receiving time) rather than in his (coding time); the writer is, in this case, showing his awareness that from the reader's perspective he belongs to the past. The alternative interpretation is that the verb is past tense simply because the sentence of which it is a part was written after the copyist had finished his main task, in which case the point of reference is coding-time. It is difficult to choose between these two possibilities; but the obvious commemorative purpose

---

[18] See N. R. Ker, *Catalogue of Manuscripts Containing Anglo-Saxon* (Oxford: Oxford University Press, 1957), No. 181 and lvi, where Latin equivalents to such English forms are also cited (e.g. Ker, No. 338, item 25: *Me scripsit Wulfgeatus scriptor wigornensis*, "Wulfgeat, scribe of Worcester, wrote me").

of these utterances suggests that the former, receiving-time-based analysis is the better reflection of the writer's intention.

What is relatively clear is that these utterances represent a writer's analysis of linguistic communication, in contrast with "Books say . . .", which is, as we saw earlier, essentially a reader's analysis. *Wulfwi me wrat* shows the scribe anticipating the reception of his work. It represents, in one way at least, the writer's equivalent of the reader's "Books say . . .". However, these colophons also represent a logical advance on "Books say . . .". To report that books 'say' things involves only the most elementary level of personification; but it takes matters a stage further when writers give books distinctively bookish utterances, things which only they could 'say'. A special discourse of books is brought into being. Books may say, or be reported as saying, things that a human being could say just as well, for example "(Books say that) the world is coming to an end." But in spite of the use of the first-person pronoun (the implications of which will be considered in a moment), no human being could sensibly say "Wulfwi wrote me"; only a book or text could 'speak' such a sentence.

These utterances also represent an obvious paradox. Their form is strikingly at odds with their content. Formally, the scribe remains in the background, deferring to the text which is allowed to 'speak' directly to the reader at receiving time; but in contrast with this formal deference, the colophon's content is wholly concerned with the scribe and his professional activity at coding time. He is named (*Wulfwi*) and his job of writing denoted in a straightforward way by the verb 'wrote' (*wrat*). The scribe's evident desire to preserve a record of his identity in relation to his own work consorts oddly with his use of such a self-effacing style to achieve it. This incongruity gives us, perhaps, a glimpse of the struggle of early writers to grasp the logic of writing and reading.

As the analysis of written communication is determined by two independent variable factors, the four main possibilities may be schematized as follows:

Written communication: alternative analyses

Conditions	*Coding time*	*Receiving time*
	Reader absent; writer presented as source of utterance.	Writer absent; book (or other medium) presented as source of utterance.
Reader's analysis	The writer 'spoke' to the book, or the book 'heard' the writer speak its text to it. (e.g. *the Husband's Message*)	The book 'speaks' to me, the reader (e.g. *þæs þe secgað bec*, "as books say").

Writer's analysis	I, the writer, 'speak' to you, the book (e.g. Chaucer's *Troilus*).	I, the book, speak to you, the reader (e.g. *Wulfwi me wrat*).

FIGURE 3.

§6. Deixis

The academic field of linguistic pragmatics has already provided us with some useful terminology for analysing utterances of the "Books say . . ." type; and we may draw further on its resources at this point. One of the most distinctive aspects of *Wulfwi me wrat* and similar scribal utterances is their exemplification of deixis, a universal linguistic phenomenon.[19] A consideration of them as deictic utterances will, I hope, clarify their nature considerably, as well as raise further questions about them.

Generally speaking, the term deixis denotes a special kind of reference which is used in some kinds of utterance but not others. Deictic elements, which may be either particular words and expressions, or grammatical features such as tense, make reference in their different ways to aspects of the context of an utterance, so that the recipient will have difficulty in understanding it as a communication if he has no independent access to this contextual information.[20] The essential nature and workings of deixis are most easily conveyed by illustrating what happens when an utterance employing deictic terms is removed from its context so that the information on which it is based is missing. Levinson's well-known example is of the discovery of a message in a bottle washed up on the seashore, the text of which reads "Meet me here a week from now with a stick about this big."[21] As Levinson comments, "we do not know *who* to meet, *where* or *when* to meet him or her, or *how big* a stick to bring." One might add that the finder does not know whether he or she is the person who was meant to find, read, and obey these instructions either, or even if the writer had a particular recipient in mind. In any case, the message fails because the writer has injudiciously included deictic terms in it which no reader could interpret without knowledge of the context in which the message was written.[22] As an utterance, it exemplifies several of the

---

[19] I attempt only a brief explanation of deixis here. A fuller account of the subject is Levinson, *Pragmatics*, 54–96. There is also a clear (and entertaining) introduction to deixis in Charles J. Fillmore, *Santa Cruz Lectures on Deixis, 1971* (Bloomington: Indiana University Linguistics Club, 1975).

[20] On the importance of the context of utterance in distinguishing spoken and written communication, see Jahandarie, *Discourse*, 136–39.

[21] Levinson, *Pragmatics*, 55.

[22] I say "was written", though there are aspects of this particular utterance which suggest that it is essentially oral and so would never be written down; see below.

commonest categories of deixis: person ("me", and the pronoun of address implicit in the use of the imperative), place ("here"), and time ("a week from now"). The words 'me', 'here' and 'now' are deictic terms, words which have no regular reference to particular persons, places or times in English but are better regarded as semantic variables or parameters to which specific 'values' are assigned by the context whenever they are used as elements of actual utterances.

In *Wulfwi me wrat* there are two deictic elements. The tense of the verb *wrat* ties the utterance to a certain period (after Wulfwi wrote his contribution to MS. BL, Cotton Otho C.i); and although, as we saw earlier, it is not certain exactly where in time the point of reference is meant to be, it is clearly an example of time-deixis. The other deictic element is *me*, 'me'. As a personal pronoun, *me* immediately invites classification as person-deixis; but analysis is complicated by the fact that the pronoun does not here refer to a person at all but to a text. It is therefore best taken as falling into the category of "textual deixis" as defined by Lyons.[23]

Levinson's example is designed simply to illustrate the main varieties of deixis; but it also demonstrates something of much more direct relevance to our discussion: the potential for the spectacular breakdown of deictic reference when an essentially oral utterance is transferred unchanged to a written medium.[24] In fact, it seems natural to take Levinson's sentence as an oral utterance because of the expression "about this big", which must have been accompanied either by a physical gesture indicating the required length, or by some appropriate physical model, visible to both speaker and hearer. There are implications here for the transition from an oral to a literate society. Levinson (following Lyons) emphasises that the very nature of deixis points to a historical and logical basis in what he calls the "canonical situation of utterance," defined as the "basic face-to-face conversational context." Deixis is fundamental to language because its origins, like the origins of language itself, lie in vocal interaction; and at least some deictic usages, such as that exemplified by "about this big" in Levinson's example, would

---

[23] John Lyons, *Semantics*, 2 vols. (Cambridge: Cambridge University Press, 1977), 2: 667. The problem of classification here is difficult because the categorization of deictic terms and features may depend either on grammatical criteria, according to which *me* is person-deixis, or semantic criteria, according to which it is textual deixis. Levinson's discussion indicates that there is still no satisfactory taxonomy of deictic forms, no doubt partly because of this overlap in the principles of classification.

[24] See Jeffrey Kittay, "Thinking through Literacies," in *Literacy and Orality*, ed. Olson and Torrance, 165–73: "The writer must write *in* those aspects of the oral communication that are not themselves uttered but are prerequisites for the successful conveyance of the message, so that, for example what is an oral deictic must in writing be specified, because the reader will not be in the situation of the writer, will be bereft of the system of possible denotations, and thus will not know what a simple 'now' or 'here' or 'that' means" (167).

never occur in actual written utterances.[25] Deixis is an inconspicuous feature of spoken language, easily ignored; it becomes conspicuous only when it fails, and it is significant for my argument that its failure is most clearly illustrated in writing. The intimate connection between deixis and the circumstances of vocal conversation means that the transfer of deictic expressions into writing, with the loss of context that inevitably involves, is bound to cause problems.

§7. The deictic gap in literacy

An important and radical question arises at this point about the effect of incipient literacy on the usage of deictic terms. As far as I know, linguists have not taken much interest in this general problem,[26] perhaps as a consequence partly of the synchronic bias in sociolinguistics generally, and partly of the general favouring within linguistics of the spoken language over the written which was discussed briefly in Chapter 1. The utterance *Wulfwi me wrat* raises a very specific question about the implications of literacy for the use of personal pronouns, particularly the first-person pronouns 'I' (OE *ic*), 'me' (*me*) and 'my' or 'mine' (*min*). It is to be expected that newly literate Anglo-Saxon writers would experience a sense of awkwardness here. Their previous experience of first-person pronouns (as of all the most fundamental aspects of their language) would have been in the context of ordinary conversation, where they would use them to refer to themselves as speakers and hear them used by others to refer to themselves when they replied. They would also, perhaps, hear them used by oral poets in speeches attributed to characters, or in other, non-poetic, verbatim quotations of the words of a third party. But they would undoubtedly associate them most closely (just as we do even now) with the canonical situation of utterance, the "basic face-to-face conversational context" to which Lyons refers, and hence with the factor of 'presence' which I identified earlier as an inevitable concomitant of face-to-face conversation. If the oral phase left any lasting legacy at all to the literate Anglo-Saxons,

---

[25] This is not to claim that the expression "about this big" could never be used in written discourse; only that if written it would not normally have the 'gestural' implication it clearly has in Levinson's example—unless it was part of a quotation in direct speech, in which case some sort of explanation by the narrator would normally accompany it.

[26] A notable exception is Suzanne Fleischman, "Philology, Linguistics, and the Discourse of the Medieval Text," *Speculum* 65 (1990): 19–37. Fleischman connects the advent of literacy with the employment of deictic terms in Middle French prose romances: she relates usage of the temporal and spatial adverbs *or(e)*, 'now', and *(i)ci*, 'here' as markers of narrative turning points in these works to the oral tradition that formed their basis and to their conversion into written prose: *or(e)* is appropriate to oral performance as the text "unfolds through the time of its recitation," *(i)ci* to the written narrative as the text moves "across the space of the page" (33).

it must surely have included the assumption that the use of first-person pronouns was inseparably bound up with the presence of human speakers.

As we have seen, however, it is in the nature of writing to detach utterances from the presence of the utterer, the writer. Writing therefore causes a 'deictic gap' to open up which might well have inhibited writers in the early stages of literacy in their use of *ic*, *me*, and *min* for self-reference. The source of this supposed inhibition would lie in the writer's realization that he or she would be absent when their writings were read. The whole business of writing—the 'planting' of a communication which the writer is unlikely to see harvested—must have seemed a strange exercise when literacy was still new; but this problem with first-person pronouns might have seemed especially intractable. What (the writer might have asked) could a future, unknown reader be expected to make of 'I' and 'me'—words inextricably linked with presence and vocal conversation—when the writer to whom they referred would not be there in person as a justification of their use?

§8. Closing the deictic gap

Utterances such as *Wulfwi me wrat* seem to represent a response to this problem: they solve it by closing the deictic gap which literacy creates. The coming of literacy meant that the traditional co-presence of utterance and (human) utterer could no longer be taken for granted; but the established, structural, deictic link between first-person pronouns and the context of utterance which gives them meaning could be salvaged if the medium were pressed into service to fill the role of the absent human source of the utterance. Earlier I tried to explain the logic behind "Books say . . ." in terms of the preservation of 'presence' in writing. Obviously there is no inconsistency between that explanation and the one I have just offered for *Wulfwi me wrat*. In fact, they are probably best regarded as different sides of the same coin, one based on the realities of human discourse, the other on more narrowly linguistic considerations. Whether we couch the argument in terms of 'presence' and its loss, or in terms of deixis and a 'deictic gap', the same conclusion emerges.

Evidently, then, first-person pronouns underwent a process akin to semantic broadening in Old English: it became possible to use them to refer to things as well as to persons. This is not, of course, to maintain that such utterances were designed simply as a way of making possible the use of first-person pronouns in writing: the utterances in question seem to reflect logical (though no doubt unconscious) thinking based on the perceived structure of linguistic communication. Nor, of course, did this process lead to a permanent banishment from written English of first-person pronouns as expressions denoting human writers, for they are used today by writers without any sign of inhibition or awkwardness. Perhaps the earliest context in which they were used easily was in personal letters, where writing was used for one-to-one communication. And once the conventions and constraints of writing were taken for granted, and writers were no longer as acutely aware of the difference between their roles as writers and as speakers, this inhibition would have disappeared. In Chapter 6 of this book I shall attempt to describe the processes whereby writers became accustomed to using the first-person pronoun to refer to themselves, and the connections between this usage and the development of new literary forms among the earliest English texts.

§9. Medium-deixis in Anglo-Saxon inscriptions

Other varieties of first-person deixis among Anglo-Saxon writings, closely parallel in form to the type represented by *Wulfwi me wrat* and its analogues, are found among the Anglo-Saxon corpus of inscriptions on material artifacts.[27] There are several sub-types using first-person deixis, the commonest of which records the name of the artifact's maker by the simple formula: *X me worhte*, or (in Latin) *X me fecit*, "X made me." An example is a censer-cover from Pershore in Worcestershire,[28] on which appears the inscription *Godric me wvorht*, "Godric made me." Almost as common is the sub-type which records the name of the artifact's owner in the formula *X me ah*, "X owns me," an example being the 'eawen' ring,[29] inscribed *eawen mie ah*, "Eawen owns me" (*eawen* is an Old English personal name). The more elusive 'commissioner' formula is exemplified by the inscription on the famous 'Alfred Jewel' from Athelney in Somerset:[30] *Ælfred mec heht gevvyrcan*, "Alfred ordered me to be made."

These epigraphical texts obviously bear a close formal and grammatical resemblance to the scribal colophons discussed earlier. They use the deictic first-person pronoun; but here a different kind of deixis operates, a variety which might be termed 'medium-deixis'. The colophon, *Wulfwi me wrat*, occurs as an appendage to Wulfwi's copy of the Old English Gospels — a much more substantial text. The personal names this and similar colophons contain are the names of scribes, not of the authors or translators of the main texts; so strictly speaking the referent of the pronoun *me* is not the work in question but a text of it, the unique copy of the work for which the scribe is claiming responsibility in

---

[27] These inscriptions are dealt with more fully in Chapter 3 below.
[28] See Elisabeth Okasha, *Hand-List of Anglo-Saxon Non-Runic Inscriptions* (Cambridge: Cambridge University Press, 1971), No. 100. Hereafter, reference to inscriptions in Okasha's *Hand-List* is by numbered item.
[29] Okasha, *Hand-List*, No. 155.
[30] Okasha, *Hand-List*, No. 4.

his use of the verb *wrat*.[31] The epigraphical texts I have just introduced into the discussion differ from the colophons in that the first-person pronoun denotes, not another text which the scribe has copied or produced, but the material artifact, the maker or owner or commissioner of which the inscription names.[32] The only uncertainty is whether or not the inscription itself is covered by the pronoun *me*. Another difference is that whereas the personal names in the scribal colophons must identify the colophons' authors ('Wulfwi' is presumably responsible not only for copying the Gospel translation in MS. BL Cotton Otho C.i, but also, as author, for the colophon which names him), the names in the inscriptions do not necessarily denote the inscribers. Thus 'Eawen' probably did not herself inscribe the ring the inscription on which names her as its owner, and 'Alfred' is probably not the inscriber of the text on the Alfred Jewel which names him as commissioner of the artifact.

There can be little doubt that inscriptions of this general type reflect, like the colophons, a receiving-time-based analysis of linguistic communication. This is suggested on the one hand by the obviously commemorative function of the maker and commissioner formulas, and on the other by the function of the owner formula as a guard against loss or theft of the artifact: it conveys a strictly contemporary message to all readers, whenever they may appear.

§10. The written 'speech'

Readers of this chapter will not have failed to notice a problem of descriptive terminology raised by all these varieties of written utterance, particularly in the case of those using the first-person pronoun. A manifestation of the problem is to be seen in my use of inverted commas to mark 'speeches' and the 'speakers' who 'say' them, whereas, of course, in reality they are and do nothing of the sort. A sentence like "Godric made me," inscribed on an artifact, is essentially

---

[31] Later I shall need to consider in more detail the distinction between the scribe of a text and the author of a work of which it is a copy, for this is a distinction definitely observed in some of the Old English texts I shall examine.

[32] My explanation of the form of these inscriptions as representing an attempt to replicate in writing the basic pragmatics of speech may be compared with the theory advanced by Jesper Svenbro, *Phrasikleia: An Anthropology of Reading in Ancient Greece*, trans. Janet Lloyd (Ithaca and London: Cornell University Press, 1993), 41–42, about comparable medium-deictic inscriptions in ancient Greece. Rejecting an 'animist' interpretation of them (which would explain such 'egocentric' inscriptions as a manifestation of the general tendency in primitive societies to attribute life to all objects), Svenbro regards such 'egocentric' inscriptions simply as a "way of drawing attention to the presence of the object before its beholder" (42). One inadequacy of this theory, it seems to me, is that a reader's apprehension of the inscribed object would inevitably precede engagement with its inscription.

a written utterance. Its material reality does not of itself make it an *essentially* written utterance, for original speeches may be transcribed; but its content seems to rule out any possibility that it is, or even has been, a speech by a human being *in propria persona*, in British English at least. The closest match to such a speech within the possible range of human utterance is no doubt "God made me," which is, of course, a special case, something which any Christian human being might be expected to claim; but "Godric made me" does not make sense if interpreted as an utterance by a human being *in propria persona*. Sense can be made of its first-person pronoun only if it is understood as a deictic reference to the artifact on which the utterance is preserved. If the text were removed from its context, it would lose almost all its significance. Roughly the same is true of "Eawen owns me": in Anglo-Saxon society, a claim on a slave's part that someone else owned her or him might have been intelligible; but in this particular case the context of the utterance militates strongly against its interpretation as an idle scribble by a literate slave about her master's identity: *me* is surely the inscribed ring, *Eawen* its owner. So far, so good. But problems arise when we try to give some kind of descriptive label to these utterances, based on an analysis of their peculiar form and pragmatic context. They are obviously and essentially writings, for the reasons just mentioned; but in practice, one seems compelled to call them (for want of a better word) 'speeches', and to label the objects so inscribed 'speakers'. The terminology is obviously inappropriate; yet the pressure to use it is strong, even greater than in the case of other kinds of writing that we customarily call 'speeches'—printed or written records of actual or fictional orations, for example—because only in the case of our text- or medium-referring utterances is the 'speaker' (the book or artifact, denoted by *me*) actually present at receiving time; in all other cases the speaker is absent or imaginary, or both. The presence of an utterer is normally a reliable distinguishing criterion of speech; and this is the main reason why these so-called 'speeches' more closely resemble real, vocal speeches than any other kind of writing I have ever encountered. Yet, as we have seen, they can only be writings. So what should we call them? Some compromise term is needed to accommodate their special doubleness, the curious discrepancy they display between form combined with 'presence' on the one hand, in which they show the immediacy of speech, and their material reality and content on the other, which indicate that they are writings. There is no real solution to this problem apart from inventing new words; but the difficulty of expression I face here is significant. The kind of utterance we are dealing with represents an overlap between speech and writing, a hybrid for which we have never had a special word in English. At the beginning of this chapter I considered the possibility that there were gaps in English vocabulary which could help to explain such expressions as "Books say . . .". In the case of the scribal colophons and inscriptions I have since introduced into the discussion, it does indeed seem that we lack (and have always lacked) appropriate and distinctive terms; and we are unlikely to develop them now, since the forms I have illustrated are no longer in common use.[33] They were born, I suggest, of logical thinking about language provoked by the advent of literacy in the early centuries of English history, and represent a significant linguistic 'bridge' between the oral past and the literate future.

§11. Summary

This chapter began with an analysis of the usage of the modern English verb 'to say' with a book or document as subject. It was interpreted as a reader's neutralization, or mediation, of the fundamental contrast between spoken and written utterances. The advent and rise of literacy in the Anglo-Saxon period (or even earlier) provides a plausible historical context for its development: it may be explained as the product of an unconscious modification of a structural model of oral communication based on temporal and spatial criteria with a view to accommodating the unfamiliar concept of writing as a variant form of language. Writing, looked at from the perspective of a society where speech forms the only available general model for language, would have seemed to lack a necessary adjunct of linguistic communication: the human speaker who was always present whenever language was used before writing became possible. Assuming that the loss of this 'presence' was keenly felt, I explain expressions of the "Books say . . ." type as attempts by newly literate Anglo-Saxon readers to make good the deficiency. The chosen replacement for the absent speaker—the only possible substitute, if any kind of presence was to be maintained in writing—was the writing-bearing medium, the book.

Other manifestations of the same basic response to this loss of presence which writing involves are to be seen in one type of Anglo-Saxon scribal colophon and also in certain types of Anglo-Saxon inscription on material artifacts. The most distinctive linguistic characteristic of these utterances is their use of a deictic first person pronoun (*me*) to refer to the scribe's copy or (in the case of the inscriptions) to the inscribed medium. First-person pronouns invite classification as person-deixis—by definition, so to speak; but in the colophons, the reference of the pronouns to written texts mean that they are properly categorized as text-deixis, whereas in the inscriptions, the reference of the pronoun to the inscribed material or object exemplifies a variety of deixis which I call medium-deixis. Like "Books say . . .", these 'speeches' meet the challenge offered by the loss of the human presence which writing entails; but they represent a logical advance on "Books say . . ." because they could be 'spoken' only by inscribed or written

---

[33] They are still used quite often, however, as a way of drawing attention to the qualities of merchandise, as on a shopping bag in my possession inscribed "I am a RENEWa-BAG. I'm made from natural fibres so I'm great for the environment—and gorgeous with it!" For other examples, see Fell, "Runes and Riddles in Anglo-Saxon England," 276.

media. Incipient literacy evidently generated a narrow, specialized discourse of books and inscribed artifacts which has now largely disappeared.

Two questions with both historical and linguistic aspects have been raised in this chapter which I shall pursue later on. First, observations on the likely impact of incipient literacy on person-deixis led to the hypothesis that the form of these colophons and inscriptions represents an attempt to fill a 'deictic gap' which literacy effectively opened up. Before literacy, the Old English first-person personal pronouns (*Ic, me(c)* and *min*, 'I', 'me' and 'my') would have been generally associated with conversation and would normally have referred to the speaker of the utterance which contained them. When literacy arrived, this invariable association broke down: 'I' and 'me' were no longer linked to a speaker who was present at receiving time. The severing of this link could scarcely fail to precipitate a crisis of uncertainty about how these pronouns should be used in writing. Utterances of the type represented by the colophons and inscriptions mentioned here, which use the first-person pronoun in reference to material referents, are to be explained partly as responses to this crisis. Writers, inscribers, and scribes might well have found it difficult to see the point of using these pronouns to refer to themselves as they sent their writings off to be read in their absence, elsewhere or in the future. Both the medium and the text offered themselves as suitable surrogates for the missing writer; for they *would* be present to distant or future readers. I shall reaffirm and develop this hypothesis later on, in Chapter 6, by arguing that certain literary forms and preoccupations which seem to be characteristic of Old English literature are reflections of this anxiety about the loss of 'presence' which writing entails.

Second, a distinction was drawn between coding time and receiving time as alternative perspectives from which to analyse linguistic communication. All the Anglo-Saxon evidence examined so far is consistent with a historical conception of receiving time as the key moment in this process. A consequence of this is that writers and authors are effectively condemned to a relatively unimportant formal role in linguistic communications of this kind; and this raises questions about the perceived status of writers and authors in relation to their utterances which need to be followed up.

The body of linguistic and textual evidence adduced so far in this chapter is small. It has become clear, however, that a search for further evidence of thinking about language and writing in Anglo-Saxon England should not be confined to manuscript writings but ought to cover inscriptions on material artifacts of the period too. Both kinds of writing were produced by Anglo-Saxon writers after the introduction of the roman alphabet which accompanied the conversion in the seventh century; but as we saw in Chapter 1, some inscriptions in runes survive from the pre-Christian period. The partial priority, in chronological terms at least, of inscriptions over manuscript writings offers some justification for the focus of the next chapter, which opens with a sketch (fuller than the one I gave near the beginning of Chapter 1) of the historical beginnings of writing as a technique in Anglo-Saxon England. It then continues with a broad survey of the various forms of utterance exemplified in Anglo-Saxon inscriptions both runic and roman, pre-Christian and post-Christian, English and Latin; and the chapter will conclude with a consideration of the relevance of these inscriptions to the discussion of deixis and the beginnings of English literacy that has been initiated here.

Chapter 3
Anglo-Saxon Inscriptions

§1. The beginnings of literacy in Anglo-Saxon England: the runic and roman alphabets

When the first Anglo-Saxons left their continental homelands to settle in Britain in the fifth century, they were not illiterate; at least, not all of them were.[1] So far as we know, they had no practical knowledge of the roman alphabet, nor of parchment, pens, ink, or books, until their conversion to Christianity in the seventh century;[2] but some Anglo-Saxons evidently knew and used the runic alphabet from the time of their earliest settlement in Britain, for runic inscriptions engraved, scratched, or stamped on a variety of hard surfaces (metal, stone, bone, ivory, wood, or pottery) are known from Anglo-Saxon England from the fifth century onwards. The rarity of runic inscriptions surviving from the preconversion period, with fewer than twenty dating from before about 650,[3] makes it difficult to assess the extent of runic expertise in England before Christianity, or to generalize about the purposes to which runic writing was put; but pre-conversion runic inscriptions are still being discovered and the picture may eventually emerge in a clearer form.

Although runes are closely associated in the popular imagination with the Scandinavian peoples in particular, runic inscriptions dating from the Dark Ages

---

[1] The introduction to this chapter expands on what has already been said about runes and inscriptions in Chapter 1.

[2] Possibly the earliest known Anglo-Saxon use of the roman alphabet is the legend on the gold medalet issued in about 580 by Bishop Leudhard, who came to Britain with Bertha, the Frankish princess, at the time of her betrothal to King Æthelberht of Kent; see Page, *Introduction to English Runes*, 213.

[3] See John Hines, "The Runic Inscriptions of Early Anglo-Saxon England," in *Britain 400–600: Language and History*, ed. Alfred Bammesberger and Alfred Wollmann, Anglistische Forschungen 205 (Heidelberg: Winter, 1990), 437–55; idem, "Some Observations on the Runic Inscriptions of Early Anglo-Saxon England," in *Old English Runes and their Continental Background*, ed. Alfred Bammesberger, Anglistische Forschungen 217 (Heidelberg: Winter, 1991), 61–83; and David N. Parsons, *Recasting the Runes: The Reform of the Anglo-Saxon 'Futhorc'* (Uppsala: Uppsala Universitet, 1999), 43–70.

and later are found over much of the Germanic language-area of Europe,[4] with the very earliest examples dating from about 200 A.D. The origin and early history of the runic alphabet, or *fuþorc*,[5] are controversial questions. No doubt invented by one person, runes were probably based on one of a number of Etruscan- or North Italic-derived alphabets.[6] There is an early concentration of runic inscriptions in Denmark. A scattering of early finds to the south and east of Scandinavia may give a misleading impression of the range of runic writing, for all of these early non-Scandinavian inscriptions occur on items of weaponry or other portable objects which may well have been inscribed far from the places where they were discovered in modern times.[7] This consideration also affects the interpretation of the concentration of early runic inscriptions in Denmark, where all the examples appear on portable artifacts. We cannot be certain that Denmark was the original centre of runic expertise in Europe, though it may well have been.

The form of runes shows an avoidance of horizontals, each symbol consisting of a distinctive arrangement of straight vertical or diagonal lines. It has long been recognized that this feature points to wood as the medium for which runes were originally designed. If we assume that the normal way of cutting runes was in a row or rows along the grain of wood, on the planed surface of a branch or twig, lines cut horizontally would have tended to merge with the grain, whereas other materials such as metal or stone would not have presented the same problem.[8] It may seem surprising, in the light of this original, formal connection between runes and wood, that only a very few runic inscriptions on wood survive from Anglo-Saxon England,[9] all of them dating from the post-conversion period; but wood is combustible and decays easily in most kinds of soil. Plenty of runic inscriptions on wood have been found on the European continent, especially in Norway, though most of them date from a later period than the few English examples.[10]

The coming of Christianity, the roman alphabet, and all the paraphernalia of writing meant that from the seventh century onwards the Christian

---

[4] See R. W. V. Elliott's map of continental runic monuments in *Runes: An Introduction*, 2nd ed. (Manchester: Manchester University Press, 1989), 21.

[5] The name is based on the first six letters of the Anglo-Saxon runic series, the order of which is established by certain inscriptions and manuscripts of the period which contain lists of all the runes. The earliest, Common Germanic runic series is called the *fuþark*; see Page, *Introduction*, 38.

[6] See Elliott, *Runes*, 1–12; cf. Bengt Odenstedt, "A New Theory of the Origin of the Runic Script: Richard L. Morris's Book *Runic and Mediterranean Epigraphy*," in *Old English Runes and their Continental Background*, ed. Bammesberger, 359–87.

[7] See Elliott, *Runes*, 21, 80.

[8] See Elliott, *Runes*, 14.

[9] An inscribed wooden spoon from York and St. Cuthbert's coffin from Lindisfarne; see Page, *Introduction*, 99.

[10] See Elliott, *Runes*, 90–94, and Page, *Introduction*, 97–98, for accounts of the Bergen rune-sticks which date from c. 1200 to the 15th century.

Anglo-Saxons possessed a choice of two alphabets, runic and roman, and a choice between inscription and book-writing in their use. We should add to these a choice of languages to represent with them, English or Latin. But some of these choices were evidently limited by considerations we do not yet fully understand. The runic *fuþorc* was used chiefly for Old English, only occasionally for Latin, the roman alphabet both for Latin and (with a few extra letters, two of them, 'thorn' and 'wynn', borrowed from the runic *fuþorc*) for Old English.[11] Runes, as we shall see in the next two chapters of this book, were sometimes used in manuscripts, though not for continuous writing; roman was preferred. On the other hand, roman was often used for inscriptions in either language as an alternative to runes; and a few inscriptions that mix runic and roman letters survive.

§2. The inscriptions

Below I offer a brief survey of the known corpus of Anglo-Saxon inscriptions, both runic and roman, Old English and Latin. Few scholars, least of all myself, are really qualified to attempt such a survey. The ideal student of Anglo-Saxon inscriptions will be expert in runology, archaeology, numismatics, Old English, Latin, social and political history, palaeography, and philology, to name only the most obvious disciplines. Other considerations are equally discouraging. Because new Anglo-Saxon inscriptions are being brought to light all the time, any generalization about the corpus is constantly subject to review. The problems of interpretation raised by inscriptions are often formidable; many of them are difficult to read, let alone understand. A distinction between runic and roman inscriptions as objects of study has normally been observed in the past, though it is difficult to appreciate the justification for it (apart from the fact that their interpretation requires rather different sets of skills and knowledge) in the absence of any attempt to summarise the whole corpus. The classification of any corpus of inscriptions is bound to be difficult, because an inscription embodies information from so many different fields. A whole range of factors cutting across the runic-roman divide—the material inscribed, the geographical or political area in which the inscribed object was discovered, its date, or the content and form of the inscription itself—could be used and correlated in any combination for the purpose of classifying inscriptions. Each chosen method of classification will obviously carry its own suppositions and prejudices, and there is probably no one perfect system. My classification here is based mainly on the linguistic form and content of the inscriptions because those are the aspects of them of most immediate interest, though I cannot neglect the nature of the artifacts and objects upon which the inscriptions appear, nor the choice between runes or roman. My classification is

---

[11] See Campbell, *Old English Grammar*, §§67–70, and Kelly, "Lay Society," 37.

not based on a rigid set of criteria. The primary classification, indicated below by A and B, is fairly straightforward, distinguishing only between deictic and non-deictic inscriptions and following on from my discussion of deixis in the previous chapter. For present purposes, 'deictic inscriptions' are those which cannot be fully grasped as communications (however easily they may be read and translated) without knowledge of the pragmatic setting in which they are placed—the material medium of the inscription, the nature or function of the artifact, and its position or environment in space or time. Non-deictic inscriptions are those the meaning or significance of which are conveyed independently of any of these features of their setting. Classifications at the secondary level are, however, based on a variety of factors. Sometimes the linguistic form of the inscription decides the class, sometimes the information the inscription contains, sometimes what is judged to be the function of the inscription. I also sometimes subdivide groups of texts according to the nature of the medium upon which they are inscribed in cases where this makes the material more manageable.[12]

Although the surviving Anglo-Saxon inscriptions offer a fair variety of form and content, a high proportion of them do not yield easily to interpretation. Damage or natural deterioration has made many incomplete or difficult to read; others, though legible enough (and this applies particularly to runic inscriptions), do not seem to spell recognizable words or names at all. A general survey of the kind attempted here cannot linger much over controversial or baffling cases and I have therefore restricted attention, wherever it has been possible to do so without excluding types that seem distinctive, to inscriptions that are relatively easy to read and interpret.[13] The chief drawback of this policy is that it leads to a neglect

---

[12] The problem of inscription classification is an old one; see, for example, A. G. Woodhead, *The Study of Greek Inscriptions* (Cambridge: Cambridge University Press, 1959), 35, and Wolfgang Meid, *Gaulish Inscriptions: Their Interpretation in the Light of Archaeological Evidence and their Value as a Source of Linguistic and Sociological Information*, Archaeolingua, Series Minor, 1 (Budapest: Archaeological Institute of the Hungarian Academy of Sciences, 1992), 5.

[13] The texts of inscriptions are here quoted in edited form, with all abbreviations silently expanded. I have decided (with reluctance) not to indicate the punctuation, ligatures, spacing, or line-division of the original inscribers. See Page, *Introduction*, 49–59 on the transliteration of runic texts, and Okasha, *Hand-List*, 44–45 on the representation of non-runic inscriptions. I do, however, follow the Dickins-Page system of distinguishing between roman and runic inscriptions by the use of roman capitals for the former and lower-case letters in inverted commas for the latter, though even here I have simplified Page's more elaborate practices: Page (*Introduction*, 59) reserves inverted commas for runic texts presented in a relatively 'raw', unedited condition, but I thought it best to dispense with this refinement here and use inverted commas even for edited runic texts. In cases where roman inscriptions make use of the (originally runic) letters 'thorn' (þ) and 'wynn', I use roman capitals for these letters as well as for the others, and I omit the inverted commas when a text combines runic and roman letters (these last two practices appear to be standard). I substitute *w* for the runic

of certain inscriptions, particularly runic ones, which may have magical purposes.[14] This is unfortunate, but I shall not neglect the possibility of magical inscriptions in my subsequent discussion.

§3. The forms of inscriptions

A. Deictic Inscriptions

1. Medium-deictic inscriptions with first-person pronouns

A particularly distinctive type of inscription, exemplified briefly in my previous two chapters, denotes by the first-person pronoun the object on which it is inscribed. All known instances date from the post-conversion period. There are several sub-types:

a. Maker formula
The commonest variety records, invariably in roman script,[15] the name of the artifact's maker by a simple formula in either Old English or Latin: X ME WORHTE, or X ME FECIT, "X made me." It appears on a variety of objects,

---

letter 'wynn' in all its instances. I have not attempted to copy the scrupulously detailed system of transcription which the editors of epigraphical texts have evolved to indicate restored and conjectural letters or words. Those interested in the particular inscriptions or types mentioned here should consult the standard editions, to which constant reference will be made. However, in cases where the edited text is the product of a good deal of conjecture or intelligent guesswork, I have tried to make this clear, for obvious reasons. My lists of examples in the main text and in the notes are not complete, but I notice and exemplify all the types I have been able to distinguish. Non-runic and mixed runic-roman inscriptions are referred to by number from four of Okasha's publications: the *Hand-List* (nos. 1–158); "A Supplement to *Hand-List of Anglo-Saxon Non-Runic Inscriptions*," *ASE* 11 (1983): 83–118 (nos. 159–184); "A Second Supplement to *Hand-List of Anglo-Saxon Non-Runic Inscriptions*," *ASE* 21 (1992): 37–85 (nos. 185–211); and "A Third Supplement to *Hand-List of Anglo-Saxon Non-Runic Inscriptions*," *ASE* 33 (2004): 225–81 (nos. 212–240). Runic inscriptions are cited from Page, *Introduction*, and/or from Elliott, *Runes*. Reference is also sometimes made to *The Making of England: Anglo-Saxon Art and Culture, AD 600–900*, ed. Leslie Webster and Janet Backhouse (London: British Museum, 1991), referred to as 'Webster and Backhouse'; and to articles in *Old English Runes and their Continental Background*, ed. Bammesberger.

[14] For a survey of the subject, see R. I. Page, "Anglo-Saxon Runes and Magic," *Journal of the British Archaeological Association*, 3rd ser., 27 (1964): 14–31, repr. in idem, *Runes and Runic Inscriptions: Collected Essays on Anglo-Saxon and Viking Runes*, ed. David Parsons, bibliography Carl T. Berkhout (Woodbridge: Boydell & Brewer, 1995), 105–25.

[15] There are no certain runic instances. The only possible example is the Cramond (Edinburgh) bronze finger-ring, which contains as part of its badly damaged runic inscription the sequence 'wor', which might be part of *worhte*; see Page, *Introduction*, 157.

chiefly metal or stone, some portable, some not (a bronze censer cover, a bronze sword-guard, leather scabbards, stone sundials, a carved stone shaft, and a carved stone slab), the earliest dating from the 9th c. A straightforward example is Okasha 100, Pershore (Worcestershire), a censer-cover, 10th-11th c., with the inscription: GODRIC ME WVORHT, "Godric made me."[16]

b. Owner formula
Almost as common is the sub-type preserving the name of the artifact's owner by the Old English formula: X ME AH, "X owns me." No Latin equivalent is known. This appears (again, always in roman, never runes) on various portable artifacts from the 9th c. onwards: finger-rings in silver or gold, brooches, a horn sword-grip, and a whalebone implement (Okasha 118) which may be a weaver's sword. An example is Okasha 27, Cuxton, a silver brooch, 10th c.: ÆLFGIVV ME AH, "Ælfgivv owns me."[17]

c. Elaborated owner formula
There are two examples, both in roman and Old English, of elaborations of the owner formula in Okasha 114, Sutton (Cambs.), a silver disc brooch of the late 10th or early 11th c., and Okasha 155, the 'eawen' gold ring, the origin of which is unestablished, dating probably from the 9th or 10th c. The first of these is poetic and may be set out as verse (though alliteration fails in the second and third lines, with rhyme and assonance taking its place):

  ÆDVWEN ME AG AGE HYO DRIHTEN
  DRIHTEN HINE AWERIE ÐE ME HIRE ÆTFERIE
  BVTON HYO ME SELLE HIRE AGENES WILLES

---

[16] Other Old English examples are Okasha 2 (i), Alnmouth, a stone shaft, probably 10th c.; Okasha 17 (ii), the silver Brussels cross, 10th-11th c. (on which see also 1 (i) below); Okasha 41 (i), Great Edstone, a stone sundial, 10th-11th c.; and Okasha 64, Kirkdale (iii), an 11th-c. stone sun-dial. Latin examples are Okasha 37, Exeter, a bronze sword-guard, 9th-11th c.; Okasha 161, Canterbury VII, a stone slab, late 10th or early 11th c.; Okasha 163, Dublin II, a leather scabbard, 11th c.; and Okasha 185, Aachen, a decorated leather scabbard, probably 11th c. Other likely examples are Okasha 199, Lund, Sweden, a carved wooden box-lid, 11th c.; and Okasha 207, Trondheim, a decorated leather scabbard, probably 11th c.

[17] Other examples (all are in Old English) are Okasha 13, Bodsham, a gold ring, probably 9th c.; Okasha 118, Wallingford II (i), (ii), a whalebone implement, 10th–11th c., where the attribution, EADBURH MEC AH ... (the text continues illegibly), is repeated; and Okasha 204, Steyning (Sussex), a gold ring, probably 9th c. Another likely example is Okasha, 179, Wareham (Dorset), a horn sword-grip, perhaps 10th c., though the text is "highly deteriorated."

"Ædvwen owns me, may the Lord own her. May the Lord curse him who takes me from her, unless she gives me voluntarily."

The inscription on the 'eawen' ring is EAWEN MIE AH SANCTVS PETRVS STAN CESE, "Eawen owns me, may St. Peter the Rock choose (her)."[18]

d. Adjacent owner and maker formulas
There is one example (in roman and Old English) of an artifact bearing both 'owner' and 'maker' formulas in Okasha 109 (i), (ii), Sittingbourne, an iron knife, late 9th to early 10th c., inscribed: SIGEBEREHT ME AH, "Sigebereht owns me," and (on the other side of the blade): BIORHTELM ME WORTE, "Biorhtelm made me."

e. Combined owner and engraver formulas
Okasha 66, Manchester (formerly attributed to Lancashire; see Page, *Introduction*, 31), a gold ring, probably 9th c., combining roman and runic letters, links the Old English 'owner' formula with an otherwise unattested 'engraver' formula, also in Old English: æDRED MEC AH EAnRED MEC agROF, "Ædred owns me, Eanred engraved me."[19] The names alliterate vocalically and it seems possible that the text was meant to be read as a line of verse.

f. Commissioner formula
An Old English 'commissioner' formula appears in roman on three artifacts, two portable, one fixed. Okasha 4, Athelney (Somerset), the 'Alfred Jewel', probably 9th c., is inscribed in embossed gold letters: AELFRED MEC HEHT GEVVYRCAN, "Aelfred ordered me to be made." Okasha 156, the silver 'sigerie' ring, of uncertain date and origin, reads: SIGERIE HEÐ MEA GEVVIRCAN, "Sigerie ordered me to be made." Okasha 73, Lincoln, a stone slab, probably late 11th c., though now partly illegible, seems to have exhibited an elaborated version of this formula: EIRTIG ME LET WIRCEAN AND FIOS GODIAN CRISTE TO LOFE AND SANCTÆ MARIE, "Eirtig had me made and endowed with possessions to the glory of Christ and St Mary." In this last case, reference is made to the church of which the slab formed part of the fabric.[20]

---

[18] The word-division, expansion of abbreviations, and the translation of the second part of this last inscription are partly conjectural.

[19] See (g) below for a comparable Latin 'inscriber' formula.

[20] See my category 6 below for other examples of such dedications without first-person pronouns.

g. Inscriber formula
A Latin 'inscriber' formula occurs as part of the Latin inscription (in roman) in Okasha 111, Stratfield Mortimer, a stone slab, probably 11th c., which according to Okasha "may have been a grave or tomb cover": TOKI ME SCRIPSIT, "Toki wrote me."[21] It is possible that *scripsit* here means "inscribed" rather than "wrote", in which case the inscription belongs with the engraver formula exemplified above under (e).

h. Defining formula
A unique 'defining' formula using the medium-deictic first-person nominative pronoun *ic* is the recently-discovered Wheatley Hill (Durham) silver-gilt ring inscription in runes (mentioned briefly above in Chapter 1): 'hring ic hattæ', "I am called ring." The inscription may be from the second half of the 8th c.[22] The final *æ* rune is not absolutely certain, but neither sense nor grammar are seriously in doubt.

i. Inscriptions on symbolic objects
Two Old English inscriptions on crosses—Okasha 17 (iii), the silver Brussels cross, 10th–11th c., in roman, and Okasha 105 (Sv), the stone Ruthwell cross, probably early 8th c., in runes—use first-person pronouns, some of them in the nominative case (*ic*), to refer, not to the inscribed artifacts as such, but to the cross of Calvary which they symbolize and with which, as 'speakers', they identify. In these inscriptions, both of which are in alliterative verse, the cross recalls the crucifixion and associates itself closely with Christ the redeemer. The Brussels cross, which also bears the 'maker' formula inscription: DRAHMAL ME WORHTE, "Drahmal made me,"[23] has as its main inscription:

ROD IS MIN NAMA   GEO IC RICNE CYNING
BÆR BYFIGYNDE   BLODE BESTEMED

"My name is 'Cross'; once, trembling, drenched with blood, I bore the mighty king."

The text of the Ruthwell inscription is incomplete because of damage sustained by the monument, but has been restored editorially to a state closer to the original by reference to lines 39–64 of *The Dream of the Rood*, a poem preserved in the late 10th-c. Vercelli Book, parts of which match the Ruthwell poem fairly

---

[21] The whole inscription is VIII KALENDAS OCTOBRIS FVIT POSITVS ÆGELWARDVS FILIVS KYPPINGVS IN ISTO LOCO BEATVS SIT OMO QVI ORAT PRO ANIMA EIVS TOKI ME SCRIPSIT ("On 24 September Ægelward son of Kypping was put in this place. Blessed be the man who prays for his soul. Toki wrote me").

[22] Page, *Introduction*, 169.

[23] Okasha 17 (ii); see 1(a) above.

closely.[24] Four fragments, separated by three lacunae of varying and uncertain size, and terminating in a fourth, are legible:[25]

39–40   '[. .]geredæ hinæ ḡod alme₃ttig,   þa he walde on ḡalḡu gistiḡa,
41   [.]odig f[. . . . . . .] men.
42   [.]ug[. . . . .]'

"Almighty God bared his body as he prepared to climb the gallows, valiant in men's sight . . . bow . . ."

44   '. . . ic riicnæ ƙyniŋc,
45   hêafunæs h*l*afard,   *h*ælda ic ni dorstæ.
48   Bismæræ*d*u uŋƙet men ba ætg̱ad[. .];   ic [. . .] *m*iþ blodæ [.]ist*e*mi[.],
49   bi[. . . . .]'

"I . . . a mighty king, lord of heaven. I dared not bend down. Men mocked the pair of us together. I was stained with blood . . . ."

56   Krist wæs on rodi.
57   Hweþræ þer fus*æ*   fêarran kwomu
58   *æ*þþilæ til anum.   Ic þæt al bi[. . . .].
59   S[. . .] ic w[.]s mi[.] so[.]g̱um gi*d*rœ[. .]d,   h[.]ag̱ [. . . . .]'

"Christ was on the cross. Yet to this solitary one there came men from afar, eager and noble. I beheld it all. I was bitterly distressed with griefs . . . bowed down . . ."

62   '*m*iþ stre*l*um giwundad.
63   Alegdun hiæ *h*inæ limwœrignæ,   gistoddu[.] him [. . . . .]ic*æ*s [. .]f[. .]m;
64   [. . .]êa[.]du[. .]i[.] þe[. . . . .]'

". . . wounded with arrows. Down they set the man weary of limb. They stood at the corpse's head. There they beheld . . ."

---

[24] For the text of *The Dream of the Rood*, see *The Vercelli Book*, ed. George Philip Krapp, The Anglo-Saxon Poetic Records 2 (New York: Columbia University Press, 1932), 61–65. On the relationship between the two texts, see further below, Chapter 4.

[25] As there are so many minor uncertainties about the readings of the Ruthwell Cross inscription, I simply reproduce Dobbie's edited transliteration of the runic text (*The Anglo-Saxon Minor Poems*, ed. Elliott Van Kirk Dobbie, The Anglo-Saxon Poetic Records 6 [New York: Columbia University Press, 1942], 115) without altering it in any way except in rearranging it to read in full verse lines rather than half-lines. Dobbie's dots, which I reproduce, represent his assessment of the likely number of lost runes. Line-numbers to the left of the text refer to corresponding lines of *The Dream of the Rood*. The modern English translation follows Page, *Introduction*, 147–48.

2. Maker formula

A maker formula, comparable with the instances collected under 1(a) above but differing from them in its omission of any explicitly deictic term, is the runic inscription in Old English on the Kirkheaton (W. Yorks.) stone: 'eoh worohtæ', "Eoh made (this *or* me)." The shape of the Kirkheaton stone indicates that it was originally meant to stand upright and independently. Later it was incorporated into the fabric of the local church.[26]

3. Repairer formula

A repairer formula is attested by a single Old English runic example: the Harford Farm (Caistor-by-Norwich) disc-brooch, excavated in 1990,[27] and inscribed 'luda gibœtæ sigilæ', "Luda mended (the) brooch." The brooch has indeed been repaired. Its date is probably mid-7th c. The historical integrity of the inscription is questioned by Page who, noting that the runes for 'Luda' are larger than those for the remainder of the sentence, suggests that the name might originally have stood alone, with the rest of the inscription added later when the brooch was repaired.

4. Memorial inscriptions

Memorial inscriptions name deceased individuals. Old English and Latin examples survive, and the script may be either runic or roman, with one instance (Falstone) using both (see under [h] below). Most examples are on stone crosses, shafts, or slabs (exceptions are Okasha 17 and 21; see under [c] and [h] below), the earliest dating from the 8th c. Classification of the subtypes is difficult because the various pieces of basic information (name of deceased person, date of death, names of relatives and of the makers or commissioners of the monument) are combined in several different ways.

a. 'Here lies X'

The most basic type consists simply of the Latin formula (in roman): "Here lies X," with minor elaborations. An example is Okasha 92, Monkwearmouth II, a carved stone slab, probably of the 9th-11th c.: HIC IN SEPULCRO REQVIESCIT CORPORE HEREBERICHT PRESBYTER, "Here in the tomb rests Herebericht the priest in his bodily form."[28]

---

[26] Page, *Introduction*, 34, 137.

[27] See Page, *Introduction*, 166.

[28] Okasha 135, Whitchurch (Hants.), a stone slab from the same period, contains a similar example, also in Latin.

b. "Here lies X, related to Y"
A slightly more informative subtype adds information about a relationship between the deceased and another named person, as in Okasha 138, Winchester I, a stone, late 10th-11th c., in Old English: HER LIÐ GVNNI EORLES FEOLAGA, "Here lies Gvnni, Eorl's companion."

c. Record and date of death of X, related to Y
Another relatively simple form, though a rare one, records only the name of the deceased person, his or her relationship to another person (in most cases, one imagines, the person responsible for the monument), and the date of death, as in Okasha 21, Canterbury III (i), a lead cross, late 11th c., in Latin: ANNO MILLESIMO LXIII V IDVS MARTII MIGRAVIT EX HAC VITA WLFMÆG SOROR WLFRICI ABBATIS, "On 11 March 1063, Wlfmæg, sister of Abbot Wlfric, departed from this life."

d. Plea for prayers for X
A commoner subtype consists of an exhortation to pray for the commemorated person (or persons). A basic example is Okasha 46, Hartlepool IV, a carved stone, 8th c., with the Latin inscription (in roman): ORA PRO UERMUND TORHTSUID, "Pray for Uermund (and) Torhtsuid."[29] The Lancaster cross fragment,[30] probably of the early 8th c., carries the (incomplete) Old English runic inscription 'gibidæþ foræ cynibalþ cuþbere. . .', "Pray for Cynibalþ, Cuþbere. . ." The lost ending of this inscription perhaps identified Cynibalþ as the son of the person denoted by the incomplete Cuþbere-. A second, somewhat more elaborate, example is the Overchurch (Cheshire) rune-stone,[31] the Old English text of which (using the forms in Page's edition of the inscription) is 'folc arærdon becun gebiddaþ fore æþelmunde', "The people erected (this) monument. Pray for Æþelmund." The attribution of the monument to "the people" here is unique.

e. Plea for prayers for X's soul
Even more commonly, however, the reader of the inscription is explicitly asked to pray, not for the dead person as such but for his or her soul. The Great Urswick stone is an Old English poetic example in runes,[32] which Page edits as follows:

---

[29] Similar examples are Okasha 47, Hartlepool V (i), (ii), 8th c.; and probably Okasha 9, Billingham (i), 8th or 9th c., and Okasha 42, Hackness (i), probably 8th or 9th c.
[30] Page, *Introduction*, 143; Elliott, *Runes*, 112.
[31] Page, *Introduction*, 55, 142; Elliott, *Runes*, 95. The stone is possibly 10th c.
[32] Page, *Introduction*, 59, 141. I modify Page's presentation here (59), but not his forms.

'tunwini setæ　　　æfter torohtredæ
bekun æfter his bæurnæ　　　gebidæs þer saulæ'

"Tunwini set up the monument in memory of Torohtredæ his child. Pray for the soul."

The Thornhill C rune-stone,[33] probably late 8th or early 9th c., may also be presented as verse (though the poet was not as assiduous as the composer of the Great Urswick inscription in the matter of alliteration):

'jilsuiþ arærde　　　æfte berhtsuiþe
bekun on bergi　　　gebiddaþ þær saule'

"Gilsuiþ raised up in memory of Berhtsuiþ a memorial on a mound. Pray for her soul."[34]

f. Prayer to God on behalf of X

Occasionally the inscription is itself a direct prayer to God for the salvation of the deceased individual, as in Okasha 43, Haddenham, a stone cross-shaft of uncertain date with the Latin inscription (roman): LUCEM TVAM OVINO DA DEVS ET REQVIEM AMEN, "O God, grant your light and rest to Ovin, Amen." A similar, runic, Old English example occurs on the copper covering of the Mortain reliquary, perhaps 8th-9th c.,[35] transcribed and translated by Page as 'good helpe æadan þiiosne ciismeel gewarahtæ', "God help Æada (who) made this *ciismeel*." The meaning of the hapax legomenon *ciismeel* is uncertain, as is the true or original function of the container itself (Page refers to evidence that it was not originally designed as a reliquary). Nor is it by any means certain that this is a memorial inscription. If Æada was himself responsible for the inscription, he may have hoped for God's help in this life rather than the next.

g. Name of the monument-maker or its commissioner

Often the person or persons who commissioned or set up the memorial object are named. We have already seen some examples under (d) and (e) above. Other runic examples are the fragmentary Thornhill stones A and B (Elliott, *Runes*,

---

[33] Page, *Introduction*, pp. 141–2; Elliott, *Runes*, pp. 114–5.

[34] Other examples are Okasha 30, Dewsbury I, roman, in Old English, 8th-9th c.; Okasha 39, Falstone, in Old English, with both runic and roman texts, 8th-9th c., on which see (h) below; and in roman and Latin, Okasha 67 and 68, Lancaster I and Lancaster II, both probably 9th c.; Okasha 150 and 152, York V and York VII, stone slabs, date uncertain; Okasha 111, Stratfield Mortimer, a stone slab, 11th c.; Okasha 161, Canterbury VII, a stone slab, late 10th or 11th c.; and probably Okasha 2, Alnmouth (ii), a stone shaft, 10th c.

[35] Okasha 93; see Elliott, *Runes*, 124; Page, *Introduction*, 162–63.

113–14, 8th to 9th c.; Page, *Introduction*, 141, who calls these Thornhill I and II), which are respectively inscribed (in Page's edited versions): 'eþelberht sette æfter eþelwini . . .', "Eþelberht set up (this memorial) after Eþelwini . . .," and 'Eadred sete æfte Eategnne', "Eadred set up (this memorial) after Eadþegn." There are few well-preserved examples in roman. Perhaps the best is Okasha 144, Wycliffe (N. Yorks.), a carved stone cross-shaft, probably 8th-9th c., though even here the text has deteriorated and is incomplete. Okasha's edited version is: BADA . . . AEFTER BEREHTVINI BECVN AEFTER . . ., "Bada (? set this) in memory of Berehtvine, a monument in memory of . . ."[36]

h. Name of monument-maker and his relation to X
Sometimes there is an accompanying reference to the relationship between the person or persons responsible for the monument and the dead man or woman. The Great Urswick runic inscription, quoted above under (e), is one example; another, in roman, is Okasha 17, Brussels I (iii), 10th-11th c.: ÞAS RODE HET ÆÞLMÆR WYRICAN ET AÐELWOLD HYS BEROÞOR CRISTE TO LOFE FOR ÆLFRICES SAVLE HYRA BEROÞOR, "Æþlmær, and Æðelwold his brother, ordered this cross to be made to the glory of Christ, (and) for the soul of Ælfric their brother." A third example is Okasha 39, the Falstone stone cross, Old English, 8th to 9th c.,[37] notable for its parallel roman and runic versions, though the name of the maker is missing:

    E. .T. . . . AE AEFTAER HROETHBERHTE BECUN AEF-
    TAER   EOMAE GEBIDAED DER SAULE
'. . . æftær roe. . .tæ becun æftær e. . . geb. . .æd þe. . . saule'

". . . in memory of Hroethberht, a monument in memory of (his) uncle; pray for the (= his) soul."[38]

i. Request for prayers for the monument-maker
A unique request for prayers for the maker (or commissioner) of the monument who presumably died before his work was complete is found on Okasha 68, Lancaster II, an incomplete carved stone cross-shaft. The Latin inscription, in ro-

---

[36] Other examples are Okasha 23, Carlisle I, Old English, a carved sandstone cross head, probably 8th-9th c., and Okasha 69, Lanteglos, a stone shaft, Old or early Middle English, probably 11th c. or post-Conquest. Two less certain examples, both in Old English, are Okasha 40, Gainford, a carved stone, probably 9th c., and Okasha 87, London I, a sandstone wheel-headed cross, 10th-11th c.

[37] See also Page, *Introduction*, 142, whose transcription differs slightly from Okasha's.

[38] Other examples are Okasha 30, Dewsbury I, sandstone, probably a cross-shaft, Old English, 8th-9th c.; and Okasha 145, Yarm (N. Yorks.), a stone shaft, Old English, 8th-9th c.

man, probably 9th c., has deteriorated, but Okasha reads: ORATE PRO ANIMA. . . CYNIBA. . . HOC OPVS . . . PERPETUARAT AD GLORIAM DOMINI, "Pray for the soul of Cynib. . . (?who) had promised this work (. . .) to the glory of the Lord."

j. Implied prayer

Okasha 94, Newent (ii), a sandstone slab which may be a pillow-stone, probably late 10th or early 11th c., is inscribed with the list: MARCVS LVCAS IOHANNES EDRED MATHEUS. *Edred* is presumably commemorated here, the inscription as a whole constituting a prayer to the evangelists for his soul. Notable is the English form of the Anglo-Saxon name beside the Latin forms of the apostles' names.

5. Personal names

Many surviving inscriptions consist simply of an Old English personal name with little or no elaboration. The earliest examples date from the 8th c., the majority appearing on stone crosses or name-stones in the north of England. There is no doubt that most of the inscriptions in this category are commemorative, though this is absolutely clear only in cases where the stone was originally found in, or close to, a grave. The numerous examples are classified below according to the inscribed material and the form of writing (runic or roman).

a. Names on stone in runes

Runic instances are rare. An example is Hartlepool I,[39] an 8th c. stone slab bearing (below the 'Alpha' and 'Omega' symbols) 'hildiþryþ', the name probably of the nun in whose grave the stone was found.[40]

b. Names on stone in roman

Examples using roman characters are numerous. Representative is Okasha 48 (ii), Hartlepool VI (Durham), from the 8th c., a limestone slab inscribed BERCHTGYD, which is a form of the known female name *Beorhtgyð*.[41]

---

[39] Page, *Introduction*, 49–52; Elliott, *Runes*, 107; Okasha, 77, footnote.

[40] Other examples are Hartlepool II (Page, *Introduction*, 49–52; Elliott, *Runes*, 107; Okasha, 77, footnote), an 8th c. stone slab inscribed 'hilddigyþ', also found in the grave of a nun; the Dover stone (Page, *Introduction*, 137; Elliott, *Runes*, 108–9), of the 9th or 10th c., inscribed 'jislheard', the stone probably "a slab to cover a grave" (Page, *Introduction*, 137); Maughold I, Isle of Man, 'blagcmon', the stone "presumably a grave headstone" (Page, *Introduction*, 137); and Monkwearmouth I, a carved stone slab bearing the name 'tidfirþ' (Page, *Introduction*, 138–39).

[41] Further examples are Okasha 3, Ardwall (Kirkcudbrightshire), a stone shaft, 8th-9th c.; Okasha 12, Bishopstone (Sussex), a stone sundial, 11th-12th c.; Okasha 45, Hartlepool III (Durham), a limestone slab, 8th c.; Okasha 52, Hexham I (Northumberland),

c. Names on stone with roman and runic letters combined
Okasha 25, Chester-le-Street (Durham), a stone slab, probably 10th or 11th c.,[42] mixes runic with roman characters in the name: EADmVnD.

d. Names on stone with parallel versions in roman and runic
There are a few examples of the presentation of a name in both roman and runic forms, for example Okasha 76, Lindisfarne II (Northumberland),[43] a stone slab probably from the 8th c.: 'osgyþ', followed by OSGYÐ. Page believes that two different persons, perhaps mother and daughter, are commemorated here because some possible examples of a similar type (the texts are incomplete) seem to record two different names by this means.[44]

e. Names on metal in runes
Runic examples are rare. An example is the silver tweezer fragment from Brandon, Suffolk,[45] bearing the name 'aldred'. The use of serifs in this inscription leads the editor (Page) to suggest that "the rune-master was literate also in the roman alphabet." A second example is the Thames scramasax (a kind of short sword),[46] bearing the name 'beagnoþ'.[47] The names might refer to either the maker or the owner of these objects, as Page suggests, though it also seems conceivable that *beagnoþ* is a name given to the sword itself.[48] Finally, a third example in runes

---

a stone slab, probably 8th-9th c.; Okasha 75, Lindisfarne I (Northumberland), a stone slab, probably 8th c.; Okasha 121, Wensley II (NR Yorks.), a stone slab, possibly 8th-9th c.; Okasha 125, Whitby IV (NR Yorks.), a stone cross, 8th-9th c. Other probable examples are Okasha 49 and 50, Hartlepool VII and VIII (Durham), stone slabs, both 8th c.; Okasha 65, Knells (Cumberland), a stone slab, possibly 8th-9th c.; Okasha 81 and 83, Lindisfarne VIII and X (Northumberland), stone slabs, both probably 8th c.; Okasha 94, Newent (Gloucestershire) (i), a stone slab, probably late 10th or early 11th c.; Okasha 101, Plymstock (Devon), a stone cross, probably 10th-11th c.; Okasha 120, Wensley I (NR Yorks.), a stone slab, possibly 8th-9th c.; Okasha 128 and 132, Whitby VII and XIV (NR Yorks.), stone crosses, both 8th-9th c.; Okasha 143, Workington (Cumberland), a stone shaft, date uncertain; and Okasha 170, Jarrow VI (Durham), a stone slab, date uncertain.

[42] Page, *Introduction*, 139, dates the stone to the late 9th c.
[43] Page, *Introduction*, 139, refers to this inscription as Lindisfarne I. See Michelle P. Brown, *The Lindisfarne Gospels* (Toronto: University of Toronto Press, 2003), 23 with fig. 9.
[44] Okasha 80, Lindisfarne VII (Northumberland), a stone slab, probably 8th c., and Okasha 91, Monkwearmouth I (Durham), a stone slab, possibly 8th to 9th c. See also Page, *Introduction*, 139–40.
[45] Webster and Backhouse, 66(o); Elliott, *Runes*, 50; and Page, *Introduction*, 167, who dates it "eighth-/ninth century."
[46] Elliott, *Runes*, 104; Page, *Introduction*, 113, who dates it to the tenth century.
[47] On the *fuþorc* inscribed on this scramasax, see under 15 below.
[48] For similar examples, see under 10 below.

is provided by a recently-excavated copper-alloy object from Wardley (Rutland) which bears the incomplete inscription '-olburg' which Page restores as the female name *Ceolburg*.[49]

f. Names on metal in roman
An example in roman letters is Okasha 174 (i), Putney (London), an iron knife, probably 10th or early 11th c., which bears the name OSMUND. The other side of the blade bears a second inscription, Okasha 174 (ii), which is damaged but may be a self-referring owner-formula of the type: X MEC AH.[50]

g. Names on metal in roman with runes
An inscription on metal which combines roman with runic characters is Okasha 86, Llysfaen, Caernarvonshire,[51] a gold ring of the 9th c., bearing the name ALHSTAn. Okasha believes that the single rune, for *n*, was probably included to achieve "symmetry of design."

h. Names on wood in roman
Of personal names inscribed on wood, only a single, uncertain example survives in a wooden comb found in Dublin (Okasha 162, Dublin I, possibly 11th c.). Two inscriptions on the comb, both deteriorated, seem likely to be names: the first may well be a name such as ÆDWARD or ÆDWALD, the other a name ending in the common second element -RIC.

---

[49] Page, *Introduction*, 167.

[50] Similar examples are Okasha 103, Rome I, a gold ring, possibly 9th c., with the name AVFRET; Okasha 115, Swindon, a gold ring, probably late 9th or 10th c., with the name BVREDRVÐ; Okasha 141, Winchester IV (Hampshire), a circular metal brooch, probably 10th c., with only the first element HERE- legible; and Webster and Backhouse 47, the York helmet from the second half of the 8th c., bearing the name OSHERE following a Latin prayer: IN NOMINE DOMINI NOSTRI IHV SANCTUS SPIRITUS DEUS ET OMNIBUS DECEMUS. AMEN, OSHERE, XPI. Okasha translates this (without OSHERE, XPI) as "In the name of our Lord Jesus, the Holy Spirit, God and with all we pray. Amen." However, the entire inscription has been reedited by J. W. Binns, E. C. Norton and D. M. Palliser, "The Latin Inscription on the Coppergate Helmet," *Antiquity* 64 (1990): 134–39. They understand the abbreviation *SCS* not as the nominative singular masculine *sanctus*, "holy", but as *sanctis* (dative pl.), "saints," which they take with *omnibus*, giving "to all the saints"; they take the abbreviation *DI* as short for genitive *Dei*, "of God"; emend the puzzling *DECEMUS* to *dicemus* (from *dicare*, "to dedicate", "to offer"), giving the meaning "let us offer up"; and interpret the final abbreviation *XPI* as for Latin *Christi* and reposition it before *ET*, "and". Thus they arrive at IN NOMINE DOMINI NOSTRI IHV CHRISTI ET SPIRITUS DEI OMNIBUS SANCTIS DICEMUS OSHERE AMEN, "In the name of our Lord Jesus Christ and of the spirit of God, let us offer up Oshere to All Saints. Amen."

[51] See also Page, *Introduction*, 165–66.

i. Names on bone in roman
A sole example survives in Okasha 198, London IV, (i) and (ii), mid-11th c., where the name AELVBRH (which Okasha thinks may represent one of the otherwise unrecorded names ÆLFBURG or ÆLFBEORHT) is inscribed twice in roman letters (some of them inverted) on a piece of bone. The name is probably that of the engraver and Okasha thinks that the object is a trial-piece.

j. Name with office in roman
An elaborated version of the simple name which adds the title or office of the named person occurs on a few items, mainly metal. An example is Okasha 70, Laverstock (Wilts.), a gold ring, A.D. 828–858, inscribed: ETHELVVLF REX, "King Ethelvvlf."[52]

k. Name-lists
A lead plaque from Flixborough (South Humberside) of the mid-8th c. (Webster and Backhouse 69[a]; Okasha 193, Flixborough II) bears a list of seven Anglo-Saxon names in roman: ALDUINI ALDHERI HAEODHAED EODUINI EDELGYD EONBERECHT EDELUIIN. The original purpose of this object is debatable, but nail-holes indicate that it was originally attached to something else. Michelle P. Brown, the contributing editor in Webster and Backhouse, comments:

> "A commemorative listing of people of importance in the history of an ecclesiastical community, or a list of those whose relics were contained in an attached reliquary, are possible functions of this piece."

Okasha thinks the plate "could . . . have been memorial, perhaps to mark the graves of the seven people, at least one of whom was a woman."

6. Dedication inscriptions
Inscriptions of dedication are rare, with only nine currently known, all of them in roman. Six are in Latin, three in Old English (Okasha 1, Aldbrough; Okasha 64, Kirkdale; and Okasha 73, Lincoln I) and one (Okasha 146, York I) combines the two languages. The inscriptions are all on stone, usually a slab which is (or was originally) built into the fabric of the church whose dedication the inscription records. In two cases the inscribed stone doubles as a sundial. These are Okasha 1, Aldbrough (ER Yorks.) and Okasha 64, Kirkdale (NR Yorks.), (i). All instances except one date from the 10th or the 11th c., the single exception de-

---

[52] Two similar examples are Okasha 107, Sherburn (WR Yorks.), a gold ring, A.D. 853–88, inscribed EAÐELSVIÐ REGNA, "Queen Eaðelsvið"; and Okasha 154, the 'Eadward' brooch, origin unknown, probably 10th c., EADWARD REX ANGLORUM, "Eadward, king of the English."

riving from the 7th, Okasha 61, Jarrow I (in Latin), closely datable to 685 from the inscription's content.

a. The name of the dedicatee
The essential component of dedication inscriptions is the name or names of the person or persons to whom the church is dedicated—a saint or saints, a member of the Holy Trinity or the Trinity as a group, or combinations of these. A simple, though possibly incomplete, example is Okasha 29, Deerhurst II (Gloucs.), probably 11th-c., reconstructed by Okasha as IN HONOREM SANCTAE TRINITATIS HOC . . . DEDICATUM EST, "In honour of the Holy Trinity this (church, altar) was dedicated."[53]

b. Commemoration of the church's commissioner or others
The only example of a dedication inscription which omits to name any dedicatee is Okasha 1, Aldbrough (ER Yorks.), an Old English inscription from the late 10th or 11th c. on a sundial set in the wall of the local parish church (the second word might be [LE]T, "caused," rather than [HE]T, "ordered"): VLF HET ARŒRAN CYRICE FOR HANVM 7 FOR GVNWARA SAVLA, "Vlf ordered the church to be erected for himself and for Gvnwaru's soul." Here the named persons are the church's commissioner and a (presumably deceased) woman, both of whom the commissioner wishes to be remembered in association with the church.[54] The names are Norse, and the form *hanum* is interpreted by Okasha as "the ON pronoun used as a reflexive."

c. Date of dedication
A record of the date of the dedication is often included.[55] The following example, Okasha 28, Deerhurst I, A.D. 1056, also includes the names of the church's commissioner and (unusually) that of a deceased person, here a brother of the commissioner, to whose memory the church is regarded as a monument. Another unique item here is the name of the bishop who presided at the dedication itself:

---

[53] A similarly spare example is perhaps the much-deteriorated Okasha 59, Ipswich II, probably 11th c., in Latin, which Okasha reconstructs as IN DEDICATIONE ECLESIE OMN . . . RVM, and translates tentatively as "At the dedication of the church of all [? saints]."

[54] This commemorative element seems to be typical; it occurs also in Okasha 28, Deerhurst I (Gloucs.), quoted below under (c); Okasha 61, Jarrow I, A.D. 685; Okasha 64, Kirkdale (i), A.D. 1055–65; Okasha 73, Lincoln I, probably late 11th c.; and Okasha 146, York I, quoted below under (d). For discussion of Anglo-Saxon dedication inscriptions generally, see John Blair, *The Church in Anglo-Saxon Society* (Oxford: Oxford University Press, 2005), 416–17.

[55] Okasha 61, Jarrow I; Okasha 64, Kirkdale (i), and Okasha 146, York I, in addition to the example quoted here.

ODDA DVX IVSSIT HANC REGIAM AVLAM CONSTRVI ATQUE DEDICARI IN HONORE SANCTI TRINITATIS PRO ANIMA GERMANI SVI ÆLFRICI QVE DE HOC LOCO ASSVMPTA EALDREDVS VERO EPISCOPVS QVI EANDEM DEDICAVIT II IDIBVS APRILIS XIIII AVTEM ANNO REGNI EADWARD REGIS ANGLORVM, "Earl Odda ordered this royal church to be built and dedicated in honour of the Holy Trinity for the soul of his brother Ælfric which (was) taken up from this place. And Ealdred was the bishop who dedicated the same on 12 April and in the fourteenth year of the reign of Eadward King of the English." The "royal church" is either the church itself or the chapel at Deerhurst.

d. Old English into Latin
Okasha 146, York I, a sandstone slab of the 10th or 11th c., is the only known Anglo-Saxon inscription which begins in one language—Old English—and finishes in another—Latin (possibly reverting again to Old English finally; see Okasha's description): ... MINSTER SETTON ...ARD AND GRIM AND ÆSE ON NAMAN DRIHTNES HÆLGES CRISTES AND SANCTA MARIA AND SANCTE MARTINI AND SANCTE C...TI AND OMNIVM SANCTORVM CONSECRATA EST AN...VIS IN VITA ET..., "...ard and Grim and Æse raised (this) church in the name of the holy Lord Christ, and to (*or* of) St Mary and St Martin and St (?Cuthbert) and All Saints. It was consecrated in the (...) year in the life of..." It is, however, in all respects a typical dedication inscription, incorporating the names of the commissioners and dedicatees, and (in its original form) the date of the dedication.

7. Inscriptions referring explicitly to the substance of the medium
There is one clear runic example of this type in the 8th-c. whalebone Auzon (Franks) casket which includes the grammatically independent expression 'hronæs ban', "whale's bone," on its front panel.[56] There are two other possible examples, both runic and both involving grammatical uncertainties. One is the Caistor-by-Norwich roe-deer astragalus,[57] probably at least as early as the 5th c., inscribed 'raihan', which Page interprets as from Gmc. *raiho*, OE *raha, ra*, "roe-deer." The inflexional ending presumably indicates an oblique case (probably either gen. or dat. sg.) of this weak noun,[58] giving the meaning: "of (*or* from) a roe."[59] Here must also be added the recently-excavated Brandon antler handle,[60] which reads 'wohs wildum deoran', "(I *or* it) grew on a wild beast." The grammar is puzzling: in view of (a) the general likelihood that a single animal on which

---

[56] Page, *Introduction*, 174.
[57] Page, *Introduction*, 179–80; Elliott, *Runes*, 46.
[58] See Campbell, *Old English Grammar*, §§236(3), 619(3).
[59] As suggested in Parsons, *Recasting the Runes*, 48.
[60] Page, *Introduction*, 169–70.

the antler grew is referred to, (b) the neuter gender of the Old English *a*-noun *deor*,[61] and (c) the inflexion of the adjective *wildum* (clearly dat., and presumably sg. neuter), one would expect the form *deore*, not *deoran*, the inflexion of which associates the noun with the weak paradigm. The only solution that has been suggested is to treat the sequence *an* as a form of the preposition *on*, 'on', here used postpositionally; but this leaves an apparently nom. sg. *deor*, which cannot be easily accommodated in this arrangement. The inscription has not been dated with any precision, but it is unlikely on archaeological grounds to be later than the end of the 9th c.[62]

8. Inscriptions referring to contents of the inscribed object

A rare type, represented by only two examples, both in roman and Latin. Okasha 106, Sandford (Oxfordshire) is a decorated bronze nonagon, possibly late 10th to 11th c., on which the Latin inscription reads INTVS QVOD LATET CVNCTO NOS CRIMINE LAXET, "May that which lies hidden within free us from all guilt." The other, perhaps less certain, example is Okasha 189, Cologne, a carved crozier head of ivory and silver, 11th c., the silver of which bears a Latin inscription reconstructed by Okasha as RELIQVIE SANCTAE MARIE ET SANCTI CRISTOFORI, "The relics of St Mary and St Christopher." The relics in question "were presumably kept inside the wooden staff" (Okasha).

9. Inscriptions referring to the bearer of the inscribed object

The only clear example of this type is Okasha 14, Bossington (Hants.), a decorated gold baptismal ring with a much-abbreviated Latin inscription in roman, possibly 9th to 10th c. Okasha's edited text is IN CHRISTO NOMEN CULLA FICTUM EST, "In Christ (my) name has been changed to Culla." A possible second example, this time in runes, is the Whitby comb,[63] with an inscription incomplete at both beginning and end which begins in Latin and then switches to Old English: '. . . dæus mæus god aluwaludo helipæ cy-', ". . . my God; may God almighty help Cy-." The last word is probably a personal name in *Cyne-* (for example, *Cynewulf*), which could be the name either of the comb's owner or of its maker. This inscription is interesting in two ways: it is a rare example of the combination of Latin and Old English in a single inscription; and it also exemplifies the rare use of runes for Latin.[64] The comb has so far been dated only within very broad limits (between 657 and the end of the 9th c.).

---

[61] See Campbell, *Old English Grammar*, §§570, 573.
[62] See Parsons, *Recasting the Runes*, 118.
[63] Page, *Introduction*, 164–65.
[64] See below, §§5 and 6.

10. Inscriptions referring to a function of the inscribed object

All examples are in roman. Two subtypes may be distinguished:

a. One-word inscriptions

Okasha 36, a decorated silver ring from Essex, date uncertain, now lost, bore the Old English compound word DOLGBOT. Okasha comments: "It is perhaps an unrecorded name *DOLGBOT, since taking it as the OE noun 'compensation for a wound' seems less meaningful." However, this word is not recorded elsewhere as a personal name, and it seems more likely that the inscription means "wound-cure," making the ring an amulet, specifically a treatment for wounds.

b. Elaborated versions

Okasha defines some inscriptions in this category as descriptive formulae "referring to the object itself" (Okasha, *Hand-List*, 7). A Latin example is Okasha 26, Crowland (Lincolnshire), a stone shaft of uncertain date, perhaps post-Conquest, with an incomplete inscription of which Okasha's edited version is . . . HANC PETRUM GVTHLACVS HABET SIBI METAM, ". . . Guthlacus has this stone as a boundary for himself."[65] An Old English example is Okasha 64, Kirkdale (NR Yorks.) (ii), a stone sundial, AD 1055–1065, which reads: ÐIS IS DÆGES SOLMERCA ÆT ILCVM TIDE, "This is the day's sun-marker at every hour." Okasha notes confusion here between OE *ælc*, 'each', and *ilca*, 'the same'.[66]

11. Inscriptions inspired by the substance or function of the inscribed object

Among the runic Old English texts on the Auzon casket (Okasha 6; Elliott, *Runes*, 126–27; Page, *Introduction*, 174) is the following poem (front panel):

'fisc flodu ahof on fergenberig
warþ gasric grorn þær he on greut giswom'

"The flood cast up the fish on to the rocky shore; the king of the sea became sad, where he swam on the shingle."

---

[65] Other Latin examples are Okasha 41, Great Edstone (NR Yorks.), a stone sundial, 10th-11th c., ORLOGIV. . . .TORIS, which Okasha reconstructs as ORLOGIVM VIATORIS, "the traveller's clock"; and Okasha 99, Orpington (iii), a stone sundial of uncertain date, OR . . .VM, which Okasha presumes to be a form of (H)OROLOGIVM, "clock."

[66] The incomplete Old English inscriptions (i) and (ii) on Okasha 99, Orpington, inscription (iii) of which is referred to in my previous note, seem to describe the function of the dial.

The translation is provisional because of grammatical uncertainties in the original, especially over which noun, *flodu* or *fisc*, is the subject and which the object of the verb *ahof*.[67] But it is quite clear what inspired this descriptive poem: the whalebone from which the casket is made. The beginnings of its manufacture are traced to the moment when the whale was cast up (according to the interpretation of the grammar that seems more convincing, reflected in my translation) on to a Northumbrian shore, and the connection is emphasised by the fact that *hronæs ban* ("whale's bone") adjoins the text of the poem.[68] A comparable roman example in Latin is Okasha 173, Potterne (Wilts.), a stone font, date uncertain, probably late, with the following Latin inscription: SICVT CERVVS DESIDERAT AD FONTES AQVARVM ITA DESIDERAT ANIMA MEA AD TE DEUS AMEN, "Just as the deer desires the water springs, so my soul desires you, O God. Amen." The water held by the font was presumably the inspiration for the quotation drawn, as Okasha notes, from St Jerome's version of Psalm 41:2.

12. Functional inscriptions

An inscription which itself constitutes a function of the artifact is Okasha 20, Canterbury II (i), on a gold and silver decorated portable sundial, probably 10th c. The Latin inscription reads: IAN DEC FEB NOV MAR OCT MAI AVG IVN IVL APR SEP, "January, December, February, November, March, October, May, August, June, July, April, September."

13. Inscriptions identifying the subjects of visual representations on the object (captions)

Over twenty examples of this type are known, extending from the late 7th c. to the 12th. Most are in roman script and Latin, the only exceptions being Okasha 58, Ipswich I (roman, Old English); Okasha 6, Auzon (one Latin example beginning in roman and finishing in runes, plus other examples in Old English and wholly in runes; see below); and Okasha 34, Durham I (St. Cuthbert's coffin, Latin, A.D. 698), with two of the five identifiable inscriptions partly in runes, partly in roman, the remaining three in roman alone. Stone, in the form of either a slab or a cross, is the usual medium, though objects in metal, bone, walrus ivory, and wood are among the examples.

---

[67] The various possibilities are explored by Page, *Introduction*, 174.
[68] See under category 7 above.

a. Personal names

Sometimes the inscription consists solely of a name or names referring to a person depicted in a carving. A straightforward example is Okasha 57, Inglesham (Wilts.), a stone slab of the 11th or 12th c., part of the fabric of the parish church, showing a carved figure of the Virgin below the inscription MARIA.[69]

b. Descriptive sentences

Sometimes descriptions of carvings on the artifact consist of complete sentences. A Latin example in roman is Okasha 172, Paris (i), a wood and porphyry portable altar framed in silver, probably of the late 10th or early 11th c., which reads DISCIPVLVS PLORAT RAPHAEL QVEM SEMPER ADORAT, "The disciple mourns him whom Raphael always worships," referring to an incised figure of St John.[70] An impressive variety of examples in different scripts and languages is found on Okasha 6, the Auzon whalebone casket,[71] including (a) a Latin inscription mainly in roman letters, partly in runes: 'HIC FUGIANT HIERUSALIM afitatores', interpreted by Okasha as "Here the inhabitants flee

---

[69] Other examples with names referring to the subjects of carvings are Okasha 11, Bishop Auckland (Durham), a stone cross-shaft, probably 8th or 9th c., with two inscriptions: (i) PAS and (ii) AND, probably abbreviated forms of the names Paulus and Andreas; Okasha 17, Brussels I (Belgium), the Brussels cross, 10th-11th c., inscription (i) of which reads AGNVS DEI, "Lamb of God"; Okasha 31, Dewsbury II (WR Yorkshire), a stone slab, perhaps late 9th c., with IHSXPVS, an abbreviated form of Christ's name; Okasha 93, Mortain (Normandy), a wooden casket gilded with copper, probably 8th to 9th c., with two inscriptions: (i) SCS MIH and (ii) SCS GAB, abbreviations of the names of St Michael and St Gabriel; Okasha 97, North Elmham (Norfolk), a walrus ivory panel, 10th-11th c., with an inscription (i): SANCTA MARIA SANCTUS PETRUS, "St Mary, St Peter"; Okasha 105, Ruthwell, stone cross, one of the inscriptions on the northern face of which (Okasha's N(v)) reads MARIA ET IO. . .TVO, "Mary and . . ." (Okasha thinks probably a version of 'Joseph' completes the inscription); Okasha 149, York IV, a limestone slab, 11th or 12th c., inscribed SANCTA MARIA, "St Mary"; Okasha 159, Brandon (Suffolk), a gold plaque, probably late 8th or early 9th c., inscribed SANCTUS EVANGELISTA IOHANNIS, "St John the Evangelist," the inscription framing the figure of John; and Okasha 166, Fletton (Peterborough), a stone slab from the wall of the chancel of the parish church, date uncertain, text probably SANCTUS MICHAEL, "St Michael." Okasha 34, Durham I, c. 698 A.D. (St. Cuthbert's coffin), an oak coffin, with at least five Latin inscriptions in this category, mostly in roman but with two partly in runes, has already been mentioned. Okasha 113, Sulgrave (Northants.), probably of the 11th c., is another possible example.

[70] Several similar examples in Latin and roman are to be found in a somewhat deteriorated condition on Okasha 105, Ruthwell, a stone cross, early 8th c., texts (Nii–iv) and (Siii–v).

[71] For an account of all the inscriptions on the Franks casket, see Elliott, *Runes*, 123–39, and Page, *Introduction*, 172–79.

from Jerusalem," in reference to part of the scene depicted;[72] and (b) an Old English inscription in runes, 'Her fegtaþ titus end giuþeasu', "Here Titus and a Jew fight."[73] Another Old English example in runes, this time in verse and very obscure in its significance and relation to the carving it accompanies, occurs on the right side of the casket:[74]

> 'her hos (*or* herh-os) sitiþ on harmberga
> agl.. drigiþ swa hiræ ertae gisgraf
> sarden sorga ond sefa torna'

> "Here Hos (*or* The temple-goddess) sits on the sorrow-mound; she suffers distress as Ertae had imposed it upon her, a wretched den (?wood) of sorrows and of torments of mind."[75]

c. Name plus descriptive sentence
A combination of (a) and (b) in runes and Old English is found on the left side of the Auzon casket:[76] 'romwalus and reumwalus twœgen gibroþær afœddæ hiæ wylif in Romæcæstri, oþlæ unneg', "Romulus and Remus, two brothers; a she-wolf fed them in the city of Rome, far from their native land."

d. Reference to the artifact as symbol
An apparently unique sub-type is represented by Okasha 63, Jarrow III, a stone slab with carved cross, possibly 8th c. The damaged Latin inscription is reconstructed by Okasha as: IN HOC SINGVLARI SIGNO VITA REDDITVR MVNDO, "In this unique sign life is returned to the world." The special feature of this inscription is the direct reference to the representation as an abstract symbol, rather than to what lies behind it, as in previous examples. One is reminded

---

[72] Runes are very rarely used for Latin; see Page, *Introduction*, 219, and §6 below.

[73] Page, *Introduction*, 176–77. A similar Old English example in roman is Okasha 58, Ipswich I (i), a carved stone slab of the 11th c., inscribed HER SANCTUS MIHAEL FEHT WIÐ ÐANE DRACAN, "Here St Michael fights (*or* fought) against the dragon."

[74] Text from Page, *Introduction*, 178–79. See also Elliott, *Runes*, 134–37.

[75] The translation given here is one of two alternatives given by Page (*Introduction*, 179), with an alternative reading offered for the first line. Elliott divides verse 2b as *swa hiri erta egi sgraf*, "just as to her Erta appointed anxiety," with *egi* understood as an early form of the noun *ege*, 'fear', 'awe'; but this gives double alliteration (here vocalic) in the b-verse, so the arrangement seems best avoided.

[76] Elliott, *Runes*, 130–31; Page, *Introduction*, 175–76.

here of the Ruthwell and Brussels cross inscriptions.[77] It has been suggested that the text draws upon Rufinus's edition of Eusebius.[78]

14. Stamps

In this category fall eight seal-dies made of ivory or bronze bearing Latin inscriptions. The earliest, Okasha 38, Eye (Suffolk), dates from the 9th c., the latest (Okasha 177, Totnes; Okasha 184, York IX) from the late 11th or early 12th c. Two types may be distinguished on the basis of the amount of information the inscription conveys.

a. Personal names
The basic type is represented by Okasha 177, Totnes (Devon), an ivory seal-die, possibly late 11th to early 12th c.: SIGILLVM ALFREDI, "The seal of Alfred."[79]

b. Personal name plus office
An elaborated version of the formula adds the office held by the owner of the seal. An example is Okasha 184, York IX, ivory, possibly late 11th to early 12th c.: SIGILLUM SNARRI THEOLENARII, "The seal of Snarri the tax-gatherer."[80]

B. Non-Deictic Inscriptions

Some inscriptions have no obvious formal or implicit connection with the object on which they appear and might be detached from it without loss of significance. Two main types may be distinguished:

---

[77] See category 1 (i) above.

[78] Okasha, *Hand-List*, 87.

[79] Other examples are Okasha 176, Sittingbourne II (Kent), ivory, late 10th-early 11th c., SIGILLVM WVLFRICI, "The seal of Wulfric"; Okasha 119, Weeke (Hants.), bronze, of the same date, SIGILLVM ÆLFRICI A, "The seal of Ælfric" (the significance of the final *A* is unclear).

[80] Other examples are Okasha 38, Eye (Suffolk), bronze, 9th c., SIGILLUM EÐILVVALDI EPISCOPI, "The seal of Bishop Eðilvvald"; and Okasha 187, Chester, a lead seal-die, probably of the late 11th c., which reads SIGILLVM PETRI CESITRENSIS EPISCOPI, "The seal of Peter, bishop of Chester"; Okasha 117, Wallingford (Berkshire), (i) and (ii), ivory, probably 10th and 11th c. respectively, SIGILLVM 8 GODWINI MINISTRI, "The seal of Godwin the priest (*or* the thane)" (the significance of the character that resembles an arabic figure 8 is uncertain), and SIGILLVM GODGYÐE MONACHE DEO DATE, "The seal of Godgyð, a nun given to God." It appears that this is a re-used seal-die, with (i) possibly later than (ii). Okasha 197, Lincoln III, a walrus ivory seal-die, probably 11th c., plainly has an even more elaborate inscription than these, but the text is incomplete.

15. *Fuþorcs* and alphabets

The Thames scramasax,[81] a 10th-c. weapon according to Page,[82] and probably of Kentish manufacture, is inscribed with a twenty-eight-rune Anglo-Saxon *fuþorc*, the letters not in the traditional order. A silver gilded pin, possibly from the late 8th or early 9th c., found at Brandon in Suffolk,[83] carries an inscription consisting of the first sixteen letters of the *fuþorc* in their traditional order. A silver gilded finger-ring from Flixborough, dating from the 8th or 9th c.,[84] is inscribed with the letters A to L in alphabetical order (J omitted "in accordance with early medieval usage"). The letter b is upside down, perhaps indicating "that the craftsman was unfamiliar with the precise nature of the letters" (Webster and Backhouse). The Webster and Backhouse editors note that this series is "perhaps the equivalent" of inscriptions of runic *fuþorcs* such as appear on the Brandon pin. A wide range of possible interpretations is suggested: ". . . they may have fulfilled a teaching role, a talismanic function, or both. Some connection with Insular abcedarial prayers such as that found in an early 9th-c. Mercian prayerbook . . . which arrange their supplications in alphabetical order, emphasised by enlarged initials, is also possible, with the ring performing a devotional mnemonic, rosary-like function." Okasha 190, Dublin V, a piece of leather with drawstring (perhaps part of a bag), late 11th or early 12th c., has the first few (probably six) letters of the alphabet incised on it (ABCDEF). Okasha 178, Waltham Abbey, is a shapeless piece of lead, probably 9th to early 11th c., bearing a full alphabet, carved probably as "practice letters" in Okasha's view. Okasha 186, Barton St David (Somerset), a piece of sandstone, "probably trial piece," has three texts, one of which (Text i) is a partial alphabet (ABCDE).

16. Biblical quotations

a. *Alpha and Omega*

One identifiable formula consists of abbreviated forms of *alpha* and *omega*, sometimes in conjunction with a personal name, as on Okasha 48, Hartlepool VI (i) and (ii), a stone slab, 8th c.; and Okasha 115, Swindon, a decorated gold ring, probably late 9th or 10th c. The function of such inscriptions may depend on the medium, Okasha 48 being presumably commemorative, Okasha 115 perhaps intended to confer spiritual protection on the wearer.[85]

---

[81] Page, *Introduction*, 80; Elliott, *Runes*, 42–43, 104.
[82] Page, *Introduction*, 113.
[83] Webster and Backhouse, no. 66 (b), 82–83; Page, *Introduction*, 80–81.
[84] Webster and Backhouse, no. 69(b), 95–96; Okasha 192, Flixborough I.
[85] The alpha and omega symbols are also found on Okasha 167, Gloucester (i), a clay bell-mould fragment from the late 9th or early 10th c., and Okasha 200, North Stoke, a stone sundial of uncertain date.

b. Miscellaneous

Biblical inscriptions probably intended to have a protective purpose are Okasha 19, Canterbury I (ii), a silver coin-brooch of the 10th c. with the Latin inscription: NOMINE DOMINI, "(In) the name of the Lord," and Okasha 33, Driffield (ER Yorks), a decorated gold ring, possibly 9th c., inscribed ECCE AGNVS DEI, "Behold the Lamb of God." The quotation is from John 1:29.

§4. Runes or roman

My own survey tends to confirm Page's observation that there is "no justification for deducing the nature of a text from the type of lettering it is written in."[86] However, although far more roman than runic inscriptions survive from the Anglo-Saxon period, it is clear that runic inscriptions are proportionately commoner from the earlier centuries than from the later ones. The 8th c. would appear to have been the high point of runic epigraphy in England, judging by the number of surviving inscriptions. Only a handful of runic inscriptions datable to the 9th c. or later survive, the main examples being the Chester-le-Street (Durham) slab (5[c] above) and the Manchester gold ring (1[e] above), 9th-11th and 9th c. respectively, neither of them fully runic; the Thames scramasax, with its name (5[e] above) and full runic *fuþorc* (15 above), which Page dates to the 10th c.; and the Dover stone (5[a] above, note), 9th or 10th c., with its single name. From the 8th c., however, my own rough calculation suggests that almost as many runic as roman inscriptions are known.

Competence in runes among inscribers, perhaps never particularly widespread in England, had evidently weakened to the point of disappearance by the end of the ninth century at the latest. We cannot know what factors determined this decline, though several possibilities suggest themselves: competition from the roman alphabet;[87] technical advances enabling the roman alphabet to be used more easily than before for inscriptions on hard surfaces; or a perception of runes as old-fashioned, or even tainted by early associations with paganism or minor superstitious practices condemned by the church. Some of these factors may, of course, have combined to condemn runes to extinction as an epigraphic script.

---

[86] Page, *Introduction*, 115.

[87] See Page, *Introduction*, 34, who doubts if the reason for the disappearance of runic inscriptions is quite as simple as this, in view of "the new finds from Brandon and Blythburgh, which indicate quite late runes in learned or ecclesiastical contexts." However, none of these recent finds has been dated very precisely so far. Page describes the Blythburgh bone writing tablet as "?eighth-century" on p. 30 (but "of unknown date" on p. 217). Of the Brandon finds, only the silver tweezers fragment is dated by Page, and that rather vaguely ("eighth-/ninth-century" [167]).

The great majority of Anglo-Saxon inscriptions are carved either in runes or in roman letters, though mixtures of the two within single inscriptions, and repeated inscriptions in both alphabets, are occasionally found. Examples of the mixture of scripts are the Auzon whalebone casket (8th c., Latin, 13[b] above); the Chester-le-Street slab (9th-11th c., Old English, 5[c] above); St. Cuthbert's coffin (A.D. 698, Latin, 13 [introductory paragraph] above); the Manchester gold ring (probably 9th c., Old English, 1[e] above); and the Llysfaen gold ring (9th c., Old English, 5[g] above). In all of these examples except St. Cuthbert's coffin, roman letters preponderate over runic. Repeated inscriptions in both runic and roman scripts are very rare, with only two examples known: the Falstone stone cross (Old English, 4[h] above), and the Lindisfarne II stone slab (Old English; see 5[d] above), both relatively early inscriptions (8th c. or, in the case of Falstone, possibly 9th c.).[88] There is probably little point in speculating about the thinking behind the production of these biliteral inscriptions. Page draws attention to evidence that the roman text on the Falstone cross was primary and that the parallel runic text represents a letter-by-letter transcription of it.[89] On the face of it, the most obvious general explanation for biliteral inscriptions is that the carvers believed that some readers would understand their texts in one or the other script but not in both, though the explanation may well be more complicated. The fact that the Falstone runes are secondary may point to a certain stage in the waning of runic traditions; but it would probably be unwise to pursue the whole question of the relationship between the two scripts any further without bringing in the evidence of manuscripts in which letters and words in runes appear in largely roman contexts. Page gives a good account of these manuscript runes but cautiously refrains from drawing any general conclusions from them.[90] This is an area for future research.

Most of the surviving Anglo-Saxon inscriptions are in prose, though a few of the ones in Old English are in alliterative verse. The majority of these poetic inscriptions, especially the earlier ones, are runic. A few inscriptions, though they contain alliterating elements, are really too brief (i.e. of half-line length or

---

[88] For discussion of English inscriptions employing both runic and roman letters, see Page, "Anglo-Saxon Runes and Magic," who suggests that runes were used in these inscriptions because "runes were a traditional script for grave furniture, at least in the north-east" (referring to St. Cuthbert's coffin and the Lindisfarne name-stones). This might account for the use of runes, but it does not explain the repetition of the message. See also Page, *Introduction*, 121–25.

[89] R. I. Page, "Roman and Runic on St Cuthbert's Coffin," in *St. Cuthbert, his Cult and his Community to AD 1200*, ed. Gerald Bonner et al. (Woodbridge: Boydell Press, 1989), 257–65, repr. in Page, *Runes and Runic Inscriptions*, ed. Parsons, 315–25 (at 322).

[90] See Page, *Introduction*, 212–25. See also Elisabeth Okasha, "Script-Mixing in Anglo-Saxon Inscriptions," in *Writing and Texts in Anglo-Saxon England*, ed. Alexander R. Rumble (Cambridge: D. S. Brewer, 2006), 62–70.

shorter) to indicate a definite intention on the part of the inscriber to produce verse. The 8th-c. runic Wheatley Hill ring inscription (under 1[h] above), *hring ic hattæ*, "I am called ring," falls within this category. Other inscriptions which show alliteration and are extensive enough to be regarded as complete single verse-lines are the 9th-c. Manchester gold ring text (1[e] above), *ædred mec ah eanred mec agrof*, "Ædred owns me, Eanred engraved me" (vocalic alliteration), which mixes runic and roman letters, and the runic memorial inscription on the Overchurch stone (4[d] above; the date may be as late as the 10th c.), *folc arærdon becun gebiddaþ fore æþelmunde*, "The people erected (this) monument. Pray for Æþelmund" (alliteration on *þ*). A number of other, more or less equally brief, memorial inscriptions included in category 4 above show alliteration, though only on names. The runic inscriptions on the two Thornhill stones (8th-9th c.) that Page numbers I and II (4[g] above) alliterate (vocalically) on names, though as in the case of the Manchester ring inscription, this could be the result of family relationships rather than poetic contrivance: the first reads *eþelberht sette æfter eþelwini*, "Eþelberht set up (this memorial) after Eþelwini"; the second differs only in its names and shows the same pattern of vocalic alliteration between the name of the memorial's maker and that of the commemorated person. In the same category (4[g]), the incomplete Old English inscription on the Wycliffe cross-shaft (8th-9th c.) is probably in verse too, with alliteration between the names and *becun*, 'monument'. The inscriptions on the Great Urswick (9th c.) and Thornhill C (8th-9th c.) stones (4[e] above) are more extensive: both consist of two-line memorial inscriptions in runes showing alliteration in the second line on *bekun*, 'monument', and *gebidæs/gebiddaþ*, 'pray' (imperative), though the name-alliteration fails in the first line of Thornhill C. The briefer and fragmentary Dewsbury I memorial inscription (Okasha 30; see under 4[e] above, note) shows the same pattern of alliteration (*becun, gebiddad*) but is in roman rather than runes. The 8th-9th c. Falstone cross inscription (4[h] above), presented in alternative runic and roman versions, is yet another example of the linking of these same two words in alliteration. The Auzon Casket, supposed to date from the beginning of the 8th c., contains two runic passages in regular Old English verse (quoted under 11 and 13[b] above), of two and three verse-lines in length respectively. The first describes the origins of the whalebone out of which the casket was made and upon which the runes are carved; the second apparently tells the story behind an image carved on the right side of the casket, though its significance is much debated. The main Ruthwell Cross inscription (probably early 8th c.; 1[i] above), in which the cross speaks in verse of its involvement in the crucifixion, is runic, but the much briefer, two-line poetic inscription on the Brussels Cross (10th-11th c.), which shows some textual overlap with the Ruthwell text and may even have been inspired by it, is in roman. Finally, the Sutton silver disc brooch (late 10th or early 11th c.; 1[c] above) is a three-line Old English poem written in roman, though here rhyme has replaced alliteration in the linking of all but the first pair of half-lines. The general prevalence of runes over roman in these poetic inscriptions is striking and may perhaps tell us something about the relationship between the two alphabets in the period. This is a question I shall return to briefly in my concluding chapter.

§5. Old English or Latin

Of the categories in which examples are numerous enough for figures to be at all significant, Old English inscriptions outnumber Latin ones in categories 1 (Old English 20x, Latin 5x, the latter all 9th c. or later, mostly 11th c.) and 5, though in the latter case this is simply a consequence of the fact that the persons whose names are preserved are Anglo-Saxons with names of English, not Latin, form. Latin inscriptions preponderate in categories 12–16. So far as period is concerned, the only noticeable tendency is in category 4 (memorial inscriptions), where Old English is commoner than Latin in the 8th c. but not later. There is, however, no general tendency for Old English to be favoured over Latin (or vice-versa) in the earlier centuries in particular.

Most Anglo-Saxon inscriptions are either in Old English or Latin, though we know two inscriptions that combine the two languages, one in roman script, the other in runes. The former is the York I stone slab (6[d] above), the latter the Whitby comb (9 above). There are no examples of double inscriptions using both Old English and Latin.

§6. Language and script

Before the conversion of the Anglo-Saxons, the only language which runes were used to represent was Old English. No doubt the inscribers knew no other languages. That the connection between runes and the vernacular came to be seen as traditional is suggested by the fact that the link extends into the post-conversion period: runes are usually reserved for Old English, only rarely used for Latin inscriptions. It is worth noting that three of the four known exceptions are fairly early: the Auzon whalebone casket, 8th c. (13[b] above); St. Cuthbert's coffin, A.D. 698 (though here Latin names only are involved; see 13, introduction, above); and probably the Ruthwell cross (early 8th c.), the fifth inscription on the south side of which includes (in a largely unreadable passage) the form 'domin-nae' (possibly for *domini*, "of the lord"; see Okasha, *Hand-List*, 111). The fourth and final example, not yet dated with any precision, is the runic Whitby comb (9 above), which contains a Latin phrase followed (probably not as part of the same sentence) by a plea for God's help in Old English. The rarity of runic Latin inscriptions in the later part of the period is probably just a reflection of the general decline of runes.

But if runes are rare for Latin, roman is used freely for both Old English and Latin inscriptions. It would thus appear that the roman alphabet encroached, after the conversion, on the vernacular, once the province of runes, though of course it would be equally true to say that after the conversion the vernacular encroached on the roman alphabet, once (on the continent) the province of Latin. The question of which of these perspectives is more appropriate historically will be taken up briefly in the final chapter of this book.

§7. The content of Anglo-Saxon inscriptions

The content of Anglo-Saxon inscriptions shows a concern with a rather narrow range of information. Our attention may be drawn to the identity of historical persons owning an inscribed object, or involved in its manufacture; we may be given the name of a deceased person commemorated by a monument, or the name of a saint to whom a church is dedicated, or the date of its consecration. Some inscriptions constitute, or include, a plea to pray for someone's soul. Inscriptions such as these offer the kind of information to readers which they might equally well receive through ordinary spoken communication; but not all inscriptions are communicative in any obvious way. If the Essex silver ring's inscription *dolgbot* means "wound-cure", as I have suggested (10[a] above), this inscription is to be associated with some of the earliest known runic inscriptions from the continent, the only possible purpose of which seems to be to confer effectiveness on the artifacts that bear them. The clearest examples of this kind of word-magic are the Øvre Stabu (Norway) spearhead, dated to the 2nd c. and inscribed *raunijaz*, "tester, prober"; the Dahmsdorf spearhead from Brandenburg in Germany, inscribed *ranja*, the sense of which Page suggests is either "assailant" or "the weapon that makes them run," dated to the 3rd c.; and the Kovel (Ukraine) spearhead, inscribed *tilarids*, perhaps "attacker."[91] Such inscriptions seem unlikely to be mere descriptions of qualities possessed by the artifacts in question; the writing of these words was probably taken to be productive of the qualities they denote, so that their inscribing was part of the weapons' manufacture. Some of the inscriptions in my category 15, particularly the *fuþorc* carved on the Thames scramasax and the half-alphabet on the Flixborough ring, are presumably of sim-

[91] The Øvre Stabu inscription is cited from Elmer H. Antonsen, *A Concise Grammar of the Older Runic Inscriptions* (Tübingen: Niemeyer, 1975), 29, and the Kovel and Dahmsdorf inscriptions from Page, *Introduction*, 108. For instances of comparable Gaulish inscriptions, see Meid, *Gaulish Inscriptions*, 40, an example being *exsops pissíiumi*, "(As one) deprived of eye-sight I shall see," part of the Chamalières lead plate inscription. Of such utterances, Meid comments: "Apparently these are effects desired by the persons in question, clothed in speech forms which purport to anticipate the result and are thus, in this context, magically performative."

ilar purpose: the inclusion of all the letters of the writing system (or, in the case of the Flixborough ring, all the letters that there is room for) suggests a desire to draw upon the full magical resources of letters, whether runic or roman, as a way of enhancing the weapon's effectiveness and developing the magical (possibly protective) potentialities of the ring.

§8. The deictic forms of Anglo-Saxon inscriptions

The various kinds of deictic reference that can be found exemplified among Anglo-Saxon inscriptions are considered below under three headings: medium deixis, place deixis, and person deixis. The first of these includes a number of subvarieties, and a few inscriptions combine two different kinds of deixis.

§9. Medium deixis

Medium deixis occurs when the full meaning or significance of an inscription depends on an awareness of what object, artifact, or material it is inscribed on. Thus in my category 1, the maker, owner, engraver, commissioner, and defining formulas (1[a]-[f] and [h]) all exemplify medium deixis: in every case, the first-person pronoun identifies the artifact as the 'speaker' of the inscription, and the assertions that most of these inscriptions embody—of manufacture, ownership, etc. of the artifact on the part of some named individual—would obviously mean little in the absence of the artifact itself. The inscriber formula (category 1[g]), represented only by the Stratfield Mortimer slab's *Toki me scripsit*, belongs with these other first-person inscriptions if (as seems likely) *scripsit* means 'engraved'. If we translate (with Okasha) 'wrote', it exemplifies the rarer text deixis: Toki is recording his responsibility for the Latin memorial inscription which precedes the attribution.

The first-person pronoun, used in all category 1 inscriptions, is a structure-word which cannot but function deictically, in English as in any other language; but other instances of medium deixis in the corpus reside in common nouns which are not essentially deictic (as they could be used in other contexts for non-deictic purposes). One example is the Harford Farm brooch runic inscription: *Luda gibœtæ sigilæ*, "Luda mended (the) brooch" (under 3 above), and there are several examples in category 4. In the Overchurch rune-stone's *Folcæ arærdon becun. Gebiddaþ fore Æþelmunde*, "The people erected (this) monument. Pray for Æþelmund" (4[d]), the noun *becun*, "monument," can refer only to the inscribed stone itself. The Great Urswick and Thornhill C runestones (4[e]) both use the same noun, *becun* (*bekun*), in exactly the same way. In other cases, the inclusion of a deictic demonstrative ('this') reinforces the reference of the common noun to the inscribed object before us, as in the runic inscription on the Mortain reliquary

(4[f]), *Good helpe Æadan þiiosne ciismeel gewarahtæ*, "May God help Æadan (who) made this casket"; the Brussels I (iii) inscription (4[h]), which includes the phrase *Þas rode*, "this cross," in reference to the inscribed cross itself; and the Lancaster II cross-shaft inscription (4[i]), with its reference to *hoc opvs*, "this work."

It is difficult to know what significance to attach, in cases of this general type, to the omission of the demonstrative before the medium-deictic noun. This omission occurs in Harford Farm, Overchurch, Great Urswick and Thornhill C. In the last three of these, the noun in question is *becun* (*bekun*), suggesting that the similarity may be due to the repetition of a standard commemorative formula which conventionally omitted the demonstrative; but the question remains. Perhaps the answer lies in a logical difficulty that the inscribers faced. In speech, a word like 'this' will point to something close to, but distinct from, the speaker; but here there is no separate 'speaker' and so no distinction. It may be that the demonstrative is omitted from these inscriptions either because it was felt to inappropriate for this reason, or because it would have seemed redundant in the context: no need was felt to specify which particular 'monument' the inscription referred to; the context itself was sufficient indication. If this is right, we must assume that the process has gone even further in some of the inscriptions listed under 4[g] above, for example the Thornhill A and B (I and II) rune-stones. The second of these is inscribed *eadred sete æfte(r) eateinne*, which Page translates as "Eadred set up (this memorial) after Eadþegn." Here there is not even a noun referring to the memorial, let alone a demonstrative to support it. There are, furthermore, several memorial inscriptions which include no deictic elements, for example the Haddenham stone cross-shaft (4[f]), inscribed *Lucem tvam Ovino da deus et reqviem amen*, "O God, grant your light and rest to Ovin, Amen"; but in such cases a deictic link between the named individual and the monument is probably implicit in the context of the inscription. Another example of implicit deixis is the Kirkheaton stone runic inscription (under 2 above) *eoh worohtæ*, "Eoh made (this *or* me)."

The three inscriptions in category 7, two on bone objects, one on horn, also exemplify medium deixis, but of a rather more specialized kind. The 8th c. Auzon casket's runic *hronæs ban*, "whale's bone," identifies the material nature of the inscribed medium and the species from which it comes, rather than the whole artifact, whereas the 5th c. Caistor-by-Norwich roe-deer astragalus's inscription: *raihan* (possibly genitive singular, "roe's") identifies only the species from which the bone derives. Even more oblique is the Brandon antler handle inscription: *wohs wildum deoran*, which seems to mean something of the order of "(I *or* it) grew on a wild beast": the inscription indicates the nature of the inscribed medium, the antler, by describing its animal origins, but the grammatical difficulties presented by this inscription mean that this is about as far as we can go. A further variation on the same type, but far more difficult to analyse, is the (?late 8th c.) Wheatley Hill ring runic inscription (1[h] above): *hring ic hattæ*, "I am called (a) ring": The object itself differs from the other examples in being an artifact rather than a natural material like bone or horn. Its first-person pronoun *ic* exemplifies a kind of medium deixis we have already identified (though the use of the nominative is unusual); and rather than simply labelling itself as what it is (in the manner of the Auzon casket), the artifact refers to the linguistic category into which it has been placed, as if (like a human being) it had been given a name.

Another minor variation on normal medium deixis is represented by the two Latin inscriptions in category 8, the Sandford nonagon and the Cologne crozier head, the first of which reads *Intvs qvod latet cvncto nos crimine laxet*, "May that which lies hidden within free us from all guilt": the inscriptions point, not to the inscribed object itself but to what it contains. All the inscriptions in category 10 exemplify another slightly oblique form of medium deixis. These are the inscription on the lost silver ring from Essex, *dolgbot* (if my suggestion that the word means "wound-cure" is correct), the Latin inscription on the Crowland stone shaft, . . . *hanc petram Gvthlacvs habet sibi metam*, ". . . Guthlacus has this stone as a boundary for himself," and the Old English inscription on the Kirkdale stone sundial, *Ðis is dæges solmerca æt ilcvm tide*, "This is the day's sun-marker at every hour." All three inscriptions focus attention on a function of the inscribed artifact rather than on the artifact itself. The deictic reference of the two inscriptions in category 11 is more enigmatic: they allude inexplicitly to some feature of the inscribed object. The Auzon casket's lyric about the beaching of a whale is naturally taken as drawing inspiration from the actual whale that supplied the whalebone from which the casket was made. An attractive interpretation of the poem would be as a riddle having as its solution the extralinguistic deictic link between inscription and medium. The inscription *hronæs ban*, which immediately precedes the poetic text, gives the game away, though it is possible that this identification is a kind of heading for the riddle. In the second of the two examples I have put in this category, the Potterne font inscription, the text employs a standard baptismal quotation inspired by the holy water kept in the font: *Sicvt cervvs desiderat ad fontes aqvarvm*, etc., "Just as the deer desires the water springs . . ." (Psalms 41:2). Finally, the seal-dies in category 14 are all medium-deictic; a representative example is Totnes: *sigillvm Alfredi*, "the seal of Alfred." There is also an element of text deixis in inscriptions like these: the words themselves are an essential functional feature of the artifact. The Essex ring's inscription *dolgbot*, discussed above, also shows a degree of text deixis: the word does not simply denote the ring's magical power; the text is what produces its power.

Some but not all of the single name inscriptions in category 5 show medium deixis. The inscriptions in this category are broadly divisible into two groups according to whether the medium is fixed (i.e. stone) or portable. The inscriptions on portable objects (5[e]-[j]) probably name, in most if not all cases, the persons who owned or made these objects, in which case they can only be classified as a variety of medium deixis (those on fixed stones exemplify place deixis; see below): the inscription does not name or otherwise define the object; so in order to appreciate what object the named person owns, we must be able to see what it is. These inscriptions fulfil the basic requirements of medium deixis, though the exact relationship between the named person and the object on which his or her name is inscribed is not always obvious. We may suspect that the names are of the owners in most cases; but in some they could equally well be the names of the craftsman—not necessarily to be identified with the owner.

The inscriptions on the Brussels and Ruthwell crosses (1[i]) represent a sigificant variant of medium deixis which we might call 'image deixis': these utterances refer deictically to the artifacts upon which they appear, though they are in fact appropriate only to the true cross with which their inscriptions identify them.

§10. Place deixis

Place deixis occurs when the full meaning or significance of an inscription depends on an awareness of the position in space of the medium that bears it. However, we must extend this definition to cover awareness of the position *on* the object of the inscription if we are to include here the inscriptions in category 13 which refer to carved figures on the surface of the inscribed medium. In such cases, reference to the picture or symbol is sometimes reinforced by a local deictic term such as 'here', as in the Auzon Casket's Latin inscription *Hic fugiant Hierusalim afitatores*, "Here the inhabitants flee from Jerusalem" (an Old English example is the same artifact's inscription: *Her fegtaþ Titus end Giuþeasu*, "Here fight Titus and the Jews"), or a demonstrative adjective, as in the Latin inscription on the Jarrow III stone slab with carved cross, *In hoc singvlari signo vita redditvr mvndo*, "In this unique sign life is returned to the world."

In the case of the (Latin) demonstrative adjectives in the dedication inscriptions of my category 6, it is often difficult to draw any strict distinction between place deixis and medium deixis. The problem is exemplified by the Deerhurst I inscription, which begins *Odda dux ivssit hanc regiam avlam constrvi . . .*, "Earl Odda ordered this royal church to be built . . .": *hanc*, "this," is medium deixis if the inscribed stone is regarded as part of the fabric of the church, place deixis if it is conceived as a separate sign pointing to the church proper; but the same inscription includes the phrase: *de hoc loco assvmpta*, "taken up from this place," in which *hoc* is unmistakably place-deictic. The memorial inscriptions that make up my category 4 include some showing similar place-deictic terms, for example Latin *hic*, "here", in Monkwearmouth II *Hic in sepulcro . . .*, "Here in the tomb . . ." (4[a]), and Old English *her*, "here", in the Winchester I stone's *Her lið Gvnni . . .*, "Here lies Gvnni . . ." (4[b]), the function of these terms being to mark the place of burial. Place deixis is also characteristic of the name-inscriptions in category 5 on fixed stones (5[a]-[d]), most of which were probably intended to mark the position of the grave in which the named individual's remains rested. The Newent slab inscription (4[j]) and the name-list on the Flixborough lead plaque (5[k]) are probably further examples of the same general type.

§11. Person deixis

Inscriptions referring deictically to a living person are rare. The only reasonably clear instance I have been able to identify is the Bossington baptismal ring (category 9) with the Latin inscription *In Christo nomen Culla fictum est*, "In Christ (my) name has been changed to Culla." Here we need to be able to see the wearer of the ring to know who it is that is called Culla.

§12. Absence of deixis

There are few inscriptions that do not use some form of deixis. Category 12 is represented by only a single inscription: the list of the months of the year on the Canterbury II portable sundial. Although it is true that the list would be of no practical value if it were removed from its medium, I am reluctant to call it a case of medium deixis because the verbal material is less of a communication than an essential part of the actual mechanism of the artifact. The runic and alphabetical letter-series which constitute category 15 are also, it seems to me, difficult to interpret as deictic utterances. Here the uncertainly arises from our ignorance of the purpose of these inscriptions. In spite of the suggestions that the editors of the Flixborough ring make, it seems to me likely that these inscriptions are not meant to be communicative in the way utterances usually are; in fact, they seem to me completely uninformative. The runes and letters were probably meant to confer magical power on the artifacts on which they are cut. As the inscriptions tell us nothing, we cannot really call them deictic, in spite of the fact that they transform the objects they appear on into objects of power. In the case of the biblical inscriptions in category 16, there is no explicit deixis and no suggestion even of an implicit deictic link between inscription and artifact—apart from the general implication of a relationship between text and medium that any inscription carries.

§13. Summary

What is most distinctive in the form and content of Anglo-Saxon inscriptions? Two general points seem worth making. The first is an obvious one: Anglo-Saxon inscriptions use runic letters far more often than manuscript texts do. Runes were, as we shall see in the next two chapters, sometimes incorporated in manuscript writings for special purposes; but the roman alphabet is established from the beginning of the Christian period (in the seventh century) as the normal vehicle of linguistic expression in manuscripts. The use of runes in manuscripts is therefore a clear manifestation of continuity with pre-Christian English culture and the epigraphic traditions associated with it. There are, however, discontinuities too, as we shall see shortly.

The second point is that Anglo-Saxon inscriptions, in runes or roman, Old English or Latin, are nearly all deictic, non-transferable texts. The type of deixis most characteristic of the Anglo-Saxon corpus of inscriptions as a whole is what I have called medium-deixis, a distinctively and exclusively literary variety (for speech involves no medium) which effectively closes the deictic gap. These inscriptions proclaim their status as written texts by the deictic link between them and the media upon which they are inscribed; and so deictic reference in manuscript writings to the inscribed medium is probably to be taken as a sign of continuity with established epigraphical practices — a point which will be developed further in the next chapter.

The examination of the corpus of Anglo-Saxon inscriptions in this chapter has revealed several distinct manifestations of medium-deixis; but three subtypes in particular are especially remarkable and relevant to the argument of this book. There is no need to repeat what has already been said about those medium-deictic inscriptions that use first-person pronouns as their main deictic element (e.g. *X me worhte*, "X made me"), collected in category 1 above: briefly, their effect is to create a 'speaking' artifact or material, though the content of the 'speech' itself excludes it from the realm of human utterances *in propria persona*. Who but God could 'make' a person? On the whole, it seems likely that these inscriptions are one of the earliest and most basic reflections of the desire to replicate in writing the broad structural or interpersonal fundamentals of spoken conversation. The form of utterance they exemplify probably developed earlier than the more elaborate text-deixis of the scribal colophons.

A second type of medium-deictic inscription, equally distinctive but more elusive and variable in form, consists of, or includes, parts of speech other than personal pronouns which are in some way applicable to the medium. Examples are collected under 7 above. The simplest and most direct type is represented by the Auzon casket's *hronæs ban*, "whale's bone," which does nothing more, on the face of it at least, than identify the medium's substance. However, comparable instances of this general type of inscription point to an interest, not so much in the substance as in the origins of the medium. Even the Auzon casket inscription tells us, not just that the medium is bone, but also what species this particular bone comes from. The Caistor-by-Norwich roe-deer astragalus inscription: *raïhan*, if it means "of (*or* from) a roe," emphasises the original connections of the bone rather than its substance. My third example, the Brandon antler-handle inscription: *wohs wildum deoran*, tentatively interpreted as "(I *or* it) grew on a wild beast" (as indeed any antler must have done), does not use a noun to identify the medium as the first two examples do, but refers discursively to its origins as part of an animal. Perhaps all three of these inscriptions may therefore be classified as condensed narratives of origins rather than mere linguistic labels, the point of which would be more difficult to explain. It seems impossible, however, to judge their antiquity in relation to the type of medium-deictic inscription using the first-person pronoun. The interest in the origins of the materials they mark may be related to similar, if more discursive, accounts of the origins of various artifacts which are found among the Old English *Riddles* of the Exeter Book. The relevant parallels will be considered in detail in Chapter 5 below.

Related to this second type of inscription is a third, exemplified by the lost and undated Essex silver ring (category 10[a] above). If its (roman) inscription: *dolgbot* means, as I have suggested, "wound-cure," the noun either identifies the ring as an amulet, or was intended to confer such properties upon it as will make it one. In either case, there are parallels with certain early continental inscriptions in the older *fuþark*, mentioned earlier: the Øvre Stabu spearhead: *raunijaz*, "tester" or "prober"; the Dahmsdorf spearhead: *ranja*, "assailant" or "the weapon that makes them run"; and the Kovel (Ukraine) spearhead: *tilarids*, "attacker", were all inscribed probably with a view to ingraining in these weapons the qualities the words denote. Such inscriptions seem to me to represent an obviously ancient, now quite unfamiliar use of words. They turn (so to speak) certain concepts or functions embodied in language back on to the physical realities of the world as a way of evoking these functions.

It is important to recognize here that deixis is not an inevitable feature of inscriptions. It would have been possible in theory for an Anglo-Saxon epigraphist to inscribe an Old English lyric poem, for example, on any stone or other suitable object, fixed or moveable, for all to see, without implying any structural connection between the text and the object itself, or its position in space. The fact remains, however, that there is no evidence at all of this kind of unimpeded flow of formally (or actually) oral utterances into the inscribed mode of linguistic presentation. The pragmatics of epigraphic literacy imposes its own requirements and limitations as a matter of course, bringing into being a distinctively literate discourse. Writing becomes the silent speech of objects with their own individual perspectives on the world—a discourse which is, of course, created by human beings, but one in which they may actually participate only as readers of the objects' utterances. If these developments in the childhood of English literacy seem strange to us, it is, no doubt, mainly because we have now developed ways of moving easily, without conscious effort or adaptation, from one mode to the other.

In Anglo-Saxon society, the earliest writings were epigraphical texts. It is not surprising, therefore, to find that the traditions of inscribed writing that were already established when book-literacy arrived receive some reflection in manuscript literature. The following two chapters trace some of the strands in this thread of continuity.

Chapter 4
From Inscription to Manuscript Text

In this chapter I shall trace formal and pragmatic relationships between the text-deictic scribal colophons and medium-deictic inscriptions described respectively in Chapters 2 and 3 and certain Old English manuscript texts: four verse-prefaces, four poems by Cynewulf, and *The Dream of the Rood*.

§1. Artifacts and books

Most of the Anglo-Saxon medium-deictic inscriptions described in Chapter 3 are preserved on artifacts with decorative, practical, or ritual uses: jewellery, sundials, a knife, a sword-guard, leather scabbards, a censer-cover, and a church. The inscriptions themselves are of incidental importance inasmuch as the artifacts would still be decorative or useful without the individualization their inscriptions confer on them. In this they differ fundamentally from books as conveyances for linguistic communication. A blank, unwritten book would be a book only in the most basic, material sense of the word. However much we may be intended to admire a particular volume for the skill with which it was made, or the beauty of its script or illumination, it is obviously the linguistic utterance represented by the text that constitutes the book's real value and distinctiveness.

It would be possible in theory for a handwritten book to devote at least part of its text to a medium-deictic description of its nature and origins as a material object in the manner of the inscribed objects considered in the previous chapter, though I know of no Anglo-Saxon manuscript that gives such an account of itself. The Old English *Riddles* of the Exeter Book, which will be considered as a group in Chapter 5, include some 'book' riddles in which the speaker mimics such an account, though the resemblance is superficial:[1] the speakers in these riddles do not identify themselves with the Exeter Book in particular and are thus not medium-deictic. They are only imaginary personifications of books, as the reader is expected to deduce from their descriptions of themselves.

---

[1] The sequence of stages in the production of books in the period is described in *Riddle* 26, on which see further below.

§2. The speaking text and the speaking work

We saw in Chapter 2 how particular manuscripts are sometimes individualized by scribal colophons using 'text-deixis': *Wulfwi me wrat*, "Wulfwi wrote me," marks the particular copy of the Old English Gospels known to us as MS. BL, Cotton Otho C.i., vol. I. Today, a printed volume is normally just one of a series of identical copies produced in a print-run. Individualization of a modern printed book is, of course, possible, if (for example) the author inscribes the fly-leaf or inside cover with his or her signature under a message or dedication addressed to a named recipient; but the printer or publisher, whose role in the modern book's production corresponds to some extent with that of the scribe of a medieval handwritten manuscript, would scarcely think of drawing attention to his role in the same way. The publisher claims responsibility for the whole print-run, not for individual copies. The individualization of the handwritten manuscript that scribal first-person colophons achieve belongs, historically and logically, to the period of early literacy in England, when every book was unique.[2] By identifying the role of individual scribes in the production of texts, however, these colophons provoke (for the modern reader) questions about the status of authors in relation to Anglo-Saxon manuscripts — an issue that was raised briefly above in Chapter 2. Was the role of author regarded as secondary to that of the scribe, or even subsumed by it? The various texts examined in the present chapter will provide some evidence relevant to this question.

From a formal and pragmatic point of view, the closest relatives elsewhere among Old English writings of scribal colophons of the "Wulfwi wrote me" type are four verse-prefaces that individualize books in a very similar way, though they exemplify, as we shall see below, more complex types of deictic reference stemming from the recognition that several individuals — decorators, scribes, and authors — contribute to the production of individual manuscripts. These four poems are *Thureth*, *The Metrical Preface to Wærferth's Translation of Gregory's Dialogues*, *The Metrical Preface to the Pastoral Care*, and the fragmentary *Aldhelm*.[3] In

---

[2] On the contrast between the uniqueness of the medieval handwritten book and the modern printed book, see Ong, "Orality, Literacy, and Medieval Textualization," 1–3. Ong writes: "In medieval manuscript culture, books were subtly assimilated more to oral utterance and less to the world of physical objects than they are in a high-technology print culture" (3). However, the uniqueness of medieval manuscripts, and the lavish decoration that was often bestowed upon them, meant that in many ways they had more of the artifact about them than the modern printed book, which is always identical with others in the same print-run.

[3] For a discussion of the context in which the first three of these poems are preserved, see Peter Orton, "Deixis and the Untransferable Text: Anglo-Saxon Colophons, Verse-Prefaces and Inscriptions," in *Imagining the Book*, ed. Stephen Kelly and John J. Thompson (Turnhout: Brepols, 2005), 195–207.

all four, we encounter first-person 'speakers' who are clearly to be identified with the books that the prefaces introduce, though there are differences of emphasis. *Thureth* exemplifies the genre in its most straightforward form:[4]

    Ic eom halgungboc;[5]   healde hine dryhten
    þe me fægere þus   frætewum belegde.
    Þureð[6] to þance[7]   þus het me wyrcean,
    to loue and to wurðe,   þam þe leoht gesceop.
5   Gemyndi is he   mihta gehwylcre
    þæs þe he on foldan   gefremian mæg,
    and him geþancie   þeoda waldend
    þæs þe he on gemynde   madma manega[8]
    wyle gemearcian   metode to lace;
10   and he sceal æce lean   ealle findan
    þæs þe he on foldan   fremaþ[9] to ryhte.

---

[4] *Thureth* survives on fol. 31ʳᵛ of BL, MS. Cotton Claudius A.iii, fols. 31–86 and 106–150, written at the end of the 10th or the beginning of the 11th c. On the manuscript, see Ker, *Catalogue of Manuscripts Containing Anglo-Saxon*, No. 141. Opinion is divided between Worcester and York as the centre in which it was written; see Craig Ronalds and Margaret Clunies Ross, "*Thureth*: A Neglected Old English Poem and its History in Anglo-Saxon Scholarship," *Notes and Queries* 246, N.S. 48 (2001): 359–70 (at 359, n. 4). The text of the poem printed here is from Dobbie, *The Anglo-Saxon Minor Poems*, 97. A more recent edition and translation of the poem appears in Ronalds and Ross, "*Thureth*," 360–61.

[5] For a discussion of the sense of the unique compound *halgungboc*, see Ronalds and Ross, "Thureth," 367–68.

[6] Þureð, who commissioned the binding of the book, has a Scandinavian name; see F. Holthausen, "Kleinere altenglische Dichtungen," *Anglia* 41 (1917): 400–4 (at 404), who compares the Old Norse names *Þórðr*, *Þorvarðr*. Ker thinks that this Þureð may be identifiable with an earl of that name with property in Yorkshire who signed charters of King Æðelred in the latter half of the tenth century (Ker, *Catalogue*, 178). See further below on the potential importance of this identification.

[7] 3 *to þance* probably means "thankfully" or "gratefully" here; cf. *Guthlac* 96.

[8] 8 *manega* is presumably acc. pl. masc., agreeing in number with gen. pl. *madma*. The *-a* inflexion of *manega* in place of the expected *-e* might be put down to the general levelling of unstressed vowels which occurred in late (11th c.) Old English; see Campbell, *Old English Grammar*, §379. The plural of *manig* with gen. pl. of the qualified noun, as here, is normal; cf. *Beowulf* 728 *rinca manige*. Cf. Ronalds and Ross, "*Thureth*," 360–61, who take *manega* as genitive plural in agreement with *madma* and translate 8–9 as "because, mindful of many treasures, he wishes to designate (me) as an offering to the Lord." It seems to me that there are two disadvantages in this arrangement: one is that (as Ronalds and Ross recognize) it creates a need to invent an object ('me') for *gemearcian*; and the other is that the significance of "mindful of many treasures" as applied to Þureð is not very clear.

[9] 11 *fremaþ* is probably a late form of *fremeþ* (from *fremman*; see note to 8 *manega* above), rather than a part of the verb *fremian*, whose meaning: "be good", "avail", does not suit the context here.

"I am a consecration book. May the Lord preserve him who thus beautifully covered me with ornaments. Þureð thus gratefully ordered me to be made in praise and honour of him who created light. He [presumably Þureð] is mindful of every mighty work, of what he [God] may accomplish on earth; and may the Ruler of nations reward him, for he intends to designate (*or* inscribe) many treasures as a gift to the Ordainer; and he must surely obtain an eternal reward for all the good works he performs on earth."

The "consecration book" with which the speaker identifies in line 1 follows the poem in the manuscript.[10] No doubt the poet of the text was Þureð himself,[11] though the extent of his contribution to the production of the manuscript is not as clear as one might wish. The speaker begins by invoking God's protection for "him who" (1–2 *hine . . .þe*) adorned the volume (*me fægere þus frætewum belegde*); then immediately we learn that Þureð "ordered" the speaker "to be made" (3 *Þureð to þance þus het me wyrcean*). Is the decorative art of an anonymous craftsman being commemorated here, in addition to the initiative of Þureð in getting the book produced? Perhaps; but there can be no doubt that the speaker is a particular manuscript; and if Ker is right in identifying the Þureð of the poem with a Yorkshire earl alive in the second half of the 10th c.,[12] it may even be that the speaker is meant to be this particular manuscript, BL, Cotton Claudius A.iii,[13] which preserves the poem, for it is dated by Ker to the end of the tenth century or the early eleventh, when this Þureð was active.[14] The speaker presents itself as a composite of text and manuscript, though it distinguishes its own essential nature as a text—specifically a consecration book, a representative of a certain literary genre—and the decoration so generously lavished upon it, rather as a warrior might show pride in the gifts bestowed on him by a generous lord. The deixis here is thus basically textual, even though the speaker acknowledges (by implication) the degree to which it has also been transformed into a 'treasure'; we learn in line 8 that Þureð means to dedicate *madma manega*, "many treasures," to God. *Thureth* seems to imply the view that the essential nature of a book lies in its literary contents, and that such decorative qualities as it possesses are extras—value added to the linguistic communication at the heart of the book's being.

---

[10] See Ker, *Catalogue*, 177–78; Ronalds and Ross, "*Thureth*," 367–68. There is some uncertainty about the extent of the *halgungboc*. First (fols. 32–38) comes a legal text, the canons of the Council of Eanham, with one version in Latin (fols. 32–35) and a second in Old English (fols. 35–38), though presumably this text fell under the rubric of *halgungboc* so far as the poet was concerned.

[11] Cf. Bragg, *The Lyric Speakers of Old English Poetry*, 45, who thinks that the scribe of the *halgungboc*, rather than Thureth himself, was the author of the poem, "since Thureth was not a cleric."

[12] See above, n. 6.

[13] See above, n. 4.

[14] See above, n. 4.

Ker calls *Thureth* an "inscription"—appropriately, because the Anglo-Saxon inscriptions considered in the previous chapter afford a number of parallels with it. The most obvious, as we have seen, is the basic formal device of the inanimate first-person speaker. Another is suggested in particular by the Lincoln I slab inscription: *Eirtig me let wircean and fios godian criste to lofe and sanctæ marie*, "Eirtig had me made and endowed with possessions to the glory of Christ and St. Mary," which draws an analogous distinction between the essential nature of the speaker (a literary text in the case of *Thureth*, a church in the case of the Lincoln I inscription) and its enrichment, either through decorative art in the case of *Thureth*, or in the case of the Lincoln church through the gift of "possessions" which glorify it. A third parallel is stylistic: line 3 of the poem, *Þureð to þance þus het me wyrcean*, "Þureð thus gratefully ordered me to be made," is reminiscent of the Alfred Jewel inscription *Ælfred mec heht gevvyrcan*, "Alfred ordered me to be made."[15] In view of the formal and pragmatic similarities between the poem and such epigraphic texts, it seems likely enough that these parallels result from the actual influence of epigraphical style and substance on the *Þureð* poet.[16]

The Metrical Preface to Wærferth's Translation of Gregory's Dialogues (hereafter *MPD*) requires more extensive discussion, partly because the text has clearly undergone modification in the course of its transmission:[17]

---

[15] As noted by Ronalds and Ross, "*Thureth*," 368, n. 46.

[16] Another possible connection with inscriptions lies in the *Thureth* poet's use of the verb *gemearcian* (9), which might mean either "designate" or "inscribe" here. For the latter meaning, see *Beowulf* 1695 *þurh runstafas rihte gemearcod*, "correctly marked in runes," referring to an inscription on a sword-guard; and T. Northcote Toller, *An Anglo-Saxon Dictionary Supplement* (Oxford: Oxford University Press, 1921), s.v. *gemearcian*, VII, "to indicate in writing, note, record."

[17] The text of the poem occurs only in MS. BL, Cotton Otho C.i, vol.2, fol. 1^r, numbered 182 by Ker, and dated to the beginning of the 11th c. The text of the Old English *Dialogues* which follows the poem in the manuscript is the work of two hands, the first the same hand that wrote the *Metrical Preface* (early 11th c.), the second, of the mid-11th c., beginning on fol. 62 (the start of Book 3 of the *Dialogues*). Ker judges the first hand "about 40 years older" than the second. The manuscript was almost certainly written at Worcester. It is not in good condition, having been damaged in the Cottonian fire in 1731. Letters once legible have crumbled away from the edge of folio 1. My text of the *Metrical Preface* is from David Yerkes, "The Full Text of the Metrical Preface to Wærferth's Translation of Gregory," *Speculum* 55 (1980): 505–13. Italicized letters are editorial. In identifying missing or illegible letters, I have relied on Yerkes's detailed examination of the manuscript.

Se ðe me rædan ðencð   teonð¹⁸ mid rihtum geðance.
He in me findan mæg,¹⁹   gif hine feola lysteð
gastlices lifes   godre biesene,
þæt he ful eaþe mæg   upp gestigan
5   to ðam heofonlican hame,   þar byð a hyht ond wyn,
blis on burgum,   þam þe bearn godes
sielfes hiora eagum   geseon motan.
Þæt mæg se mon begytan,   se þe his modgeðanc
æltowe byþ,   ond þonne þurh his ingehygd
10   to þissa haligra   helpe geliefeð,
ond hiora bisene fulgað,   swa þeos boc sagað.
Me awritan het   Wulfs*ige*²⁰ bisceop,
þeow ond þearfa   þæs þ*e* alne þrym a*h*of,²¹
ond eac walden is   wiht*a*²² gehwelcre,
15   an ece god   eallra gesc*ea*fta.²³
Bideþ þe²⁴ se bisceop,   se þe ðas boc begeat²⁵

---

[18] 1 *teonð* presents difficulties. Keynes and Lapidge (*Alfred the Great*, 333, note) complain, justifiably, that Yerkes's translation of line 1 ("He who thinks to read me troubles himself with a good intention") "makes little sense." They suggest that *teonð* (from the verb *tynan*) be understood in the sense of 'to close', with reference to "the reward the reader will have gained by the time he has read through the book and finally closed it," and I adopt their translation.

[19] The first one and a half lines of the poem are in capitals in the MS. Dobbie (*The Anglo-Saxon Minor Poems*, 202) thought that the first half-line of the poem was missing, and printed simply *[.]e ðe me rædan ðance* for line 1; but Yerkes's fresh examination of the manuscript (see n. 17 above) revealed line 1 as given here. The final letter of 2 *mæg* is illegible in the manuscript.

[20] The manuscript reads *wulfstan*, but the last three letters are on an erasure and original *-ige* may be deduced if not read; see Kenneth Sisam, *Studies in the History of Old English Literature* (Oxford: Clarendon Press, 1953; repr., with corrections, 1962), 200–3, 225–27. Ker, *Catalogue*, 236, thinks the emendation was made "to make it appear as though the manuscript had been written for Bishop Wulfstan I of Worcester," the dates of whose bishopric are 1002–1023. Wulfsige was bishop of Sherborne in the time of Alfred. Keynes and Lapidge (*Alfred the Great*, 187) calculate that Wulfsige's episcopacy lay within the period 879–900. See further below on this modification of the text.

[21] 13 *ahof*, MS *aof* with no space between *a* and *o* (cf. *hiorð-* for *iorð-* in 27).

[22] 14 *wihta*, MS *wiht*.

[23] 15 *gesceafta*: letters are lost after *c* at the end of the written line in the MS.

[24] 16a *þe* is followed in the manuscript by an erasure of about two letters, the second of which Yerkes suspects was *e*.

[25] Keynes and Lapidge (*Alfred the Great*, 334, note) derive their translation of 16b, "had this copy made" from Sisam (*Studies*, 225); but although this translation clarifies the process the poem describes, *þas boc* really means "this book"; so to translate as "this copy" undermines the manuscript's claim to individuality and independent status as an artifact.

4. From Inscription to Manuscript Text

   þe þu on þinum handu*m*[26] nu hafast ond sceawast,
   þæt þu him to þeossum halgum helpe bidde,
   þe heo*ra* gemynd her on gemearcude siendon,
20 ond þæt him god ællmihtig
   forgyu*e*[27] þa gyltas þe he ge*o*[28] worhte,
   ond eac resðe mid him, se ðe ah ealles rices gewe*ald*,[29]
   ond eac swa his beahgifan, þe him ðas bysene forgeaf,
   þæt is se selesða sinces brytta,
25 Ælfryd mid Englum, ealra cyninga
   þara þe he sið oððe ær fore secgan hyrde,
   oððe he iorðcyninga[30] ær ænigne gefrugne.

"He who sets out to read me through will close me with appropriate recompense. If he wants many good examples of the spiritual life, he may find them in me in order that he may very easily ascend to the heavenly home where there is ever joy and rapture—bliss in those dwellings for those who may see the Son of God Himself with their own eyes. That may the man perceive whose mind is sound and then through his understanding trusts in the help of these saints and carries out their example—as this book explains. Bishop Wulfsige commanded me to be written, the poor servant of Him who created all majesty and is also the Ruler of each of His creatures—one eternal God of all creation. The bishop who had this copy made (which you are now holding in your hands and looking at) begs that you beseech help for him from those saints whose memories are here recorded, and that God Almighty, who wields power over every kingdom, forgive him the sins which he formerly committed, and also that he may come to rest with Him and likewise with his ring-giver who gave him the exemplar: Alfred of the English, the greatest treasure-giver of all the kings he has ever heard tell of, in recent times or long ago, or of any earthly king he had previously learned of."[31]

Sisam argued convincingly that the poet of *MPD* was Wulfsige, bishop of Sherborne at the end of the ninth century, in the time of King Alfred of Wessex.[32] The manuscript, which dates from the early eleventh century, reads *wulfstan* in 12; but *-tan* stands on an erasure and Sisam established a strong likelihood that

---

 [26] 17 *handum*: Yerkes sees only two minims, presumably of *m*, at the end of the manuscript line. Dobbie (*Minor Poems*, 112) reads *handum* without comment.
 [27] 21 *forgyue*: final *e* illegible.
 [28] 21 *geo worhte*, MS *geworhte*.
 [29] 22 *geweald*: Yerkes suspects *a* after the second *e*, but cannot read *l* or *d*.
 [30] 27 *iorðcyninga*, MS *hiorð cyninga*.
 [31] Translation from Keynes and Lapidge, *Alfred the Great*, 187–88. The earlier translation by A. S. Cook, "An Unsuspected Bit of Old English Verse," *MLN* 17 (1902): 7–10 (at 8), is less reliable.
 [32] Sisam, *Studies*, 225–31. Sisam's discussion of the text and its significance (200–3, 225–31) is the foundation of all subsequent commentary on the poem.

the original reading was *wulfsige*.[33] The implications of this scribal amendment require discussion; but as it was made some time after the poem had been copied (see below), it seems best to consider first the text as it stood before it was interfered with in this way.

If we take *wulfsige* as the reading in 12, the line (12 *Me awritan het Wulfsige bisceop*) tells us that Wulfsige ordered the present manuscript to be written; a later passage (16–17 . . . *ðas boc . . . þe þu on þinum handum nu hafast ond sceawast*) emphasises that the manuscript in which we are reading the poem is one and the same as this copy commissioned by Wulfsige; and ll. 23–25 of the poem record King Alfred's gift to Wulfsige of a copy of Wærferth's Old English translation of Gregory's *Dialogues* which was used as the exemplar of the present manuscript (23–25 . . . *his beahgifan, þe him ðas bysene forgeaf . . . Ælfryd mid Englum* . . ., "... his ring-giver who gave him the exemplar: Alfred of the English . . ."). It is therefore clear that the 'speaker' of the poem must be the copy of Wærferth's translation that Wulfsige had made; that this was a copy of the manuscript of that translation that Alfred gave to Wulfsige; and that *MPD* was composed (quite possibly by Wulfsige himself) to introduce this new copy.

But in spite of the poem's claim that this new copy is the one the reader holds in his hands (16–17), the date (early eleventh century) and Worcester provenance of MS. BL, Cotton Otho C.i, vol.2, which alone preserves the text of the *MPD*, are enough to establish that this is not the actual manuscript produced at Sherborne on Wulfsige's instructions; it must be a descendant of it. The text of the poem as we have it is thus at at least one remove from the poet's own version;[34] and the statement in line 16–17 to the effect that the Otho manuscript is itself the copy that Wulfsige had made is obviously false. That statement was true only of the manuscript prepared by Wulfsige's command, from which Otho descends. Because the poem refers deictically to the manuscript written by Wulfsige's orders (the reference to the Alfredian exemplar is the crucial element in confining the deictic reference to the manuscript that was copied directly from this exemplar), the poetic text is (like the inscriptions on individual artifacts discussed in the previous chapter) technically non-transferable; it cannot preface a later copy of the translation—even one made by another bishop—and be true of that copy as well. Even so, it *has* been transferred, with the inevitable consequence that it misrepresents the true history and status of the Otho manuscript to which it is now attached.

---

[33] See n. 20 above.

[34] Cf. Keynes and Lapidge, *Alfred the Great*, 333, note, who refer, rather misleadingly, to the MS (Cotton Otho C.i, vol. 2) as "a later copy of an exemplar which Alfred had originally sent to Wulfsige, bishop of Sherborne": our manuscript preserves, not a direct copy of the Alfredian manuscript Wulfsige received, but a copy of Wulfsige's copy of it; otherwise the inclusion of Wulfsige's preface would be hard to explain.

4. From Inscription to Manuscript Text

These observations are based on the text of the poem as it originally stood in the Otho MS, before line 12 was emended. Next we must explore the significance of the emendation of *wulfsige* to *wulfstan*. Sisam and Ker agreed in thinking that the alteration was made in the second half of the eleventh century,[35] after completion of the copying of both *MPD* and the Old English *Dialogues* text it introduces.[36] The substitution of Wulfstan's name for Wulfsige's was not necessarily made with the deliberate intention of deceiving readers; on the contrary, it may have been done partly to remove the misrepresentation that the text clearly embodied, as we have seen, after it had been reproduced in the Otho manuscript. As Sisam remarks, the emender may have believed, or even known for a fact, that Otho (written, we should remember, in the early to mid-eleventh century) was copied at Worcester on the instructions of Wulfstan I sometime before his death in 1023.[37] The way Wulfsige expresses himself in the sentence beginning in line 16 ("The bishop who had this copy made," with no mention of his own name) might have appeared to provide an opportunity for a later bishop to be commemorated for commissioning a new (post-Wulfsige) copy of the translation (i.e. Otho) with the minimal adaptation of the poem's text represented by changing 12 *wulfsige* to *wulfstan*; but an obvious misrepresentation still remained: the bishop in question is said to have received his exemplar-text directly from King Alfred. Wulfstan I could scarcely claim to have received a gift from a king who had died over a hundred years before.

MPD is thus doubly misleading. In its unaltered state in the eleventh-century Otho manuscript, it claimed to introduce the actual copy of Wærferth's *Dialogues* translation commissioned by Wulfsige, though Wulfsige had been dead probably for a hundred years or so when Otho was written. This discrepancy was simply a consequence of the text of *MPD* being copied unchanged from manuscript to manuscript. The emendation of *wulfsige* to *wulfstan* is best explained as an attempt to update the text of the poem to make it true of a manuscript of the Old English *Dialogues* written at the instigation of Wulfstan I of Worcester;[38] but the reference to the gift of the exemplar by King Alfred himself remained unmodified, with the result that the poem cannot be true of the Otho manuscript either. These aspects of the text's history are both excellent illustrations of how text-deixis renders literary works uncopiable; or rather, that if they are copied unchanged, they cease to be true of the manuscripts in which they are reproduced.

---

[35] Ker, *Catalogue*, 236; Sisam, *Studies*, 202, n. 1. Sisam suspected that the alteration was made "during the bishopric of Wulfstan II" (bishop of Worcester from 1062 to 1095) because "the prayer would be more appropriate in his lifetime."

[36] The third and fourth books of the *Dialogues* are written by a hand Ker dates to the mid-11th c.; see n. 17 above.

[37] Sisam, *Studies*, 226.

[38] Cf. Dobbie, *Minor Poems*, cxvii, who seems to miss the point of Sisam's argument.

Keynes and Lapidge's translation of the poem, which I have used here, renders *MPD* 23 *ðas bysene* as "the exemplar," in spite of the fact that *ðas* would normally mean 'this' in Old English. Here they follow Sisam, who translated the phrase as "the pattern copy,"[39] because he could not square 'this' with the supposed circumstances of the poem's composition. Sisam's objection seems to be founded on the idea that Wulfsige would have realized that "this exemplar" would puzzle future readers because they would not have the Alfredian exemplar before them when they read the copy Wulfsige had made. But 'this' would make good sense to Wulfsige himself if he had the exemplar at his elbow when he composed *MPD*, as he might well have done. So *ðas*, 'this', is defensible in this period as a deictic reference to Wulfsige's Alfredian exemplar for his text of the *Dialogues*. Modern writers automatically avoid deictic reference to non-transferable features of the writing environment; we make allowances for the inevitable differences between future readers' circumstances and our own. Anglo-Saxon authors might well have been less alert to the potential for confusion when deictic terms are employed unguardedly in writing; but in any case, "this exemplar" is perfectly intelligible in the context; we are given enough information in the poem to enable us to project ourselves into Wulfsige's circumstances as he wrote, probably with Alfred's exemplar-text in front of him. In Chapter 2 we found that deictic references used by early English writers characteristically reflect a receiving-time-based analysis of linguistic communication. Wulfsige's *ðas bysene* reflects his coding-time-based analysis of the utterance that constitutes *MPD*. Perhaps Wulfsige still had some way to go in ridding himself of the unthinking habits of deictic reference inculcated by preliterate linguistic communication; but nevertheless, a reference to "this exemplar" causes the reader no real difficulty: it cannot refer to the copy Wulfsige had made; it must refer to its exemplar.

Finally, we may note that 12 *Me awritan het Wulfsige bisceop*, "Bishop Wulfsige commanded me to be written," provides another stylistic echo (not quite so close, admittedly, as *Þureth* 3 *Þureð to pance pus het me wyrcean*) of the Alfred Jewel inscription: *Ælfred mec heht gevvyrcan*, "Alfred ordered me to be made." Three passages all of which include the first-person pronoun used impersonally in the accusative, *het* (*heht* in the Alfred Jewel inscription) the past tense of the *hatan*, 'to command, order', and the proper name of the human commissioner, have a good deal in common. Again, it seems likely that all three instances represent a loose formula that originated in epigraphic texts.

The Metrical Preface to the Pastoral Care (hereafter *PCP*), attached to King Alfred's Old English translation of Pope Gregory's *Cura Pastoralis*, survives in

---

[39] Sisam, *Studies*, 225: "Here *ðas bysene* is translated 'the pattern copy' as if it were *ða bysene*. Unless a vague use is allowed, the rendering 'this' troubles all the interpretations to be discussed." Keynes and Lapidge defend their decision (*Alfred the Great*, 334).

four extant copies of the Alfredian translation.[40] The text given here is based on the Hatton manuscript:

  Þis ærendgewrit Agustinus
  ofer sealtne sæ suðan brohte
  iegbuendum,[41] swa hit ær fore
  adihtode dryhtnes cempa,
5 Rome papa. Ryhtspell monig
  Gregorius gleawmod gindwod
  ðurh sefan snyttro, searoðonca hord.
  Forðæm[42] he monncynnes mæst gestriende
  rodra wearde, Romwara betest,
10 monna modwelegost, mærðum gefrægost.
  Siððan min[43] on englisc Ælfred kyning
  awende worda gehwelc, and me his writerum
  sende suð and norð, heht him swelcra ma
  brengan bi ðære bisene, ðæt he his biscepum
15 sendan meahte, forðæm hi his sume ðorfton,
  ða ðe lædenspræce læste cuðon.

"Augustine brought this written message from the south over the salt sea to the islanders, as the Lord's champion, the Pope of Rome, had composed it beforehand. The wise Gregorius was steeped in many true doctrines through wisdom of mind, a hoard of skills; therefore he, best of Romans, most talented of men, most celebrated in glories, won over most of mankind to the guardian of heaven. Afterwards King Alfred translated every word of me into English, and sent me to his scribes south and north; ordered more such

---

[40] These are MSS. Oxford, Bodleian Library, Hatton 20 (known as H; Ker, *Catalogue*, no. 324), fol. 2ᵛ/10 - 19, written between 890 and 897; Cambridge, Corpus Christi College, 12 (D; Ker, no. 30), fols. 3ᵛ/11 - 4ʳ/1, written in the latter half of the 10th c.; Cambridge, Trinity College R.5.22 (T; Ker, no. 87), fol. 72ʳ/1–9, late 10th or early 11th c.; and Cambridge University Library Ii.2.4. (U; Ker, no. 19), fols. 6ᵛ-7ʳ, from the third quarter of the 11th c. The text printed below, based on H, is from Dobbie, *Minor Poems*, 110. The few substantial variants from the other three texts are described in my notes to the text.

[41] 3 *iegbuendum*, T *eorðbugendum;* the *iegbuendum* ("island-dwellers") of H and D are the English, to whom Augustine brought Gregory's message across the sea. T's *eorðbugendum*, "earth-dwellers" (presumably in the sense of 'mankind'), is too broad a term, for obvious reasons.

[42] 8 *Forðæm*, T *forþæm þe*: T's "because" (H, D have "therefore") gives poor sense: Gregory's wisdom and studies were the basis of his effectiveness as a winner of converts, not the result of it.

[43] 11 *min*, T *me*: here T's scribe (or a predecessor), presumably impatient for a direct object for 12 *awende* (actually *worda gehwilc*, "each word"), has produced one by replacing *min* ("of me") with accusative *me*.

agreeing with the exemplar to be produced for him which he might send to his bishops, for some of them who knew least Latin needed it."

In the first part of *PCP* (1–10), there is nothing to indicate who or what is 'speaking'—no sense, indeed, of any particular narrator: Gregory's work is just "this written message," where "this" suggests a perspective on the prefaced text which is very close to that of the reader himself. But when the first-person pronoun is used in 11 and 12, and we learn of the translation of Gregory's book from Latin into English and of its subsequent duplication, it becomes clear that the speaker is Gregory's book in an essential, irreducible form, independent of any particular language into which it might be translated or any particular manuscript into which it might be copied. It may be that only a single volume was circulated amongst Alfred's "scribes south and north" (12–13 *his writerum . . . suð and norð*); but certainly several more copies resulted from the exercise. Benson is, I believe, mistaken in thinking that the two first-person pronouns in the poem refer to the poem itself.[44] It seems likelier that 1 *ærendgewrit*, "message", undoubtedly a reference to the *Cura Pastoralis*, is their antecedent. In the last four lines of the poem, which deal with the rather complicated business of distributing and reproducing copies of Gregory's work, the personification is no longer in evidence. The speaker does not identify itself with the Alfredian master-exemplar (14 *ðære bisene*); but this is consistent with the text's self-identification as a work transcending any one version of itself, a 'strong' text which neither translation nor copying can transform or weaken.

The survival of this poem in no fewer than four manuscripts of the period is a function of its transferability, in which it contrasts with both *Thureth* and *MPD*. Because it uses what we might call 'work-deixis' instead of text- or manuscript-deixis, this poem could preface any text of the Alfredian translation of the *Cura Pastoralis*, however far removed from the original: the speaker here is not an individual manuscript but the abstract text or work. Because of this special feature of the poem, the personification can go deeper to include a memory of the 'youth' of the work as a Latin text prior to Alfred's translation of it into English, and an account of its travels.

Finally we may look briefly at the fragmentary and obscure poem *Aldhelm*, which is mostly in Old English but incorporates Latin and Greek words:[45]

---

[44] Benson, "The Literary Character of Anglo-Saxon Formulaic Poetry," 335.

[45] On Aldhelm, who was born c. 640, see Michael Lapidge, "The Anglo-Latin Background," in *A New Critical History of Old English Literature with a Survey of the Anglo-Latin Background by Michael Lapidge*, ed. Stanley B. Greenfield and Daniel G. Calder (New York: New York University Press, 1986), 9–13; idem, "The Career of Aldhelm," *ASE* 36 (2007): 15–69. The poem *Aldhelm* is preserved only in MS. Cambridge, Corpus Christi College 326 (Ker, *Catalogue*, no. 61), written in the second half of the 10th c. at Christ Church, Canterbury. The text given here is Dobbie's (*Minor Poems*, 97–98).

    Þus me gesette   sanctus et iustus
    beorn boca gleaw,   bonus auctor,
    Ealdelm, æþele sceop,   etiam fuit
    ipselos on æðele[46]   Angolsexna,[47]
5   byscop on Bretene.   Biblos ic nu sceal,
    ponus et pondus   pleno cum sensu,
    geonges geanoðe   geomres iamiamque,
    secgan soð, nalles leas,   þæt him symle wæs
    euthenia   oftor on fylste,
10 æne on eðle   ec ðon ðe se[48] is
    yfel on gesæd. Etiam nusquam
    ne sceal[49] ladigan   labor quem tenet
    encratea,   ac he ealneg[50] sceal
    boethia   biddan georne
15 þurh his modes gemind   micro in cosmo,
    þæt him drihten gyfe   dinams[51] on eorðan,
    fortis factor,   þæt he forð simle . . .

A partial translation (up to line 5) of *Aldhelm* is offered by Bernard F. Huppé, *Doctrine and Poetry: Augustine's Influence on Old English Poetry* (Albany: SUNY Press, 1959), 74; for translations of the full poem, see L. G. Whitbread, "The Old English Poem *Aldhelm*," *English Studies* 57 (1976): 193–97; Fred C. Robinson, "'The Rewards of Piety': Two Old English Poems in their Manuscript Context," in *Hermeneutics and Medieval Culture*, ed. Patrick J. Gallagher and Helen Damico (Albany: State University of New York Press, 1989), 193–200 (at 197); and Andy Orchard, *The Poetic Art of Aldhelm*, Cambridge Studies in Anglo-Saxon England 8 (Cambridge: Cambridge University Press, 1994), 282. Arthur S. Napier, *Old English Glosses Chiefly Unpublished* (Oxford: Oxford University Press, 1900), xiv-xv, notes that comparable mixtures of Old English and Latin are found in *A Summons to Prayer* (of which see Dobbie's edition in *The Anglo-Saxon Minor Poems*, 69–70), and in the closing lines of *The Phoenix* (see *The Exeter Book*, ed. G. P. Krapp and E. V. K. Dobbie, The Anglo-Saxon Poetic Records 3 [New York: Columbia University Press, 1936], 112–13).

[46] 4 *æðele*, MS *æðel*. Napier retained the MS form; Holthausen (*Anglia* 41 [1917]: 403) printed *eðle* (dat. sg. of *eþel*, "patria") for the sake of grammar and metre: *on*, 'in', requires a dative noun after it, and type A verses of this kind do not normally end with two unstressed syllables. Dobbie prefers *æðele* because *eþel* is occasionally spelt with *æ* in the first syllable.

[47] 4 *Angolsexna*, MS *angel sexna* with *o* added above the first *e*.

[48] 10 *se*: Napier comments: "One would rather expect *him*—'that to *him* was always euthenia . . ., fame, moreover (*ec ðon*), in the land, to *whom* evil has been attributed (who has been spoken of badly)'." My own rendering implies a comparative clause introduced by *ðon* (which I interpret as an error for *ðonne*, "than") after the comparative *oftor* in 9.

[49] 12 *sceal*, MS *seal*.

[50] 13 *ealneg* with final *g* almost illegible.

[51] 16 *dinams*, Holthausen (*Anglia* 41 [1917]: 403) *dinam[i]s*.

> "Thus the holy and righteous (*sanctus et iustus*) good author (*bonus auctor*) Aldhelm, a man wise in books, a noble poet, composed me—one moreover who was eminent (*etiam fuit ipselos*) in the native land of the Anglo-Saxons, a bishop in Britain. As a book now, (?) a work and a weighty one (*ponus et pondus*), I must tell the truth, not falsehood, with full sense (*pleno cum sensu*), in lamentation of recent sorrow at this very moment (*iamiamque*), that abundance (*euthenia*) was ever in his aid, fame (*æne*) in (his) native land, more often than that evil was attributed to him. Nowhere, moreover, (*etiam nusquam*) must the labour which a man occupies (*labor quem tenet*) excuse him self-control (*encratea*), but he must always zealously pray for support (*boethia*) through the thought of his heart in the little world (*micro in cosmo*) so that the Lord, the powerful maker (*fortis factor*), may give him strength (*dinamis*) on earth, so that he ever after . . ."[52]

This poem, difficult though it is, represents a more straightforward example of work-deixis than *PCP* because Aldhelm's poem *De Virginitate*, which it prefaces, remains in the language of composition so that the text does not have as complicated a life-history as the Old English *Pastoral Care*.

These four texts divide easily into two pairs: *Thureth* and *MPD* are both text-deictic and untransferable, even though the latter was in fact tranferred;[53] *PCP* and *Aldhelm* are both work-deictic and transferable, and the former was indeed often transferred, appearing in four surviving manuscripts of the period.[54] The first pair are formally and pragmatically closely related to the scribal colophons discussed in the previous chapter. Both include prayers for the salvation of the poets who wrote them as a reward, not of course for the poems themselves, but for the piety of the poems' authors in commissioning manuscripts which redound, in different ways, to the glory of God. It is more difficult to generalize about the second pair. *PCP* is much taken up with the literary history of the work it introduces, though it also has something to say both of Gregory's missionary achievements and of Alfred's reasons for Englishing the work. *Aldhelm* includes an account of the poet himself as a man of distinction and piety, but this merges with more general remarks on the place of humility and prayer in our daily lives. Although *Aldhelm* refers to Aldhelm as a "good author" and a "noble poet," neither poem shows any particular concern with the literary qualities of the works they introduce, though both poems are significant in showing an interest in the

---

[52] The syntax of all but the first five lines of this poem is very obscure, and it is with considerable diffidence that I offer my translation. The text ends abruptly and Aldhelm's *De Virginitate* follows immediately.

[53] Cf. Ronalds and Ross, who identify *Thureth* as "the only specifically identifiable book . . . that 'speaks' to us from the Anglo-Saxon period" ("*Thureth*," 368), and exclude *MPD* from the same category on the grounds that "it is the *text* which speaks to us, not the specific book, as is the case with *Thureth*" (369, n. 49).

[54] Bragg (*Lyric Speakers*, 46) divides the four poems in this way.

authored work. *Thureth* and *MPD* direct the reader's attention to the copied manuscript, an artifact regarded as a splendid achievement in its own right; but *PCP* and *Aldhelm* treat the literary work as a reproducible object of real value even in abstract form.[55] It is not, of course, possible to place the two types of text in a chronological relationship to each other; we cannot say which type came first. The latter two poems do, nonetheless, reflect the more modern conception of the text as an abstraction, capable of realization in various manuscripts. There is still no cult of the author as exercising mysterious proprietary rights over his work;[56] but there is a sense of basic authorship which we have not seen in any other texts discussed so far.

In their commentary on *MPD*, Keynes and Lapidge have this to say about the origins of the first-person pronoun usage it exemplifies:

> The convention adopted here, that of the book speaking in the first person by way of preface to what is to follow, is fairly common in Old English poetry and owes its origin to the tradition of riddles. Other examples are the verse preface which Alfred added to the *Pastoral Care* . . . and the poems called by editors "Thureth" and "Aldhelm". . .

This comment seems to me open to challenge. For one thing, it lumps all four poems together: "the book speaking" is too all-embracing an expression to use in this context in view of the distinctions between these poems in the type of deixis they exemplify. The link with riddles also seems questionable. The difference between these poems and riddles is one of pragmatics: riddles impose on the audience or reader the task of identifying a concept of something in the world; and they all involve, to a greater or lesser degree, an element of disguise. In the four poems just discussed there can be no disguise because what corresponds to the riddle's 'solution' is present to the reader; there is no puzzle to solve. We have also seen how the first pair of poems show stylistic parallels, not with the riddles but with certain medium-deictic inscriptions examined in the previous chapter; and formally the same pair are closely allied to the scribal colophons also discussed earlier (Chapter 2). Riddles, whether in Old English or Latin, have, I suggest, nothing particular in common with either pair of poems except, of course, the impersonal usage of first-person pronouns—not enough, perhaps, to establish that this formal feature of these four poems was riddle-inspired.

---

[55] According to one definition, writings must be reproducible to count as literature; see Ruth Finnegan, "The How of Literature," *Oral Tradition* 20 (2005): 164–87 (at 165).

[56] Compare Amodio, *Writing the Oral Tradition*, 14, who identifies "the proprietary impulse" of literate poets as conspicuously lacking in oral or oral-derived poetry.

§3. The name of the poet

A major part of the function of *PCP* and *Aldhelm* is to identify the authors of the works they introduce; but whereas Aldhelm himself might have been the poet of *Aldhelm*, Gregory the Great was certainly not the author of *PCP*. *Thureth* and *MPD* each name individuals, Þureð and Wulfsige respectively, who are probably to be taken as the authors of the poems themselves, though their primary purpose is clearly to identify persons responsible for the production of specific manuscripts of the works they introduce. The naming of their authors is not the primary purpose of these poems.

Although the explicit naming of the authors of Anglo-Latin and Old English prose works is not unusual, most of the Old English poems which have come down to us in contemporary manuscripts are anonymous. This might seem an odd circumstance from one point of view, for Old English poems contain fairly frequent references to individual poets and verse-composition, some of which indicate that it was possible for Germanic and Anglo-Saxon oral poets to achieve, if not widespread renown, at least an acknowledged position on a scale of artistry. The best evidence for this comes from *Deor*, a poem in the Exeter Book, in which an oral poet (or *scop*) so named describes how he was supplanted in his lord's favour by a rival named Heorrenda, "a man skilled in song" (40 *leoðcræftig monn*). It is a common assumption among modern scholars that both these named poets are "fictitious,"[57] though I shall question the appropriateness of this epithet for these figures in a later chapter.[58] Although Deor is unknown outside this poem, it has been suggested that Heorrenda, named by Deor as his rival as a poet, is to be identified with the Horant of German tradition, a poet of legendary skill.[59] In *Widsith*, another Exeter Book poem, a scop of that name ("far-journey[er]") boasts of the many tribes he has visited and the famous rulers in whose courts he has found welcome and reward. Widsið's travels extend all over the Germanic world and beyond into the Middle East—a fantastic geographical and chronological range which identifies him as not so much a fictitious as a generic poet, a kind of super-scop whose experience encompasses the whole of the heroic age and more.[60] No doubt Widsið is a highly symbolic figure, an embodiment of the

---

[57] See Kemp Malone, ed., *Deor*, rev. ed. (Exeter: University of Exeter, 1977), 16, where the speaker of the poem is identified with the poet ("In this section the poet speaks in the first person . . ."), although Malone adds that "This tale of the poet's own trouble is to be regarded as fictitious."

[58] See below, Chapter 6.

[59] See Malone, ed., *Deor*, 40, on the Heodeningas and Heorrenda; and more recently, Joyce Hill, ed., *Old English Minor Heroic Poems* (Durham: Durham Medieval Texts, 1983), 17 and 89, s.v. *Heorrenda*.

[60] See Kemp Malone, ed., *Widsith* (London: Methuen, 1936), 1, 3, who calls Widsið a "fictitious scop," and later (11) an "ideal figure." That Widsith is not a scop but a seer or

idea that the individual scop, standing as he does at the apex of an ancient Germanic poetic tradition, is heir to the collective knowledge of story and skills in composition, not just of all the poets he had ever heard himself, but also of poets of earlier generations from whom they had learnt in their turn. Indeed, Widsið may even be an instance of the kind of legendary poet that Foley finds recognized in South Slavic oral poetic tradition: an "ancestral master bard," a uniquely gifted practitioner from whom living poets trace their "personal bardic lineages," and who constitutes "an anthropomorphization of what we name by the abstraction 'tradition'."[61] The poem *Beowulf*, although it does not record the names of any poets, mentions individual scops as men with special skills and access to an ancient store of historical lore and stories.[62] One of these passages, describing the original poeticization by a Danish *scop* of Beowulf's fight against Grendel—a version from which, I think we are meant to infer, the first part of the actual Old English poem *Beowulf* ultimately descends—constitutes the fullest contemporary account we have of the actual processes of oral composition of alliterative poetry:

	Hwilum cyninges þegn,	
	guma gilphlæden,	gidda gemyndig,
	se ðe ealfela	ealdgesegena
870	worn gemunde,	word oðer fand
	soðe gebunden;	secg eft ongan
	sið Beowulfes	snyttrum styrian
	ond on sped wrecan	spel gerade,
	wordum wrixlan.	(*Beowulf* 867b-874a)

"At times the king's thane, a warrior laden with poetic eloquence, recalling stories, who recollected old traditions without number, found different words linked properly together; he afterwards proclaimed wisely Beowulf's adventure, and told the story skilfully, varying his words."

---

woðbora is suggested by Ida Masters Hollowell, "Was Widsið a Scop?", *Neophilologus* 64 (1980): 583–91.

[61] See John Miles Foley, *Homer's Traditional Art* (University Park, PA: Pennsylvania State University Press, 1999), 50. See also Mark C. Amodio, "Res(is)ting the Singer: Towards a Non-Performative Anglo-Saxon Oral Poetics," in *New Directions in Oral Theory*, ed. idem, MRTS 287 (Tempe: Arizona Center for Medieval and Renaissance Studies, 2005), 179–208: Amodio surveys the "reports of scopic activity" in the surviving texts of the period and argues that they are all "idealized and fictionalised accounts of how legendary figures composed vernacular poetry" rather than records of "contemporary Anglo-Saxon cultural praxis" (184–85).

[62] See *Beowulf and the Fight at Finnsburg*, ed. Fr. Klaeber, 3rd ed. (Lexington: Heath, 1950), lines 90–98, 867–874.

In this description, *word . . . soðe gebunden* might well be a reference to alliteration, the main structural principle of Old English verse composition, and [*word] oðer fand* refers either to original composition simply or to variation, the most distinctive stylistic device of Old Germanic poetry, whereby poets used two or more expressions to refer (often from different perspectives) to a single referent. The other emphasis in this passage is on the extent of the store of stories held in the poet's memory, and their antiquity. Despite all this, this poet is not given a name; he is only "the king's thane."

We saw earlier how the poem *Aldhelm* calls Aldhelm (born c. 640) a "noble poet" (3 *æþele sceop*). Bede's story of the poet Cædmon in his *Historia Ecclesiastica* gives us the name of another historical oral poet some sixty years after his death.[63] Cædmon was important to Bede chiefly, it seems, for his abilities as a poet and for the divine origin of his poetic gift;[64] but the preservation of his name in Bede's *Historia* looks rather casual, for it is mentioned only once in the Latin, in an address to Cædmon delivered by the mysterious angelic figure who appears to him in his sleep and encourages him to compose the nine-line Old English 'Hymn' for which he was remembered. The name is included in the address chiefly, one suspects, in order to show the speaker's power and foresight: he knows who Cædmon is already and may even have marked him out for the task of introducing Christian subject-matter into English vernacular poetry for the first time.

Evidently, then, it was not the usual practice for Old English poets to record their own names when committing their work to parchment, or for the scribes who handled their work to attach the poets' names to the copies they produced. Oral poets would not, of course, have needed to attach their names to their performances: they would have been in a position to introduce themselves to their audiences. Furthermore, the concept of a fixed text, which is so closely bound up with the modern notion of authorship, may not have become a familiar one until literacy made the preservation of performances possible. The scribes who, when literacy arrived, were in a position to write down poems they heard recited, or to

---

[63] Cædmon flourished at Whitby in Yorkshire, probably during the abbacy of Hilda, 657–680; see *Bede's Ecclesiastical History of the English People*, ed. Bertram Colgrave and R. A. B. Mynors (Oxford: Oxford University Press, 1969), 4.24: 414–21. For a broad account of Cædmon's significance and a survey of recent critical views, see Daniel Paul O'Donnell, "Material Differences: The Place of Cædmon's Hymn in the History of Anglo-Saxon Vernacular Poetry," in *Cædmon's Hymn and Material Culture in the World of Bede*, ed. Allen J. Frantzen and John Hines (Morgantown: West Virginia University Press, 2007), 15–50. On the importance of Cædmon and Bede's account of him for the emergence of the idea of authorship, see Toby Levers, "The Construction of Subjectivity in the Cædmon Story," *Quaestio Insularis* 6 (2005): 98–119.

[64] See Peter Orton, "Cædmon and Christian Poetry," *NM* 84 (1983): 163–70.

write down the poems they themselves composed as writers, would thus have had no tradition of recording poets' names to draw upon.

§4. Cynewulf

Against this background of generally anonymous oral or oral-derived poetry, the Old English poet Cynewulf is an particularly interesting figure. Cynewulf devised a way of ensuring that his identity would be permanently associated with his own poems as they were copied from manuscript to manuscript; and the fact that he used runic letters to record his name points, as I shall argue later, to a more or less direct dependence on established epigraphic traditions.

Cynewulf's methods of preserving his name within the texts of his poems will be examined in detail below; but we may begin by considering such evidence as there is for the kind of man he was and his methods of composition. We know little about him apart from his name and four of his poems. One of the ways in which his name is spelt—'*Cynewulf*'—combined with the linguistic evidence resulting from his use of rhyme in one his poems, suggests that he lived in the ninth century and composed in an Anglian, probably Mercian, dialect.[65] Cynewulf incorporated his signature in runic letters in four surviving Old English poems: *The Fates of the Apostles* and *Elene* in the Vercelli Book, and *Christ II* and

---

[65] See further below on the likelihood that Cynewulf was a Mercian. The linguistic and metrical evidence for Cynewulf's date and dialect was set out very clearly by P. O. E. Gradon, ed., *Cynewulf's Elene* (London: Methuen, 1958), 13–15, and more recently by R. D. Fulk, *A History of Old English Meter* (Philadelphia: University of Pennsylvania Press, 1992), 351–68, who dates the Cynewulf poems to the period 750–850. Fulk places Cynewulf's works in his second, "middle" group of Old English poems which also includes *Guthlac B*, *Andreas*, and *The Phoenix*. The earliest, "Cædmonian" group contains *Beowulf*, *Genesis A*, *Daniel*, and probably *Exodus*, *Guthlac A*, and most of the *Riddles*. Fulk's third, "Alfredian" group is constituted by the *Meters of Boethius*, *The Metrical Preface to the Pastoral Care*, *The Metrical Epilogue to the Pastoral Care*, the tenth-century poems of the *Anglo-Saxon Chronicle*, and *Judith*; and his fourth, latest group has as its chief members *The Battle of Maldon*, the *Paris Psalter*, and *The Seasons for Fasting*. This classification is reaffirmed in R. D. Fulk, "Cynewulf: Canon, Dialect, and Date," in *Cynewulf: Basic Readings*, ed. Robert E. Bjork (New York and London: Garland, 1996), 3–21, though here Fulk is inclined to regard the second or "middle" group, which includes Cynewulf's poems, and the third or "Alfredian" group as one, chiefly on the evidence of Cynewulf's date presented in the same volume by Patrick Conner, "On Dating Cynewulf" (*Cynewulf: Basic Readings*, 23–55). Conner identifies Usuardus's version of the Latin *Martyrologium*, compiled "circa 875" (Conner,"Dating," 46), as the source of *The Fates of the Apostles*, though it may be that more precise knowledge about the antecedents of Usuardus's version is needed if Conner's source-identification, and its implications for the date of Cynewulf's works, are to be regarded as completely secure.

Juliana in the Exeter Book. Both these manuscripts were written in the second half of the tenth century,[66] which means that the Cynewulf texts they contain are probably not the poet's originals but copies, perhaps separated from the original texts by several stages of transmission. There are two different spellings of Cynewulf's name in these poems: in *Elene* and *Juliana* the runes spell '*Cynewulf*', but in *Fates* and *Christ II* they resolve to '*Cynwulf*'. We do not know what this variation signifies, though it seems to be generally accepted that the two forms are simply variants of the same name, indicating the same poet.

We can be reasonably certain that Cynewulf (or Cynwulf) is the poet of these four poems, not the name of a scribe who copied them, for in two of his poems, in passages coming shortly before the runic signatures, the poet refers explicitly to himself as author. In *The Fates of the Apostles* 96–98, the sentence *Her mæg findan for(e)þances gleaw . . . hwa þas fitte fegde*, "Here the man of wisdom may discover . . . who composed this poem," introduces the signature passage; and in *Elene* 1237, Cynewulf says that he "wove (the fabric of) verbal art" (*wordcræft wæf*), and in 1250 of the same poem he tells us that God "unlocked the poetic art" in him (*leoðucræft onleac*). The runic signature follows in lines 1257–1270. In both poems, reference is made, not to Cynewulf's general status as a poet, but to his composition of these poems in particular.

The question of Cynewulf's literacy raises some difficult issues. As we saw in Chapter 1, the term 'literacy' covers such a wide range of abilities and cultural attitudes. Academics, who constitute a highly literate subgroup within modern societies, tend to have an exaggerated regard for literacy, seeing it as the essential mark of education and civilization.[67] Thus if we are to value or admire Cynewulf as an educated man living in a civilized world, we would prefer to be able to think of him as a writer and a reader; but the evidence we have that he could do either is not all of the same quality.

The evidence that Cynewulf could read is strong. Cynewulf could spell his own name, and the method he chose to preserve it would obviously not have occurred to an illiterate. To this extent, at least, Cynewulf must have been literate. He used Latin works as the sources for his poems,[68] and there are numerous references in the latter to knowledge gleaned from books: *Fates* 64 *we þæt gehyrdon*

---

[66] See Ker, *Catalogue*, nos. 116, 394.

[67] See Street, *Literacy in Theory and Practice*, 38–43, on the limited and distorting definitions of literacy that the study of it by academics may lead to. Ward Parks, "The Textualization of Orality in Literary Criticism," in *Vox Intexta: Orality and Textuality in the Middle Ages*, ed. Doane and Pasternak, 46–61, accuses modern academics of "vocational class prejudices" against oral or oral-derived literature (46): we find it "hard to renounce the sense of superiority that highly developed literacy affords" (47).

[68] For a survey of Cynewulf's written sources, see D. G. Calder and M. J. B. Allen, *Sources and Analogues of Old English Poetry: The Major Latin Texts in Translation* (Cambridge: Boydell & Brewer, 1976), 35–39, 59–69, 78–83, 121–32, though cf. n. 65 above.

þurg halige bec, "Holy books tell us," repeated in *Elene* 364; *Elene* 1254b *swa ic on bocum fand*, "as I found in books"; *Christ II* 453b *Hwæpre in bocum ne cwið*, "Yet it does not say in books," 547b *swa gewritu secgað*, "as the scriptures say," 701b *Swa hit on bocum cwiþ*, "as it says in books," 785b *Us secgað bec*, "books tell us," and 792–793 *þæt me hælend min on bocum bibead*, "what my saviour commanded me in books." The rather unspecific nature of these references (usually "books," with "holy books" and "scriptures" as variants) carries at least a suggestion of the naive perspective of an outsider, visualizing a world of literacy which is somewhat mysterious to him, though this impression is countered by *Elene* 1254, and perhaps also by *Christ II* 792–793, which refer explicitly to Cynewulf's personal reading of books.[69]

If Cynewulf could read (and understand Latin), did he also write his own vernacular poems with his own hand? The ability to read was not necessarily accompanied by writing skills in this period. The passages from *Fates* and *Elene* quoted above as evidence of Cynewulf's claimed authorship of these poems are not helpful in this regard, for the verbs *fegde* and *wæf* mean respectively 'joined' and 'wove'—general terms for composition which cannot tell us whether its mode was oral or literate. Cynewulf might have worked with a scribe who wrote at his dictation (and under his detailed instruction when it came to the runic signatures), though there is no positive evidence of this way of working in any of his four poems.

Cynewulf's poems also lack any indication of how he might have learnt to compose alliterative poetry. This is a question that has been rather pushed to one side by the closely related but distinct question of whether Cynewulf was an oral or literate poet. F. P. Magoun accepted the runic signatures as evidence that Cynewulf was "a lettered person,"[70] but took the generally formulaic character of "the narrative parts" of his poems as a sign that "those parts at least he composed in the traditional way," and that he "subsequently got them written down, whether dictating to himself, as it were, or to another person . . . ."[71] By "composed in the traditional way," Magoun means "extemporized orally": Cynewulf, in Magoun's view, was an oral poet of the kind defined by Parry and Lord in their work on Homer. Benson, whose reply to Magoun was mentioned earlier in Chapter 1, demonstrated the formulaic nature of certain Old English poems "which we can be sure were not orally composed,"[72] namely *The Metrical Preface to the Pastoral Care* (quoted in full above), *Riddle* 35 (based on Aldhelm's riddle

---

[69] See Jeff Opland, *Anglo-Saxon Oral Poetry: A Study of the Traditions* (New Haven: Yale University Press, 1980), 158, who also lists *Elene* 204, 290, 369, 670, 825, 852; idem, "From Horseback to Monastic Cell: The Impact on English Literature of the Introduction of Writing," in *Old English Literature in Context*, ed. Niles, 30–43, 161–63.

[70] Magoun, "The Oral-Formulaic Character of Anglo-Saxon Narrative Poetry," 212.

[71] Magoun, "Oral-Formulaic Character," 212.

[72] See Benson, "The Literary Character of Anglo-Saxon Formulaic Poetry."

De Lorica), the Old English poetic *Psalms*, *The Phoenix*, and *The Metres of Boethius*. Benson concluded from this that literate Old English poets could "write in a formulaic style," though it seems to me that all Benson really shows is that some Old English poets were probably able to commit their work to parchment themselves. Their methods of composition are (or might have been) another matter entirely. But in any case it seems clear that this scholarly disagreement over the mode of composition has tended to obscure the question of how Cynewulf came to compose Old English poetry at all. As someone who could read, he might have learnt to compose in the traditional alliterative style by reading poems in manuscripts and imitating them; but it is difficult to see how he could have become the poet he did without learning from the recitations of experienced oral poets.[73] In fact, it seems to me very questionable if any Anglo-Saxon poet could have learnt his craft by reading, for a number of reasons. The fact that some modern scholars have managed to produce fair imitations of Old English poetry in a spirit of experimentation must not be mistaken for a demonstration that a literate Anglo-Saxon who had never heard poetry recited would have been able to do the same thing. The modern scholar has the advantage of literate ways of thinking, of analytical methods and techniques, of texts, paper, concordances, and computers. So far as we know, Old English poets did not analyse the form of their poetry as a series of abstract rules in the way modern critics have attempted to do. We must assume that they learned through the ear.[74] Another reason for doubting the idea of the self-taught, book-based poet is the shortage of surviving manuscripts from the relevant period. The fact that many manuscripts of Old English poetry may have been destroyed by the Viking attacks on Anglo-Saxon England in the late eighth and ninth centuries does not allow us to assume that such manuscripts were ever plentiful. A third consideration is that an Old English poet would quite clearly have needed a wide knowledge (no doubt unconsciously acquired through the ear in the oral phase) of the alliterative tradition in order to compose competently. Although we still do not fully appreciate the complexity of the conventions of Old English versification, we already know that they were exacting. We should be wary of accepting without proof that any Anglo-Saxon poet operated independently of oral tradition. We should also remember that literacy does not destroy oral tradition inevitably. As Opland has written,[75] "Writing as such is not the enemy of oral poetry; it is the altered social conditions or attitudes that

---

[73] The question of whether Cynewulf was an oral or literate poet is no longer as controversial as it once was; most scholars now seem to agree that he was a literate poet well versed in the Old English poetic tradition; see (for example) Michael D. Cherniss, "The Oral-Traditional Opening Theme in the Poems of Cynewulf," in *De Gustibus: Essays for Alain Renoir*, ed. Foley, 40–65 (at 40–41).

[74] See further Peter Orton, "Anglo-Saxon Attitudes to Kuhn's Laws," *RES* N.S. 50 (1999): 287–303 (at 301).

[75] Opland, *Anglo-Saxon Oral Poetry*, 74.

writing brings with it that may operate to the detriment of an oral tradition."[76] For all we know of Cynewulf, he may well have had a footing both in the new world of Latin literacy and also in the older, oral world of Anglo-Saxon England.

Cynewulf's technique in recording his name varies somewhat in the four 'signature' passages. This makes nearly all generalizations about his methods subject to qualification. The following remarks are intended only as an introduction to what seems, on the evidence of three out of the four signature passages, to have been his standard method.

Cynewulf always chose runic letters rather than roman to preserve his name in his poems; but this policy presented him with certain difficulties of integration and expression which he was unable to surmount completely. Today (and no doubt this was so in the Anglo-Saxon period), each letter of the roman alphabet has its own name. These names are largely confined to the spoken form of the language, for when we are writing and wish to nominate a letter of the alphabet it is natural to use the letter itself—'a', 'b', and so on. In a few cases the name of the letter has developed a special, written phonetic form, the most familiar examples in British English being "aitch" and "zed", though the existence of variants ('zee' in American English, for example) is probably significant: there is not often any occasion to use these 'words' in writing. Each letter of the runic alphabet also had a name. In most cases, as with the roman alphabet, the name began with the vowel or consonant which the rune represented; but the special feature of the runic alphabet which distinguishes it most clearly from the roman is that each rune-name seems, at least at an early stage in the history of runes, to have been a common or proper noun denoting a familiar object, idea or person. Examples are *wynn*, 'joy', for the *w*-rune, *lagu*, 'water', for the *l*-rune, *Ing* (a divine or legendary personage) for the *ng*-rune. Some rune-names, however, including those of three of the runes spelling Cynewulf's name, are unrecorded in Old English except as rune-names; they are not attested as ordinary words. Most of our information about the meaning of these names comes from the Old English *Runic Poem*.[77] The *c*-rune was called *cen*, 'torch'; the *y*-rune was *yr*, which seems to have meant 'bow'; and the *u*-rune was *ur*, 'aurochs'. We cannot state unequivocally that these names had no currency as common nouns in Old English—our records of the language are not extensive enough to permit that inference—but

---

[76] See also Amodio, *Writing the Oral Tradition*, 1–32, on the complex interactions of orality and literacy once the latter is established in a particular culture. Amodio warns against casting the transition from orality to literacy "in evolutionary terms" (2).

[77] *The Runic Poem* is printed in Dobbie, *The Anglo-Saxon Minor Poems*, 28–94, and (with a translation) in T. A. Shippey, *Poems of Wisdom and Learning in Old English* (Cambridge: Brewer, 1976), 80–85. The manuscript, the text, its analogues in Norwegian and Icelandic, the runes, and the meanings of their names are all discussed thoroughly by Page, *Introduction*, 63–76.

we have no positive evidence that they did, unless we regard Cynewulf's usage as such evidence.[78]

Cynewulf's usual aim in his signatures is to spell out his name in runes in the text of his poems; but he also incorporates the names of the runes into the verse-structure, and accommodates the meanings of the names of all seven or eight runes into his narrative. He thus uses each rune both phonemically, to represent an individual vowel or consonant of his name as spelt, and as a logogram for the rune's name, the name being incorporated as a common noun both metrically into the verse-structure and also syntactically and semantically into the narrative context. We shall see this method in operation when we come to look at the signature passages themselves. There have been several modern interpretations of Cynewulf's signatures that depend on substituting broadly similar words for some of the runic names, for example the adjective *cene*, 'brave', for the noun *cen*, 'torch'.[79] Such interpretations seem unnecessarily speculative and difficult to trust because, as Kenneth Sisam pointed out long ago,[80] any departure from the standard names of the runes would have placed a heavy burden on his readers who would have had to guess what words the runes were meant to stand for. The evidence for the names of the runes making up the name '*Cyn(e)wulf*' in Anglo-Saxon England is, as Sisam showed, unequivocal, even though we cannot be sure exactly what, if anything, some of those names meant as ordinary Old English words. There is no reason to think that Cynewulf did not stick to these fixed names of the runes spelling his name. There is, however, one speculation of a somewhat less radical kind that seems to me very persuasive. This concerns Cynewulf's exceptional handling of the name of the *u*-rune in three out of the four signature passages. The *u*-rune was called *ur*, 'aurochs', the European bison *Bos primigenius*, now extinct worldwide, and probably not an indigenous animal in Anglo-Saxon England. In all his signatures except the one in *Juliana* (where the meaning of *ur* is probably immaterial, as we shall see below), the narrative context very strongly suggests that the *u*-rune is a logogram, not of 'aurochs', but of its homonym *ur*, 'our', the first-person plural possessive pronoun.[81] Either Cynewulf did not know (or thought his readers would not know) *ur* as an ordinary Old English word in the sense of 'aurochs'; or the difficulty of incorporating an aurochs into his narrative was so acute as to make the semantic substitution of *ur*, 'our', desirable or necessary. Cynewulf may, of course, have been influenced by

---

[78] See Roger Lass, "Cyn(e)wulf Revisited: The Problem of the Runic Signatures," in *An Historic Tongue: Studies in English Linguistics in Memory of Barbara Strang*, ed. Graham Nixon and John Honey (London: Routledge, 1988), 17–30 (at 28, n. 11).

[79] The most recent supporter of this interpretation is John D. Niles, "The Trick of the Runes in *The Husband's Message*," *ASE* 32 (2003): 189–223, at 214–15.

[80] Kenneth Sisam, "Cynewulf and his Poetry," *Proceedings of the British Academy* 18 (1932): 3–31 (at 22). The article is reprinted in Sisam, *Studies*, 1–28.

[81] 'our' for the *u*-rune is preferred by Niles, "The Trick of the Runes," 215.

both these considerations; but in any case, his substitution (if that is what it is) is a small but telling piece of evidence for the dialect in which he composed. The usual spelling of the first-person plural possessive pronoun in Old English was *ure*, with final *e*. The form lacking the final *e* is confined, according to Campbell,[82] to the Mercian dialect of Old English (the corresponding Northumbrian forms being *user, usra*). In view of the fact that only the Mercian form of the pronoun is homonymic with the runic name *ur*, 'aurochs', Cynewulf's substitution (if that is what it was) suggests that he composed in a Mercian, not a Northumbrian, dialect.[83]

§5. Cynewulf's runic signatures

Below I quote and translate the four passages in which Cynewulf records his name. In the Old English texts, each runic letter is represented (for convenience) by its roman equivalent, with the Old English name of the rune following it in brackets. In the modern English translations below each Old English text, the name of the rune follows its gloss (except in the case of *Juliana*, on which see the commentary following the translation).

1. *Fates of the Apostles* 96–106:[84]

```
       Her mæg findan      for(e)þances[85] gleaw,
       se ðe hine lysteð    leoðgiddunga,
       hwa þas fitte fegde.   .F. (feoh) þær on ende standeþ,[86]
       eorlas þæs on eorðan brucaþ;  ne moton hie awa ætsomne
100    woruldwunigende.     .W. (wyn) sceal gedreosan
       .U. (ur) on eðle,    æfter tohweorfan
       læne lices frætewa,  efne swa .L. (lagu) toglideð.
```

---

[82] See Campbell, *Old English Grammar*, §702.

[83] Cf. Lass, "Cyn(e)wulf Revisited," 29, n. 14, who suggests that monosyllabic *ur*, "our," may have been "a poetic koiné form, which poets from anywhere could use if they wanted to work with runes." This is, of course, a possibility; but as Lass himself points out, the rhyming passage in *Elene* (on which see Sisam, "Cynewulf and his Poetry", 4) is good evidence that Cynewulf composed in an Anglian dialect of some kind, so I prefer the simpler explanation that he used the *u*-rune to mean *ur*, "our," because he was a Mercian composing for Mercian-speaking readers who would have been able to understand his method.

[84] Text from *Andreas and The Fates of the Apostles*, ed. Kenneth R. Brooks (Oxford: Oxford University Press, 1961), 59.

[85] 96 *foreþances*, MS *forþances*.

[86] 98 *standeþ*, MS *standaþ*.

Þonne .C. (*cen*) ond .Y. (*yr*)   cræftes neotað
nihtes nearowe,   on him .N. (*ned*) ligeð,
105   cyninges þeodom.   Nu ðu cunnon miht
hwa on þam wordum wæs   werum oncyðig.

"Here the man of wisdom who enjoys poetry may discover who composed this poem. Last stands wealth (*feoh*) which noblemen enjoy on earth, (though) dwellers in the world cannot do so for ever. The joy (*wyn*) which is ours (*ur*) in our homeland must fail, the brief trappings of the body afterwards decay, just as water (*lagu*) ebbs away. When torch (*cen*) and bow (*yr*) exercise their power with labour in the night, constraint (*ned*), the king's service, lies upon them (*or* him). Now you may know who is revealed to men in these words."

A unique feature of this signature is that it is an anagram (resolving to '*Cynwulf*'), though the order of presentation is such that the two elements of the compound name ('fwul-cyn' for 'cyn-wulf') are kept separate. The indications at the beginning of the passage that *F* is the last letter of the name, and at the end that the signature is concluded, assist the reader in solving the anagram. The meanings of most of the runes' names are ingeniously integrated into the narrative structure of the passage (one notes especially the association of *cen*, 'torch', with nocturnal activity), though strain is evident in the incorporation of the names of the *y*- and *n*-runes towards the end.[87]

2. *Christ II* 797–807a:[88]

Þonne .C. (*cen*) cwacað,   gehyreð cyning mæðlan,
rodera ryhtend,   sprecan reþe word
þam þe him ær in worulde   wace hyrdon,
800   þendan .Y. (*yr*) ond N. (*ned*)   yþast meahtan
frofre findan.   Þær sceal forht monig
on þam wongstede   werig bidan
hwæt him æfter dædum   deman wille
wraþra wita.   Biþ se .W. (*wyn*) scæcen
805   eorþan frætwa.   .U. (*ur*) wæs longe
.L. (*lagu*) flodum bilocen,   lifwynna dæl,
.F. (*feoh*) on foldan.

---

[87] We may note here the use of hypermetric lines in 98, 99, and 102—the only hypermetric lines in this poem and in any of the signature passages, though Cynewulf does use them elsewhere in parts of *Christ II* and *Elene*; see A. J. Bliss, *The Metre of Beowulf*, 2nd ed. (Oxford: Blackwell, 1967), 163–64.

[88] Text from *The Exeter Book*, ed. Krapp and Dobbie, 25.

"Then the torch (*cen*) will tremble, he will hear the king speak, the ruler of the heavens say angry words to those who had been feeble in obeying him in this world, while the bow (*yr*) and necessity (*ned*) could find solace most easily. In that place many a one, terrified, shall await wearily what harsh penalties he will adjudge him in consequence of his deeds. The joy (*wyn*) of earthly treasures will have passed away. Our (*ur*) portion of life's delights will long have been encompassed by the water's floods (*lagu*), our wealth (*feoh*) in the world."

In this passage the letters of the name (again 'Cynwulf', as in *Fates*) are in their natural order. The meanings of the names of *wyn*, *ur*, *lagu*, and *feoh* are satisfactorily integrated into the narrative; but *cen*, 'torch' for the *c*-rune, *yr*, 'bow' for the *y*-rune, and *ned*, 'necessity' or 'need' for the *n*-rune are not; as in the *Fates* signature, the effect is forced. *Cen* might stand, by a kind of metonymy, for Cynewulf himself (as in the *Juliana* signature, on which see below); but *yr* and *ned* seem to be opposed to *cen* and it is not clear how they are to be understood.

3. *Juliana* 699b–711a:[89]

	Min sceal of lice	
700	sawul on siðfæt,	nat ic sylfa hwider,
	eardes uncyðþu;	of sceal ic þissum[90]
	secan oþerne	ærgewyrhtum,
	gongan iudædum.	Geomor hweorfeð
	.C. (*cen*) Y. (*yr*) ond .N. (*ned*).	Cyning biþ reþe,
705	sigora Syllend,	þonne synnum fah,
	.E. (*eoh*) W. (*wyn*) ond U.(*ur*)	acle bidað
	hwæt him æfter dædum	deman wille
	lifes to leane;	.L. (*lagu*) F.(*feoh*) beofað,
	seomað sorgcearig.	Sar eal gemon,
710	synna wunde	þe ic siþ oþþe ær
	geworhte on worulde:	

"My soul shall go forth from the body on its journey, I know not whither, to what unknown land; I must go hence to seek another place, according to my earlier doings, my former deeds. Sadly *cen*, *yr*, and *ned* will journey. The king, giver of victories, will be stern when *eoh*, *wyn*, and *ur*, stained with sins and terrified, await what he will adjudge them according to their deeds, as a reward for the life they have led. *Lagu*, *feoh* will tremble, will lie sorrowful. I shall remember all the torment, all the wounds of sins I ever wrought in the world:"

---

[89] Text from *Juliana*, ed. Rosemary Woolf, 2nd ed. (London: Methuen, 1966), 53–54.
[90] *þissum* with one letter erased after *i*.

The runes are again in natural order (here spelling '*Cynewulf*'), but there are several features unique to this signature-passage. The runes are divided into groups of three, three, and two runes, each group occupying a single line of verse. As Sisam noticed,[91] the grammatical number of verbs and adjectives dependent on the rune-groups varies. The fact that each group contains two or three runes would lead one to expect that a verb having any one of the groups as its subject will show plural inflexion, as in *Fates* 103 *neotað* and *Christ II* 800 *meahtan*, both plural verbs having as their subjects pairs of runes linked by 'and'. One would also expect any adjective qualifying one of the groups to be plural too. However, there are singular inflexions in 703 *Geomor* and *hweorfeð*, adjective and verb, both associated with the first group; plural inflexions in 706 *acle* and *bidað*, adjective and verb, beside the singular adjective *fah* in 705, all associated with the second group; and singular inflexions on the verbs *beofað* (708) and *seomað* (709) and the adjective *sorgcearig* (709), all associated with the third group. I shall return to these inconsistencies in a moment. Meanwhile, another unique feature of the *Juliana* signature is that only here is it necessary to draw a distinction between the pronunciation of the names of individual runes and their meaning. For example, in the first group, C, Y, and N (again, morphological groups are preserved, as in *Fates*), the name of each rune is no doubt meant to be *pronounced* (vocally or mentally) by a reader in the usual way of Cynewulf's signatures; otherwise the verses in which they occur would not scan; but there is no sign here of the attempt we see in the other three signature passages to integrate the names of the runes into the meaning of the passage. Sisam argued,[92] I think very persuasively, that each of the three groups of letters into which Cynewulf's name is divided in *Juliana* transcends the meanings of the individual rune-names and refers, by a kind of orthographic metonymy, to Cynewulf himself: each is semantically equivalent to 'Cynewulf' in the context of the passage as a whole.

One of the advantages of this theory is that it helps to explain some of the singular verbs and adjectives associated with the three rune-groups. The singular verb 703 *hweorfeð*, associated with the first group of runes, might be explained as an illustration of an observation of Mitchell's that in Old English "two or more singular subjects joined by *and* may have a singular verb ... when the verb precedes the first subject and is not repeated with any following subject(s)";[93] but the number of the verb could also be explained according to another of Mitchell's observations: a series of singular subjects linked by *and* may have a singular verb "when they are thought of as a unit."[94] If we can accept either of these explanations, we

---

[91] "Cynewulf and his Poetry," 31, n. 29; see also Woolf, ed., *Juliana*, 54, note to line 705 *fah*.
[92] Sisam, "Cynewulf and his Poetry," 18.
[93] Bruce Mitchell, *Old English Syntax*, 2 vols. (Oxford: Oxford University Press, 1985), 1: §30(2).
[94] Mitchell, *Old English Syntax*, 1: §30(1).

probably need look no further for a justification of the singular number of the adjective *Geomor* (703) which precedes the verb *hweorfeð*: it is singular for the same reason that the verb is singular. The only singular form associated with the second group of runes is *fah* (705). Again, the rune-group consists grammatically of a series of singular subjects linked by *and*; but Mitchell's observations apply to verbs, not adjectives, so singular *fah* is perhaps more easily defended on the basis of Sisam's theory: it is the rune-group's reference to a single entity, 'Cynewulf', which makes a singular qualifying adjective appropriate. The two singular verbs 708 *beofað* and 709 *seomað*, and the singular adjective *sorgcearig*, associated with the third group of runes, might be justified in two ways: either by the fact that the *l-* and *f-*runes are consecutive and so would have been pronounced as if they constituted a single, singular compound noun *lagu-feoh*; or, again, by Sisam's theory that they are to be understood as equivalent semantically to 'Cynewulf'. Thus Sisam's theory and Mitchell's observations together enable us to dispose of the problem represented by singular forms in these contexts where we might expect plural ones, though it seems impossible to be certain exactly how Cynewulf expected his readers to interpret him in this respect.

Sisam's solution to the problem of the *Juliana* signature is not accepted by everyone. Of rivals to it, the most popular takes the three groups of runes as standing for the three words they spell—*cyn, ewu,* and *lf*.[95] However, only the first two are recorded Old English words—*cyn*, 'race', and *ewu*, 'ewe'; *lf* is meaningless. Furthermore, neither of the two words which do exist in Old English fits happily into the context: *cyn* might be acceptable if it were regarded as equivalent to *mancyn*, 'mankind'; but Sisam remarks that 'ewe' produces a meaning which is "plainly ridiculous."[96] Sisam also notes that immediately before and after the runic passage, "Cynewulf speaks in his own person"—a point which favours his interpretation of each group of runes as standing for the poet. The runic passage both continues and is continued by remarks by Cynewulf about himself.

---

[95] This interpretation is favoured by Niles, "The Trick of the Runes," 214–17.

[96] Cf. Christine Fell, "Runes and Riddles in Anglo-Saxon England," in *"Lastworda Betst"*, ed. Hough and Lowe, 277, who defends *ewu*, 'ewe', as Cynewulf's reference to his soul, translating: "The king, giver of victories, will be stern when *ewu* (the sheep, my soul) stained with sins awaits in terror . . ." etc.: Cynewulf, aware of the wolfish connotations of the second element of his dithematic name, is associating himself with Christ's flock. Niles similarly favours 'ewe', unbothered by the sexual specificity of the word (Niles, "The Trick of the Runes," 216 and n. 66).

4. *Elene* 1256b–1270a:[97]

                      A wæs sæcg[98] oð ðæt
cnyssed cearwelmum,   C. (*cen*) drusende
þeah he in medohealle   maðmas þege,
æplede gold.   .Y. (*yr*) gnornode,
1260   .N. (*ned*) gefera   nearusorge dreah,
enge rune   þær him .E. (*eoh*) fore
milpaðas mæt,   modig þrægde,
wirum gewlenced.   .W.[99] (*wyn*) is geswiðrad,
gomen æfter gearum,   geogoð is gecyrred,
1265   ald onmedla.   .U. (*ur*) wæs geara
geogoðhades glæm;   nu synt geardagas
æfter fyrstmearce   forð gewitene,
lifwynne geliden   swa .L.[100] (*lagu*) toglideð,
flodas gefysde.   .F. (*feoh*) æghwam bið
1270   læne under lyfte;

"Until then the man was always tossed by the waves of care, a sinking torch (*cen*), though he received treasures in the meadhall, embossed gold. Bow (?) (*Yr*), his comrade in need (*ned*), mourned, felt affliction, an oppressive secret, where formerly the steed (*eoh*) measured the mile-paths, ran proud, adorned with filigree work. Joy (*wyn*) has faded, happiness after the years, youth, the old pomp, is changed. Once the radiance of youth was ours (*ur*). Now the old days have passed away in due course of time, the joy of life departed just as water (*lagu*) ebbs away, the driven floods. Wealth (*feoh*) is transitory for every man beneath the heavens."

The runes are in natural order and spell '*Cynewulf*', as in *Juliana*. The ebbing of the joy of life compared with that of the sea is a simile Cynewulf also uses in *Fates*. There is the same difficulty in incorporating the rune-names *cen*, *yr*, and *ned* in the passage as we saw earlier in *Fates* and *Christ II*; but this signature passage contains no other problems or individual features.

---

[97] Text from *Cynewulf's Elene*, ed. Gradon, 72–74.
[98] 1256 *sæcg*, MS *sæcc*.
[99] In 1263 the *w*-rune was written twice, the first instance erased.
[100] In 1268 an erasure occurs before the *l*-rune.

§6. The reception of Cynewulf's poems

It has long been recognized that Cynewulf's use of runes in his signatures has important implications for the way in which he planned the reception of his poetry, but critics have differed over what those implications are. Sisam envisaged a circle of listeners around a speaker reading the poems aloud from a book:

> Cynewulf used runes because, while they were obvious to a reader, they made possible the communication of his name to an audience in a way at once memorable and sure. An Anglo-Saxon hearing *cen, yr,* would know at once that he was dealing with runes; his attention would be directed at once to the task of solution because runes sometimes played a part in Old English riddles; and he would listen closely for the succession.[101]

Sisam's reaction to the poor integration of the meanings of the rune-names *cen* and *yr* in the signature passages is that Cynewulf, far from attempting to embody their meanings in his narrative, welcomed the awkwardness as a way of signalling to the audience that they formed part of a spelling of his own name:

> [Cynewulf] was content to let *cen* and *yr* be what they are—simple letter-names that would serve as warnings of less obvious letter-names to follow. So far from regretting that *cen* and *yr* were not ordinary words, he probably blessed his luck in having a name that began so unambiguously in runes.[102]

The reader would not, of course, have needed any such warnings because he would be able to see the runes. Other commentators, however, have doubted Sisam's idea of the reception of Cynewulf's poetry, arguing that it would have been impossible to appreciate the full significance of the runic passages without actually seeing the runes.[103] This objection seems to me a weighty one. In a recitation

---

[101] Sisam, "Cynewulf," 21–22.

[102] Sisam, "Cynewulf," 22.

[103] This was implied by Magoun, "The Oral-Formulaic Character of Anglo-Saxon Narrative Poetry," 212: "... Cynewulf was surely a lettered person, else how could he have conceived a plan to assure mention of his name in prayers by means of runic signatures which depend on a knowledge of spelling and reading for their efficacy?" Benson ("The Literary Character of Anglo-Saxon Formulaic Poetry," 335) puts the matter more explicitly: "... the visual punning of the runic signatures shows that he [Cynewulf] wrote for readers ...". Benson's view is repeated by Opland, *Anglo-Saxon Oral Poetry,* 159: "Clearly the poems of Cynewulf are designed to be read: it is difficult to understand how else the runic signatures might appeal to an audience." The older view of Sisam has been defended by Ursula Schaefer, "Hearing from Books: The Rise of Fictionality in Old English Poetry," in *Vox Intexta,* ed. Doane and Pasternack, 117–36 (at 28): "Kenneth Sisam convincingly proved a long time ago that the runic signature could be perceived as such by somebody who only received the poem by listening. Moreover, it is unlikely that an early

of the kind Sisam envisages, the names for the individual runes making up Cynewulf's name would have been enunciated, as the metre requires; but it would have taken remarkable concentration on the audience's part to piece together Cynewulf's name simply by hearing the names of the appropriate runes read out, even when allowance is made for the fact that some of these rune-names apparently had no application other than as rune-names (and so might have alerted an audience to the signature, as Sisam suggests). The difficulty would have been particularly acute in *Fates*, where the letters of the name are presented as an anagram. I therefore agree with those critics who argue that the decipherment (and hence the preservation) of Cynewulf's name would have been possible only for someone who was in a position to *see* the text, and impossible for any audience we might imagine sitting at the reader's feet. Furthermore, Sisam's tableau of a reader reciting Cynewulf's poetry from a book to an audience carries an implication that tends to undermine his own argument: it implies that this audience was illiterate. If they had been able to read, they would not have needed to have the manuscript book read out to them; they would have been able to take it and read it for themselves. But as illiterates, the audience would not have been able to spell, and so could scarcely have been competent to put the letters of Cynewulf's name together as his name when they heard the runes spelling it. Much favours the view that Cynewulf intended his work to be read out loud, not to an audience but by a reader to himself. He wrote for the solitary monastic. It is often said, no doubt justly, that all Old English poetry and most Middle English poetry too was composed for reading aloud; but reading aloud in a medieval European—especially a monastic—context does not necessarily imply any audience other than the reader himself. Chaytor showed long ago how recent a development in western culture is silent reading and suggested that a medieval library or scriptorium would have been full of "the buzz of whispering and muttering" made by solitary readers.[104] The medieval reader "had learnt to rely on the memory of spoken sounds, not upon the interpretation of written signs. And when he had deciphered a word, he pronounced it audibly."[105] These, it seems to me, must have been the conditions under which Cynewulf's poetry was read, if it was read at all.

---

medieval poet composed poetry for such a small audience as the community of literates of the time"; but cf. Samantha Zacher, "Cynewulf at the Interface of Literacy and Orality: The Evidence of the Puns in *Elene*," *Oral Tradition* 17 (2002): 346–87.

[104] Chaytor, *From Script to Print*, 19.

[105] Chaytor, *From Script to Print*, 14. See also Ong, *Orality and Literacy*, 119: "[Medieval] readers commonly vocalized, read slowly aloud or *sotto voce*, even when reading alone ..." Ong makes the same point in his article: "Orality, Literacy, and Medieval Textuality," 1. On silent reading, see now Paul Saenger, *Space Between Words: The Origins of Silent Reading* (Stanford: Stanford University Press, 2000).

4. From Inscription to Manuscript Text

A passage towards the end of *Juliana* has been taken by some commentators as supporting Sisam's idea of the reception of Cynewulf's poetry; but this is based on a misunderstanding of the Old English. The passage in question is:

>   Bidde ic monna gehwone
>   gumena cynnes,   þe þis gied wræce,
> 720 þæt he mec neodful   bi noman minum
>   gemyne modig, . . .   (*Juliana* 718b-721a)

So far as I can discover, all previous editors and translators of this passage have understood the antecedent of the relative clause *þe þis gied wræce* in 719b to be the indefinite pronoun *gehwone*, 'each' (718), in the phrase *monna gehwone gumena cynnes*, "each man of the race of men." Grein's early translation into German and S. A. J. Bradley's more recent English rendering both illustrate this interpretation:

"Ich bitte der Menschen jeglichen, der dieses Lied wird lesen, der Leute jeden, daß er meiner angelegentlichst bei meinem Eigennamen geistesmutig gedenke . . ."[106]

"I pray each person of humankind who recites this poem that, diligent and magnanimous, he will remember me by name . . ."[107]

I would argue, however, that the antecedent of the relative clause is not *gehwone* but 718 *ic*, 'I', the subject of the principal clause; in other words, that the verb *wræce*, a variant of West Saxon *wrece*, 'utter', is first person singular present indicative, denoting current action (Cynewulf's composition of *Juliana*), not third person singular present subjunctive, denoting possible future action (readings of *Juliana* by others). Cynewulf himself is, I believe, the verb's subject, so that my preliminary translation would be:

"I, who am uttering this story, pray each man of the race of men that, diligent and magnanimous, he remember me by name. . ."

The case for this interpretation rests largely on the normal semantic range of the verb *wrecan* in the general sense of 'utter' in Old English: it never refers elsewhere to the recitation by one person of another's original poem, as Grein's and Bradley's interpretations of *Juliana* 719b would imply; nor does it ever suggest verbatim repetition by one person of another person's composition (or, indeed, of his or her own composition). In most of its occurrences the verb quite clearly denotes the utterance of an original, orally delivered poem; and in those where

---

[106] C. W. M. Grein, *Dichtungen der Angelsachsen stabreimend übersetzt*, 2 vols. (Göttingen: Wigand, 1857–1859), 2: 66.

[107] S. A. J. Bradley, *Anglo-Saxon Poetry* (London: Dent, 1982), 319.

this implication is not definite it is probable.[108] If Cynewulf composed pen-in-hand, he used the verb in a slightly unusual way, to refer to written composition of poetry rather than to oral delivery; but he does not depart far enough from the standard usage to confuse his readers. He simply adapts the verb to the new, literate conditions under which he himself worked. My preliminary translation above has "am uttering"; according to this interpretation, "am writing" should, perhaps, replace it, though I should be inclined to retain 'uttering' in a sense comparable to the way in which the noun 'utterance' is used throughout this book: as a linguistic production of either kind, spoken or written.

§7. Runic and roman in Cynewulf's poems

Cynewulf's ingenuity ensured that his name could not easily be detached from his work without a major deletion; but it will be clear from my discussion of the individual signatures that the poet was unable to resolve a basic incompatibility between the meanings of the runes' names and the narratives in which they are embedded. The unfamiliarity as ordinary words of the names of three of the runes spelling his own name, namely *cen*, *yr*, and *ur*, contributed largely to this incompatibility. It is possible that Cynewulf's policy on *ur* was guided by the consideration that his readers were unlikely to know what an *ur* ('aurochs') was; but it could equally well have been an attempt to solve a different problem: that of incorporating all seven or eight of the relevant rune-names in a brief passage of poetry. It cannot have been easy to think up a short passage in which joy, water, wealth, and constraint all feature, not to mention a torch, an aurochs, and a bow. Cynewulf's method in *Juliana*—a less ambitious one than elsewhere, if we accept Sisam's interpretation of the runic signature—deals very effectively with this problem, though it does produce its own difficulty: a certain straining of grammar arising from the failure of number-concord between the plurality of clusters of runes on the one hand, and the singularity of the ultimate signification of each cluster ('Cynewulf') on the other. In none of his surviving signatures did the poet manage fully to resolve the incompatibility between runes as letters and runes as logograms.

In Cynewulf's poems there is a clear functional distinction between runic letters and the roman writing in which they are embedded: runes are used for the author's name, roman for his work. The implications of this distinction are important. We have already seen (in Chapter 2) how, in a pre-literate society, the very existence of an utterance depends entirely on the presence and voice

---

[108] The other instances of the verb *wrecan* in this sense are *Christ and Satan* 35, *Andreas* 1548, *Seafarer* 1, *Order of the World* 12, *Vainglory* 15, *The Wife's Lament* 1, *Beowulf* 873, 1065, 2154, 2446, 3172, *Menologium* 70. There are no examples of the verb in this sense in Old English prose.

of the speaker, for all human speech disappears in the course of being uttered. The receiver (in the case of speech a hearer) must also be present at the moment of utterance; otherwise no communication will occur.[109] In writing, utterances achieve permanence though their materialisation, and may be received repeatedly through time, whenever anyone chooses to read them. From the reader's point of view, the loss involved in writing is, of course, the loss of the speaker's presence; but the loss is to a degree compensated for if the writer can preserve his name in association with his writings. This is, one imagines, how the idea of authorship first arose—from the same desire to restore the connection between utterance and utterer that led, as I suggested in Chapter 2, to medium-deictic usage of the first-person pronoun. A speaker is automatically and naturally associated with his own utterances; he could not escape responsibility for them even if he wanted to. The most that a writer can do in this direction is to attach his name to his writings as firmly as possible. Thus it is true, up to a point at least, to say that authorship is a response to the structural analogy between writing and speech.

These considerations suggest that Cynewulf used runes for his name because of their original association with inscriptions. Runes represented one of the ways—quite probably the only way—by which men in a largely preliterate past had managed to preserve their identities in relation to anything that they had made. According to this analogy, the written work is an artifact on the surface of which the maker—the author—may inscribe his name because he enjoys the use of two distinct alphabets, the letters of one of which might do double duty as letters and words. The runes are thus partly writing, partly writing on writing. As names, they tend to go against the grain, so to speak, of the texts in which they are incorporated, against the syntax of the poetry; but this friction contributes to the visibility (metaphorically speaking) of the runes on the poetic surface. The true analogy here is not between books and artifacts but between written texts and artifacts; for texts are as much made objects as other artifacts are, products of skill, experience and technology. A text can be reproduced in copies—all four of the texts of Cynewulf's poems that have survived to us are copies, as we saw earlier—but the reproduction of his work by copyists has not obscured Cynewulf's authorship or diminished his authority. On the other hand, Cynewulf was all but defeated by the combined breadth and antiquity of the frame of reference to which the runic names refer. These names had to be comprehensible if his experiment in authorship was to work; but many of them belonged to a lost, continental Germanic world, a world of pagan superstition and superseded agricultural priorities; and their sweep, as a system, made them virtually unusable in the way Cynewulf wanted to use them.

This is, I suggest, the kind of thinking that lies behind Cynewulf's runic signatures and their incorporation in his poems. Sisam and Rosemary Woolf both

---

[109] For a useful description of the different assumptions underlying oral and literate poetic composition in Anglo-Saxon England, see Opland, *Anglo-Saxon Oral Poetry*, 83–85.

argued that Cynewulf drew some inspiration for his runic signatures from Latin poetry in which the poet's name is preserved by an acrostic made out of the first letters of the first words of a series of poetic lines. It should be pointed out, however, that acrostics are essentially spatial devices: the letters of the name are given in 'natural' (i.e. spelling) order at regular, predictable intervals in the verse-structure. Cynewulf's runic signatures do not depend on such regularity: the runes may or may not alliterate; they may or may not be given in natural order; and they never occur in any kind of regular or predictable pattern in an unbroken sequence of lines in any of the four surviving signatures. Thus the influence of acrostics on Cynewulf was probably minor. They may have given him the idea that he could, in theory, preserve his name as a poet; but the actual procedure he followed looks very much as if it was inspired by the runic epigraphic tradition, most probably by artifacts which bore simply the name of the maker. There seems little doubt that Cynewulf's readers would have made the connection with inscriptions: runes must have been closely associated with them in the minds of most Anglo-Saxons who knew what runes were, for that was their first, and before Christianity their only, function. Any use of runes in manuscript literature would have been likely to recall their original epigraphic applications. In the case of Cynewulf's signatures, the memory of their original epigraphical role would also have helped the reader to understand their purpose and significance.

§8. The Ruthwell Cross inscription and *The Dream of the Rood*

The Ruthwell Cross inscription, quoted earlier in Chapter 3, consists, as we saw there, of four fragments of a speech attributed to the cross of Calvary and therefore 'spoken' (in a sense) by the Ruthwell Cross itself. All four fragments show a close verbal resemblance to passages distributed among lines 39–64 of the Old English poem *The Dream of the Rood*, which survives only in the late-tenth-century Vercelli Book.[110] The level of correspondence between the two texts in these passages is high enough to justify our regarding them as variants of a single composition. What is less clear is which version of the poem represents the earlier stage in its transmission and development. The question has often been considered by scholars but cannot really be regarded as settled. Of the two texts, the shorter Ruthwell inscription survives earlier than the longer Vercelli Book version; but that does not rule out the possibility that the longer version was already in existence in some form when the shorter was inscribed on the Ruthwell monument in the late seventh or early eighth century. The existence of other versions now lost connecting our two surviving texts obviously cannot be ruled out either.

---

[110] The Ruthwell text and the corresponding parts of *The Dream of the Rood* are printed, translated and compared in Orton, *The Transmission of Old English Poetry*, 144–48.

But there are two main possibilities: either the Ruthwell Cross poem is an abbreviation of the longer poem to which *The Dream of the Rood* is a late witness; or *The Dream of the Rood* represents an expansion of the poem inscribed on the Ruthwell cross.[111]

The prevailing view seems to be that Ruthwell consists of excerpts chosen by the inscriber from a lost, longer, probably eighth-century Northumbrian poem (whether oral or written), comparable in length and overall structure with *The Dream of the Rood*.[112] Some critics, however, are not convinced that matters are quite so simple: they suggest that the Vercelli text may have been subjected during transmission from its Northumbrian original to deliberate expansion and (possibly) extension—even that the whole of the second half of the poem, from line 78, is an addition.[113] The theory I advance below that the Ruthwell text was independently composed (like almost all other surviving Anglo-Saxon inscriptions), and for inscription on the Ruthwell Cross in particular, not quoted from a preexisting poem, and that it formed the core around which the longer version was assembled by a later poet or poets is not, so far as I know, accepted by anyone else. Michael Swanton mentions it as a possibility,[114] but rejects the idea mainly because of the presence in the text of single-verse lines which he regards as intended by the inscriber to stand as metrically unattached. He cites in this connection 39–40 *þa he walde on ğalğu gistiğa*, 56 *Krist wæs on rodi*, and 62 *miþ strelum giwundad*. Swanton comments: "Had the verse been composed especially for the monument it is inconceivable that it should have contained such defective lines."[115] The second and third of these unattached half-lines are also regarded as intended and original to the monument by Christopher Ball.[116] However, as R. D. Fulk has pointed out,[117] the first of the allegedly unattached half-lines mentioned by Swanton, 39–40 *þa he walde on ğalğu gistiğa*, is actually the b-verse of

---

[111] The question raised here is distinct from that of the relative authority of the textual variants in the passages where the texts overlap. My own answer to this last question is that "appeal to metrical considerations tends to favour RCr [the Ruthwell Cross text] as having the best, and so probably the original, text" (Orton, *Transmission*, 148).

[112] See, for example, Michael Swanton, ed., *The Dream of the Rood* (Manchester: Manchester University Press, 1970), 39–41, and Éamonn Ó Carragáin, *Ritual and Rood: Liturgical Images and the Old English Poems of the Dream of the Rood Tradition* (London: The British Library and University of Toronto Press, 2005), 331–32.

[113] See, for example, Bruce Dickins and Alan S. C. Ross, ed., *The Dream of the Rood* (London: Methuen, 1963), 17–18, who suggest that the whole of the second half of the poem (from line 78 to the end) may be a later addition, and Orton, *Transmission*, 159–61.

[114] Swanton, ed., *The Dream of the Rood*, 39–41.

[115] Swanton, ed., *The Dream of the Rood*, 41.

[116] Sir Christopher Ball, "Inconsistencies in the Main Runic Inscriptions on the Ruthwell Cross," in *Old English Runes and their Continental Background*, ed. Bammesberger, 107–23 (at 113–15).

[117] Fulk, *A History of Old English Meter*, 342–43, n. 155.

the hypermetric line with which the Ruthwell runic poem begins;[118] and we must also note that the other two unattached half-lines identified as odd by Swanton, 56 and 62, each immediately follow on from a gap in the text caused by damage to the monument, so that it is conceivable that the lacunae originally contained the missing a-verses corresponding to them. These issues are all closely bound up with the vexed question of how much text has been lost from the Ruthwell cross as a result of the damage it has suffered.[119]

The question of priority is not normally discussed in terms of the different pragmatics of the 'speeches' which the two texts represent, though an approach along these lines reveals differences that seem relevant to the problem. The speech of the cross in *The Dream of the Rood* is an example of the rhetorical device of personification or prosopopoeia, the imaginary attribution of human capacities and qualities to animals or inert objects.[120] Personification creates a concept of a humanized object in the reader's mind; and although it need not necessarily involve the attribution of speech to the personified object, the impression of humanity is particularly vivid if it does, as in *The Dream of the Rood*. The cross is described by a narrator, the dreamer, who introduces its speech with a 'reporting clause', just as if it were a human character (*Dream of the Rood* 27 *Ongan þa word sprecan wudu selesta*, "The best of trees spoke these words:"). The poem reports a conversation (a one-sided one), and the conceptualization of the cross by the reader as a speaking character follows inevitably: we read its speech just as we would any other written speech, internalising it as a 'voice'.

This 'hearing' of a literary speech is a perfectly normal effect in much poetry or prose, both Old English and later. The speeches of human characters in *Beowulf*, for example, provide numerous instances; but the impact of the Ruthwell text is very different. From one point of view, the inscribed monument offers us something one step closer to the reality of a speaking cross. The reader of the inscription is not required to conceptualize the speaker as he is when reading the Vercelli text; for at Ruthwell, where the artist created it, the cross is present to the reader's perception and waking mind. This intimate, structural relationship between medium and text make Ruthwell's runic inscription seem appropriate, one might almost say more naturalistic, as the silent speech of the silent object upon which it is carved. There is no need for any mediating narrator-dreamer to introduce its words to us: the obvious relationship between the monument and its inscription makes any interference of that kind unnecessary. The link between the cross and the reader is as direct as that between a human speaker and his interlocutor. I can think of no other text in the reading of which we are less aware

---

[118] See my text of the poem, reproduced from Dobbie's edition, in Chapter 3 above.

[119] A fresh investigation of these interconnected problems might be fruitful.

[120] See M. Schlauch, "*The Dream of the Rood* as Prosopopoeia," in *Essays and Studies in Honor of Carleton Brown*, ed. Percy W. Long (New York: New York University Press, 1940), 23–34.

of the original writer, the inscriber. And although we read, just as we read the Vercelli text, we do not 'hear' the cross's speech in the way we do there because the pragmatics of the inscription—the cross's assumption, simply by its use of the first person pronoun, of the role of 'speaker'—insists on our apprehending it *directly* as writing, not as something to be converted imaginatively into speech. We are not told that anyone or anything is speaking to us. The Ruthwell monument embodies a paradox: the only form of speech possible for material objects is writing. Written speeches by human beings are mimetic: they copy actual speech; but here there is no mimesis of the normal kind: writing is made to appear as the natural language of objects, directly apprehended. This thoroughgoing integration of setting, linguistic mode, and form is what makes the impact of the Ruthwell poem so much more immediate, more dramatic, than the speech of the cross in the longer, manuscript version. The difference in effect is similar to the difference between seeing a play performed and reading it, except that one aspect of the situation is inverted: the Ruthwell cross is comparable to an actor speaking the part the poet has written for it in a crucifixion drama, though here reading, not hearing, is the primary mode of reception. We experience a drama of writing.

I cannot, of course, prove that the Old English cross-poem did not began its life as a speech attributed to the cross in an oral poem, or in a manuscript text such as Vercelli's; but the carving of the Ruthwell monument seems to me so much more convincing as a occasion for the composition of the earliest version, inspired by the potential of the artistic setting. I offer this as a legitimate consideration in judging the relative priority of the two versions, and suggest that the Ruthwell cross is the poem's original context; that it was composed for inscription on an actual cross, in all likelihood for the Ruthwell cross itself. So far as the Vercelli version is concerned, it is easy to see how the separation of the text from its original pragmatic setting on a stone cross would have required a narrative framework, and how appropriate a choice was that of the dream-vision form as a means of authenticating the idea of an object which can speak.

§9. Summary

In turning, in this chapter, from Anglo-Saxon inscriptions on hard surfaces to Old English manuscript texts, we encounter further examples of the impersonal first-person pronoun used deictically. But instead of the medium-deixis characteristic of the inscriptions, here we confront two poems, *Thureth* and *The Metrical Preface to Wærferth's Translation of Gregory's Dialogues*, that illustrate text-deixis: an impersonal first-person pronoun refers to a particular written text produced by a particular person. We have observed text-deixis in action before, in Chapter 2, in certain scribal colophons attached to other Old English texts (e.g. *Wulfwi me wrat*). Colophons of this general type may have helped to shape these two poems; but they contain stylistic features pointing to the probable influence of the epigraphic medium-deictic 'commissioner' formula, best exemplified by the Alfred Jewel inscription: *Aelfred mec heht gevvyrcan*, "Alfred ordered me to be made," and suggesting a perceived analogy between certain artifacts and books as beautiful, ornate, made objects.

Text-deixis renders a text that uses it uncopiable, a point clearly illustrated by our only extant copy of *MPD*: the poem, composed for and attached to a lost manuscript (to which it makes direct deictic reference) of the Old English translation of Gregory's work, was originally simply reproduced in a later copy, the Otho manuscript (originally, that is, before *wulfsige* in line 12 was altered to *wulfstan* in Otho) without any adaptation to its new environment, so that even before the modification of line 12 (which did not improve matters, as we saw earlier) the poem already misrepresented the true history of the copy it introduced. Here we see some evidence of the unguarded use of deictic terms by writers, probably because their use of deictic elements was still attuned to speech.

Two other poems—*The Metrical Preface to the Pastoral Care* and *Aldhelm*—exemplify a third type of deixis: work-deixis, unattested in either inscriptions or colophons. Unlike texts that use text-deixis, those using work-deixis may be reproduced without misrepresentation. Thus the first of these poems survives from the period in four manuscript versions, all of which constitute appropriate introductions to the Old English translation of Gregory's work. Another important feature of both *PCP* and *Aldhelm* is that by focusing attention on the literary work itself as a production, they introduce their writers as individual, historical persons in association with their works and so create embryonic conceptions of the author and authorship comparable with modern notions of these things. To this extent, these are works that in their own time pointed to the future rise of the author.

The general rarity with which Old English poets are identified by name in copies of their work is no doubt to be explained chiefly by reference to the circumstances of oral composition and recital: an oral poet would have had social opportunities to register his or her identity with an audience, and in any case, there could be no point in trying to attach one's name to a fleeting oral performance. The fact that the Anglian poet Cynewulf names himself indicates a desire on his part (for whatever reason) to associate his identity with his compositions as they were transmitted into the future. Prayers for his soul, rather than lasting fame as a vernacular poet, were probably what Cynewulf was hoping for here; but his signatures also suggest that he operated in a milieu affected by literacy, and even by inscriptions in particular. Although almost certainly trained as a poet in the traditional way, through the ear, Cynewulf must have been able to read, and could probably write as well. The runic passages he constructed, and the way they reveal his name, suggest that he composed with readers in mind, not listeners. As spellings of his name integrated into the very fabric of his verse, Cynewulf's signatures constitute a superimposition of one kind of writing on another—runic on roman writing. The inspiration for this imaginative technical innovation may have come partly from Latin acrostics; but inscriptions consisting of a single name (of owner or maker) on artifacts were probably a stronger influence on Cynewulf.[121] Again, as in the case of *Thureth* and *MPD*, the structural parallel suggests a perceived analogy, though in this case between the manufacture of a decorative or useful artifact and the composition of an edifying work of literature. In fact, all the texts discussed in this chapter seem, in their different ways, to suggest that artifacts, books, and literary works were regarded as products of an inseparable combination of art, craft, and piety.

The influence of a particular extant inscription on a particular manuscript text is, I argue, uniquely illustrated by the relationship between the Ruthwell Cross inscription and the Old English manuscript poem *The Dream of the Rood*. The Ruthwell text, though exceptional in several respects, is in others a typical medium-deictic inscription: the stone cross, to which the text's first-person pronouns point, constitutes a 'presence' which 'speaks' (in the now-familiar manner of Old English writings) directly to the reader. The impact of this very direct address, in which nothing stands between the reader and the cross, is considerably muted in *The Dream of the Rood*, where the reader is required to imagine a speaking cross experienced in a dream by a third party. The greater dramatic impact of the Ruthwell inscription does not make it the better poem; but it is preserved much earlier than the *Dream*, and fits so easily into a well-attested category of deictic inscriptions, composed specifically for carving on particular objects, that it would seem perverse to insist on (and much more difficult to argue for) the priority of the *Dream*, which stands alone as an example of the dream-vision genre in Old English verse. Several considerations combine to suggest that the *Dream*, like all the other texts considered in this chapter, owes a strong debt to the Anglo-Saxon epigraphic tradition.

---

[121] See above, Chapter 3, §3, category 5(e)-(i).

Chapter 5
Experiments in Literacy:
The Old English *Riddles*

This chapter is concerned mainly with the Old English *Riddles*, but also includes a consideration of the lyric poem *The Husband's Message* which is closely associated with the *Riddles* in the only manuscript that preserves them and shows certain formal connections with them. The *Riddles* are relevant to this study on several counts. First, many of them (as well as *The Husband's Message*, according to the majority view) consist of first-person utterances by non-human speakers, a feature that naturally invites comparison with many of the texts considered in the previous two chapters, especially the first-person medium-deictic inscriptions discussed in Chapter 3. Secondly, some of the *Riddles* use runes to spell the word or words that denote the solution, a device that might well be related, not only to the use of runes in inscriptions, but also to Cynewulf's use of runes in the four signatures examined in Chapter 4. The use of runes in *The Husband's Message* has (I shall argue) clear connections with their use in inscriptions. Finally, some of the *Riddles* describe the material paraphernalia of literacy and their uses in such a way as to provide revealing evidence of contemporary attitudes to the written word and its relationship to orality.

§1. The Old English *Riddles*

The Old English *Riddles* are preserved in the Exeter Book, a poetic anthology copied by a single hand of the second half of the tenth century.[1] There are between ninety-one and ninety-five *Riddles* in the manuscript, the total depending on editorial decisions about where some texts end and their successors begin. They are divided in the manuscript into two main sequences, *Riddles* 1–59 and

---

[1] A recent editor narrows the manuscript's date down to the period 965–975; see Bernard J. Muir, ed., *The Exeter Anthology of Old English Poetry: An Edition of Exeter Dean and Chapter MS 3501*, 2 vols. (Exeter: University of Exeter Press, 1994), 1: 1.

61–95.² A number of short poems of various kinds intervene between these two major blocks, among them two more *Riddles*: a second version of *Riddle* 30 usually designated 30b, immediately followed by *Riddle* 60. *The Husband's Message* immediately follows *Riddle* 60.³

Some of the Old English *Riddles* have proved difficult to solve, and new solutions are still being offered for many of them, even for some long regarded as satisfactorily solved. These uncertainties do not, however, prevent us from making some generalizations about the genre the Old English *Riddles* represent. A riddle presents itself to the reader as a challenge; and although the solver is never in doubt about what is required (sometimes an explicit challenge to name the solution is included at the end of the poem), the mental operations involved are quite varied. The account I give below of processes and effects is meant to offer a representative sample of the kind of thinking which the *Riddles* reflect on the part of their composers and demand from the solver. This account is intended to prepare the way for the more detailed discussion that follows of those *Riddles* that seem, for one reason or another, to provide evidence of Anglo-Saxon reflections on literacy and its relation to orality.

A riddle typically provides the would-be solver with a narrative description of the solution. The description may be concerned with the solution's origins, activities, appearance, or function, in any combination. The solution itself can be human, animal, vegetable, artifact, or immaterial phenomenon. Often it is something of which there are many individual examples in the world, as for example in the case of *Riddle* 34 (Williamson 33), 'Rake', quoted below. Only occasionally is the solution something unique, represented in the world by only a single instance. *Riddle* 6 (Williamson 4), 'Sun', is an obvious example of this last type; another is the relatively famous *Riddle* 46 (Williamson 44), 'Lot and his Family'. Sometimes the solution is generic in the sense that, for example, the solution to *Riddle* 65 (Williamson 63), 'Onion', is not an individual specimen but the vegetable as a species:

---

² Fols. 101^r-115^r and 124^v-130^v respectively. I follow the numeration of the Old English *Riddles* in *The Exeter Book*, ed. Krapp and Dobbie, because this edition still represents the textual divisions most familiar to scholars; but when referring to individual texts I add in brackets the numbering in Craig Williamson, ed., *The Old English Riddles of the Exeter Book* (Chapel Hill: University of North Carolina Press, 1977), which sometimes reflects a more convincing identification of textual divisions.

³ Anne L. Klinck, *The Old English Elegies: A Critical Edition and Genre Study* (Montreal and Kingston: McGill-Queen's University Press, 1992), 26, explains this sequence as arising from a misunderstanding by the compiler of the manuscript: "Since the subjects of *Riddle* 30 and *60* are both objects made of wood, and *The Husband's Message* features a rune-stave, the compiler must have thought he was putting together a series of tree-riddles at this point."

5. Experiments in Literacy: The Old English Riddles

      Cwico wæs ic, ne cwæð ic wiht,   cwele ic efne seþeah.
      Ær ic wæs, eft ic cwom.   Æghwa mec reafað,
      hafað mec on headre   ond min heafod scireþ,
      biteð mec on bær lic,   briceð mine wisan.
5   Monnan ic ne bite,   nymþe he me bite;
      sindan þara monige   þe mec bitað.
                          (*Riddle* 65 [Williamson 63], 'Onion')

"I was alive, I said nothing, but even so I die. I existed before, I shall return. Everyone despoils me, has me in confinement, and shears my head, bites me on the bare body, breaks my neck. I do not bite a man unless he bites me; many are those who bite me."

No one onion could possibly lay claim to this range of experiences.

The description of a riddle's solution is (for obvious reasons) never straightforward and is normally figurative, expressed in terms foreign to the solution's real nature as the riddler sees it. For example, in the 'Onion' *Riddle* 65 just quoted, a vegetable solution is described as if it were animate. In other *Riddles*, material artifacts may be described as if they were animate, e.g. *Riddle* 34 (Williamson 33), 'Rake', quoted below, or animal species as if they were human, e.g. *Riddle* 15 (Williamson 13), 'Fox', or possibly 'Badger'.[4] The solver needs to convert these presenting terms to an underlying, analogous set that they are designed to suggest. The riddler's linguistic technique is, of course, comparable with that of the allegorist.

The presenting image may be more or less developed. Sometimes it is conceived in such imaginative terms as almost to distract attention from the task of solving the riddle, as for example in the remarkably dramatic 'Inkhorn' *Riddle* 93 (Williamson 89), in which the artifact recalls its previous existence as an antler, riding on the head of a stag until it fell in the moult to be replaced by a new horn, and its carving into a new shape for human use:[5]

                       . . .
      hwilum stealc hliþo   stigan sceolde
10   up in eþel,   hwilum eft gewat
      in deop dalu   duguþe secan
      strong on stæpe,   stanwongas grof
      hrimighearde,   hwilum hara scoc
      forst of feaxe.   Ic on fusum rad
15   oþþæt him þone gleawstol   gingra broþor
      min agnade   ond mec of earde adraf.

---

    [4] Other species of animal have been suggested as the solution to this *Riddle*; see Williamson, *The Old English Riddles*, 173–75.
    [5] The text is somewhat damaged in the manuscript, hence the lacunæ at beginning and end.

>   Siþþan mec isern   innanweardne
>   brun bennade;   blod ut ne com,
>   heolfor of hreþre,   þeah mec heard bite
> 20   stiðecg style.   No ic þa stunde bemearn,
>   ne for wunde weop,   ne wrecan meahte
>   on wigan feore   wonnsceaft mine,
>   ac ic aglæca   ealle þolige,
>   þæt [..]e bord biton.   Nu ic blace swelge
> 25   wuda ond wætre, . . .   (Riddle 93 [Williamson 89], 'Inkhorn')

> ". . . Sometimes he [*sc.* the stag] had to mount the steep slopes up to his domain, sometimes descend again into the deep valleys to seek his followers, strong in step, he dug through the stony pastures when they were hard with frost, sometimes shook the grey frost from his hair. I rode on the hastening one until my younger brother possessed the glee-stool and drove me from my dwelling-place. Later the shining iron wounded me within. No blood came forth, no gore from my breast, even though the strong, sharp-edged steel bit me. I did not mourn that time nor weep for my wound, nor might I avenge my misery on the life of the warrior, but I rather suffer pain, wretch that I am, from all those who bit the shield. Now I swallow black wood and water . . ."

But however elaborate the presenting image may be, it must obviously be unrecognizable as a known type of person, creature, or thing if the reader is to be provoked into the mental operations required to solve the mystery. Elements of unreality, monstrosity, or paradox are deliberately incorporated to encourage us to reject the presenting image and search for the consistent image of the reality underlying it. Thus in the 'Onion' *Riddle* quoted earlier, the apparent immortality of the onion is obviously inconsistent with the statement that it dies; the inconsistency is resolved when these figurative images are decoded to reveal a vegetable solution which may be consumed as an individual but naturally reproduces itself as a species. The way in which the preparation of the onion for the table and its consumption are run together as a sequence of attacks on its life mounted by "everyone" projects an image of a creature subjected to universal persecution which clearly does not correspond with any known reality: only allegorical interpretation will make sense of these images. Similarly, in the 'Inkhorn' *Riddle* just quoted, the paradox of the bloodless wounds suffered by the speaker points to something inanimate, an object with no capacity for independent action, let alone revenge, against its human shaper.

    A distinctive psychological effect of riddles is to disrupt the system of conventional categories we have devised to impose order on the external world. A riddle substitutes new, *ad hoc* classifications which makes it possible, for example, to describe a rake as if it were a rooting animal such as a pig:

> Ic wiht geseah   in wera burgum,
> seo þæt feoh fedeð.   Hafað fela toþa;
> nebb biþ hyre æt nytte,   niþerweard gongeð,
> hiþeð holdlice   ond to ham tyhð,
> 5 wæþeð geond weallas,   wyrte seceð;
> aa heo þa findeð,   þa þe fæst ne biþ;
> læteð hio þa wlitigan,   wyrtum fæste,
> still stondan   on staþolwonge,
> beorhte blican,   blowan ond growan.
>   (*Riddle* 34 [Williamson 33], 'Rake')

"I saw a creature in the settlements of men which fed the herd. It has many teeth; its nose is useful as it turns down, plunders gently and proceeds home, hunts by walls, seeks plants; always it finds them when they are not firmly fixed. The comely ones it lets stand quietly, firm in their roots in the field they grow in, shine brightly, bloom and grow."

An anthropological-structuralist analysis of the Old English *Riddles* has emphasised this basic manoeuvre as a deliberate subversion of conventional categories, designed to reveal their arbitrariness: a riddle-collection, the argument runs, has a cumulative effect, bringing home to us that "all the world's a riddle and all our classifications merely unconfirmed solutions."[6] There is certainly some truth in this, though it seems doubtful if the metaphysical implications of riddles are quite so profound. Novel methods of classification need not invalidate or even pose a challenge to the traditional order; they merely draw attention to the possibility of different perspectives on the world. The 'rake' riddle encourages us, not to reclassify rakes and pigs under a new heading ('dentates'), or even to question the validity of our classifications of the rake as an agricultural tool and the pig as an agricultural animal, but to admire the ingenuity of the poet who contrives to hide (but not totally obscure) the identity of the rake under a linguistic and conceptual camouflage woven from animal terms alien to its actual nature. Riddles play games with ideas and with the figurative possibilities offered by language, partly for our mystification but chiefly for our entertainment.

---

[6] Nigel Barley, "Structural Aspects of the Anglo-Saxon Riddle," *Semiotica* 10 (1974): 143–75 (at 144). For a stimulating and accessible analysis of the *Riddles* generally from this standpoint, see Elaine Tuttle Hansen, *The Solomon Complex*, McMaster Old English Studies and Texts 5 (Toronto: University of Toronto Press, 1988), 126–43.

§2. Speaker or observer? Two forms of *Riddle*

It was mentioned earlier that the Old English *Riddles* are divided in the Exeter Book into two main sequences. It has not, so far as I know, been noticed before that the texts as ordered in the manuscript are divisible into three fairly distinct sequences according to whether the solution speaks from within the narrative and refers to itself in the first person (such narrators are classified as 'homodiegetic' in terms of narratological theory), or whether the solution is described by an external ('heterodiegetic') narrator.[7] The fact that the division between the second and third blocks corresponds with the scribal division between the two main groups in the manuscript indicates that this formal criterion has some significance for the textual history of the Exeter Book *Riddles*. The three sequences may be defined as follows:

1. *Riddles* 1–27 (Williamson 1–25), all with homodiegetic speakers except two, 13 and 22 (Williamson 11 and 20). A third, 19 (Williamson 17), is an amalgamation of two forms, beginning with a heterodiegetic narrator but terminating with the homodiegetic utterance: *Saga hwæt ic hatte*, "Say what I am called."[8]

2. *Riddles* 28–59 (Williamson 26–57), all of which are narrated heterodiegetically except three: 30, 35, 40 (Williamson 28, 33, 38). *Riddle* 59, the last of this group, is also the last of the first block of *Riddles* in the manuscript.

3. *Riddles* 60–95 (Williamson 58–91), a mixed group in which the homodiegetic form preponderates (twenty-three instances, or twenty-two in Williamson's division of the texts, compared with twelve clear heterodiegetic exceptions in 64, 67, 68, 69, 70, 75, 76, 82, 84, 87, 89, and 90 [ten in Williamson's edition: 62, 65, 66, 67, 73, 78, 80, 83, 85, and 86]). One, 94 (Williamson 90), is uncertain, and a second, 86 (Williamson 82) begins, like 19

---

[7] See Gérard Genette, *Narrative Discourse: An Essay in Method*, trans. Jane E. Lewin, intro. Jonathan Culler (Oxford: Blackwell, 1980), 244–45. There is a difficulty of definition and nomenclature here. The distinction between the two types cannot, unfortunately, be made by calling one 'first-person' and the other 'third-person', because in riddles narrated heterodiegetically the first-person pronoun is often used with reference to the observer-narrator, as in the first line of *Riddle* 34 (Williamson 33), 'Rake', quoted above; but on the other hand, it is questionable if all the *Riddles* I define here as heterodiegetic are properly so labelled because their narrators sometimes present themselves as occupying the same world as the riddle-objects they describe (for example, in those that begin with "I saw . . ." or some similar formula). I shall use 'homodiegetic' and 'heterodiegetic' as terms here simply for the sake of convenience. The basic distinction between the two types is, at least, reasonably clear-cut in practice.

[8] On *Riddle* 19, see further below.

under 1 above, with a heterodiegetic narrator but terminates with the homodiegetic imperative: *Saga hwæt ic hatte.*

It would thus appear that at some stage (not necessarily the latest) in the transmission of the first major sequence of *Riddles* (*Riddles* 1–59; Williamson 1–57) in the Exeter Book, either an Anglo-Saxon editor has attempted to organize the texts of his exemplar according to this formal criterion, or two collections which already differed in this regard have been placed in sequence. In either case, it seems clear that some awareness existed in the period of a formal distinction between the two types.

They differ in effect. Heterodiegetic narrators normally adopt the perspective of an inexperienced or alien observer who views the solution with a naive and uncomprehending eye. The 'Rake' *Riddle* 34, quoted earlier, is an example: we are invited to contemplate a mundane artifact through the consistently distorted perception of a narrator who appears (from one perspective) to have a very limited grasp of the way the world is organized. Homodiegetic riddles, on the other hand, are expressed from an internal, subjective point of view related to the speaker's own individual (or generic) nature: we are shown how such an object or creature might describe itself were it capable of description. This interior perspective gives the homodiegetic *Riddles* an extra dramatic dimension: the 'voice' adds a level of imaginative ingenuity and coherence to our picture of the solution. The relationship between the solution and the character of this individual 'voice' is sometimes based on natural analogies between the solution and its closest human counterpart, as when, for example, a weapon or item of war-gear is personified as a warrior.[9] Such links, once they have been repeated in several *Riddles*, acquire the value of conventions contributing to the solver's sense of the sort of parallels he may expect to find between the presenting image and the true nature of the solution. The speaker of *Riddle* 5 (Williamson 3), 'Shield', exemplifies this method particularly well:

```
     Ic eom anhaga      iserne wund,
     bille gebennad,    beadoweorca sæd,
     ecgum werig.       Oft ic wig seo,
     frecne feohtan.    Frofre ne wene,
5    þæt me geoc cyme   guðgewinnes,
     ær ic mid ældum    eal forwurðe,
     ac mec hnossiað    homera lafe,
     heardecg heorosccarp,   hondweorc smiþa,
     bitað in burgum;   ic abidan sceal
10   laþran gemotes.    Næfre læcecynn
```

---

[9] On heroic convention in the *Riddles*, see Eric Gerald Stanley, "Heroic Aspects of the Exeter Book Riddles," in *Prosody and Poetics in the Early Middle Ages: Essays in Honour of C. B. Hieatt*, ed. M. J. Toswell (Toronto: University of Toronto Press, 1995), 197–218.

> on folcstede   findan meahte,
> þara þe mid wyrtum   wunde gehælde,
> ac me ecga dolg   eacen weorðað
> þurh deaðslege   dagum ond nihtum.
>
> (*Riddle* 5 [Williamson 3], 'Shield')

"I am a solitary, wounded by iron, injured by the sword, tired of battle-work, weary of swords. Often I see battle, fierce fighting. I know no consolation, that relief from battle-struggle should come to me, before I utterly perish among men, but the legacies of hammers buffet me, hard-edged and fearfully sharp, the handiwork of smiths, bite me in the fortresses; I must await a more hateful encounter. Never might I find the kind of doctor on the battlefield who could heal my wounds with herbs, but wounds from swords increase on me through mortal strokes day and night."

Here the presenting image of a warrior badly hurt but still fighting on is vivid and largely consistent in its own terms, though the fact that the speaker seems extraordinarily passive and resilient, capable of sustaining wounds indefinitely, points the solver towards some material object wielded by human beings as the solution to the puzzle.[10] A similar motif of a warrior unable to avenge the wounds he suffers appears in *Riddle* 93, 'Inkhorn', quoted earlier.

§3. The homodiegetic *Riddles*

So far as the homodiegetic *Riddles* in particular are concerned, the solver is expected to accede to one of the implications of the oral model of linguistic communication defined in Chapter 2 as the 'canonical situation of utterance': a speech presupposes a speaker. The solver hears (or reads) the words of a disembodied voice (properly, of course, an unembodied voice, because the voice of a homodiegetic riddle with a non-human solution was never embodied in the first place; the voice is a kind of forgery) and is challenged to discern the distinctive imprint of a speaker's form in its utterance. The game, which is essentially an oral game to the extent that no one would imagine that the speakers of such riddles were expressing themselves in writing,[11] requires an understanding that the 'speaker'

---

[10] The idea that the real solution to *Riddle* 5 is not 'Shield' but 'Chopping board', a humble item of kitchen equipment, has been revived recently; see Jennifer Neville, "Joyous Play and Bitter Tears: The *Riddles* and the Elegies," in *Beowulf and Other Stories: A New Introduction to Old English, Old Icelandic and Anglo-Norman Literatures*, ed. Richard North and Joe Allard (Harlow: Pearson Education, 2007), 130–59 (at 131–33).

[11] For an exception to this generalization, see my discussion below of *Riddle* 60 (Williamson 58), 'Reed-pen'.

is not so much absent as hidden from the solver. Superficially, the speech is a speech like any other; but the reader knows that he must regard it, not as an ordinary communication, but as a thoroughly artificial utterance seeded with clues to the speaker's nature.

The homodiegetic Old English *Riddles* occupy an uncertain position in relation to the kinds of first-person literary forms that we have been chiefly concerned with so far in this book. If we attempt to place them in relation to the transfer of the linguistic subject from human speaker to inscribed medium that was illustrated in Chapter 2 and dealt with more extensively in Chapter 3, they seem to exhibit a combination of reactionary, stable, and progressive aspects. The reactionary element resides in their elimination of the 'speaking' medium, in which respect they appear to restore the old, pre-literate conception of an utterance as something issuing directly (i.e. vocally) from a speaker. The element of stability, which effectively undermines the basis of the reactionary element, is constituted by the implication that non-human subjects may be admitted into the essentially human world of language-use. I label this element 'stable' because, as we have seen, this is also an implication of the medium-deictic first-person inscriptions dealt with in Chapter 3. On the other hand, this stability is in its turn subverted by new factors constituting the progressive element of the *Riddles*. One of these factors is connected with their obviously playful purpose: the idea that non-human objects, animals, and phenomena can use language is only a pretence, one of the rules of the game that the reader is invited to play. The sense of genuinely impersonal utterance that we may observe in the medium-deictic first-person inscriptions is absent from the *Riddles* because of our awareness of this. The second factor has more important implications for the development of literate consciousness which all the texts explored in this book are intended to illustrate: the 'hidden' utterers of the homodiegetic *Riddles*, whom the solver is expected to unveil, are in some respects analogous with human first-person narrators of written literature, who are characteristically absent when their writings are received. The riddle-solver's work in constructing an identity on the basis of the solution's words is comparable (as we shall see in Chapter 6) with the work a reader has to do to identify and place the human subject of a written text on the basis of a deictic, nameless 'I' or 'me'.

In speaking of reactionary, stable, and progressive features, I do not mean to imply that the Old English *Riddles* represent a definite stage in an orderly sequence of historical developments affecting the linguistic subject; only that their formal character, combined with their pragmatics, make them fit happily into the structural context of early literacy. In Anglo-Latin verse, the riddle genre flourished in the late seventh century and the first half of the eighth in Anglo-Saxon England, which was also the earliest period of English roman literacy. The surviving collections are the work of named authors: Aldhelm, who produced a hundred riddles and died in 709 A.D. or thereabouts; Tatwine, identified with the cleric of that name who became archbishop of Canterbury in 731, responsible for forty riddles; Eusebius, perhaps a *nom de plume* of Hwætberht, abbot of Wearmouth from 716 to 747, who added to Tatwine's collection to bring the number of riddles up to one hundred; and Boniface, martyred in 754, to whom twenty riddles are attributed.[12] These various collections of Anglo-Latin riddles are found assembled in a single eleventh-century manuscript, Cambridge, University Library, MS. Gg.5.35, in a context suggesting that they may have been used for educational purposes.[13] Some of the Old English *Riddles* have long been regarded as translations or adaptations of extant Latin riddles,[14] though it has recently been suggested that some of the Anglo-Latin riddles may be based on sources among the Old English *Riddles*.[15] The Anglo-Latin riddles are preponderantly homodiegetic (Aldhelm's are all of this type); and part of their function might have been to acclimatize newly literate readers to the absence of the first-person utterer which written texts inevitably involve. The lesson (according to this perspective) that homodiegetic riddles teach is that in the new world of literacy, words, and words alone, must do all the work previously done by self-declared identity, appearance, gesture, and circumstance if the reader is to know his writer as well as the hearer knows his speaker. If the riddle is solved, the potential of

---

[12] See Fr. Glorie, ed., *Collectiones Aenigmatum Merovingicae Aetatis*, Corpus Christianorum, Series Latina, 133 and 133A (Turnhout: Brepols, 1968), vol. 133 containing the riddles of Tatwine, Eusebius, and Aldhelm (165–208, 209–71, and 359–540 respectively), vol. 133A those of Symphosius (611–723). For Aldhelm's riddles, see also *Aldhelm: The Poetic Works*, trans. Lapidge and Rosier, 61–69 and 242–47. Manuscripts are listed in Nancy Porter Stork, *Through a Gloss Darkly: Aldhelm's Riddles in the British Library MS Royal 12.C.xxiii* (Toronto: PIMS, 1990), 25–26.

[13] See Patrizia Lendinara, "The World of Anglo-Saxon Learning," in *The Cambridge Companion to Old English Literature*, ed. Malcolm Godden and Michael Lapidge (Cambridge: Cambridge University Press, 1991), 264–81, at 275–77. The same manuscript also includes the collection of one hundred three-line hexameter riddles in Latin attributed to Symphosius, several of which have been identified as possible sources of some of the Old English *Riddles*. See further below, n. 14.

[14] English translations of all the most convincing Latin sources (or analogues) for the Old English *Riddles* are available in Michael J. B. Allen and Daniel G. Calder, *Sources and Analogues of Old English Poetry: The Major Latin Texts in Translation* (Cambridge: Brewer, 1976), 162–74. For a recent discussion of Anglo-Saxon riddles in both Old English and Latin, see Andy Orchard, "Enigma Variations: The Anglo-Saxon Riddle-Tradition," in *Latin Learning and English Lore: Studies in Anglo-Saxon Literature for Michael Lapidge*, ed. Katherine O'Brien O'Keeffe and idem (Toronto: University of Toronto Press, 2005), 284–304.

[15] See Fell, "Runes and Riddles in Anglo-Saxon England," in *'Lastworda Betst'*, ed. Hough and Lowe, 264–77 (at 267). Appeal to the comparative evidence of the other early Germanic poetic corpora in Old Icelandic, Old High German, Old Frisian, Old Saxon, and Gothic reveals nothing to indicate a very widespread tradition of riddling in early Germanic oral culture, though riddles were clearly part of native tradition in medieval Scandinavia.

the written word to convey the identity of missing speakers is satisfactorily demonstrated; and conversely, failure to achieve the solution would draw attention to the possibility of communicative failure in writing—the ever-present threat of the 'deictic gap' that haunts the written word.

§4. The runic *Riddles*

Whatever generic or genetic relationships may exist between the Old English *Riddles* and the Anglo-Latin riddles, some of the texts of the vernacular group show a very clear link with the native runic epigraphic tradition that constitutes the earliest identifiable stage of Anglo-Saxon literate culture: there are six *Riddles* (75, 19, 63, 24, 58, and 42) that incorporate runic letters that the solver has to put in the right order to spell the name of the solution.[16] The exploitation of runic script in manuscript literature written largely in the roman alphabet represents a combined utilisation of the two orthographies available in the period of early literacy in England that is obviously of interest here. Below I shall consider the various ways that runes function in the runic *Riddles* as part of the puzzle presented to solvers, and measure the success achieved by the poets in integrating runic characters and their names into their texts. This last operation will form the basis of an assessment of the runic *Riddles* as attempts to incorporate runic characters, which belong firmly in the realm of written linguistic expression, into the originally and essentially oral verse-form of alliterative poetry.

The six runic *Riddles* exemplify a number of different procedures in their use of runes. The simplest is to present the letters of the name of the solution in reverse order. It has been noticed that the scribe of the Exeter Book always encloses in single points runic groups that are intended to be taken together to make the letters of words.[17] *Riddle* 75 (Williamson 73), a one-line text with four runes appended,[18] is clearly of this type. The text reads:

---

[16] I exclude from consideration here six instances, some less certain than others, of isolated runes written in the margins of the Exeter Book in association with *Riddles* 5, 6, 7 or 8, 12, 16 or 17, and 64 (Williamson 3, 4, 5 or 6, 10, 14 or 15, and 62). Williamson, who provides facsimiles of these runes in his edition (52–59), doubts if any of them (with the possible exception of the *s*-rune in association with *Riddle* 5 [Williamson 3]) is the work of the main scribe of the manuscript.

[17] See *The Exeter Book*, ed. Krapp and Dobbie, xxiii.

[18] It is possible that the extrametrical runic group is a scribal addition to the one-line text; but on the other hand, the text itself is very uninformative and would probably have been found impenetrable but for the runes.

Ic swiftne geseah   on swaþe feran
.D N L H.   (*Riddle* 75 [Williamson 73])[19]

"I saw a swift creature travelling on its way."[20]

No one doubts that in this *Riddle* the solution is spelt out when the runes are read backwards; indeed, there are parallels to the spelling of words in runes from right to left among the hard-surface inscriptions that survive from the Anglo-Saxon period);[21] but reverse-reading gives (in roman orthography) the non-word 'hlnd'. There is no consensus of opinion about what word this obscure sequence of letters is meant to indicate, though it has been suggested that the scribe's *l*-rune may be an error for the *u*-rune which it somewhat resembles formally, because with this emendation the runic sequence read backwards gives *hund*, 'dog', to which the description of a swiftly travelling creature might well apply. Alternative solutions, though somewhat less convincing because they do not match the one-line description as well as *hund* does, do not require any emendation of the text, though they do involve the assumption that the poet employs runes in a special, cryptic way to indicate the spelling of the solution. Thus Williamson, taking the runic characters as they stand and reading them backwards, derives from them the word *hland*, 'urine', assuming that the *a* was deliberately omitted according to a system of cryptic vowel-deletion.[22] Mackie, also assuming that the poet is using vowel-deletion, reads the runes as *Hælend*, 'Saviour',[23] though it seems to me that both these interpretations place considerable strain on the one-line text

---

[19] Williamson combines *Riddle* 75 with *Riddle* 76, also a single-line text (*Ic ane geseah idese sittan*, "I saw a woman sitting alone") and treats them as one.

[20] Translation from Page, *Introduction to English Runes*, 190.

[21] See Page, *Introduction*, 41: "At first there was no recognised direction of writing. An inscription, and so its letter forms, could run from left to right or right to left, and some inscriptions mix the two." Left to right is, however, the commoner direction.

[22] Williamson, *Riddles*, 252–55. *Riddle* 36 contains a line, almost certainly interpolated into the original text, which uses vowel-substitution (not vowel-omission, as possibly in *Riddle* 75) to indicate the solution (or what the interpolator thought was the solution) to the riddle. The line reads (in Krapp and Dobbie's text) *monn.h.w.M.wiif.m.x.l.kf wf.hors.qxxs.* which has been decoded to *monn homo, wiif mulier, hors equus*, "man, woman, horse," each part of the solution represented by the English and Latin word for it, and the Latin word concealed by the vowel-substitution code, according to which, as Williamson (*Riddles*, 248) explains, "consonants *b, f, k, p* and *x* are substituted for their respective preceding vowels—*a, e, i, o* and *u*." There can be little doubt that this is the correct interpretation of the code, though the passage seems to have suffered somewhat in transmission; for example, instead of *p* for the first *o* of *homo*, *w* (i.e. *wynn*) appears; and the *f* that stands for the *e* of *equus* is misplaced.

[23] W. S. Mackie, "Notes on the Text of the 'Exeter Book'," *MLR* 28 (1933): 75–78 (at 77).

of the riddle which describes, in Williamson's view, an act of male urination, and in Mackie's, "Christ as a hunter in pursuit of sin." Both solutions exemplify a tendency in riddle-criticism to prefer difficult to simple solutions—an understandable tendency in a way, because difficult and ingenious solutions reflect well on the poem and its author (as well, of course, as on the critic).

The runic riddles in the Exeter Book vary considerably in the degree of metrical integration of the names of the runic letters in the text. From this point of view, *Riddle* 75 is not a success: the runic sequence is simply extra-metrical, because the non-runic, descriptive line is metrically complete, and the 'line' that results from reading of the runes by their names—*dæg nyd lagu* (or *ur*) *hægl*—neither scans as a pair of half-lines of attested metrical type, nor provides any alliteration.[24] In spite of the way *Riddle* 75 is presented by the editors, with the runic sequence as line 2, this is really a one-line text with a runic supplement. Other runic *Riddles* achieve a greater degree of metrical integration of the runic letters, as we shall see.

Riddle 19 is another poem that uses groups of runes to spell words backwards:

> Ic on siþe[25] seah   .SRO
> H. hygewloncne,   heafodbeorhtne,
> swiftne[26] ofer sælwong   swiþe þrægan.
> Hæfde him on hrycge   hildeþryþe
> 5 .NOM.   nægledne rad
> .AGEW.   Widlast ferede
> rynestrong on rade   rofne .CO
> FOAH.   For wæs þy beorhtre,
> swylcra siþfæt.   Saga hwæt ic hatte.   (*Riddle* 19 [Williamson 17])

"I saw a horse (*sroh* = *hors*) in motion, proud in spirit, bright of head, running quickly over the fertile plain. It had on its back a war-troop, a man (*nom* = *mon*). The warrior (*agew* = *wega* =[?] *wiga*) rode the nailed (?one). The wide track, strong in its course, carried on its journey a bold

---

[24] If it is assumed that the second and fourth rune-names in the sequence are subordinate metrically to the first and third, the results somewhat resemble certain rare verse-types attested in *Beowulf* that consist of two compounds in sequence, e.g. *Beowulf* 1719a *breosthord blodreow*, or 193a *nydwracu niþgrim* (Bliss's types 2A4(i) and 2A4(ii) respectively; see Alan Bliss, "The Scansion of *Beowulf*," ed. Peter J. Lucas, *Old English Newsletter*, Subsidia 22 [1995]: 30); but the double alliteration that is normal in *Beowulf* in verses of these types fails here.

[25] 1 *on siþe* is an editorial addition.

[26] 3 *swiftne*, MS *swistne*.

hawk (*cofoah* = *haofoc*). The course was the brighter, the journey of such as these. Say what I am called."[27]

Again, as in the case of *Riddle* 75, no one seems to doubt that here the runes represent the individual letters of words, and that each runic sequence is to be read backwards as a word, as indicated in my translation above. Once this principle of reading the runes from right to left to spell words is grasped, the words themselves are accessible to any Old English reader literate in runes. The only puzzle that arises as a result of following this procedure is 6 *wega*, which has runic *e* rather than the *i* we would expect if (as most assume) the intended word was *wiga*, 'warrior'. Copying error might, of course, have been involved here.

As for the answer to the riddle, some commentators have been content to conclude that *Riddle* 19's solution is sufficiently defined by the four nouns spelt backwards by the runic groups: 'horse', 'man', 'warrior', and 'hawk': the solution, some believe, is a warrior on horseback with a hawk on his hand. Critical dissatisfaction with this conclusion seems to be based, not on any doubts about the interpretation of the runes, but partly on a feeling that this solution is too easy to derive, and partly on a general expectation, here apparently disappointed, that the solution to any riddle will be an object, individual, or phenomenon, not the composite and apparently random image which these four nouns represent when taken together. The achievement of the mental image of a riding warrior must, it is felt, be only the first step in the chain of deduction that is required of the solver; allegorical interpretation of these images is necessary to reach the solution that the riddler had in mind. Thus Williamson suggests that the true solution to *Riddle* 19 is 'Ship'.[28] He compares the 'horse' spelt by the first runic group with Old English kennings for ships meaning 'sea-horse', for instance *merehengest* or *sæmearh*; he links the adjective *heafodbeorhtne* in 2 to the kind of ornamental figureheads that have survived from the period; he would connect 5 *nægledne*, 'nailed' (the place of which in the syntax is far from certain), with the *nægledcnearr* or 'nailed clinker' mentioned in *The Battle of Brunanburh* 53, and compares the nailed ship excavated at Sutton Hoo; and the hawk is the sail. This interpretation has been boosted by Griffiths, who noticed that the initial runes in each of the four sequences spell (when read forward) *snac*, a possible form of the Old English word for a speedy ship attested (in the plural forms *snacca* and *snaccum*) in eleventh-century annals in some manuscripts of the *Anglo-Saxon Chronicle*.[29] That

---

[27] My translation, especially of 5b-6a, is offered very tentatively. In the main, it follows Williamson's interpretation of the syntax and grammar of the poem (Williamson, *Riddles*, 186–92).

[28] Williamson's interpretation is accepted in the more recent edition of Hans Pinsker and Waltraud Ziegler, *Die altenglischen Rätsel des Exeterbuchs* (Heidelberg: Winter, 1985), 181.

[29] Mark Griffiths, "*Riddle* 19 of the Exeter Book: *snac*, an Old English Acronym," *Notes and Queries* 237, N.S. 39 (1992): 15–16. The word in question seems to occur in Old

two interpretations of the riddle based on independent evidence should converge in this way gives credibility to the 'Ship' solution, as Griffiths points out; but how much faith we place in 'Ship' depends ultimately on how testing we think Anglo-Saxon readers would have found the basic runic puzzle. It is difficult to judge how hard even relatively simple runic spelling games would have seemed to Anglo-Saxon readers; but the fact that such puzzles are set at all suggests that they were probably felt to represent a respectable challenge. It should be noted here that one of the Old English *Riddles* incorporates a retrograde spelling of its solution in roman: *Riddle* 23 (Williamson 21) begins: *Agof is min noma eft onhwyrfed*, which might be rendered "'wob' (*boga* = 'bow') is my name reversed." This is perhaps even more of a giveaway than the runic sequences in *Riddle* 19, though here there is a complication in the form *agof* instead of the *agob* we would expect, and it has been suggested that this extra obscurity might be deliberate.[30] At any rate,

---

English only in the plural inflected forms *snacca* and *snaccum*, the former in the C and D texts of the *Chronicle* annal for 1052 (see *Two of the Saxon Chronicles Parallel*, ed. Charles Plummer, 2 vols. [Oxford: Oxford University Press, 1892 and 1899; repr. 1952], 1: 178 and 179), the latter in the D and E texts of the annal for 1066 (1: 197). Both forms show retraction of Old English *æ* to *a* before back vowels in the following syllable, so that a nominative singular *snæc(c)* would have been a likely alternative to the analogical form *snac* that Griffiths reads in *Riddle* 19; see Campbell, *Old English Grammar*, §160, for comparable variations in words of similar phonological type.

[30] See Williamson, *Riddles*, 204–5. The problem is rather complex. Williamson argues, probably justifiably, against the ingenious suggestion of Wyatt (A. J. Wyatt, ed., *Old English Riddles* [Boston: Heath, 1912], 81) that the reverse-spelling *agof* instead of the form *agob* (which the reader must achieve if he is to reverse it and obtain the solution *boga*), is a deliberate attempt on the poet's part to make the solution more of a challenge. The Primitive OE voiced labial consonant [v] was written *b* in final position by Anglo-Saxon scribes before about 800 A.D.; thereafter, *f*, already used for the voiced labio-dental fricative that had arisen in prehistoric Old English from [f] between voiced sounds, was used as well for older [v], presumably indicating a convergence of the two originally distinct sounds (see Campbell, *Old English Grammar*, §§57[1], 398, 444; Stanley, "Heroic Aspects of the Exeter Book Riddles," 208). Wyatt, taking up Sievers' comments on the significance for the dating of the *Riddles* of *agof* for *agob* (Eduard Sievers, "Zu Cynewulf," *Anglia* 13 [1891]: 1–25, at 15), thought that the poet was working about 800, when *b* (as in *agob*) was still remembered as a spelling for final [v] but had been supplanted by *f* (*agof*) as the standard representation of this sound. The solver was thus required (a) to remember that words formed on the model of the poet's bogus word *agof* were once spelt *agob*, (b) substitute this 'older' spelling for *agof*, (c) reverse it to reveal *boga*; and (d) recognize the result as Old English for 'bow' (in which word *b* is the bilabial voiced plosive, not [v]). One of the main reasons for rejecting this reconstruction is that a post-800 reader would have no way of knowing that *agof* needed to be restored to the 'older' spelling *agob* (stage [b]) prior to the reversal of the letters (stage (c)), unless, of course, he read the remainder of the text and worked out what the solution was likely to be on the basis of its narrative. It is much easier to believe that, following what amount to the poet's instructions in 1, the

problems with solutions and with the poets' technique make it hard to decide if the runic *Riddles* are designed to test readers' knowledge of an old and recondite mode of writing, or if they are basically spelling games of the kind that modern crossword puzzles play.

Riddle 19 (quoted above) shows an imperfect integration of the names of its runes into the structure of the verses. In five of the six half-lines that contain runes (1b, 2a, 5a, 7b, 8a), the first rune of the series (the sole rune in the case of 2a) carries the alliteration. This arrangement is in accordance with the general rule in Old English poetry that the first stressed word of any half-line will alliterate: the runes, pronounced as their names, each represent a noun which is (by definition in metrical tradition) a stressed word. This system breaks down only in 6a: the headstave (i.e. the alliterating sound in the b-verse) is clearly the initial consonant of *Widlastas*, though in the a-verse, *w* is the last rune of the group, not the first. Nor is *Riddle* 19 successful in integrating the names of the runes into the metre of the half-lines in which they occur: problems of scansion similar to the one noted above in connection with the runic sequence in *Riddle* 75 become apparent when the runes are read as their names (in the nominative singular); only in verse 2a is the runic name satisfactorily integrated within the metrical structure of the verse.[31] Nevertheless, *Riddle* 19 marks a technical advance on *Riddle* 75 (considered earlier) in its attempt to integrate the runes into the text and its largely successful accommodation of the runes to the alliterative structure of the lines in which they appear.

If the most obvious solution to *Riddle* 19 has seemed, to modern critics at least, too easy, *Riddle* 64, in spite of the fact that a similar solution to *Riddle* 19

---

reader would have produced *foga* and be stumped by this non-word. Thus Williamson is probably right in thinking that *agof* is a substitution by a scribe who, oblivious to the fact that *agob* was a reversed spelling of *boga*, adjusted the spelling because *-of* finally seemed more in conformity with modern spelling practices than the relatively archaic *-ob*.

[31] In verse 1a the runes for the sequence *sro* become *sigel rad os*, which is metrically short of a syllable for a standard half-line (dissyllabic *sigel*, with short *i*, resolves to the metrical equivalent of a single long monosyllable); and the same problem is apparent in 5a *nyd os mon*. In 6a (*ac gifu eoh wynn*) and 8a (*feoh os ac hægl*), we are faced with the same problem as the rune-sequence appended to *Riddle* 75 presents: the sequence of four stressed long monosyllables gives no recognizable metrical contour (6a *gifu*, like 1a *sigel*, is subject to resolution), and there is no double alliteration. In 7b, a verse: *rofne cen os* might bear comparison with certain verses in *Beowulf* that terminate in compounds with secondary stress on the second element, e.g. 1522a *grædig guðleoð* or 690a *snellic særinc*, classified by Bliss as type 2A2(i) (see Bliss, "The Scansion of *Beowulf*," 28); but such verses always occur in the first half of the line in *Beowulf*, and double alliteration is invariable in them, neither of which conditions is fulfilled by *Riddle* 19.7b when the runes are given their names. In 2a, the verse reads as *hægl hygewloncne*, which is a regular verse of Bliss's type 1D2, with the double alliteration that is normal for this type in *Beowulf* (cf. *Beowulf* 2408a *hæft hygegiomor*, or 1847a *hild heorugrimme*; see Bliss, "Scansion," 23).

seems to be indicated, has been found too difficult. The text is given below, followed by a translation in which very little confidence can be placed:

>   Ic seah .W. ond .I.   ofer wong faran,
>   beran .B.E.;   bæm wæs on siþþe
>   hæbbendes hyht   .H. ond .A.
>   swylce þryþa dæl,   .Þ. ond .E.
> 5   Gefeah .F. ond .Æ.   fleah ofer .EA
>   S. ond .P.   sylfes þæs folces.   (*Riddle* 64 [Williamson 62]).

"I saw a horse (*wi* = *wicg*) going over the field carrying a warrior (*be* = *beorn*). For both of them on the journey the hawk (*ha* = *hafoc*) was the owner's joy, and also a thane (*þe* = *þegn*), part of the forces. The falcon (*fæ* = ?*fælca*) rejoiced, flew over the arrow (*ea* = ?*earwe*) and spear (*sp* = ?*spere*) of those people."

There seems to be general agreement about how the runes are meant to work in *Riddle* 64: each pair is to be interpreted as representing, in natural order, the first two sounds of a particular word. On the other hand, there is no general agreement (as the question-marks in my translation are intended to indicate) about which words in particular are meant, especially by the groups towards the end of the poem.[32] Williamson solves *Riddle* 64 as 'ship', again mainly on the basis of figurative expressions in Old English which describe ships and their equipment in terms of horses, birds, and so on,[33] and identifies the poem as "a companion piece" to *Riddle* 19; but again, although the 'ship' solution seems possible, the case for it can scarcely be regarded as absolutely compelling because it requires faith in the associative force of standard poetic kennings for ships and their equipment.[34]

Metrical integration is more successful here than in either of the two other runic *Riddles* considered earlier. The names of the runes fit in with the alliterative requirements of the lines in which they occur: runes appear in all six lines of the text, and in the five places where there is a pair of runes, the first rune of the pair carries the alliteration, in accordance with the rule (stated above in connection

---

[32] It is uncertain whether the rune in 5b, *ea* in roman transliteration, is to be taken on its own (e.g. as *earh*, 'arrow'), or in combination with the pair of runes that follows in 6a; see Williamson, *Riddles*, 329–30; Frederick Tupper, Jr., ed., *The Riddles of the Exeter Book* (Boston: Ginn and Company, 1910; repr. Darmstadt: Wissenschaftliche Buchgesellschaft, 1968), 206.

[33] Williamson, *Riddles*, 325. Pinsker and Ziegler, *Die altenglischen Rätsel*, 290, agree with this solution, though they differ (105) over the detailed interpretation of the runic groups in the final two lines of the text.

[34] Jackson J. Campbell's review of Williamson's edition (*MP* 77 [1979–1980]: 315–17, at 316) casts doubt on Williamson's 'Ship' solution to *Riddles* 19 and 64 (Williamson 17 and 62).

with *Riddle* 19) that the first stressed element of a half-line should alliterate. In 5b there is only one rune, and it does not alliterate, though this is simply because the alliterative requirement of the half-line in question has already been fulfilled by the finite verb *fleah*. On the other hand, the rune-names make good metre only in three (at most) out of seven cases (1a, 5a, 5b).[35] A general pattern is emerging in the runic *Riddles*: the runes' names are often well integrated into the standard alliterative pattern of the Old English half-line; but full metrical integration was clearly more difficult to achieve.

A more straightforward type of runic puzzle is represented by *Riddle* 24, 'Jay', in which the name of the solution is concealed in a runic anagram. This is the only runic *Riddle* in which the narrator is homodiegetic. It begins with the solution's account of its ability to vary its voice (1 *Ic... wræsne mine stefne*) in imitation of a variety of animals and birds: dog, goat, goose, hawk, eagle, kite, and seamew (otherwise known today as the 'common gull'). The puzzle concludes:

```
                .G.³⁶ mec nemnað,
    swylce .Æ. ond .R.      O. fullesteð,
    .H. ond .I.      Nu ic haten eom
10  swa þa siex stafas    sweotule becnaþ.
                        (Riddle 24 [Williamson 22], 7b-10))
```

"G (*gifu*) names me, as also do Æ (*æsc*) and R (*rad*); O (*os*) helps, H (*hægl*) and I (*is*). Now these six letters clearly signify what I am called."

There is unanimous agreement among critics about how the runes are to be read in *Riddle* 24 and what the solution must be: taken together, the runes spell *higoræ*, the name of one of the corvidae family of birds, possibly the magpie but more probably the jay, famous for its powers of mimicry.[37] The final sentence of the text implies nothing about the order in which the letters of the solution-name are given, though in fact it turns out that while the two sequences *ÆRO* and *HI* are both in 'natural' order, the groups themselves need to be transposed in reconstructing the name of the solution.

In the hierarchy of skill and sophistication which is beginning to emerge from my account of the Old English runic riddles, *Riddle* 24 stands higher than *Riddles* 75, 19, and 64, partly because of the more satisfying (and solvable) ana-

---

[35] Verses 1a (*Ic seah wynn ond is*) and 5a (*Gefeah feoh ond æsc*) are both normal verses of type 2B1b (see Bliss, "Scansion," 31). 5b *fleah ofer ear* also represents an attested type, though a very rare one in *Beowulf* (type 2B2-; see Bliss, "Scansion," 32); but 2a *beran beorc eoh*, 3b *hægl ond ac*, 4b *þorn ond eoh*, and 6a *sigel ond peorð* are all metrically 'short' verses.

[36] The scribe has written a capital roman *X* here instead of the formally similar *g*-rune, no doubt in error.

[37] On the question of the species, see Tupper, *Riddles*, 121–22, and Williamson, *Riddles*, 207–8. Pinsker and Ziegler, *Rätsel*, 198, prefer the jay (Häher).

grammatic puzzle it poses, and partly because of its largely successful metrical deployment of the runic letters: all the half-lines containing runes except 9a scan as well-attested metrical types, and alliteration is unfailing.[38]

Riddles 42 and 58 remain to be considered. In both, runic characters are represented in the text by their names written out in roman script rather than by the letters themselves. In *Riddle* 42 (on which see further below), the runes are an anagram of the solution. A slightly different technique is employed in *Riddle* 58, in which a heterodiegetic narrator describes a complicated mechanism made partly of metal and incorporating a container for liquids. The poem concludes:

>   Þry sind in naman
> ryhte runstafas,   þara is *Rad* foran.[39]
>   (*Riddle* 58 [Williamson 56], 14b-15)

"There are three true rune-letters in the name, of which *Rad* is at the front."

Here it seems pretty clear that the word *Rad* stands for the rune of that name (the *r*-rune), so that the solution ought to be a three-letter word beginning with *r*; but we are left to deduce what the other two letters might be on the basis of the object as described. There is no very obvious candidate for the word in question. Williamson thinks *rod*, 'rod', is the likeliest of the various suggestions that have been made. His own solution is 'well-sweep', an arrangement for lowering and raising a bucket into a well, and this certainly fits the description of the mechanism very well. The word *Rad* is satisfactorily integrated metrically, and supplies the alliteration for the b-verse in which it appears.

The other *Riddle* in which runic letters are represented not by the runes themselves but by their standard names written out in roman letters is the relatively well-known *Riddle* 42, 'Cock and Hen', quoted in its entirety below. It resembles *Riddle* 24, considered earlier, in presenting the reader with a runic anagram, but differs from it in its thoroughgoing integration of the runic names, with inflexions added where appropriate, into the grammar of the sentence in which they are included. In the text presented here, words denoting runes are italicized editorially:

---

[38] The runic verses scan as follows: 7b as 1A1a(i) (see Bliss, "Scansion," 18), 8a as 2B1b ("Scansion," 31), and 8b as 1D1 ("Scansion," 23). Verse 9a, *hægl ond is*, is metrically short. In 7b, *g* alliterates with *glado* in the a-verse; in 8, vocalic alliteration, carried by the runes for *æ* and *o*, links a-verse and b-verse; and in 9 alliteration is on the *h*-rune in the a-verse and *haten* in the b-verse.

[39] The manuscript reads *furum*; *foran* is Krapp and Dobbie's suggestion (*The Exeter Book*, 351, note).

	Ic seah wyhte	wrætlice twa
	undearnunga	ute plegan
	hæmedlaces;	hwitloc anfeng
	wlanc under wædum,	gif þæs weorces speow,[40]
5	fæmne fyllo.	Ic on flette mæg
	þurh runstafas	rincum secgan,
	þam þe bec witan,	bega ætsomne
	naman þara wihta.	Þær sceal *nyd* wesan
	twega oþer	ond se torhta *æsc*
10	an an linan,	*acas* twegen,
	hægelas swa some.	Hwylc[41] þæs[42] hordgates
	cægan cræfte	þa clamme onleac
	þe þa rædellan	wið rynemenn
	hygefæste heold	heortan bewrigene
15	orþoncbendum?	Nu is undyrne
	werum æt wine	hu þa wihte mid us,
	heanmode twa,	hatne sindon. (*Riddle* 42 [Williamson 40])

"I saw two wondrous creatures openly enjoying sexual intercourse out of doors. The fair-haired woman, exultant beneath her dress, was impregnated if that work succeeded. I am able to tell warriors in the hall by means of runic letters, those who know books, the names of both these creatures together. *Nyd* ('affliction', or 'need') must be there, one of two, and the bright *æsc* ('ash'), one in the line, two *acas* ('oaks'), likewise *hæglas* ('hails'). Which one has unlocked by the power of the key the fetters of the treasure-door that kept the riddle safe in the mind against runemen, its heart concealed by ingenious bonds? Now is revealed to men at wine how these creatures, the two base-hearted ones, are called amongst us."

The runic passage indicates that the solution contains *n* twice, *æ* once, and both *a* and *h* twice, giving *hana*, 'cock', and *hæn*, 'hen' as the mating pair described in the

---

[40] 4 *speow*, MS *speop*.

[41] Williamson, *Riddles*, 277, note to line 11, dissatisfied with interpretations of the manuscript's *hwylc* as a relative or interrogative ("Which"), replaces it with *Swa ic* ("Thus I . . ."; see further below). Krapp and Dobbie (*The Exeter Book*, 346) translate *hwylc* as "Which riddler," but add: "that is, 'who has solved the riddle'," from which one must assume that they really mean "Which solver." See also Pinsker and Ziegler, *Rätsel*, 255. Williamson's emendation gives the whole sentence to the poet: his translation begins: "Thus I have unlocked . . ."; but this seems to me most unsatisfactory: the poet locks up, rather than 'unlocks', his riddle; if anyone unlocks it, it will be the solver, as Lerer's translation (*Literacy and Power*, 116), like my own, implies. See also Roberta J. Dewa, "The Runic Riddles of the Exeter Book: Language Games and Anglo-Saxon Scholarship," *Nottingham Medieval Studies* 39 (1995): 26–36 (at 28), who retains *Hwylc* (as interrogative "Who").

[42] 11 *þæs*, MS *wæs*.

first five lines. All of the runic names are satisfactorily integrated into the metrical and alliterative structure of the verses in which they appear,[43] making *Riddle* 42 perhaps the most technically accomplished of the Old English runic riddles.

But why did the poet give the names of the runes rather than the runes themselves? The answer becomes fairly obvious if we attempt to replace the names with the runes they denote. No problems arise in 8b and 9b, in each of which a single rune appears; but in 10b and 11a, all manner of metrical irregularities result if a pair of runes are substituted for the grammaticalized plural names *acas* and *hæglas*.[44] We can therefore be certain that the representation of the runes by their names rather than by the letters themselves is an original feature of the poem, not a scribal imposition during its subsequent transmission.

In my discussion of the runic *Riddles* I have tried, not altogether successfully, to make questions connected with their solutions secondary to more technical matters: the way in which the runes work as clues to the solution, and the level of their metrical integration when they are pronounced as their names. The relationship between these and some other criteria that I have noted in my discussion may be expressed schematically as follows:

Riddle	*Rune-order*	*Rune-presentation*	*alliteration*	*metre*
75 'Dog'	retrograde	rune-group	none	no
19 'Ship'	retrograde	rune-groups	yes (not 6a)	yes (not 2a)
64 'Ship'	natural	individual (not 2a)	yes	mixed
24 'Jay/Magpie'	anagram	individual	yes	yes (not 9a)
58 'Well-sweep'	anagram?	individual, by name	yes	yes
42 'Cock and Hen'	anagram	individual, by name	yes	yes

FIGURE 3.

---

[43] 8b is Bliss's type 2C2b, 9b type 3B1b, 10b type 2A1a(i), and 11a type 2E1a (see Bliss, "Scansion," 36, 39, 27 and 37 respectively).

[44] In 10b, where two *a*-runes are indicated, the substitution of a single *a*-rune would result, when the rune was named, in the verse: *ac twegen*, which would be ungrammatical (*twegen* requires a plural noun, not a singular), as well as unmetrical (the verse would be a three-syllable verse and so too short). Another way of presenting the runes as runes in lines 10 and 11 might have been to repeat them, giving, in the case of 10a, a verse that would invite pronunciation as *ac ac twegen*, or simply as *ac ac*, if *twegen* were omitted; but either arrangement would involve unacceptable repetition, as well as the double alliteration strictly avoided by Old English poets in b-verses, and *ac ac* would be metrically short. If we substituted one *h*-rune for *hæglas* in 11a, the resulting verse would also be metrically short, and two *h*-runes in sequence would be unacceptable because of the repetition involved.

What emerges clearly from this table is a correlation between an anagrammatic ordering of runes presented individually, and successful alliterative and (particularly) metrical integration (*Riddles* 24, 58, and 42). The least successful *Riddles*, when measured according to the metrical criterion, are those in which the order of letters of the word they spell is reversed and the letters are presented in groups (*Riddles* 75 and 19). The explanation for this correlation is clear enough. The Old English metrical half-line is structured as an alternation of stressed and unstressed syllables in a limited number of patterns; but runic names are mostly either monosyllabic (e.g. *ac*, 'oak', the *a*-rune) or dissyllabic with short first syllable, making the result metrically equivalent to a monosyllable (e.g. *sigel*, 'sun', the *s*-rune), with the result that almost any bare sequence of runic characters amounts, when the runes are converted to their names and spoken, to a string of (stressed) monosyllabic words with no unstressed syllables available to form the metrical dips that regular Old English half-lines require. Although many of the permissible verse-patterns can accommodate single stressed monosyllables, Old English metrical half-lines of conventional type cannot be constructed entirely from unbroken strings of stressed monosyllables. But when runic letters are presented individually and their names are grammatically contextualized within the verse by other linguistic material, the difficulty, for the poet, of fitting a rune-name into normal metrical patterns is much reduced. An example of a reasonably successful attempt along these lines is provided by *Riddle* 24, 'Jay', the runic part of which is quoted above, though even here one of the runic verses (9a) does not 'work' as a normal half-line. On the other hand, *Riddle* 42, 'Cock and Hen', represents complete success in this regard.

To assess the runic *Riddles* according to the degree of alliterative and metrical integration of the runic names is to impose value-judgements on these poems, and the historical implications of full, partial, or failed integration must now be considered. We might begin by asking if there is a straightforward positive correlation between the level of technical integration of the runes and intellectual or aesthetic achievement in the text as a whole. The problem is closely bound up with the connected question of how these poems were composed, and under what circumstances they were meant to be received. Were they composed pen-in-hand? Or rather (to use O'Keeffe's more nuanced conception of a continuum between the theoretical extremes of pure orality and pure literacy),[45] where should these poems be placed along the oral-literate continuum? The fact that the main body of the *Riddle* text is in all cases written in the roman alphabet is obviously not decisive on this point, because there is always a possibility that an Old English poem preserved in roman script was composed and delivered orally and only subsequently committed to parchment. The roman alphabet is not, as such, built into the form of any of these poems; it is only a mode in which the poems might

---

[45] See my account of O'Keeffe's *Visible Song* above, Chapter 1, 30–32.

have been composed originally, or (if composed orally) into which they could have been transcribed.

The runic *fuþorc*, on the other hand, *is* an aspect of their form: runes (or their names written in roman) are always used to indicate the spellings of words which either name the solution directly or (possibly, in a few cases) are intended to suggest it figuratively, and it seems clear that the runic character of these letters is authorial: there is no reason to think that roman letters were used originally and have been replaced by runes during transmission. But this employment of runes does not settle the question of where in the oral-literate continuum these poems fall in terms of their composition and reception. The use of runes to indicate the spellings of words demonstrates the poets' literacy, in runes if not in the roman alphabet, because an illiterate would obviously be ignorant of spelling, either in theory or in practice; but it would still have been possible for poets to exploit their literacy to compose in the traditional, oral way poems that incorporated runic spelling puzzles. Every rune had its name, a word which could, in theory at least, be incorporated and metrically integrated into an oral poem. *Riddles* 24, 58, and 42 all show good integration of the names of the runes in the versification, and all of them could therefore have been composed orally and later (or on the occasion of their composition) recorded in writing, with the runes either written as runes, as they are in *Riddle* 24, or as their names in roman, as in *Riddles* 58 and 42. The fact that, of these last two *Riddles*, one at least (42, the 'Cock and Hen' *Riddle*) is still, even today, solvable to the satisfaction of all shows that the 'romanization' of runes as their names in written texts need not obscure the structural role of runes as letters.

But if the use of runes (in various ways) as an indication of the spellings of words does not in itself place these poems near the 'literate' extreme of the orality-literacy continuum, their function as part of the puzzle certainly does suggest, not just a literate target-audience, but more specifically a readership. The notion that English medieval vernacular texts were recorded in writing with a view to their subsequent recitation by a reader to an audience of (presumably) illiterate listeners is a popular one, though I have argued in the previous chapter that Cynewulf's runic signatures would have been impenetrable to an illiterate audience, and it is equally difficult to imagine this kind of reception for the runic *Riddles*. For the Anglo-Saxons, as for us today, it was doubtless not nearly as easy to reorder a jumble of sounds mentally into a known word than it was if the letters were actually visible in their written form. Furthermore, if the main justification for the recitation hypothesis is the assumption that poems were composed to be read to illiterate audiences, it is obvious that such an audience would not be able to play the kind of spelling game that the runic *Riddles* all involve. Spelling puzzles imply a high level of literacy.[46]

---

[46] See, for instance, Scholes and Willis, "Linguists, Literacy, and the Intensionality of Marshall McLuhan's Western Man."

These considerations affect the interpretation of the different levels of metrical integration of the rune-names that we have found in these poems. It seems possible that to the readers of these *Riddles*, metrical integration of the runes had no particular virtue, at least at the functional level of solving the puzzle: the runes do their job (except, perhaps, in *Riddle* 64), however well or poorly integrated they may be in the verse-structure. The romanization of runes as their names in written texts of these poems does not seem to have a serious impact on our ability to solve the puzzle, and no doubt this was also true for Anglo-Saxon readers; indeed, romanization, as well as the grammaticalization of the runic names that romanization involves in the case of *Riddle* 42, might have been positively valued on the grounds that it imposed an extra test on the solver. Furthermore, even if the degree of metrical integration of the runes mattered little to the reader *qua* solver, integration might well have been valued as an index of the riddle-poet's skill in burying his solution within the text while still leaving it accessible to the intelligent solver — a skill which could be appreciated fully only after the riddle had been solved. Runes simply attached (as in *Riddle* 75) to the main text not only create an impression of casualness, but are excluded from the total aesthetic effect created by the poem.

It is, of course, much easier to rank these runic *Riddles* in terms of the technical skill with which the runic elements are incorporated than it is to assess them in broader terms, as examples of literary art. We cannot pass literary judgement on a riddle until we have solved it; and in the case of the runic *Riddles*, we are obviously hampered by the fact that we cannot agree on the solutions to several of them. Only *Riddle* 24, 'Jay/Magpie', and *Riddle* 42, 'Cock and Hen', are now solved to most critics' satisfaction. The others may attract new interpretations in the future that are simpler or more accessible than those they have already received; but it seems more likely that any new solutions will be more ingenious than those already proposed, as demonstrated by Griffith's relatively recent case for the deliberate incorporation of the acronymic *snac* in *Riddle 19*. Perhaps the more difficult runic *Riddles* will emerge in a new light in the future; for the moment, we are not in a position to measure them according to literary standards appropriate to the genre. Fortunately, we are not handicapped in this way in relation to *Riddle* 42, 'Cock and Hen', which forms the focus of the next section.

§5. *Riddle* 42, 'Cock and Hen': form, orality, and literacy

In all the runic *Riddles*, the use of runes for spelling purposes effectively emphasises their graphic nature as visual representations of the sounds of speech; but our appreciation of this aspect of runes is deeper when the poet fails to integrate the runes metrically or alliteratively, bringing out their distinctiveness as linguistic objects of a different nature from the 'speakable' text to which they are attached. When, on the other hand, the runes are fully incorporated into the texture of the verse—by the integration of their names into the verse-structure and alliteration, and their inflexion according to their grammatical role in the sentences in which they occur—this has the obvious effect of bringing their 'speakable' quality more into the foreground. Thus although all the runic *Riddles* represent, to a greater or lesser degree, a confrontation between language as writing and language as speech, *Riddle* 42, 'Cock and Hen', seems to me to create the most pointed opposition of all between speech and writing, and even accomplishes a kind of structural mediation of the two in the way it handles the runes.[47] These aspects of the poem have little to do with the functional level of its interpretation as a riddle with a solution, which is straightforward enough, or with the description of the fowls' activities at the beginning of the poem, which constitutes (along with the runic spelling) the basic riddling content. As with all the texts discussed in this book, the aspects of *Riddle* 42 that are most relevant to my discussion have to do with its linguistic and literary form. At this level of composition and organization, the poem exposes certain implications of writing and reading and their relationship with speech and hearing.

The course of this exposure is more conveniently traced from the point of view of the reader than of the writer, and we might begin at the most elementary level of reception. The reader is faced, in *Riddle* 42, with a text in the roman alphabet. This aspect of the encounter between the reader and the text is, of course, the same for most Old English texts, prose or verse, that were originally composed, or eventually preserved, in writing, the only clear exceptions being runic inscriptions. A text in roman does not rule out the possibility that what we are reading is an originally oral composition that has been transcribed. What does rule out this possibility in the case of *Riddle* 42 is the use of runes, which as we saw earlier need to be seen, not just heard, to be interpreted in the way the poet clearly intended. The runes establish the basic literary character of this particular poem's reception with exceptional definiteness; and although it is possible that it was composed orally in the traditional way and subsequently committed to parchment, the fact that its form predicates a literate audience makes it difficult to imagine its transmission orally to a succession of literate audiences. Much points to its being a literary production from the beginning.

On the other hand, *Riddle* 42 is an alliterative poem, written in a style and metre which connects it unmistakably with oral traditions more deeply embedded in Anglo-Saxon culture than the literacy that its understanding as an utterance requires, and upon which its preservation depends. Furthermore, this poem claims explicitly, with a degree of emphasis exceptional not just in the context of the *Riddles* but among Old English poems generally, to be an oral utterance

---

[47] See Lerer, *Literacy and Power*, 115–25.

(5–6 *Ic . . . mæg . . . secgan*, "I am able to tell . . ."), delivered "in hall" (5 *on flette*)⁴⁸ to "warriors" (6 *rincum*), or to "men at their wine" (16 *werum æt wine*); the poet is clearly attempting to create an impression of oral composition and delivery in a standard heroic setting. On the other hand, the mention of "runic characters" (6 *runstafas*), and the appeal to an elite, lettered audience — "those who know books" (7 *þam þe bec witan*), and "runemen" (13 *rynemenn*) — cuts across this impression of the text as heroic oral entertainment. Although an audience literate in runes might have been able to recognize the runic anagram and solve it without actually seeing the text (partly because the rune-names make so little sense in the context if taken as common nouns), it seems very doubtful if this riddle could have been solved by illiterates who could get no help from the runic anagram: a pair of creatures of almost any species of animal or bird would be covered by the brief description of the mating in lines 1–5a.⁴⁹

Against this background of a simultaneous and contradictory appeal to common oral tradition and the clear expectation of a literate readership, the poet's paradoxical presentation of the runic letters as their names spelt out in roman assumes special significance. Like all the runic riddles, *Riddle* 42 sets up a basic functional distinction between the two modes: roman for the description of the solution, runic for the letters of its name. In the light of the narrator's insistence that *Riddle* 42 is an oral performance, a homology between two pairs of oppositions, one spoken vs. written, the other roman vs. runes, seems to emerge as the foundation upon which the poem's form is based. This conclusion may be supported by general historical considerations. As we saw in Chapter 3, runes were the only mode of writing at the earliest stage of Anglo-Saxon culture, and must therefore have been at least as closely identified with the written mode as roman was. When the roman alphabet was adopted by the Anglo-Saxons in the seventh century, it was of course already inextricably linked with books and book-production, though for the Anglo-Saxons, roman was only as old as the new religion that brought it in its wake. We have also seen (in Chapter 3) how epigraphic

---

⁴⁸ Cf. Lerer, *Literacy and Power*, 116, who translates 5b-6: "I can announce to men, through runestaves on the floor, to those who know books," etc., and then, interpreting the passage, explains that the poet "writes [the runes] on the floor for all to see." This is an attractive interpretation suggesting an elaborate dramatization of the process of setting and solving the riddle, though it perhaps involves a degree of logical conflict with the poet's presentation of the runes within the text.

⁴⁹ This aspect of the poem has great interest for what it might imply about levels of runic literacy in Anglo-Saxon England. It looks rather as if roman and runic literacy were not regarded as the province of different groups; that those who possessed the ability to read and to spell were expected to do both in either runes or roman. Cf. Lerer, *Literacy and Power*, 116, who sees a paradox here in the poem's linking of books with knowledge of runes because "runes are not a 'bookish' but an epigraphical script." The obvious fact remains, however, that runes are here used in a book, not in an inscription.

texts in runes and roman alike are often medium-deictic: they mimic speech in some respects, though they remain essentially writings by virtue of their pragmatic setting. Runes, furthermore, do not appear to have been used to transcribe actual speech (such as oral poetic performances).[50] It fell to the roman alphabet to fulfil this function and so form a genuine bridge between the oral past and the literate future. Perhaps, therefore, the roman alphabet came to be thought of as the most natural mode of transcription for what were originally, or essentially, oral utterances, such as alliterative poems, leaving runes available to fulfil something approximating to their original function: to represent utterances that could not possibly issue from a human mouth but could only be the work of the human hand. When viewed against this background of the historical relations between runes and roman, *Riddle* 42 seems to produce a kind of balance between oral and literate modes of expression; and right on the fulcrum of this balance are situated the runic names written out in roman: as runes, they are rooted in the exclusively literate world of epigraphy, and as letters they spell words, which is a procedure that only the literate can follow; but as names written in the roman alphabet and worked into the grammatical and metrical structure of the poem, they are an integral part of what is formally and traditionally a spoken utterance. The runes thus encapsulate, or perhaps 'mediate', the oppositions between speech and writing implied in the poem's form. *Riddle* 42 is a poem embodying some important aspects of the relationship between spoken and written language; and although one might speculate about a possible allegorical relationship between the intercourse of the cock and hen and the curious mingling of spoken and written modes that the poem's form accomplishes, I repeat that it seems unlikely that the solution to *Riddle* 42 has any connection with these intellectual aspects of the poem. Perhaps the sheer triviality of the solution is meant to provide a kind of foil against which they emerge with particular clarity and force.

§6. *Riddle* 47, 'Bookmoth' and *Riddle* 60, 'Pen': the materiality of writing

In section 4 of this chapter I maintained that the runic *Riddles*, taken as a group, exhibit a dichotomy, or at least a clear distinction, between the ostensible meaning and function of the text as a puzzle with a solution, and certain implications of the riddle as a formal utterance—implications that have no real bearing on the solution and represent a probing of certain aspects of writing and reading that seem paradoxical when juxtaposed with established traditions of speech and

---

[50] A possible exception is the Auzon Casket's runic poem about the death of the whale on whose bone the inscription appears (see above, Chapter 3); but the close deictic link with the medium makes this is a special case. The poem would make little sense if recited, copied into a manuscript, or even transferred to some other non-whalebone object.

oral poetic composition. But there are other *Riddles* in the Exeter Book collection that face up to these paradoxes more directly and even explicitly, by taking the materials, equipment, and products of writing as their subject-matter and playing intellectual games with them. Perhaps the most basic level of thinking is represented by the various 'Book' *Riddles*, the clearest example of which is *Riddle* 26 (Williamson 24).[51] Here, the nature of the book as an artifact with a history and a distinctive physical nature is explored in detail. A splendid imaginary volume speaks of its own origins, manufacture, and present function: after being 'killed' by an enemy (7–8 *Mec feonda sum feore besnypede*; the reference is to the slaughter of the animal that provided the skin for its pages), the speaker, now reduced to a hide, is soaked in water, dried in the sun, scraped clean with a knife, folded into pages, written upon with a quill pen (7b-8 *ond mec fugles wyn geond speddropum spyrede geneahhe*, "and the bird's delight went over me with useful drops"),[52] bound in leather, and decorated with gold leaf and other ornamentation. A book is, however, obviously more than just a physical artifact. It is useful to men as a repository for language; it has an abstract nature too and exists to be read. Accordingly, the second half of *Riddle* 26 is devoted to the functional value of the book's contents (evidently it is a religious work, possibly a Bible)—how men would be happier, wiser, safer, more successful socially and materially if they read it. The poem thus draws our attention to the composite nature of books: like all artifacts, they have a tangible presence and a physical history beginning, in the case of Anglo-Saxon parchment books, with the previous existence of their pages as the skins of living animals; but their nature is really defined by the language they capture. A book is essentially a linguistic product, a source of knowledge, wisdom, and spiritual profit, rather than just a bound series of parchment gatherings. As a physical object, the book thus represents a purer or more neutral conveyance for its text than comparable inscribed artifacts whose functional value is to a large extent independent of their inscriptions. As objects, books function only as media for language; however decorative they may be, they have no independent uses.

If *Riddle* 26 is about the making of books, one might say that *Riddle* 47 (Williamson 45), 'Bookmoth', is about their destruction. Unlike *Riddle* 26, whose reflections on books seem (to modern readers, at least) obvious enough, the 'Bookmoth' riddle is a poem of considerable ingenuity which, as Robinson

---

[51] A similar solution is generally accepted for *Riddle* 67 (Williamson 65). *Riddle* 92 (Williamson 88) and *Riddle* 95 (Williamson 91) may also be book-riddles, though there are serious doubts about both, especially the latter; see Williamson's commentary, *Riddles*, 391–93, 397–402.

[52] See Krapp and Dobbie, *The Exeter Book*, 335, note to line 8.

has shown in a much-admired article,[53] wittily incorporates several ambiguous words chosen to suggest conceptual parallels between the intellectual assimilation of verbal meaning and the ingestion of food:

> Moððe word fræt.   Me þæt þuhte
> wrætlicu wyrd,   þa ic þæt wundor gefrægn,
> þæt se wyrm forswealg   wera gied sumes,
> þeof in þystro,   þrymfæstne cwide
> 5   ond þæs strangan staþol.   Stælgiest ne wæs
> wihte þy gleawra,   þe he þam wordum swealg.
>
> (*Riddle* 47 [Williamson 45])

"A moth devoured words. That seemed to me a strange event, when I heard about that marvel, that the caterpillar swallowed some man's tale, a thief in darkness, the glorious saying and the foundation of that mighty (utterance). The thieving stranger was none the wiser for swallowing those words."

The most significant and unmistakable ambiguities found by Robinson are 6 *swealg*, the past tense of *swelgan* the literal meaning of which is 'to swallow' but also open to interpretation here in the more abstract sense of 'to take into the mind, accept, imbibe (wisdom)'; 5 *staþol*, literally 'foundation', in reference to the parchment that the moth-caterpillar is eating, but also attested in Old English in the sense of 'abstract meaning'—the intellectual content of an utterance that the moth might be taken as consuming; and 4 *cwide*, here with the primary sense of 'saying' or 'utterance', but also acceptable as a form of the noun *cwidu*, 'what is chewed'. Robinson recognizes, however, that these ambiguities are not enough to make the poem a riddle. Like *Riddle* 19, the 'Bookmoth' *Riddle* seems too easy. Is not the first verse, "A moth devoured words," so explicit as to destroy any intellectual challenge that a riddle with this solution might have posed? Robinson echoes Malone's view that the poem is not so much a riddle as "something merely paradoxical, and even this only by identification of the ink-marks with the words they symbolize,"[54] though Robinson finds a "richly equivocal quality" in *Riddle* 47 that compensates for the apparent lack of any real challenge to the reader's deductive powers.

This view of the poem as a non-riddle has, however, been challenged, in my view convincingly, by Williamson. He points to another, functional level of

---

[53] Fred C. Robinson, "Artful Ambiguities in the Old English 'Book-Moth' Riddle," in *Anglo-Saxon Poetry: Essays in Appreciation For John C. McGalliard*, ed. Nicholson and Frese, 355–62.

[54] Robinson, "Artful Ambiguities," 356, quoting Kemp Malone, "The Old English Period (to 1100)," in Kemp Malone and Albert C. Baugh, *The Middle Ages*, 2nd ed., A Literary History of England 1 (London: Routledge & Kegan Paul, 1967), 3–108, at 89.

ambiguity in *Riddle* 47 that effectively reinstates it as an instance of the riddle genre.[55] Words that would normally refer in Old English generally to spoken language are here used exceptionally to suggest (as part of the solution) written language. The surface-meaning is that the moth (or its larva, strictly speaking) consumes human speech; but in order to achieve the solution, this startling, not to say incomprehensible, proposition needs to be resolved as a riddling reference to the consumption of words in written form on the parchment which is, in reality, the larva's only interest. Williamson shows that the stumbling-block upon which interpretations of *Riddle* 47 as a non-riddle have foundered is the Old English word *word*, here operating as a subspecies of the 'false friend': a word that tricks the modern reader into an unhistorical interpretation because of its stable written form over time and its use in a context that obscures crucial semantic developments it has undergone. It appears both in the first verse of the poem, *Moððe word fræt*,[56] and in the last, *þe he þam wordum swealg*, "for swallowing those words" in my translation. Elsewhere in Old English, *word* invariably denotes spoken utterances; it is not attested in the sense of a written sequence of letters until the sixteenth century (1521).[57] One consequence of this is that interpretation of these two instances of the noun as enigmatic references to written words required, for Anglo-Saxon readers, an imaginative leap that the poet expected them to be able to perform in order to achieve the solution. Williamson makes the same point about 4 *cwide* and 32 *gied*, both of which normally denote vocal utterances in Old English. *Riddle* 47 has been misinterpreted as a non-riddle by modern readers because they have assumed that *word* is being used in the (modern) sense of written letters as part of the fabric of the text's surface meaning, rather than as part of the concealed, contextual meaning that the riddle requires the reader to uncover. As a riddle, the poem is founded on the contrast between spoken and written language; and it constitutes clear evidence that linguistic concepts such as the one represented by the word *word* were still thought of in terms of speech in the period of the poem's composition, not in terms of written language. The solution to *Riddle* 47, and the mental operations required to achieve it, indicate that the modification of linguistic concepts required by literacy was under way; but the gulf between orality and literacy was still sufficiently wide to be used as the basis of an intellectual puzzle.

Of all the Old English *Riddles*, the one that seems to me to represent the most provocative and entertaining exploration of the relationship between speech and writing is *Riddle* 60, now usually solved as 'Reed-pen'. The text of the poem, followed by a translation, is given below:

---

[55] Williamson, *Riddles*, 285–86.

[56] In line 1, *word* is probably to be taken as plural in the sense of 'spoken words' or 'speech', as Williamson (*Riddles*, 285) suggests.

[57] *OED*, s.v. **word**, meaning XII (281). The *OED* editors cite *Riddle* 47 1 *word* as the only instance of the word in this sense before 1521.

	Ic wæs be sonde,	sæwealle neah,
	æt merefaroþe,	minum gewunade
	frumstaþole fæst;	fea ænig wæs
	monna cynnes,	þæt minne þær
5	on anæde eard beheolde,	
	ac me uhtna gehwam	yð sio brune
	lagufæðme beleolc.	Lyt ic wende
	þæt ic ær oþþe sið	æfre sceolde
	ofer meodubence[58]	muðleas sprecan,
10	wordum wrixlan.	Þæt is wundres dæl,
	on sefan searolic	þam þe swylc ne conn,
	hu mec seaxes[59] ord	ond seo swiþre hond,
	eorles ingeþonc	ond ord somod,
	þingum geþydan,	þæt ic wiþ þe sceolde
15	for unc anum twam[60]	ærendspræce
	abeodan bealdlice,	swa hit beorna ma
	uncre wordcwidas	widdor ne mænden. (*Riddle* 60 [Williamson 58])

"I was by the sand, near the sea-wall, at the water's edge; I was firmly established in my place of origin. There were few of humankind who beheld my dwelling-place there in that solitude; but every dawn the brown wave encompassed me in its watery embrace. Little did I expect that I ever, sooner or later, should speak mouthless across the mead-bench, mix words. That is a kind of wonder, marvellous to such a mind that does not know how the point of the knife and the right hand, a man's purpose and the point together, have fashioned me so purposely that I should boldly announce to you a message for us two alone, so that no other men may repeat our words more widely."

The reed-pen, looking back on its solitary, undisturbed existence as a growing plant, marvels at its own transformation into something which, though "mouthless" (9 *muðleas*), is able to "speak" (9 *sprecan*)—or produce written language, in terms of the riddle's solution as a pen. The miracle of silent speech, which is an aspect of literate communication likely to impress a society new to literacy, is a major preoccupation here.[61] The closing lines reflect on another breakthrough made by the advent of reading and writing: the potential for secret, one-to-one

---

[58] 9 *meodubence*, MS *meodu*.
[59] 12 *seaxes*, MS *seaxeð*.
[60] 15 *twam*, MS *twan*.
[61] The expression "silent speech" will be familiar to students of the Old English *Riddles* from Marie Nelson's article "The Paradox of Silent Speech in the Exeter Book Riddles," *Neophilologus* 62 (1978): 609–15; but Nelson's topic is mainly the paradox whereby speech is, by implication, attributed to voiceless inanimate or non-human objects and creatures. She includes *Riddle* 60 in her study, but does not consider the text from the point of view of the orality-literacy opposition.

verbal communication between two people even when they are surrounded by others, an emphasis which may be taken to suggest a view of reading and writing as esoteric accomplishments confined to a minority.[62]

These are aspects of the riddle's explicit or implicit content; it is only when we reflect on the pragmatics of *Riddle* 60 that its real individuality emerges. This is no ordinary riddle. As a puzzle, it functions in just the same way as other homodiegetic *Riddles* in the Exeter Book collection, such as *Riddle* 26, 'Book', summarized briefly above, by dramatizing the solution by means of an imaginary, self-identifying speech. In this respect, *Riddle* 60 is conventional enough; its individuality lies in the way the discovery of the solution transforms our idea of the text we have been reading, and promotes a shift in our perception of the solution itself. In general terms, the difference between a pen and any other riddle-solution is that a pen does (in a sense) actually produce language, and is thus a more direct source of utterances than any other inanimate object known to Anglo-Saxon culture. A consequence of this realization is that we also come to appreciate that this pen's "message" (15 *ærendspræce*) is in fact the poem itself. Furthermore, because the text of the poem we have read issues *directly* from a pen, it is unmistakably a piece of writing, rather than just an imaginary speech in written form of the kind we find in other *Riddles*. Nor is this writing imaginary in the usual way (though of course it is imaginary insofar as no pen writes without human guidance): the text as we read it in the manuscript is itself a product, not of a generic pen, nor of just any pen, but of a particular and actual pen, the instance of the category 'pen' that wrote the Exeter Book. In the other Old English *Riddles*, as we saw earlier, the solution may be individual or generic, but it is never token-specific, as it is here. We do not know whether or not *Riddle* 60 has a history of literary transmission in writing; perhaps many pens have copied it. But the functional link between instrument and utterance means that what 'speaks' (at another level, of course, what writes) to the reader of the Exeter Book is the actual pen used to write the text in that manuscript. However many times the text of *Riddle* 60 may have been reproduced during the Old English period, the pen that 'spoke' to any reader of this poem would always have been the pen used to write the actual manuscript in which the riddle was being read. Here I differ from Marie Nelson, who writes of the pen-speaker: "the non-living reed says that he delivers a message that has no sound, and, since it is not quoted ... we do not know what it is."[63] In my interpretation, the soundlessness of the message is the

---

[62] The theme of the secrecy that writing makes possible should remind us of the connections with secrecy that several instances of the Old English words *run*, 'rune', and its cognate (*ge*)*ryne*, suggest in their contexts, though the question is somewhat controversial; see Page, "Anglo-Saxon Runes and Magic," 106–13; cf. Christine E. Fell, "Runes and Semantics," in *Old English Runes and their Continental Background*, ed. Bammesberger, 195–229, at 196–99.

[63] Nelson, "Silent Speech," 613–14.

silence of all written language, and the secret message (15 *ærendspræce*) that only the speaker and the recipient can know is the riddle-text, itself a direct manifestation of the pen's ability to produce 'speech'.

The theme of secrecy is a central and distinctive one in this poem. Because it is in the nature of a pen to communicate directly through writing, the speaker in *Riddle* 60 is in a position to establish a uniquely intimate—one might even say 'personal'—connection with any reader. Accordingly, the individual reader is buttonholed by the singular second-person pronoun *þe*, 'you' (14);[64] and the pen draws the reader into a relationship with itself by its use of the dual first-person pronouns *unc*, 'us two' (15) and *uncre*, 'of us two' (17). The idea of the secrecy of writing which, as we have seen, the pen emphasises explicitly, sets the seal on this enclosure of reader and pen in a private world of literate communication.

Although this is clearly a poem very much taken up with reading and writing, the author of *Riddle* 60 nevertheless draws heavily on the basic conversational model of language which I defined in Chapter 2 of this book. By dramatizing the reading of the text in terms of a conversation between the pen-speaker and the reader, the poet invokes the structural essentials of oral communication, with its co-presence of utterer and hearer in the same place and at the same moment in time. Given the conventions of riddle-composition, he achieves a convincing (if ultimately artificial) version of that 'deictic simultaneity' which is of the essence of speech but not normally achieved in writing because writer and reader are usually divided temporally and spatially. Here, because writing is the 'voice' of the pen, and because any written text is a direct manifestation of that voice, rather than just a secondary, visual codification of an underlying oral reality, the sense of being directly addressed here by the pen is abnormally vivid. We are reminded here of the extraordinary directness with which the Ruthwell Cross addresses its readers in writing. Because our access to the pen's utterance is as direct and unmediated as it is to a real spoken utterance, the impression that the pen too is present, or at least close by, is very powerful. By having the pen speak in such a mode as to make the reader forget that reception of the text has been subject to the normal delay between coding-time and receiving-time, the poet creates the illusion that the pen is communicating *now*, as its story unfolds before the reader—any reader, medieval or modern. It is, of course, the basic manoeuvre of the riddle-composer—the playful attribution of speech to an inanimate, inhuman object—that enables the poet to postulate a situation in which the distinction between conversation and written communication is minimalized; but whereas the reader may admire the ingenuity by which this minimalization is achieved, he will also be provoked into reflections on the pros and cons of conversation as opposed to writing. By exploiting the unique position of the pen as the source of writing and also its unique ability to communicate directly and immediately

---

[64] This seems to be the only place in the *Riddles* where the second person pronoun is used to address the solver.

to anyone confronted with any of its products, the poet manages to stimulate a whole range of reflections on the differences between spoken and written language: the silence of written communication compared with the sound of speech; the enclosure of writer and reader in a private world that results from this silence; and the immediacy of spoken communication compared with the spatial and temporal separation of utterer from receiver than writing typically entails.

§7. *The Husband's Message*

The poem that immediately follows *Riddle* 60 in the Exeter Book is *The Husband's Message*. The text has been damaged by the fire to which the later folios of the manuscript have at some time been exposed. The version given below reproduces R. F. Leslie's edition,[65] in which dots indicate the approximate number of missing letters, round brackets indicate readings based on fragmentary letters, and square brackets mark letters editorially supplied. The translation of parts of the poem is, naturally, somewhat conjectural.

```
       Nu ic onsundran þe      secgan wille
       . . . . . . . (n) treocyn.⁶⁶     Ic tudre aweox;
       in⁶⁷ mec æld[a]. . . . . . . . . . .sceal
       ellor londes setta(n) . . . . . . . . . . . . . . . . .lc,
 5     sealte streamas . . . . . . . . . . . . . . . . . . . .sse.
       Ful oft ic on bates [bosme] . . . . . . . . . .gesohte,
       þær mec mondryhten      min      . . . . . . .
       ofer heah h[a]fu;       eom nu her cumen
       on ceolþele,      ond nu cunnan scealt
10     hu þu ymb modluf[a]n      mines frean
       on hyge hycge.      Ic gehatan dear
```

---

[65] *Three Old English Elegies*, ed. R. F. Leslie (Manchester: Manchester University Press, 1966), 49–50. I prefer Leslie's to Krapp and Dobbie's text chiefly because its punctuation seems to me the better reflection of the sentence-structure of the original. For a more recent edition and account of the manuscript and its problems, see Klinck, *The Old English Elegies*, whose line-divisions and judgements of the number of missing letters in the lacunae often differ from Leslie's.

[66] A hole in the margin of the folio immediately after *treocyn* creates the possibility that the scribe wrote an inflected form such as *treocynne*.

[67] The *n* of 3 *in* is not certain in the manuscript, and John C. Pope, "Palaeography and Poetry: Some Solved and Unsolved Problems of the Exeter Book," in *Medieval Scribes, Manuscripts and Libraries: Essays Presented to N. R. Ker*, ed. M. B. Parkes and Andrew G. Watson (London: Scolar Press, 1978), 25–65 (at 44–45), thinks that the letter is probably a wynn, giving *iw*, 'yew'. If so, the word probably denotes the "species of tree" to which, in a more general way, 2 *treocyn* refers. See next note; but cf. Klinck, *The Old English Elegies*, 200, note to line 3, who cannot confirm a wynn in the manuscript.

  þæt þu þær tirfæste treowe findest.
  Hwæt, þec þonne biddan het, se þisne beam agrof,
  þæt þu sinchroden sylf gemunde
15 on gewitlocan wordbeotunga
  þe git on ærdagum oft gespræcon,
  þenden git moston on meoduburgum
  eard weardigan, an lond bugan,
  freondscype fremman. Hine fæhþo adraf
20 of sigeþeode. Heht nu sylfa þe
  lustum læra[n] þæt þu lagu drefde,
  siþþan þu gehyrde on hliþes oran
  galan geomorne geac on bearwe.
  Ne læt þu þec siþþan siþes getwæfan,
25 lade gelettan, lifgendne monn.
  Ongin mere secan, mæwes eþel;
  onsite sænacan, þæt þu suð heonan
  ofer merelade monnan findest,
  þær se þeoden is þin on wenum.
30 Ne mæg him [on]⁶⁸ worulde willa [gelimpan]
  mara on gemyndum, þæsþe he me sægde,
  þonne inc geunne alwaldend God,
  [þæt git] ætsomne siþþan motan
  secgum ond gesiþum s[inc brytnian],
35 næglede beagas. He genoh hafað
  fædan gold[es], ...
  [geon]d⁶⁹ elþeode eþel healde,
  fægre folda[n] . . . .
  [hold]ra hæleþa, þeahþe her min win(e)
40 . . . .
  nyde gebæded, nacan ut aþrong,
  ond on yþa gel(a)g[u ana] sceolde
  faran on flotweg, forðsiþes georn
  mengan merestreamas. Nu se mon hafað
45 wean oferwunnen; nis him wilna gad,
  ne meara, ne maðma, ne meododreama
  ænges ofer eorþan eorlgestreona,
  þeodnes dohtor, gif he þin beneah.
  Ofer eald gebeot incer twega,
50 gehyre ic ætsomne .S.R. geador
  .EA.W. ond .M. aþe benemnan
  þæt he þa wære ond þa winetreowe,

---

  ⁶⁸ Klinck (*Elegies*, 101, 203) judges that about three letters have been erased between *him* and *worulde*. She thinks the final letter was more probably an *r* than an *n*, and so supplies *ofer* (Klinck, *Elegies*, 101) instead of Leslie's *on*.
  ⁶⁹ Cf. Klinck, *Elegies*, 100, who sees -*ed* in the manuscript before 37 *elþeode*.

> be him lifgendum   læstan wolde,
> þe git on ærdagum   oft gespræconn.

"Now I intend to tell you apart (*or* apart) . . . species of tree. I grew up from a shoot (*or* child), on to me . . . of men . . . must elsewhere set on land . . . . salt streams . . . . . Very often in the bosom of a boat . . . sought, where my liege lord . . . . me across the deep seas; I am now come here in a ship, and now you must know how you think in your mind about the love in my lord's heart. I dare promise that you will find glorious fidelity there. Lo! He who engraved this tree commanded (me) to beseech you that you, richly adorned, remember in your mind the promises that you two often agreed upon in former days, while you could dwell in the mead cities, inhabit one land, display your love. Feud drove him from the victorious people. Now he himself has commanded me joyfully to persuade you that you should stir the sea, after you have heard at the hillside's edge the mournful cuckoo singing in the grove. Let no living man divert you from the journey, hinder you from your course. Seek out the sea, the homeland of the gull; embark, so that you find the man southwards across the ocean track, where the prince awaits you. No desire in the world may be greater for him in his mind, as he said to me, than that almighty God grant to you two that you together may later distribute treasure to men and to companions, studded bracelets. He owns plenty of burnished gold, . . . Amongst a foreign people he holds a homeland, the fair earth, . . . of devoted men, although my lord here . . . . compelled by necessity, pushed out a boat, and on to the expanses of the waves alone had to travel on the sea, eager for departure, stir up the sea currents. Now the man has overcome his woes. He is not lacking in pleasures, nor in horses nor treasures nor festive joys nor any of the noble treasures on earth, prince's daughter, if he possess you. In the matter of the old promise of you two, I hear together the sun-road (*sigel, rad*), the earth-joy (*or* sea-joy; *ear, wynn*), and the man (*monn*) declare together, according to the oath, that he would implement those pledges and those vows of love which you two often voiced in days gone by."

Some commentators on *The Husband's Message* believe that it is not a distinct text but a continuation of *Riddle* 60.[70] The question is affected by critical uncertainty

---

[70] Those who take this view include Ralph W. V. Elliott, "The Runes in *The Husband's Message*," *JEGP* 54 (1955): 1–8; R. E. Kaske, "A Poem of the Cross in the Exeter Book: *Riddle 60* and *The Husband's Message*," *Traditio* 23 (1967): 41–71; Margaret E. Goldsmith, "The Enigma of *The Husband's Message*," in *Anglo-Saxon Poetry: Essays in Appreciation for John C. McGalliard*, ed. Nicholson and Frese, 242–63; Pope, "Palaeography and Poetry"; and Bragg, *Lyric Speakers*, 53. The case for taking *Riddle* 60 and *The Husband's Message* as two distinct works is made by R. F. Leslie, "The Integrity of Riddle 60," *JEGP* 67 (1968): 451–57; F. J. Whitman, "Riddle 60 and its Source," *PQ* 50 (1971):

about the nature of the speaker of the poem. It is clear that the speaker is aiming his words at a woman, and a noblewoman at that, for she is addressed as *peodnes dohtor*, "prince's daughter," in line 48; but there is no broad agreement about whether the speech is to be understood as the explanatory words of a courier who brings her an inscribed piece of wood (the inscription on which is given in lines 50–51), or as a speech ascribed to the wooden medium of the runic message. The latter interpretation is probably more popular at the moment; but whatever position one takes on this question, the basic reference made in the poem to an inscribed wooden object is reasonably clear: line 13 *se pisne beam agrof*, "He who engraved this tree," must be taken in combination with the runic passage, which can scarcely be interpreted as anything other than a representation of the runes that this *beam* bears. Evidently the poet is referring here to the use of epigraphic runes carved on a piece of wood to convey a message between individuals, in which regard *The Husband's Message* is unique amongst Old English texts, and indeed constitutes the only evidence for this practice in Anglo-Saxon England.[71]

The question of the nature and identity of the speaker is a particularly thorny one. Some years ago I published an article arguing that the speaker is the inscribed staff;[72] but suspecting as I now do that uncertainty about the identity of the speaker is something the poet intended to create (I now see the poem as more of a riddle than I did, which is why I have included a consideration of it in this chapter rather than the next), I prefer to allow the nature of the speaker to emerge in the course of a general reading of the poem, rather than to pin it down by direct confrontation with the question. This procedure will, I hope, bring out the way in which the poet equivocates about the nature—human or material—of the speaker, and keeps the reader guessing.

108–15; Stanley B. Greenfield, *The Interpretation of Old English Poems* (London: Routledge & Kegan Paul, 1972), 152–53; and Klinck, *Elegies*, 27, 57.

[71] See Page, *Introduction*, 101–2.

[72] Peter Orton, "The Speaker in *The Husband's Message*," *Leeds Studies in English* N.S. 12 (1980–1981): 43–56. A more recent variant of this interpretation that will, I suspect, please many is that the speaker is not a loose piece of wood but the inscribed mast of the boat which brings the runic message to its recipient. A suggestion to this effect is made in passing by Lois Bragg, "Runes and Readers: In and Around 'The Husband's Message'," *SN* 71 (1999): 34–50 (at 41): ("[Robert Kaske and Margaret Goldsmith] were right in feeling that the word *beam* has to refer to something large, like a ship's mast or, at the very least, a walking staff"), and it is developed by John D. Niles, "The Trick of the Runes," 202–6. Niles examines the likely meanings of the words *ceolpele* (11, '(on the) keel or keel plank') and (following Bragg) *beam* (13, 'beam', i.e. a large piece of timber rather than a mere stick, and so 'mast') in their contexts. The case is well made, though the urgings of lines 26–7a, *Ongin mere secan, mæwes epel, onsite sænacan* ("Seek out the sea, the homeland of the gull; embark, . . .") might seem redundant if the woman is to be envisaged as reading the runic message on the mast of a boat.

In line 1, the woman is addressed in language some at least of which would certainly not be out of place in the mouth of a human messenger:

> Nu ic onsundran þe   secgan wille
> . . . . (n) treocyn.   Ic tudre aweox;
> in mec æld[a]. . . . . .sceal

"Now I intend to tell you especially (*or* apart) . . . species of tree. I grew up from a shoot (*or* child); on to me . . . of men . . . must", etc.

Elliott thinks that 1 *Nu* and *onsundran* demonstrate textual continuity with *Riddle* 60;[73] but "now" and "especially" (or "apart") may simply mark the beginning of the address by the messenger (whether he is human being or personified rune-bearing medium) to the intended recipient of his message: now that his quest for the woman is over, he may deliver himself of the message with which he has been entrusted. The verb *secgan* means 'to tell' or 'to say' in Old English generally, and (as we saw earlier in Chapter 2) normally takes a certain kind of object: a noun denoting an utterance, a noun-clause expressing what is said or told, or an actual quotation of the words spoken.[74] It is therefore likely that verse 2a, which contains at its beginning the first of several short lacunae in these opening lines, continued the sentence begun in 1. Exactly how it continued it we obviously cannot say,[75] though in my earlier article I argued that the metrical grammar of the following b-verse, *Ic tudre aweox*, and its relation to the nearest readable text on either side of it, indicate that it begins a new sentence, so that the first sentence of the poem will have ended at the close of verse 2a.[76] If I am right on this point, the speaker begins (1–2a) by saying that he intends to tell his addressee something about, or something connected with, a *treocyn(-)* (perhaps *treocynne* originally, before the manuscript was damaged);[77] but although this "species of tree" seems most unlikely to be anything other than the rune-staff (or the species of tree from which it was cut), the incomplete nature of the opening sentence of the poem means that the reference does not settle the question of the speaker's nature: the speaker may be the *treocyn* himself, or he may be saying something about a *treocyn*.

---

[73] Elliott, "The Runes in *The Husband's Message*," 21; see also Goldsmith, "The Enigma of *The Husband's Message*," 243.

[74] See Bosworth and Toller, *An Anglo-Saxon Dictionary*, s.v. *secgan*; also above, Chapter 2.

[75] On the suggestions that have been made for filling the gap, see Leslie, *Three Old English Elegies*, 59, note, and Orton, "The Speaker in *The Husband's Message*," 53–54 and n. 7.

[76] See Orton, "Speaker," 44 and n. 7. Cf. Krapp and Dobbie's punctuation (*The Exeter Book*, 225), and Klinck, *Elegies*, 100 (see also her note to line 2 [200]), both of whom take 2b as part of the same clause as 2a.

[77] See my note to line 2 above.

Verse 2b, *Ic tudre aweox*, is undamaged. The range of meanings that the noun *tudor* can support in Old English generally means that verse 2b might mean either "I grew up from a child" or :"I grew up from a sucker" (i.e. from a shoot growing from the base of a tree).[78] Goldsmith has suggested that the word *tudor* was chosen for its ambiguity and that the poet is deliberately hedging about the nature of the speaker here. This is an attractive idea, though interpretation should also take account of Pope's observation (made in a different connection) on the sentence if its meaning is "I grew up from a child": this would be true of any human being and so is, in Pope's view, "as mindlessly self-evident a statement as can well be imagined."[79] If we agree with Pope about the redundancy, it seems likely that the reading of *tudre* as "from a child" was meant as a 'surface' meaning that the reader was expected to penetrate at some stage—perhaps here, but more probably later on—in the course of working his way through the poem. The underlying meaning to which the reader would penetrate is, of course, "from a sucker," establishing the piece of wood as the 'solution' to the riddle of the speaker's nature. It is perhaps significant that the syntax and vocabulary of verse 2b find a close parallel in *Riddle* 73 (Williamson 71) 1a *Ic on wonge aweox*, in which the speaker, a spear, refers to its earlier existence as a growing tree before it was forced to "bow to the will of a slayer" (7 *on bonan willan bugan*).

In the heavily damaged passage that follows (3–7), the various legible fragments seem to belong to an account of the speaker's previous travels (6 *Ful oft*) across the sea (5 *sealte streamas* and 7 *ofer heah h[a]fu*) by boat (6 *on bates*), no doubt as a messenger, according to the instructions of his "liege lord" (7 *mondryhten min*; see also 10 *mines frean* and 39 *min wine*, both "my lord"). For Leslie, the reference to frequent voyages militates against the rune-staff as speaker because such an object would not be used over and over again for messages; and although an original message could have been planed off and a new one inscribed in its place, it is obviously true that the same staff could not be reused indefinitely. R. I. Page, however, has drawn attention to a rune-staff from Bergen in Norway, dating probably from between c. 1200 A.D. and the fifteenth century, which contains two runic messages carved by different hands. The first is an instruction to someone (perhaps the inscriber's husband) to come home, and the second is a text which, though obscure, is no doubt a reply from the hand of the recipient of the original message.[80] This is evidence that rune-staves inscribed with messages could sometimes be recycled. But another possibility here which, if allowed, would lend support to the rune-staff hypothesis is that in referring to its various travels the staff is regarding itself generically rather than as a particular staff. As we saw earlier in this chapter, some of the Old English *Riddles* have generic speakers, for example the 'Onion' *Riddle*, quoted in full above. There are also

---

[78] See Bosworth and Toller, *An Anglo-Saxon Dictionary*, s.v. *tudor*, I and III.
[79] Pope, "Palaeography and Poetry," 45.
[80] Page, *Introduction*, 97.

parallels to this procedure in *The Dream of the Rood*, in which the cross sometimes speaks of its experiences in such a way as to suggest that it sees itself, not just as the cross of Calvary, but as a representative of all crosses used for execution, as for example in 87–88 *Iu ic wæs geworden wita heardost, leodum laðost*, "Previously I was made to be the most severe of torments, most hateful to men." Perhaps in the early lines of *The Husband's Message* the speaker is saying, in effect: "This is the kind of service I and my kind render to our masters"; and having described this role, it returns to the job in hand and speaks of itself as an individual.

Next the speaker begins to convey the particular message that he is currently charged to deliver. He speaks first of fidelity and of earlier vows made between his lord and the woman in happier times, when they were able to live under one roof, before feud drove the man abroad (19–20). It is in the course of this passage that the speaker refers to his lord as *se þisne beam agrof* (13b), "he who engraved this tree." Leslie takes this expression to imply that the speaker is a human messenger, not the staff, because a rune-staff would not refer to its own substance in this way, as if to something separate from himself. One way in which this point might be countered is by comparison with other examples of the same kind of unexpected objectivity in *The Dream of the Rood*, when the cross says (of Christ): *gestah he on gealgan heanne* (40), "he climbed up on to the high gallows," and *Crist wæs on rode* (56), "Christ was on the cross." Both of these statements are also represented in the Ruthwell Cross inscription, where the 'body' of the cross is present to the reader in the way described in Chapter 4. Another factor which it may be appropriate to invoke here is that the rune-staff is not just any object but an inscribed one. If the staff is itself the speaker, clearly its ability to 'speak' is related to the inscription it bears: the gift of language confers upon it what is, in reality, an exclusively human capacity. From this point of view, the staff's reference to its own substance might seem no more remarkable than a human speaker's reference to his own body.

The next part of the poem (20–48) consists of elaborate instructions to the woman to make a journey across the sea to her lord's country of exile. The messenger also assures the woman of his lord's passionate desire to be reunited with her: there is nothing in the world he wants more than to have her at his side as he distributes largesse to his retainers in his adopted homeland. The sincerity of his wish is emphasised by the speaker's use of a reporting clause, *þæspe he me sægde*, "as he said to me," to introduce in indirect speech an account of the lord's own expression of his longing. Leslie regards this reporting clause as another sign that the speaker of the poem is human, not wooden: the verb *sægde* is, in Leslie's view, "much more appropriate to a human messenger than to a rune-stave whose function is essentially the conveyance of a written message."[81] If, however, we allow the possibility that the rune-staff is the speaker of the poem, perhaps its per-

---

[81] Leslie, *Three Old English Elegies*, 14.

sonification as an inscribed object logically entails the presentation of whatever message is inscribed upon it as something that was 'said' to it, not something that was written upon its body.[82] In fact, it seems possible that all the textual evidence Leslie finds in favour of a human messenger as speaker can equally well be interpreted as a consequence of the poet's decision to personify the rune-staff, not as just any human being, but as a messenger in particular. Of course, as a rune-staff, it carries only the bare five-rune message contained in lines 50–51; it is only its personification that permits it to elaborate on the message in the way it does. I shall pursue the implications of this expansion of the runic message below.

The runic message inscribed on the staff is given near the end of the poem:

gehyre ic ætsomne   .S.R. geador
.EA.W. ond .M.   aþe benemnan

"I hear together the sun-road and sea-joy and the man declare by oath . . ."

There is no general agreement about how the five runes are to be interpreted,[83] though it is assumed that they are meant to be sounded by the reader as their names, all of which are well integrated into the metre and alliteration of the verses in which they occur. The first four runes are divided in the manuscript into two pairs. The first pair means 'sun' (or possibly 'sail') and 'road', the combined meaning of which might be 'sky' or 'sea'; the second pair, 'sea' (or possibly 'earth'),[84] and 'joy', are combined in a similar way. The fifth rune has the name 'man'. The whole may, of course, be a pre-arranged, coded message, without much, if any, explicit meaning, making sense only to the intended recipient as a signal that the time has come for her to rejoin her lord abroad; but if we feel compelled to give meaning to the three runic units in the text, the first, 'sun-road' or 'sail-road', might indicate the direction or mode in which the woman should travel; the second pair, 'sea-joy' or 'earth-joy', might suggest a journey leading to love and happiness; and 'man' might indicate the lord who will provide these things for her at the end of her voyage. I need scarcely point out that this interpretation involves a good deal of speculation.

---

[82] This point was anticipated above in Chapter 2, pp. 44–47.

[83] For a careful discussion of the meaning of the runes, see Leslie, *Three Old English Elegies*, 15–18; but so completely have they eluded interpretation that modern commentators on the poem are beginning to suspect the poet of 'ludic' intentions. Thus Bragg ("Runes and Readers," 38) insists that the runes are the letters of some word, but reaches no conclusion about what the word might be and seems to imply that the poet may be deliberately teasing his readers with a puzzle without any solution. Niles ("The Trick of the Runes," 209) suggests that the reader is given considerable freedom to expand the runes imaginatively "within the context of the monologue," for example as *segl-rad*, "bridle-path of the sail," and *eadig wif ond mann*, "a happy woman and man."

[84] See Klinck, *Elegies*, 207.

A crucial feature of this passage is the use of the verb *gehyre*, 'hear', in relation to a runic message.[85] A human messenger could scarcely claim to 'hear' a runic message he carried. A personified rune-staff, however, could logically make such a claim: if the written nature of any inscription it carried were emphasised, the personification would collapse. The rune-staff, personified as a human messenger, apparently 'speaks' its runic message; and the illogicality of this scenario were the speaker a human messenger seems to settle the question of the speaker's identity in favour of the staff.

But (to revert to a question raised briefly above) how can the rune-staff 'speak' in words additional to its runic inscription? As in the runic *Riddles* examined earlier, the distinction between runic and roman script has a clear formal function in this poem: runic is writing, roman is 'speech'. It seems to follow that staff and inscription together constitute the 'speaker'. The runes are more than just the message the staff happens to be carrying on this particular journey; they are an essential part of its nature, a gift of language which confers on it a competence to 'speak' in explanation of its actual inscription. In this sense, then, it is the runes on the staff that humanize it and (so to speak) loosen its tongue.

It is worth pausing for a moment to admire the ingenuity of the poet's characterisation of the speaker and its logical consequences. Even though better sense can be made of the poem if the speaker is the rune-staff rather than a messenger, the staff's personification as a messenger is very elaborately and carefully developed. In the first line, we are probably meant to understand that the staff's communicative power, its ability to 'speak', is released the moment ("Now") the woman's eyes fall on the runes—at 'receiving time', the moment which would correspond with the arrival of a human messenger in an oral society where letters were unknown. It follows logically from this that the lord's original inscription of the staff should also be presented as a spoken communication, this time between the inscription's engraver and his 'messenger', the staff; so that in lines 30–35, the staff describes the man's desire to share with the woman the distribution of rewards to his followers in terms of indirect speech, as something 'said' to it by him (31 *þæspe he me sægde*, "as he said to me"). Finally, the presentation of inscription as a human being's way of speaking to an object is confirmed in line 50 by the rune-staff's claim to 'hear' the runes inscribed upon it. In reality, runes are, of course, an exclusively literary mode; one can no more hear them than speak in them. Although the runes are probably to be read as their names in recitation, this does not obscure their status as a strictly silent system of linguistic represen-

---

[85] The *h* of *gehyre* is by no means certain in the manuscript; see Orton, "Speaker," 49–50. Klinck (*Elegies*, 206–7) and Muir (*The Exeter Anthology*, 2: 654, note to line 50) both summarise more recent opinions. Even more recently, Bragg ("Runes and Readers," 34–35) has preferred *gecyre*, which she translates as "put together." Niles ("The Trick of the Runes," 191–92) does not commit himself to any reading, though he quotes the *gehyre* of Muir's edition.

tation. And yet, if linguistic objects such as rune-staffs are to speak or hear at all, it is perfectly logical that they should be described as doing so in terms of writing and reading. One is strongly reminded here (again) of the Ruthwell Cross, discussed in the previous chapter, whose inscription constitutes its special way of talking to those who visit it.

The staff's 'messenger' persona is clearly based on an analogy with pre-literate modes of linguistic communication over distance: both oral human messengers and letters (the rune-staff is essentially a letter) carry messages from person to person. However, the analogy is not perfect. A human messenger will not present the message he is carrying to its recipient in exactly the form he received it from the sender. He will not mimic the sender's words, but will use indirect speech to express them, and this gives him a certain amount of freedom of expression. A letter, however, may communicate nothing more nor less than its text. The messenger-persona in *The Husband's Message* does indeed use indirect speech, as we saw earlier. But at another, more dramatic level of meaning, the only message the woman actually receives is the runic message included by the staff in its speech; the situation the poem realizes is that of a woman reading a runic text. The contrast between the actual written message, terse and (to us, at least) mysterious, and the speech, courteous and elaborate, seems very pointed, and one cannot doubt that the poet wanted us to notice it. But what is the precise relationship between the two? If, as I believe, the poem describes (at the most basic level of its meaning) nothing more than the reading of a letter written on a piece of wood, we must conclude that the speech is some kind of expansion of the runic text. But whose expansion is it? One possible answer to that is 'the poet's', but that would evade the real question of who expands the runic message in its diegesis. 'The messenger-persona' is another unsatisfactory and evasive answer, for its speech is evidently a rhetorical device, the product of mere personification or prosopopoeia. There is no actual messenger in the situation the poem describes. And so it seems that the only person to whom this expansion may be attributed is the woman herself as she reads the letter alone. A closer examination of the content of the speech tends to confirm this deduction; for it contains no information which the woman could not know or infer on the basis either of the arrival of the rune-staff and the message it carries, or of the history of her relationship with her lord. The speech must therefore be essentially an account of her own perceptions, thoughts, memories, feelings, and inferences on reading the runic message, projected forth and converted into the kind of speech a human messenger might have made under similar circumstances if he had been sent instead of the rune-staff. On another level, the fact that the speech is addressed to the woman is ironic in view of its redundancy from her point of view; she has the runic message before her and needs no help in interpreting it. The implication of the speech's content is thus that there is no need for any kind of presence or speech in the couple's communication. The runic message is quite sufficiently eloquent.

A kind of deconstructive logic seems to operate in *The Husband's Message*. A vivid, clearly defined image of a human messenger is created in the course of the rune-staff's speech; and although it eventually becomes clear that this is only a 'surface' image, it is easy to be taken in by it. It is only when we reach the runic passage that we become aware that the woman-recipient has no need of any spoken message, so that the image of a messenger and his speech collapses, sucked in, so to speak, by the runic text, like the genie into Ali Baba's lamp. A basic implication of the poem, I suggest, is that the analogy between speech and writing is imperfect; that in spite of the eloquence of the 'speaker' here, writing is really an autonomous mode of language, effective in its own right. The astonishing thing about writing is that it works on its own, without the support of any human or deictic 'presence'.[86] If this is a valid reading of the poem, *The Husband's Message* represents a more advanced and sophisticated perspective on writing and reading that any of the other texts examined in this book.

This interpretation of the poem also helps to explain the juxtaposition of *Riddle* 60 and *The Husband's Message* in the manuscript. I say 'juxtaposition' because it seems to me that these are separate works, not two parts of a single poem. *Riddle* 60 begins with a description of what is clearly a semi-aquatic plant, and it is easier to believe that this is a reed (and therefore that the speaker is a reed-pen) than any plant that could be described as a "kind of tree" (*Husband's Message* 2 *treocyn-*; see also 13 *beam*, 'tree' or possibly 'branch'). Another point in favour of the integrity of the two poems is that both contain early passages in which we are given a description of the speaker's origins as a growing plant (*Riddle* 60 1–7a, *Husband's Message* 2 *Ic tudre aweox*), the separation of which would seem odd if they were parts of one *Riddle*. I have to admit, however, that these considerations are not decisive, even in combination; and it is clear that the two texts (if that is how they should be designated) do have some very specific things in common that account for their presentation in sequence in the manuscript. One is that the texts themselves are, to a degree, part of the poems' subject-matter: the text of *Riddle* 60 in the Exeter Book is, as we saw earlier, an actual manifestation of the actual, specific pen that is the riddle's solution, creating the effect of 'presence' that I described. Similarly in *The Husband's Message*, the runes are not just a sample of the sort of message the speaker may carry, but a specific message related to the circumstances of the sender and the recipient, and are an important part of the speaker's individuality. Whereas *Riddle* 60 presents the reader with a manifestation of the solution's existence in the form of its text, *The Husband's Message* goes one better by presenting us with an aspect of the speaker's own nature actually built into the text. Language, whether spoken or written, is normally used to evoke concepts in the hearer's or reader's mind; and all the other

---

[86] See Olson, *The World on Paper*, 183: "... texts ... in a sense, speak for themselves. They lose the 'voice' of the speaker or writer to become what has been called 'autonomous' or 'authorless text'."

Exeter Book *Riddles* work in this way. These two poems are alone and alike in managing (to some extent) to bypass the imaginary-conceptual level of linguistic signification, which gives them a special communicative immediacy comparable, perhaps, with that of medium-deictic inscriptions, though in *The Husband's Message* one might almost claim that runic writing itself 'speaks' to the reader. Both poems, however, create something comparable with the deictic simultaneity that is normally the province of speech.

§8. Summary

In this chapter, one of the main themes of this book—the use of the impersonal first-person pronoun—is restated and developed in the distinctive mode of the Old English *Riddles*. In the homodiegetic type of riddle, the solution is an 'I' to which the poet gives a description of itself and then, so to speak, removes the speaker from our apprehension. The reader is put in a position comparable with that of the reader of a medium-deictic inscription which, though technically untransferable, has somehow become detached from its medium: he must construct a viable image of the speaker on the basis of its speech alone. The inscribers of medium-deictic inscriptions have found a way of closing the deictic gap; but here it is the reader who must perform the task: the riddle is solved once the reader discovers the speaking 'presence' that the poet has hidden from him.

Such poems exhibit a dizzying mixture of effects and implications. The 'speech' is, of course, the poet's creation; but his deliberate subtraction of the speaker from the pragmatics of its utterance creates an impression—more disconcerting, no doubt, to readers who were unaccustomed to this characteristic effect of literacy than we are today—of unanchored, disembodied language, at least until an image of the speaker begins to take shape in the reader's mind. The notion, embodied in medium-deictic inscriptions, of written language as a mode of utterance appropriate to impersonal subjects is sustained in the homodiegetic *Riddles*; but on the other hand, the poet's concealment of the utterer also creates an experience for the reader comparable with that of reading a text written by a narrator who refers to himself as 'I' but fails to supply any information about his identity. Homodiegetic riddles thus function as a model for solving the more general problem (addressed in my next chapter) of the deictic gap created by literacy, when writers use the first-person pronoun *in propria persona*. These *Riddles* demonstrate the possibility (as well as the difficulty) of knowing the writer from his writings.

Those Old English *Riddles* that use runic characters for the individual letters of the solution's name naturally invite comparison with Cynewulf's runic signatures, examined in the previous chapter. One contrast with Cynewulf's method is that no serious attempt is made in the runic *Riddles* to incorporate the meaning of the runes' names into the narrative context. Cynewulf, as we saw, attempted semantic integration of the names but did not make a great success of it in any of his signatures, defeated by the heterogeneous and archaic frame of reference of the runes' traditional names. Cynewulf usually managed to integrate his runic letters into the standard metrical and alliterative patterns of his verse, whereas the runic *Riddles* vary considerably in this regard, again partly for technical reasons: the metrical structure of the Old English half-line will not accommodate bare sequences of runic names. Cynewulf found ways round this problem (by using conjunctions), but the poets of the runic *Riddles* seem not to have been particularly concerned with this kind of integration, perhaps because they knew that the runes were essential clues to the solutions of their riddles and so were unlikely to be obliterated by copyists, whether or not they fitted into the metre. The runic sequences in the *Riddles* are spelling games within the more conventional riddling context of enigmatic descriptions in roman.

Riddle 42, 'Cock and Hen', uses the names of runic characters written out in roman rather than the runic characters themselves to indicate the spelling of the solution. Here, the runic names are exceptionally well integrated, metrically and grammatically, into the fabric of the verse, which contributes to a 'speakable' quality in the text which the other runic *Riddles* do not, on the whole, share. The poem also proclaims itself an oral utterance, delivered in a standard heroic setting; but on the other hand, it appeals to "runemen" and "those who know books," and there are other technical aspects of the poem that show it to be a literate production from the first. These conflicting aspects of the poem, rather than being confusing or confused, probably reflect a deliberate demonstration of the basic structural opposition between orality and literacy, and other contrasts linked with it: speech versus writing, roman versus runes, roman for transcribing oral language versus runes for the language of the hand. The runic names spelt in roman emerge here as a perfect mediation of all these oppositions.

Riddles 47, 'Bookmoth', and 60, 'Reed-pen', are both (as well as being puzzles) meditations on the written word in books in particular; but they wittily provoke reflections on the oral-literate interface with a freshness that centuries of literacy have scarcely reduced. The 'Bookmoth' *Riddle* uses the Old English metalanguage of the spoken word (*word, cwide, gied*) as a source of innovative cognitive images of the written word. The poet's choice, as shown by Robinson, of terms (*fræt, (for)swealg, cwide, stapol*) for the caterpillar's activity that blend the notions of ingestion and reading draws attention, through the blend, to language, its use, and its understanding as exclusively human capacities. The poem reads now like a snapshot of a particular stage in the process of the modification of linguistic concepts necessitated by the rise of literacy; but it also seems to indicate a new level of reflection on the essential aspects of language in general. *Riddle* 60 focuses on writing as silent speech, and its potential for secret one-to-one communication; but here the pragmatics of the riddle have other, unique implications: the text itself is produced by the riddle's solution, so that the pen can communicate directly (and secretly) with any reader (14 *þe*, 'you') who encounters its work in this or any other manuscript. Again, reflections are here provoked on oral-literate distinctions and contrasts: spoken versus written communication, vocal versus silent communication, public versus private language, and the spatial and temporal implications of the two modes.

The Husband's Message is probably best understood as a poem mainly about reading rather than writing. The modern critical controversy over the nature—human or material—of the speaker is in this case a significant indication of the poet's deliberate ambiguity. Here again (as in the runic *Riddles*), runes are for writing, roman for speech. The speech in roman is based on the woman's feelings and thoughts as she reads the runic message. The poem reveals how writing, given the right pragmatics (here the context of an existing relationship between the man and his wife), can communicate autonomously, without the support of any human presence. In both *HM* and *Riddle* 60, the texts themselves are part of the poems' subject-matter, and both have a special immediacy comparable with medium-deictic inscriptions. Deictic simultaneity (as in speech) is mimicked in both these poems.

Chapter 6
The Disembodied Speaker

§1. The speaker *in propria persona*

In Chapter 2 of this book I argued that a first-person 'speech' inscribed on, and attributed to, a material artifact (e.g. "X made me") obeys a logical implication of writing as a variant of speech. My argument was based upon the idea of authorial 'presence' and on the concepts of coding time and receiving time, borrowed from pragmatics theory. To recapitulate briefly: in oral communication, coding time and receiving time necessarily coincide, whereas in written communication, receiving time normally lags behind coding time. The reader must therefore come to terms somehow with the absence of the writer when he or she receives his or her message; and the writer must also adjust to the idea of an absent and perhaps unknown readership—something for which oral communication, in which the speaker can always see and hear everyone he or she addresses, provides no preparation. In these circumstances, only the inscribed object or written book can satisfactorily bridge the 'deictic gap', created by writing, between coding time and receiving time, by acting as a surrogate presence of the absent utterer—the writer—at receiving time. First-person medium-deictic inscriptions represent an attempt to mimic—one might even say restore—the essential structural components of spoken communication in writing. These inscriptions also represent an apt arrangement from the point of view of natural law, because writing is silent, and so is an appropriate form of language for the medium of writing—the inscribed object, dumb and inert—to employ in its 'utterances'. We have already looked at some texts, notably the Ruthwell Cross inscription (Chapter 4) and *The Husband's Message* (Chapter 5), the form and content of which seem to reflect an awareness of this notion of writing as the special speech of inanimate things.

How, then, was the Anglo-Saxon writer to represent his own subjectivity in writing? The transfer of the first-person subject to the inscribed medium seems to represent (in retrospect, at least) an evasion of the most profound implications of writing for the human subject—the writer *in propria persona*. Perhaps this manoeuvre is to be taken as a sign that the newly literate do not find it easy to take up writing immediately and use it as an alternative to speech, as if the substitution of visible letters for audible sounds represented no more than a simple exchange of one set of symbols for another. Preliterate societies are likely to regard the audible voice as the essence of linguistic communication, whereas the intervention, inevitably involved in writing, of a material medium disconcertingly removes voice from the process. Thus silenced, language is placed outside the traditional sphere of human use. From this perspective, the question raised in Chapter 2 of how Anglo-Saxon writers managed to reclaim writing (if one can put it like that) for direct subjective expression and communication is a challenging one. In what spirit, with what readers in mind, and in anticipation of what degree of comprehension and sympathy does a newly-literate individual pick up a stylus or pen and write of himself or herself as 'I'? This question, as it presents itself in the context of incipient literacy in Old English poetry, will be the main focus of this chapter. The Old English texts I shall use as the basis of discussion are a group of six poems which were for a long time called "elegies" by modern scholars but are now more often, and probably more appropriately, referred to as "lyrics".

§2. The Old English lyrics, the *Riddles*, and wisdom poetry

There are several kinds of link between the Old English *Riddles* and the seven lyrics (*The Wanderer*, *The Seafarer*, *Deor*, *Wulf and Eadwacer*, *The Wife's Lament*, *The Husband's Message*, and *The Ruin*). All seven lyrics are anonymous; and all are preserved, like most of the surviving Old English *Riddles*, only in the Exeter Book. The position in the manuscript of some of them might indicate that the compiler of the collection saw some kinship between them and the *Riddles*. The sequence of texts at the end of the Exeter Book is as follows (lyrics and *Riddles* italicized):

Soul and Body II (fol. 98ʳ);
Deor;
Wulf and Eadwacer;
Riddles 1–59;
The Wife's Lament;
The Judgement Day I;
Resignation;
The Descent into Hell;
Alms-Giving;
Pharaoh;
The Lord's Prayer I;
Homiletic Fragment II;
Riddle 30b;
Riddle 60;
The Husband's Message;
The Ruin;
Riddles 61–95 [End of MS].

Four of the lyrics—*Wulf and Eadwacer*, *The Wife's Lament*, *The Husband's Message* and *The Ruin*—actually abut on *Riddles*, and a fifth, *Deor*, precedes *Wulf and Eadwacer*. The fact that both *Wulf and Eadwacer* and *The Husband's Message* have been interpreted by some modern critics as riddles (though this is not a popular view of them at the moment) might be related in some way to this distribution: perhaps the compiler of the Exeter Book also regarded these four lyrics as somehow related to riddles. However, the position, earlier in the collection, of the two remaining lyrics, *The Wanderer* and *The Seafarer*, suggest connections with a different class of poetry. The sequence of texts in the manuscript which includes these two poems is as follows:

Juliana
The Wanderer
The Gifts of Men
Precepts
The Seafarer
Vainglory
Widsith
The Fortunes of Men
Maxims I
The Order of the World
The Riming Poem
The Panther
The Whale
The Partridge
Soul and Body II
Deor

All of the poems in this list with the exception of *Juliana*, *Widsith*, and the three bestiary poems (*The Panther*, *The Whale*, *The Partridge*) are included by T. A. Shippey in a list of twenty-three Old English poems (fifteen of them extant only in the Exeter Book) sharing the following characteristics:

> Most . . . are around a hundred lines long; in most the poet makes a direct appeal to his audience; many contain gnomic generalisations, or use the figure of an old man instructing his disciple; minor similarities of tone or conclusion are pervasive.[1]

---

[1] See Shippey, *Poems of Wisdom and Learning*, 1, footnote.

§3. Genre and form in the lyrics: autodiegetic narratives, explicitly autobiographical

Although few, if any, recent critics would argue that all seven of the lyrics represent a single genre, they are connected (rather as Shippey's group of wisdom poems are) by a series of features which link each of them to some, and in a few cases to most, of the others. A significant formal link between all of them except *The Ruin* is that they consist of, or incorporate, narratives in which the narrator plays an important part in the story he or she tells, and is referred to by the first- person pronoun. *The Ruin* differs from the other lyrics in several other ways and it seems best to exclude it from discussion from now on. In this respect the remaining six lyrics resemble the first-person *Riddles* discussed earlier, though on the other hand, as Shippey notes, it marks them off from most of the wisdom poems he identifies, few of which contain "more than a perfunctory line or two in the first person."[2] In the previous chapter we noted that this general type of narrative, in which the narrator has a role in the story he or she tells, is called 'homodiegetic' in the terminology developed by Genette for his narratological theory.[3] A homodiegetic narrative is the opposite of a heterodiegetic one, in which the narrator remains entirely aloof from the story. Heterodiegetic narratives among the Old English *Riddles* were exemplified in Chapter 5. A more familiar example from Old English poetry is *Beowulf*, in which the narrator, though occasionally referring to himself in the first person,[4] is not himself a character in the story he tells, which is one of the doings of men and women (and monsters) in the past. The homodiegetic speakers of the lyrics are always nameless except in *Deor*, where the speaker identifies himself in 37 *Me wæs Deor noma*, "Deor was my name."[5] That the narratives produced by these first-person speakers are autobiographical is explicitly claimed in three of them, *The Seafarer*, *The Wife's Lament*, and *Deor*, in which the speaker says that it is his or her own experiences that are recounted in the poem. Thus *The Seafarer* begins (1–2) *Mæg ic be me sylfum soðgied wrecan, siþas secgan, . . .*, "I can utter a true lay about myself, tell of my experiences . . ."; *The Wife's Lament* begins (1–2a) *Ic þis giedd wrece bi me ful geomorre, minre sylfre sið*, "I utter this lay about myself, very sad [as I am], my own experience"; and *Deor* includes the statement (35–6): *Þæt ic bi me sylfum secgan wille, þæt ic hwile wæs . . .*, "I wish to say this about myself, that I was for a time . . ." Genette reserves the

---

[2] Shippey, *Poems of Wisdom and Learning*, 2.
[3] Above, 144.
[4] *Beowulf* 38, 62, 1197, 2163, 2172 *Hyrde ic* (or *ic. . . hyrde*), "I heard . . ."; 74, 1011, 1027, 1196, 2752, 2773 *gefrægn ic* (or *ic gefræg[e]n*), "I heard . . ."; and 776, 837, 1955, 2685, 2837 *mine gefræge*, "as I heard."
[5] The significance of this statement is considered below, 198–200.

term 'autodiegetic' for homodiegetic narratives like these, in which the narrator is not just any character in the story he tells but a central one.[6]

A remaining question, raising issues beyond the strictly narratological, concerns the relationship between the speakers in these poems and their authors. Are they one and the same, or are these speakers fictional creations of the poets? A cluster of theoretical difficulties adhere to this problem and I put off discussion of it until later in this chapter.[7]

§4. The content of the lyrics: the speaker in space and time; past happiness, present misery; separation and absence

The Old English lyrics all express powerful emotions, but they share several more specific preoccupations. In all except *The Husband's Message*, the speaker has suffered or is suffering, and looks back nostalgically to an earlier period of happiness, contrasting it, sometimes bitterly, with a miserable present. This suffering is in several cases occasioned by separation from someone dear to the speaker. In *Wulf and Eadwacer* the speaker is physically divided from another character called 'Wulf' whose absence she laments; and in *The Wife's Lament* the speaker mourns the departure overseas and protracted absence of her 'lord' (6 *min hlaford*, "my lord," 33 *frean*, "lord," also called *min freond*, "my friend" in 47 and *min wine*, "my friend," or possibly "my lover," in 50). In *The Husband's Message*, the speaker—a wooden object bearing an inscription, as we have seen—refers to its sender as *mondryhten* (7), "liege lord," *frean* (10), "lord," *þeoden* (29), "prince," and *se mon* (44), "the man," though in this poem the speaker is not presented as suffering as a result of this absence. It would be surprising if it were, for it is only an intermediary between the man and the woman to whom the rune-staff's speech is addressed.[8] In *The Wanderer*, lines 22–23 indicate a permanent separation because the speaker's lord is dead and in his grave (. . . *siþþan geara iu goldwine minne hrusan heolstre biwrah*, probably to be translated as "since long ago I covered my lord in the darkness of earth");[9] and in *The Seafarer* also, the speaker is apparently bereaved (16 *winemægum bidroren*, "bereft of dear kinsmen"). In some lyrics, the separation suffered by the speaker results from travel, either by the speaker or another character, often across the sea (see *The Wife's Lament* 6–7, *The Husband's Message* 4–9, 21, 26–27, 40–41, *The Wanderer* 3–5 and *passim*, and *The Seafarer* 1–66). In *Wulf and Eadwacer* the speaker refers to Wulf's terrestrial wanderings (9 *widlastum*, "wide-ranging tracks").

---

[6] Genette, *Narrative Discourse*, 245.
[7] See below, §8.
[8] For a detailed discussion of this poem, see Chap. 5 above.
[9] See *The Wanderer*, ed. T. P. Dunning and A. J. Bliss (London: Methuen, 1969), 108, note to 23a.

§5. The problem of identification

The experience of reading a first-person speech by a textual 'voice' which fails to identify itself in clear terms is rather like receiving an anonymous letter, or being set a riddle to solve. The modern reader of the lyrics feels the need to identify the speakers, either as individuals or types. Any attempt to reconstruct the stories told in these poems inevitably runs up against the question of what kind of person or being the speaker is, though the exact form of the question varies from poem to poem. In two cases, *The Husband's Message* and *Wulf and Eadwacer*, the very humanity of the speaker is questionable; indeed, in the case of the former poem most readers would probably now agree that the speaker is not a human messenger but a wooden object upon which the inscription, given as part of the text (50–51), is supposed to be inscribed. As we saw in the previous chapter, the probability that the speaker in *The Husband's Message* is non-human inspired a theory that the poem is not a whole but part of a larger unit, a lengthy riddle of which the first part is the text known as *Riddle* 60 which immediately precedes it in the manuscript; but this view lost much of its popularity after the inconsistencies it entails were identified.[10] As for *Wulf and Eadwacer*, W. J. Sedgefield, writing in 1931, identified the speaker and other characters in the poem as wolves.[11] Sedgefield propounded this theory very briefly and it has attracted no supporters since, though I attempted a reassessment of it some years ago and found more in its favour than I expected.[12] Sedgefield also maintained, in line with some earlier critics, that *Wulf and Eadwacer* is not a lyric poem but the first of the Exeter Book *Riddles*—a view which, as noted earlier, receives some support from the text's position immediately before the first undisputed *Riddle* in the Exeter Book. It seems fair to say, however, that Sedgefield made a genre of necessity by turning the puzzling nature of the poem into an aspect of its form as the poet himself conceived it. He also ignored one obstacle to his theory: if *Wulf and Eadwacer* is a riddle, its solution is a dramatic situation rather than a familiar nominal concept of the kind which forms the solution of most of the Old English *Riddles*. We cannot say that the solution is 'wolves', because it would be self-defeating in a riddle to name the solution openly, as the poet of *Wulf and Eadwacer* does (the character 'Wulf' is mentioned by name five times, in lines 4, 9, 13 [twice] and 17).

The sex of the speakers in two of the Old English lyrics was regarded, at least until fairly recently, as a matter for debate. In both *The Wife's Lament* and *Wulf and Eadwacer*, a female speaker seems to be indicated by the grammar.[13] The relevant

---

[10] See Leslie, "The Integrity of Riddle 60."

[11] W. J. Sedgefield, "Old English Notes," *MLR* 26 (1931): 74–75.

[12] P. R. Orton, "An Approach to *Wulf and Eadwacer*," *Proceedings of the Royal Irish Academy* 85C (1985): 223–58.

[13] See Marilynn Desmond, "The Voice of Exile: Feminist Literary History and the Anonymous Anglo-Saxon Elegy," *Critical Inquiry* 16 (1989–1990): 572–90, who

forms in *Wulf and Eadwacer* are two adjectives, *reotugu* (10, nom. sg. f.), "lamenting", and *seoce* (14, acc. sg. f.), "ill", both used by the speaker with reference to herself; and in *The Wife's Lament*, the adjective *geomorre* (1, dat. sg. f.), "sad", and the combination *minre sylfre* (2, both dat. sg. f.), "my own", in the phrase *minre sylfre sið*, "my own lot", again in reference to the speaker. Bruce Mitchell,[14] in a reply to an attempt to show that the speaker in *The Wife's Lament* might be a man,[15] makes a strong case for a female speaker in that poem on the basis of these grammatically feminine forms. Both poems consist entirely of speeches in the first person; there is no heterodiegetic narrator to introduce the speaker to the audience. If the speakers' stories had been told by an external narrator, the use of names or sex-specific nouns (for example *wif*, 'woman' or *mann*, 'man') or third-person pronouns (*heo*, 'she' or *he*, 'he') might have indicated the sex of the main characters; as it is, we are forced to rely on gender-inflexions to establish the sex of the speakers. Of course, the speakers might still have had occasion to refer to themselves by sex-specific nouns, or given their own names, but neither of them do. In *The Wife's Lament* 1, the easiest interpretation of the form *geomorre* is that it is the dat. sg. f. of the strong adjective *geomor*, 'sad', agreeing in its case and number with the dat. sg. first person pronoun *me* (dative because governed by the preposition *bi*) in the same verse. The form of the gen. sg. f. of the adjective would also be *geomorre*, but a genitive cannot be accommodated by the context. The idiom does not translate easily into modern English, but ". . . about sad me," or "about me, sad as I am" is perhaps the best we can do. The feminine gender of *geomorre* cannot be explained by agreement with a grammatically feminine noun for the simple reason that there is no feminine noun in the context upon which it might depend (*sið* is masculine). Mitchell finds a close parallel for *The Wife's Lament* 2 *minre sylfre sið* in *Christ I* 339 *þinre sylfre sunu*, "your own son," referring to Christ in a speech addressed to his mother Mary. In this phrase, the masculine noun *sunu* is acc. sg. and the possessive plainly agrees with the feminine gen. *sylfre*. This seems to constitute an almost exact grammatical parallel to *The Wife's Lament* 2 *minre sylfre sið*. In the case of *Christ I* 339, the context establishes that the person addressed "is and must be feminine" (Mitchell) — "must be" because no other explanation will account for the feminine inflexions of both *þinre* and *sylfre*. The same may probably be said of the speaker of *The Wife's Lament* 2 *minre sylfre sið*. The kind of argument Mitchell is able to mount here could never be matched in relation to a Modern English text because the English language

---

illustrates how the female voices in these two poems have in the past "occasionally disturbed the patriarchal sensibilities" of modern editors and been silenced by emendation. Desmond urges the assimilation of these female (anonymous) voices to those of the later middles ages (Margery Kempe, Julian of Norwich): women's language (if not women's literature) in English begins in Anglo-Saxon England, not in the fifteenth century.

[14] Bruce Mitchell, "The Narrator of *The Wife's Lament*," *NM* 73 (1972): 222–34; and idem, *Old English Syntax*, 1: §1175 (494).

[15] Martin Stevens, "The Narrator of *The Wife's Lament*," *NM* 69 (1968): 72–90.

no longer possesses the means of marking sex by gender-inflexions on first- and second-person possessives and reflexive pronouns. If Old English had not still retained gender-marking inflexions on words in these categories, it would have been much more difficult to demonstrate that the speakers in these poems were female.

Various attempts, none of them very successful, have been made to identify the speakers in the Old English lyrics with named characters in traditional medieval stories known from other (not exclusively Anglo-Saxon) sources. Henry Schofield's attempt to identify *Wulf and Eadwacer* as a speech of Signý, a female character in the Old Icelandic *Völsunga saga*, is a relatively persuasive example of this kind of approach,[16] and one subsequent critic has tried to support it.[17] It has been suggested that *The Wife's Lament* is a version of one of the stories, very widespread in the Middle Ages, of banished or exiled wives associated with the names of Constance and Crescentia;[18] but the parallels are not nearly specific enough to enable us to identify the speaker in the Old English poem with the heroine of any particular version of these 'banished wife' stories. On the whole, it seems fair to say that the search for sources for, or even analogues to, these poems has contributed very little to our knowledge of their speakers.[19]

§6. Narratological issues: speaker, narrator, poet

Most of the Old English lyrics are fairly clearly utterances by a single speaker. *The Wanderer*, however, has a more complex narratological structure which creates special difficulties; and *Deor* presents a peculiar narratological problem of its own. Most modern editors of *The Wanderer* use inverted commas to mark off the words of the homodiegetic (and autodiegetic) 'wanderer' of the modern title—the 'I' of the poem, to whom most of the text is certainly to be assigned—from other passages which are given to a heterodiegetic narrator;[20] but they disagree about where this narrator's interventions occur. Dunning and Bliss

---

[16] Henry Schofield, "Signy's Lament," *PMLA* 17 (1902): 262–95.

[17] See Richard North, "Metre and Meaning in *Wulf and Eadwacer*: Signý Reconsidered," in *Loyal Letters: Studies on Medieval Alliterative Poetry and Prose*, ed. L. A. J. R. Houwen and A. A. MacDonald (Groningen: Egbert Forsten, 1994), 29–54.

[18] See Leslie, *Three Old English Elegies*, 9–10.

[19] Bragg (*Lyric Speakers*, 110) thinks that in four Old English poems (*Wulf and Eadwacer*, *The Wife's Lament*, *Deor*, and *Resignation*) the speaker is a fictional character, well known to the audience, who is "speaking from his or her situation in folktale or literature," though she does not insist on particular identifications.

[20] In an attempt to avoid confusing the reader, I shall refer throughout this discussion to the first-person speaker as "the wanderer" rather than as "the *eardstapa*", because at least one editor (Hamer) evidently regards this Old English word as designating not the main speaker but a person whose words the main speaker quotes verbatim (see further below). I use "the narrator" for the heterodiegetic narrator of the poem—assuming

attribute lines 6–7, 88–91, and 111 to him,[21] whereas R. F. Leslie would limit his contribution to lines 6–7 and 111.[22] The punctuation of the opening of Krapp and Dobbie's text, reproduced below, indicates that they take lines 1–5 as belonging to the narrator as well:[23]

```
     Oft him anhaga      are gebideð,
     metudes miltse,     þeah þe he modcearig
     geond lagulade      longe sceolde
     hreran mid hondum   hrimcealde sæ,
5    wadan wræclastas.   Wyrd bið ful aræd!
       Swa cwæð eardstapa,   earfeþa gemyndig,
     wraþra wælsleahta   winemæga hryre:
     "Oft ic sceolde ana uhtna gehwylce
     mine ceare cwiþan.  Nis nu cwicra nan
10   þe ic him modsefan  minne durre
     sweotule asecgan.      ...        (Wanderer 1–11a)
```

"Often the solitary one experiences grace, the mercy of the creator, even though, troubled in thought, he has often had to set in motion with his hands the ice-cold sea throughout the sea-way, travel the paths of exile. Fate is fully determined!

Thus spoke the wanderer, mindful of hardships, of cruel slaughters accompanying the fall of kinsmen: 'Often I have had to bewail my sorrow alone at break of each day; there is now no longer any man alive to whom I dare reveal my heart openly'."

The most controversial aspect of this presentation is its implication that 6 *Swa*, "Thus," refers only forward to the speech which, in Krapp and Dobbie's view, begins in line 8.[24] Both Dunning and Bliss and Leslie, by enclosing lines 1–5 in

---

he exists: again, as we shall see shortly, Hamer punctuates the poem in a way that implies that there is no heterodiegetic narrator, only a homodiegetic one—"the wanderer."

[21] See Dunning and Bliss, *The Wanderer*, 80, 106, 120–22.

[22] R. F. Leslie, ed., *The Wanderer* (Manchester: Manchester University Press, 1966), 61–64.

[23] It is not easy to summarize the arguments about who says what in *The Wanderer* without quoting most of the text. The reader is referred to Leslie's lucid account, in the introduction to his edition (2–25), of the various arrangements that editors had suggested by the middle sixties, and to the more recent discussion by Gerald Richman, "Speaker and Speech Boundaries in *The Wanderer*," *JEGP* 81 (1982): 469–79.

[24] An unsatisfactory feature of this edition is that these inverted commas are opened but never closed, though the speech contains within it a further speech, lines 92–110, marked by opened and closed inverted commas, uttered by the man *frod in ferðe* (90); see further below.

inverted commas and opening them again at the beginning of line 8,[25] make the wanderer (identical with the *eardstapa*, according to this interpretation) begin his speech in 1–5 and then resume it in 8. But a third pattern of punctuation, exemplified by Richard Hamer's edition and translation of the poem,[26] represents a much more profound difference of narrative structure than is implied by any of the variations between these other three editions. By enclosing lines 1–5 in inverted commas, but not opening them again at the beginning of 8, Hamer puts lines 6–7, as well as the lines that immediately follow them, into the mouth of the wanderer. Accordingly, lines 1–5 become a quotation by the wanderer (the 'I' of the poem) of another speaker whom he designates *eardstapa*—a minor, exemplary figure, according to this conception of the poem, whose words are briefly quoted by the wanderer as a prelude to an account of his own experiences. As there is no pressing evidence for any subsequent change of speaker until line 88 at the earliest, Hamer's punctuation changes the whole narrative structure of the poem: most of it is still spoken by the wanderer, as other patterns of editorial punctuations imply; but the heterodiegetic narrator reflected in the other editions disappears. Instead we have a homodiegetic narrator, a nameless 'I' of the kind we find in most of the other lyrics, though with a difference: this 'I' begins his speech with a quotation of someone else's (i.e. the *eardstapa*'s) words. It is, admittedly, difficult to exclude the possibility that 8 *Oft* does open a speech by the wanderer, or indeed the alternative possibility that it continues what he has already started to say in lines 1–5; but Hamer's punctuation of the early part of the poem seems to me no less defensible an arrangement than any of the alternatives.

Another notable feature of *The Wanderer* is its abrupt changes from first- to third-person narrative and back again. Some of the other lyrics exhibit these switches in person too,[27] though only in *The Wanderer* have they been taken to indicate a change of speaker. In detail, it has been suggested that the wanderer's speech ends at line 29 because the speaker switches to the third person in 30 and does not revert to the first person again until 58, though most recent critics accept such changes into the generalizing (or 'gnomic') third person as a feature of the wanderer's speech. Another view, also currently out of favour, is that the poem is a dialogue, with a second (nameless) speaker beginning unheralded in 58—an idea encouraged by the fact that, after the long passage from 30 to 57 in the third person, the first person is resumed in 58. A variant form of this dialogue theory takes 62b rather than 58 as the beginning of the second speaker's contribution.

Uncertainties also attach to the ontological status of certain speakers in *The Wanderer*. Doubts have arisen about whether the person described in 88–91 as

---

[25] Dunning and Bliss dispense with inverted commas by italicizing the narrator's utterances instead.

[26] Richard Hamer, ed. and trans., *A Choice of Anglo-Saxon Verse* (London: Faber and Faber, 1970), 174.

[27] Their significance is considered further below, §8.

uttering the famous 'ubi sunt' passage, which all editors agree begins in 92, is to be regarded as a new speaker, distinct from the wanderer himself, or merely as a literary creation, a "man of straw," or "puppet," as Leslie calls him, whom the wanderer invents. The point where his speech ends is also controversial: Leslie ends it with line 96,[28] and takes lines 97–110 as a resumption of "the impersonal elegy of lines 73–87 [. . .] by the wanderer in his own person";[29] but some other editors, among them Dunning and Bliss and Hamer, extend the speech to the end of line 110. This is a particularly felicitous policy in Hamer's edition in view of his presentation of the opening lines, for it gives the whole poem a relatively simple narrative structure: it becomes a homodiegetic narrative by a single, nameless speaker incorporating two quotations from other persons (1–5, 92–110), each quotation followed by the sequence: *swa cwæð* . . ., "So spoke . . ." (6, 111). Finally, whereas most editors take lines 112–115 as spoken by the wanderer, some, for example Krapp and Dobbie and Hamer, take them as continuing the narrator's words in 111.[30]

These editorial problems in *The Wanderer* interconnect with each other in such a way as to make it difficult for the modern reader to maintain a grasp of them as he or she reads the poem; but many of them involve one or more of four basic questions: how many speakers there are in the poem; which parts of the text are to be attributed to which speakers; whether a distinction is to be made between genuine and hypothetical speakers; and whether the poem's organizing consciousness is a heterodiegetic narrator or a homodiegetic first-person narrator ('the wanderer', as I have been calling him) who sometimes quotes the words of other speakers. It is, perhaps, enough for the moment to call attention to these problems of narrative structure in *The Wanderer*, though I shall need to take fresh account of them briefly in connection with further developments in my argument towards the end of this chapter.

Deor presents a different kind of problem of narrative form. An outline of the poem's structure will bring out the nature of the difficulty. *Deor* opens with an allusive account of the misfortunes of Welund, the archetypal smith of Germanic legend whose story is known to us from other sources, notably the Old Norse Eddic poem *Völundarkviða*. The account is concluded with a comment (7) which seems to link the pattern of Welund's experiences (*Þæs*, "As for that") with troubles, as yet unspecified (*þisses*, "this"), endured by the narrator:

> Welund him be wurman   wræces cunnade,
> anhydig eorl   earfoþa dreag,
> hæfde him to gesiþþe   sorge ond longaþ,

---

[28] Leslie, ed., *The Wanderer*, 19–20.
[29] Leslie, ed., *The Wanderer*, 20.
[30] See Krapp and Dobbie, *The Exeter Book*, 137; Hamer, *Choice*, 180–83.

```
        wintercealde wræce;    wean oft onfond,
5       siþþan hine Niðhad on    nede legde,
        swoncre seonobende    on syllan monn.
            Þæs ofereode,    þisses swa mæg.        (Deor 1–7)
```

"Welund experienced persecution (?) by the sword, the resolute warrior endured torments, had sorrow and longing for his companions, winter-cold exile. He often experienced woe, after Niðhad with supple sinew-bonds imposed bondage on the better man. As for that, it passed; so too may this."

There follow four more sections (8–27) of varying length in which the miseries or difficulties of named persons, several of them known from other sources for the heroic age, are shown to have resolved themselves, with the 'refrain' line, represented in the passage quoted above by line 7, repeated at the end of each section. It is not until the very end of the poem that the speaker confronts his own misfortunes directly and tells us his name:

```
35      Þæt ic bi me sylfum    secgan wille,
        þæt ic hwile wæs    Heodeninga scop,
        dryhtne dyre.    Me wæs Deor noma.
        Ahte ic fela wintra    folgað tilne,
        holdne hlaford,    oþþæt Heorrenda nu,
40      leoðcræftig monn londryht geþah,
        þæt me eorla hleo    ær gesealde.
            Þæs ofereode,    þisses swa mæg.        (Deor 35–42)
```

"I wish to speak about myself, how for a time I was poet of the Heodenings, dear to my lord. My name was Deor. For many years I had a good position, a loyal lord, until Heorrenda, a man skilled as a poet, received my estate which the protector of men previously gave to me. As for that, it passed; so too may this."

The significance of the repeated final line is more difficult to understand in this, its final occurrence: is it Deor's earlier prosperity and happiness which forms the basis of comparison, or his more recent reversal of fortune? It seems to make better sense to take *Þæs* as referring to his earlier prosperity and *þisses* to his present misfortunes: just as prosperity is fleeting, so too is its opposite. Perhaps Deor may hope for better things in the future.

The formal problem posed by *Deor* is why the speaker says that his name *was* Deor (37 *me wæs Deor noma*), rather than that his name *is* Deor. Presumably the tense of the verb does not mean that the speaker's name, once Deor, has now changed, or that the poem is an utterance of Deor's ghost. Richard Hamer suggests that the use of the past tense "merely stressed the fictitious nature of the poet's attribution of the story to himself."[31] I take this to mean that the poet is mimicking Deor's voice, speaking as if he were him, though revealing his ploy only by the tense of 37 *wæs*: he stops short of claiming Deor's identity as his own. But why should the poet have arrogated to himself someone else's story, only to explode the fiction?[32] An analysis of the tense of *wæs* as a deictic term points to a conclusion different from Hamer's. Much hinges on the time relative to the poem's composition which the tense of *wæs* takes as its point of reference — the present in terms of which the verb is past. Does this implied present coincide with coding time, when the poem was composed, or with a distinctly later, anticipated receiving time? Hamer's interpretation seems to imply that coding time and receiving time coincide here; that the audience is present to the poet as he speaks. However, it is more likely that *wæs* shows a momentary switch from coding time (when it would have been appropriate for the poet to say "My name is Deor") to a future receiving time ("My name was Deor") as the temporal-deictic centre of reference. The poet, according to this theory, is either himself Deor, or is expressing himself as if he were; but he is a writer and so has no audience (or rather, more properly, like all writers, no immediate readers). He knows that his readers will not be able to see or know him; anticipating their difficulty, he adopts — momentarily — their perspective on his story. It is, perhaps, helpful to think of the speaker as saying, in effect: "By the time you read this I shall no longer be here; but I wrote this and my name is Deor." If this interpretation is right — and I think it is to be preferred to Hamer's, for the reason I gave earlier — the effect is very striking: the tense of *wæs* converts the voice of the speaker, if only for a moment, from an immediate voice into a 'dead' voice from the past echoing in the present. This interpretation also has obvious implications for the mode of the poem's composition. It is only written communication that involves a distinction between coding time and receiving time; so it would follow from my analysis that *Deor* is a poem composed in writing and designed for readers. In fact, according to my view of it, *Deor* is an excellent illustration of the sense of "the pastness of the past" that Goody and Watt identify as one of the consequences of acquiring literacy.[33] I shall return to *Deor* later in this chapter, in the

---

[31] Hamer, *Choice*, 92, note to 37.

[32] Other views on 37 *wæs* have been expressed. Norman E. Eliason, "Two Old English Scop Poems," *PMLA* 81 (1966): 185–92 (at 191, n. 34) derives the name *Deor* from the adjective *deore*, 'dear', which appears as *dyre* in the same line of the poem. On this basis, Eliason explains the past tense of *wæs* as "calling attention to his [Deor's] former, more fortunate lot." Morton W. Bloomfield, in "The Form of Deor," in *Old English Literature: Twenty-two Analytical Essays*, ed. Martin Stevens and Jerome Mandel (Lincoln: University of Nebraska Press, 1968), 212–28 (at 226), suggests that the tense of *wæs* "may imply that the poet is taking on his [Deor's] personality, or it may indicate that it was the nickname of a well-known minstrel."

[33] Goody and Watt, "The Consequences of Literacy," 34.

context of a general discussion of the question of oral versus literary composition of the lyrics.

The last two sections of this chapter have consisted largely of a survey of the various approaches that modern critics have adopted in their attempts to discover the individuality of the speakers of the Old English lyrics — their sexes, their circumstances, even, in some cases, their actual identities as figures from known heroic or legendary tradition. The result of all this scholarly effort, which has much in common with attempts to solve riddles, has been very diverse; modern critics have had to work very hard to reach even the most tentative conclusions. The Old English lyrics clearly pose difficult problems for us today. Information which we need — or think we need — to make sense of them is missing, though it is not easy, at this distance in time from their composition and without a sense of the genre or genres to which they belong, to define the exact nature of the problem. Is it a weak sense of any individual, consistent and dramatically unified 'voice' — something we have come to expect from modern lyric poetry? One might contrast, for instance, Browning's dramatic monologues in which the utterances of the speakers, though designed to achieve an effect of naturalism, are obviously also highly artificial, intended by the poet to reveal the speakers for the kinds of people they 'really' are. It is tempting to treat the Old English lyrics as early dramatic monologues, for of the poetic genres that are familiar to us from later literature this is the one that seems to suit them best; yet the texts elude this classification. Our sense of the speakers as individuals remains unclear; and the obscurity is compounded, in some of them at least, by the way in which the speaker sometimes seems to turn abruptly and inexplicably into somebody else, a phenomenon which we are inclined to explain by theories of dialogue, or at least of unsignalled switches between the speaker and another person — another character in the story, or a narrator. The disjunctions which lead us to such conclusions are not stylistic, but more a matter of apparent shifts in point of view (as in the fairly frequent oscillation between first- and third-person grammatical subjects), an uneasy balance between the particular and the general, obscure narrative structure, and (very often) a lack of circumstantial information which would help us to see the speaker's place in a recognizable situation.

These frustrations may mean that we are misinterpreting the generic signals emitted by the Old English lyrics. Perhaps understanding depends on a familiarity with conventions of lyric verse of the period which we lack, though it is difficult to imagine what these conventions might have been. It is, however, possible to look at the problem from a different perspective. There is more to any speaker than his or her identity. No one, after all, speaks all the time; we speak only in response to certain pressures and conditions. Perhaps, therefore, we may gain a different, if not necessarily clearer, view of these poems if we ask, not who the speakers are, but under what circumstances they are speaking. This kind of approach — a pragmatics-based approach — will, I hope, lead to a better idea of the formal nature of these lyrics, and also reveal special qualities they possess that may be related to their composition at a time when the Anglo-Saxons were coming to terms with the implications of the use of the written word.

§7. The solitary writer

An unobtrusive feature of the vocabulary of the Old English lyrics is that in most of them (*Wulf and Eadwacer* is the only exception in this regard) the speakers refer to their own acts of utterance by common Old English verbs meaning 'to speak' or 'to utter (orally)'. Thus *The Wife's Lament* opens:

> Ic þis giedd wrece   bi me ful geomorre,
> minre sylfre sið.   Ic þæt secgan mæg,
> hwæt ic yrmða gebad,   siþþan ic up weox, . . .   (*The Wife's Lament* 1–3)

"I utter this tale about myself, sad as I am, my own lot. I am able to say what hardships I have experienced since I grew up, . . ."

The two verbs used here, *wrecan* and *secgan*, are normal in similar contexts in the other lyrics. The second also occurs in the first line of *The Husband's Message*:

> Nu ic onsundran þe   secgan wille   (*Husband's Message* 1)
> "Now I wish to tell you especially . . ."

and in the final, autobiographical passage of *Deor*:

> Þæt ic bi me sylfum   secgan wille,   (*Deor* 35)
> "I wish to say this about myself, . . ."

Both verbs are used in the opening lines of *The Seafarer*:

> Mæg ic be me sylfum   soðgied wrecan,
> siþas secgan,   (*Seafarer* 1–2a)

"I am able to utter a true tale about me, tell of my journeys, . . ."

In *The Wanderer*, the verbs *cweðan* and *acweðan* are used to denote the utterances of the wanderer (or perhaps, in the case of lines 91b and 111, of a different speaker, depending on the editorial attribution of speeches):[34]

> Swa cwæð eardstapa,   earfeþa gemyndig,   (*Wanderer* 6)
> "So spoke the wanderer, mindful of hardships, . . ."

---

[34] See above, 194–97.

>   . . . ond þas word acwið: (*Wanderer* 91b)
> "... and speaks these words:"

> Swa cwæð snottor on mode,   gesæt him sundor æt rune. (*Wanderer* 111)
> "So spoke the wise one in his heart, he sat apart in meditation."

The implications of this last example from *The Wanderer* are of special interest and I shall return to it shortly. Meanwhile, as we are apparently faced with self-professed speakers in these poems, we might repeat an earlier question about them: to whom do they speak? Any utterance may, in theory, be directed externally or internally. In external (or extradiegetic) address, the speaker speaks to an audience or readers whom he may address explicitly as "you" or implicitly by "we." The opening lines of *Beowulf* provide an example of the second type:

> Hwæt, we Gardena   in geardagum,
> þeodcyninga   þrym gefrunon,
> hu ða æþelingas   ellen fremedon!   (*Beowulf* 1–3)

> "Lo! We have heard of the glory of the kings of the people of the Spear-Danes in days of yore—how those princes did valorous deeds!"

There is a similar example in the pious conclusion of *The Wanderer*:

> Wel bið þam þe him are seceð,
> frofre to fæder on heofonum,   þær us eal seo fæstnung stondeð.
> (*The Wanderer* 114b–15)

> "Well it is for him who seeks mercy, solace from the Father in heaven, where all security lies for us."

We should note that this remark may possibly be spoken by the narrator rather than by the wanderer himself.[35] A third example is found near the end of *The Seafarer*:

> Uton we hycgan   hwær we ham agen,
> and þonne geþencan   hu we þider cumen . . .   (*The Seafarer* 117–18)

> "Let us think where we have our home, and then consider how we may come thither . . ."

These, then, are all extradiegetic utterances. An internally-directed, or intradiegetic, utterance is one addressed to an interlocutor within the story the speaker

---

[35] See above, 197.

tells. Of our six lyrics, only *Wulf and Eadwacer* contains an intradiegetic 'narratee' of this kind:

>   Wulf min, Wulf,   wena me þine
>   seoce gedydon,   þine seldcymas,
> 15   murnende mod,   nales meteliste.
>   Gehyrest þu Eadwacer, uncerne earne hwelp?
>   (*Wulf and Eadwacer*, 13–16)

> "My Wulf, Wulf, it is expectation of you that has made me ill, your rare visits, a sorrowing heart, not lack of food. Do you hear Eadwacer, our cowardly whelp?"

There is, however, a logical problem arising from these implications of the presence of an audience: it is difficult to understand how any of these speakers can be addressing any interlocutor, whether extradiegetic or intradiegetic, because the content of their utterances indicates that they are all *alone*—isolated socially, as well as culturally or spatially displaced.[36] In fact, some of these speakers make the fact that they have no one to talk to a theme of their utterances. This has important implications. It seems to follow that these are not the 'speeches' they purport to be, but inwardly-directed monologues. The speakers are talking to themselves, using language in an attempt to make sense of their own experiences. As modern readers, we may find it quite unremarkable that poets should speak from a position of isolation; but I suggest that this feature of the lyrics would have been much more striking to a contemporary audience or reader, accustomed to thinking of language as a means of interpersonal and immediate communication. As the isolation of these speakers is crucial for my discussion, the evidence for it in each individual lyric must be evaluated before pursuing its implications any further.

Taking *The Wanderer* first, we may look more closely at line 111 which I quoted earlier:

> Swa cwæð snottor on mode,   gesæt him sundor æt rune. (*Wanderer* 111)
> "So spoke the wise one in his heart, he sat apart in meditation."

My translation reflects the generally accepted interpretation of the key expressions *on mode*, *sundor*, and *æt rune*:[37] they indicate that the "wise one" is not to

---

[36] Bragg (*Lyric Speakers*, 85), in her discussion of the speakers of these and other Old English lyrics, notes that "all the fictive speakers but Deor are alone and seem for the most part to be unaware of their audiences," though she notes the implication of *Seafarer* 117 *Uton*.

[37] See Leslie, *The Wanderer*, 89, note to 111b: "That the wanderer is communing with himself is indicated by the reflexive *him*; that his reflections are inwards is suggested by

be envisaged as actually addressing anyone.[38] Whether this wise man is the wanderer himself, or another speaker whom the wanderer has just quoted in lines 92–110, he is evidently alone, a solitary survivor of a once prosperous heroic community; and if *on mode* is indeed, as the editors think, an adverbial phrase describing the manner in which he "spoke" (*cwæð*),[39] he is not so much talking to himself as thinking silently. A question we are faced with at this point, however, is how the wanderer (or the narrator; again, the choice depends on the decision of the editor) knows what the *snottor* man is thinking if he speaks only "in his heart" and "apart." This is part of a much larger question about the truth-status—fiction or fact—of *The Wanderer* which I shall explore in more general terms later in this chapter.

Line 111 reminds us, however, of earlier indications in the poem that both the wanderer and the man he calls *frod in ferðe* in line 90 are alone. (We must consider the position of both these personages because either might be the *snottor* man of line 111.) Much of the first part of the wanderer's speech is chiefly concerned with his social and physical isolation:[40]

```
       Oft ic sceolde ana        uhtna gehwylce
       mine ceare cwiþan—  nis nu cwicra nán
10     þe ic him modsefan        minne durre
       sweotule asecgan.     Ic to soþe wat
       þæt biþ in eorle      indryhten þeaw
       þæt he his ferðlocan      fæste binde,
       healde his hordcofan,     hycge swa he wille.
15     Ne mæg werig mod          wyrde wiðstondan,
       ne se hreo hyge       helpe gefremman:
       forðon domgeorne      dreorigne oft
       in hyra breostcofan       bindað fæste,
       swa ic modsefan       minne sceolde
20     (oft earmcearig,      eðle bidæled,
       freomægum feor)       feterum sælan,
       siþþan geara iu       goldwine minne
       hrusan heolstre biwrah,   ond ic hean þonan
       wod wintercearig      ofer waþema gebind,
25     sohte seledreorig     sinces bryttan,
       hwær ic feor oþþe neah    findan meahte
       þone þe in meoduhealle    minne myne wisse,
```

---

on mode, and that his meditations are private is indicated by *sundor*": quoted approvingly by Dunning and Bliss, *The Wanderer*, 123, note to line 111.

[38] I do not call the subject of *cwæð* here "the wanderer" because, as we saw earlier, the verb's subject may be the (perhaps imaginary) man "wise of mind" (90 *frod in ferðe*) who has just finished speaking lines 92–110, rather than the wanderer himself.

[39] See Leslie, *The Wanderer*, 22, for discussion of this question.

[40] Text from Dunning and Bliss, *The Wanderer*, 106–11.

```
            oþþe mec freondleasne      frefran wolde,
            wenian mid wynnum.      Wat se þe cunnað
30          hu sliþen bið       sorg to geferan
            þam þe him lyt hafað      leofra geholena:
            warað hine wræclast,      nales wunden gold;
            ferðloca freorig,      nalæs foldan blæd;
            gemon he selesecgas      ond sincþege,
35          hu hine on geoguðe      his goldwine
            wenede to wiste— wyn eal gedreas!        (Wanderer 8–36)
```

"Often I have had to bewail my sorrow alone at break of each day; there is now no longer any man alive to whom I dare reveal my heart openly. I know as a fact that it is a noble custom in a man that he bind his heart firmly, whatever he may think. A weary heart cannot alter the course of events, nor may the fierce mind provide help: therefore those eager for glory often bind firmly in their breasts a sad heart, just as I have had to seal my heart with fetters (often wretched, deprived of native land, far from noble kinsmen), since long ago I covered my lord in the darkness of earth, and went wretched thence, desolate as winter, over the frozen waves, and sought, sad at the loss of the hall, a giver of treasure wherever I might find, far or near, someone in the mead-hall who would know my thought, or would comfort me, friendless as I am, entertain me with delights. He who makes trial of it knows how cruel sorrow is as a companion to him who has few beloved friends. The path of exile claims him, not the twisted gold, a frozen breast, not the glory of earth; he remembers retainers and the receiving of treasure, how in his youth his lord accustomed him to feasting—joy has gone completely."

The speaker bewails his sorrows "alone" (8 *ana*), and has no one in whom he dares confide (9–11)—a remark which is not, I think, to be taken to imply that he is surrounded by unsympathetic strangers. He has buried one lord, and wanders unhappily in search of a replacement, with sorrow (30 *sorg*) his sole companion. The fact that his awareness of what he has lost is expressed in images of the pleasures of life as a member of a *comitatus* (32–36) emphasises that he no longer enjoys these pleasures himself.

The speech of the man called *frod in ferðe* in *The Wanderer* opens with a litany of absent tokens of standard heroic culture:

```
            Hwær cwom mearg? Hwær cwom mago?      Hwær cwom maþþumgyfa?
            Hwær cwom symbla gesetu?      Hwær sindon seledreamas?
            Eala beorht bune!      Eala byrnwiga!
95          Eala þeodnes þrym!      Hu seo þrag gewat,
            genap under nihthelm,      swa heo no wære!        (Wanderer 92–96)
```

"What has become of the horse? What has become of the youth?
What has become of the banqueting halls? Where are the revelries of hall?
Alas for the bright cup! Alas for the mailed warrior!
Alas the pomp of the chieftain! How that time has passed away,
grown dark beneath the cover of night, as if it never were!"

Here, surely, is a man who has lost all he values, including his friends, and it is difficult to escape the conclusion that like the wanderer he is now entirely alone.

In *The Seafarer*, the speaker has had to endure social displacement and isolation at sea:[41]

>   Þæt se mon ne wat
>   þe him on foldan   fægrost limpeð,
>   hu ic earmcearig   iscealdne sæ
> 15 winter wunade   wræccan lastum,
>   winemægum bidroren,
>   bihongen hrimgicelum;   hægl scurum fleag.
>   Þær ic ne gehyrde   butan hlimman sæ,
>   iscaldne wæg.   Hwilum ylfete song
> 20 dyde ic me to gomene,   ganetes hleoþor
>   ond huilpan sweg   fore hleahtor wera,
>   mæw singende   fore medodrince.
>   Stormas þær stanclifu beotan,   þær him stearn oncwæð
>   isigfeþera;   ful oft þæt earn bigeal,
> 25 urigfeþra;   ne ænig hleomæga
>   feasceaftig ferð   frefran meahte.
>   Forþon him gelyfeð lyt,   se þe ah lifes wyn
>   gebiden in burgum,   bealosiþa hwon,
>   wlonc ond wingal,   hu ic werig oft
> 30 in brimlade   bidan sceolde.   (*Seafarer* 12b-30)

"The man whose lot is cast most happily on land knows not how I, wretched, bereft of beloved kinsmen, bedecked with icicles, passed a year on the ice-cold sea in the paths of an exile; hail flew in showers. There I heard nothing but the roaring sea, the ice-cold wave. Sometimes I had the song of the swan for my entertainment, the call of the gannet, the song of the curlew instead of the laughter of men, the gull singing instead of mead. Storms beat against the cliff there, the icy-feathered tern replied; very often the dewy-feathered eagle cried; no protective kinsman might comfort the desolate heart. Thus he who has known the joy of life in the settlements, few bitter experiences, proud and flushed with wine, little believes how I, weary, have often had to endure a voyage."

---

[41] Text from Krapp and Dobbie, *The Exeter Book*, 143–44.

Although the speaker in *The Seafarer* is not quite so obviously alone *as he speaks* as the wanderer is, the sustained emphasis on the incommunicability of his experiences suggests that he probably is. Like the wanderer, the seafarer is without confidants, and seems unlikely to find any in the future, because of the frustrating inability of those who know only life on land to appreciate the extent of his sufferings as a solitary seafaring exile—a theme he returns to repeatedly.[42] Physical isolation, and the social isolation that this entails, have placed the seafarer beyond the reach of normal communal ties; his chief complaint seems to be that no one can properly *know* him any more. Like the wanderer, he is acutely aware of the contrast between present misery and past happiness, and expresses it in a very similar way, by a series of bitter, ironic comparisons between the social joys he misses and the meaningless chatter of the birds who are his only companions. So the seafarer plainly has been alone; and although he may have returned to land to tell his story, one of the curious features of the poem is the difficulty of imagining any audience to whom such a person might speak in this vein. If there were an audience for his thoughts and feelings, much of the difficulty he is experiencing would disappear. This leads me to conclude that the seafarer's speech, like the wanderer's, is an internal monologue.

In *Deor*, the speaker does not describe his immediate circumstances as directly as the speakers in *The Wanderer* and *The Seafarer*. As we saw earlier, most of the poem consists of examples, many of them drawn from a fund of traditional heroic stories, of adversity and unhappiness overcome, and it is not until the end of the poem that Deor is explicit about his own misfortunes, hoping that they, too, will pass, as Welund's (and others') did. Deor may well be alone, like the wanderer and the seafarer, but his problem is more specific than theirs: he has lost his position, and with it his right to land (*londryht*). Deor's situation is ironic: the rejected poetic gift which he once used to entertain others he now uses to console himself for its rejection. The poem, as some critics have noticed, resembles a performative utterance:[43] Deor's speech is his way of healing his own wounds and he is his own audience. So although he is not so obviously alone as the wanderer, his speech does represent an attempt to raise his own depressed spirits by putting his own plight into a recognizable framework of precedents. The poem presents an intriguing picture of oral poetry turning in on itself and so becoming a silent, interior activity.

In none of the Old English lyrics is our sense of the speaker's isolation greater than in *Wulf and Eadwacer*. The speaker's physical separation from her beloved 'Wulf' is stated with stark simplicity:[44]

---

[42] *The Seafarer*, lines 12–17, 27–30, 55–57.

[43] See T. A. Shippey, *Old English Verse* (London: Hutchinson, 1972), 78.

[44] Quotations are from the text in Krapp and Dobbie, *The Exeter Book*, 179–80, though I have altered the punctuation slightly.

> Wulf is on iege, ic on oþerre.
> Fæst is þæt eglond, fenne biworpen. (*Wulf and Eadwacer* 4–5)

"Wulf is on an island, I on another. That island is firm, surrounded by marsh."

She sits miserably in the rain, apparently tracking the wandering Wulf in her imagination:

> Wulfes ic mines widlastum wenum dogode
> 10 þonne his wæs renig weder and ic reotugu sæt.
> (Wulf *and Eadwacer* 9–10)

"In my thoughts I dogged (?) my Wulf's wide-ranging tracks when it was rainy weather and I sat lamenting."

Then she addresses Wulf directly, in the passage (13–16) quoted earlier: the frustration of unfulfilled expectation has made her ill; but she is evidently unheard by him because she finally reverts to the soliloquy-mode with which the poem began, reflecting sadly on the pathos of a *giedd* ("tale") so easy to break off because there is so little to tell. Her life with Wulf has had little of what the narratologist calls 'story':

> Wulf min, Wulf, wena me þine
> seoce gedydon, þine seldcymas,
> 15 murnende mod, nales meteliste.
> Gehyrest þu Eadwacer, uncerne earne hwelp?
> Bireð wulf to wuda.
> Þæt mon eaþe tosliteð þætte næfre gesomnad wæs,
> uncer giedd geador. (*Wulf and Eadwacer* 13–19)

"My Wulf, Wulf, it is expectation of you that has made me ill, your rare visits, a sorrowing heart, not lack of food. Do you hear Eadwacer, our cowardly whelp? He will carry Wulf to the wood. What has never been put together is easily interrupted, this tale of the pair of us."[45]

Finally, in *The Wife's Lament* the speaker is plainly quite alone:[46]

---

[45] The situation at the end of the poem corresponds closely with the typical ending of what Genette (*Narrative Discourse*, 227) calls the "subsequent-narrating" novel: ". . . the temporal (and spatial) interval that until then separated the reported action from the narrating act becomes gradually smaller until it is finally reduced to zero: the narrative has reached the *here* and the *now*, the story has overtaken the narrating."

[46] Text from Leslie, *Three Old English Elegies*, 47–48.

```
            Heht mec mon wunian      on wuda bearwe,
            under actreo      in þam eorðscræfe;
            eald is þes eorðsele,      eal ic eom oflongad.
30          Sindon dena dimme,      duna uphea,
            bitre burgtunas      brerum beweaxne,
            wic wynna leas;      ful oft mec her wraþe begeat
            fromsiþ frean.      Frynd sind on eorþan,
            leofe lifgende      leger weardiað,
35          þonne ic on uhtan      ana gonge
            under actreo      geond þas eorþscrafu,
            þær ic sitta[n] mot      sumorlangne dæg,
            þær ic wepan mæg      mine wræcsiþas,
            earfoþa fela,      forþon ic æfre ne mæg
40          þære modceare      minre gerestan,
            ne ealles þæs longaþes      þe mec on þissum life begeat.
                                                 (Wife's Lament, 27–41)
```

"I was ordered to dwell in a grove of the woods, beneath the oak-tree in this earth-cave; this earth-hall is old, I am assailed by longing. The valleys are dark, the hills high, bitter are the precincts, overgrown with briars, a place bereft of joys; very often the departure of my lord has been grievously brought home to me. There are lovers on earth, living loved ones, who keep to their beds, while I at dawn walk alone beneath the oak-tree, round these earth-caves, where I may sit the summer-long day, where I may weep over my miseries, my many hardships, because I can never get any relief from the cares in my heart, nor from all the longing which has afflicted me in this life."

The burden of the speaker's lament is her sexual and emotional isolation. Like the wanderer and the seafarer, she inhabits an entirely natural landscape; and like them, she sees it, not as a place of beauty, but as a desert, a scene of uncultivated disorderliness, unredeemed by any mark of human culture. Again, as in some of the other lyrics, we find the bitterly ironic contrast between the social and cultural security so sorely missed and the depressing reality of the speaker's circumstances, here encapsulated in the phrase *bitre burgtunas*, "bitter precincts," a wilderness overgrown with briars, the antithesis of the orderly precincts of the settlements which the word *burgtunas* would normally suggest.[47]

It thus seems fair to maintain that in five of the Old English lyrics the speakers are socially isolated and miserably lonely. The two exceptions are *The Ruin*,

---

[47] Leslie, *Three Old English Elegies*, 56, note to 31, points out that although *burgtun* is unrecorded elsewhere, its existence as an Old English word is indicated by placenames such as Bourton, Broughton, and Burton, many instances of which derive from it; see Eilert Ekwall, *The Concise Oxford Dictionary of English Place-Names*, 4th ed. (Oxford: Clarendon Press, 1960), s.v. **Bourton, Broughton** (sense 2), and **Burton** (1).

excluded from the group near the start of my discussion, and *The Husband's Message*, in which, as we saw in Chapter 5, the speaker addresses an intradiegetic woman-character. Even the speaker in *Wulf and Eadwacer*, who alone stands some chance of achieving communication with another individual in the world of the poem, seems to remain unheard. On the other hand, these speakers' utterances are introduced to us using the standard Old English verbs of speaking (*secgan, cweðan, acweðan*) or composing orally (*wrecan*), and in *The Seafarer*, at least, the speaker's use of the plural first-person pronoun unmistakably implies an awareness of a mass of common humanity to whom his experiences have some relevance. But if these are speeches, who hears them? The question would no doubt have seemed more pointed to an Anglo-Saxon audience than it does to us, familiar as we are with the voice of the poetic 'speaking' writer who addresses the reader directly from his or her isolation, by long-established literary convention. It would not normally occur to us to question how such direct address can be achieved in an internal monologue; we would assume that the 'speaker', though formally talking to himself or herself, was really a writer who expects to be 'overheard' by his readers.[48] But this breach between form and pragmatic convention in English literature must have had a beginning. I suggest that that beginning is unlikely to have preceded the advent of literacy, for the simple reason that oral speakers who have no one to talk to are logically prevented from expressing the actual fact of their isolation directly to anyone else. If an audience can be found, they are no longer isolated; and if they are to speak (literally) of their isolation, it must be done in the past tense. The speakers of the Old English lyrics generally describe their isolation and loneliness as present conditions, the only possible exception being the speaker in *The Seafarer*: the loneliness he speaks of has passed, though his reincorporation into human society seems doubtful as he contemplates a journey to a "land of foreigners far away" (37–38 *feor heonan elþeodigra eard*).

A writer, on the other hand, whose utterances predicate the future arrival of an audience which is absent at the moment of writing, *is* in a position to present reflections on his or her own isolation directly (though not immediately) to his or her addressees, who will, of course, be readers, not hearers. Although isolation and silence are the normal lot of writers everywhere, these restrictions are surmountable to the extent that the writer can 'speak' over time to future readers who will look back sympathetically on his or her loneliness. Writing is thus not merely the true medium of the internal monologue of isolation, but a necessary factor of its composition. It may be possible to maintain even that the internal or introspective monologue is the only form of first-person 'speech' permitted by the logic of the written word, because writing precludes any *immediate* one-to-one (or one-to-many) communication. The writer cannot tell his or her readers

---

[48] See Bragg, *Lyric Speakers*, 85: "These lyrics are thus best thought of as soliloquies, internal monologues intended to be overheard by the reader."

anything in the normal sense of that verb, for writers cannot normally have the kind of close contact with their readers that 'telling' normally implies; but it is only to these readers, waiting in the wings for their entrances in the drama of linguistic communication, that the writer may open his or her consciousness. The combination of isolation and utterance in the Old English lyrics becomes much more understandable if these are poems composed in writing.

But if this is the case, why do they use the vocabulary of speech? As a residuum of oral ways of thinking about language surviving into the period of literacy? Joyce Coleman's recent eloquent attack on the whole idea of residual orality in late Middle English literature cautions us against accepting this obvious answer too readily.[49] However, the difference between Coleman's period and the Anglo-Saxon period is not insignificant. In the England of the fourteenth and fifteenth centuries, vernacular literacy had already existed for seven hundred years. Old English verse as we know it emerges in written form in the late seventh or early eighth century from a centuries-old oral tradition of versifying. The first-person writer *in propria persona* was not in a position to use the inscribed medium as his surrogate at receiving time in the way that the early Anglo-Saxon inscribers did; he had to speak to his readers directly if he was to speak to them at all. While the intimacy of immediate address was beyond his reach, the only model of direct address he knew was speech; so it is easy to see why what is normally inexpressible in speech—thought-language, the only true language of silence—is expressed through the metalanguage of speech. Here in the Anglo-Saxon period one may, I

---

[49] Joyce Coleman, *Public Reading and the Reading Public in Late Medieval England and France*, Cambridge Studies in Medieval Literature 26 (Cambridge: Cambridge University Press, 1996). Here we may compare Ursula Schaefer, *Vokalität: Altenglische Dichtung zwischen Mündlichkeit und Schriftlichkeit*, Scripta Oralia 39 (Tübingen: Gunter Narr Verlag, 1992), which invokes the idea of *Vokalität* ('vocality') in preference to *Mündlichkeit* ('orality') as a means of capturing the special kind of orality that resulted when texts were vocalized as they were read in the medieval period. She writes: "Die Welt, in welche die altenglische Dichtung eingebettet war, dürfen wir uns also weder denken als eine kommunikative Welt, die primär—und damit ausschließlich—mündlich gewesen, noch als eine, in der Schriftliches unvermittelt von Lesern rezipiert worden wäre. Es scheint mir deshalb dringend notwendig, für diese vokale Welt das, was da kommuniziert wird, begrifflich neu zu überdenken. Dieser Begriff muß zum einen der Tatsache Rechnung tragen, daß auf der Senderseite Schriftliches vorliegt, das auf der Empfängerseite hörend aufgenommen wird" (43). ("We should therefore think of the world in which the Old English poem was embedded neither as a primarily—and so exclusively—oral communicative world, nor as a world in which what was written was received by readers in an unmediated form. It therefore seems to me a matter of urgency to rethink in conceptual terms what was communicated in this vocal world. This new concept must take account of the fact that on the sender's side there is a written text, the receiving of which is done on the receiver's side by hearing.")

think, reasonably invoke the idea, denounced by Coleman and many other writers on literacy, of a historical 'great divide' between orality and literacy.

Although the connections I have just made between the Old English lyrics and incipient literacy might suggest that these poems were actually composed in writing, it is of course possible that the literate mentality which, I believe, lies behind them might, once established, have affected the form of poetry produced in the traditional oral mode as much as it affected verse produced pen-in-hand. There seems no need to insist that the poets of the Old English lyrics were able to write themselves, though there is no evidence either that they were unable to do so. One of the biggest gaps in our understanding of the composition of Old English verse in the literate period lies in the area of possible modes of interaction between the act of composition and the recording of its fruits in writing and later transmission. Were the words of reciting poets transcribed on parchment by trained scribes as they spoke? Surely not, unless the poets modified their normal speed of delivery. Did some of the poets whose work has survived in manuscripts transcribe their own performances? Cynewulf, as we saw in Chapter 4, was probably such a poet; but the general lack of firm evidence which might provide answers to these questions is frustrating.

Another obvious historical question arises here: is form the cause and content the effect, or vice versa? Are the Old English lyrics taken up with the plight of isolated individuals because the poets are writers, more or less compelled to produce internal monologues by the logic of the written word they have chosen to use? Or were the poets compelled to write rather than speak because the theme of personal isolation they chose demanded the internal monologue, a genre which is logically and essentially textual? Silence and solitude go together; but the first explanation seems the likelier of the two: that it was the availability of writing which precipitated this significant advance in the development of literary forms, rather than a new desire to explore the nature of human consciousness from within; otherwise we would need to explain the convenient coincidence of the arrival of literacy with the very moment when new artistic aspirations required it.

§8. The Old English lyrics: history or fiction?

Another question, impossible to ignore but unfortunately much more difficult to answer in any definite way, follows on from my argument that the Old English lyrics are products of a literate culture. This is the problem, raised briefly earlier in this chapter, of the relationship between the speakers of these poems and the poets who composed them. To argue, as I have done, from a pragmatic datum revealed by the content of the Old English lyrics—the apparent isolation of the speakers—to the conclusion that the mode of their composition was either actually literary or influenced by a literate mentality might seem to entail the assumption that the first-person 'speakers' of these poems must be identical with their poets. Again, this is certainly possible, I would say even probable; but the question has complex ramifications.

We might open discussion of it by trying to envisage the situation at the moment of literacy's first impact in England. When writing was a complete novelty, no doubt any writer who wrote without any narrative frame about the thoughts of someone whom he or she designated 'I' would be understood to have written about his or her *own* thoughts. The whole weight of established sociolinguistic practice in the oral phase would support the poet in this usage of the first person: people would normally speak in their own voices; they would not habitually borrow or imitate other people's. On the other hand, precedents for the imitation of the voices of others will almost certainly have already existed in the oral poetic tradition (as well as in everyday speech). In telling a traditional story a poet would, no doubt, be expected to produce speeches (involving the use of the first-person pronoun) made by the characters in his story. In *Beowulf*, the narrator distinguishes clearly between his own words and those of his characters by his use of a standard reporting-clause (usually *X* (name) *maþelode*, 'X spoke', which occurs twenty-six times in the poem) to introduce direct speeches by characters. It is, of course, possible that *Beowulf* is itself the work of a literate poet, a view which has gained much ground in recent years. However, the fact that this particular feature of narrative style may be exemplified from the Old High German *Hildebrandslied* suggests that it may have its origins in Germanic oral alliterative tradition.[50] The Old English *Riddles*, furthermore, demonstrate that Old English poets sometimes adopted non-human personae without warning or preamble, though it is difficult to judge how old this aspect of riddle-style might be. But the convention that 'I' and the oral poet were one must surely have been the default convention when writing was new and unfamiliar.

It is clear, however, that under literacy this convention eventually weakened, for we now take it entirely for granted that writers may pretend to be, not only somebody other than themselves, but also people who have never existed—imaginary, or fictional, persons. Perhaps we may detect the presence of an early forerunner of the truly fictional speaker in one of the Old English lyrics, *The Wanderer*. Before examining the evidence for this view, however, it will probably help the discussion if I return briefly to some points made earlier about the origins of deixis in spoken language, and then consider in general terms some of the consequences of literacy for deictic reference, before turning back to the lyrics.

Lyons and others have pointed out that the foundations of deixis as a linguistic phenomenon are firmly grounded in speech, not writing. 'I', 'me', 'my', and 'mine' (Old English *ic*, *me* or *mec*, and *min*) refer, in spoken language, to the speaker of the utterance in which they occur; but they are not referential in

---

[50] For the text of the *Hildebrandslied*, see Klaeber, *Beowulf and the Fight at Finnsburg*, 290–92. Line 14 reads *Hadubrant gimahalta, Hiltibrantes sunu*, "Hadubrant spoke, son of Hildibrant," introducing direct speech, and similarly in 7, 36, and 45.

the way most other words are. The difference between these pronouns and other words in their referentiality is brought out clearly by Benveniste, who wrote that a noun (for example) refers to "a fixed and 'objective' notion, capable of remaining potential or of being actualized in a particular object and always identical with the mental image it awakens," whereas instances of the first-person pronoun "do not constitute a class of reference since there is no 'object' definable as *I* to which these instances can refer in identical fashion. Each *I* has its own reference and corresponds each time to a unique being who is set up as such."[51] A word such as 'parsnip' can refer to the concept of a parsnip in the absence of any such vegetable and still be fully meaningful. Not so first-person pronouns, which obviously cannot be used in normal speech to refer to an absent speaker. They can scarcely be used even to refer to the concept of a particular speaker, because unlike most other words they do not have a stable referent; each 'I' is different, unique. The first-person pronoun is thus not quite a linguistic sign in the Saussurean sense. A sign is composed of word and conception, whereas 'I' does not refer to any stable conception. The only stable element in its use is its indication of the speaker of whatever utterance it appears in, whoever he or she may be. Lyons' discussion of person-deixis is worth quoting at length here:

> It must not be thought, however, that the meaning of 'I' and 'you' is accounted for by saying that 'I' means "the one who is (now) speaking" and that 'you' means "the one who is being addressed". In so far as 'the speaker' and 'the hearer' are substitutable for 'I' and 'you' in ordinary English, they are conventionalized pseudo-descriptions which (like 'the author' and 'your lordship') depend for their interpretation upon our intuitive understanding of how person-deixis operates. Furthermore, the proposed analysis of 'I' in terms of some underlying definite description meaning "the one who is (now) speaking", if it is pressed to the point at which it will do the job that it is intended to do, must be relativized to the very utterance that contains the first-person pronoun whose meaning it, allegedly, explicates. In other words, if 'the speaker' is to serve as the equivalent of 'I' in *The speaker is hungry*, the proposition that is expressed must be understood to be, not just "The person who is speaking is hungry", but "The person who is uttering this very utterance is hungry"; and the logical status of propositions like this, which necessarily involve token-reflexivity . . . is, if anything, even more obscure than is the analysis of propositions containing terms that refer to the self.[52]

---

[51] Emile Benveniste, *Problems in General Linguistics*, trans. Mary Elizabeth Meet, Miami Linguistics Series 8 (Coral Gables: University of Miami Press, 1971), 217–22, "The Nature of Pronouns" (at 218).

[52] Lyons, *Semantics*, 2: 647.

These problems of logical analysis do not, however, question the unerring aim of deictic pronouns, at least in speech. In practice they are as unambiguous as any other word, despite the fact that they do not refer to any "objective" meaning, because the invariable presence of whatever person is using them to refer to himself or herself makes the lack of a common reference irrelevant. They *point* unmistakably to the speaker who is, necessarily, present and available to the perception of the receiver of the spoken utterance.

In speech, then, deictic terms operate effectively—one is tempted to say 'naturally'—as part of the linguistic machinery that makes verbal communication possible. Writing, however, creates a new set of circumstances which interferes radically with the working of this machinery. A writer may, as we have seen, use the first-person pronoun to refer to his or her medium or his or her text, or to the characters whose speeches he or she quotes in the stories he or she tells, or (in *Riddles*) to a cloaked identity. The writer does not have to use it to refer to himself or herself; but if he or she chooses to do so, a serious difficulty of communication looms up. 'I' will not 'carry' in space or time like other words. It forms an indissoluble link between the individual utterer and the utterance of which it forms a part, pointing directly to the speaker, as a kind of aural signpost. But the utterer needs to be present to the recipient if the latter is to know what he needs to know: to whom exactly 'I' refers in a sentence such as Lyons's example: "I am hungry." The trouble is that writers remain when (so to speak) and where they are, in their own times and places; but their texts carry the authorial 'I' away with them as they begin to scan the future for readers. The writer's 'I' positions him or her with one foot in the text and the other outside it, in his or her own space and time. Thus a split (or perhaps, rather, a stretch) opens up between the writer and 'I' as his or her text begins its journey in time, space, or both. In the absence of the writer, 'I' no longer does the job it does in speech and is left pointing into thin air. This is, of course, a manifestation of the deictic gap defined in Chapter 2.

For speakers, this problem does not arise, because their words cannot in any case travel beyond the immediate hearing-range, nor can they achieve the permanence secured by writing. In an oral culture, speakers will not develop ambitions to transmit their actual words beyond the immediate circle of listeners, except, perhaps, by messenger. Writers, however, aim for both permanence and transferability in their utterances; otherwise they would stick to speech. Much of the point of writing is to 'speak' to the future and to the world; but it would seem that if writers refer to themselves as 'I', their desire must be frustrated by the rules of deictic reference. The writer is, of course, represented (in a limited sense) by 'I' in his or her text; but the actual and observable link between the writer as an individual and his or her utterance which the word 'I' secures in the oral situation is severed. The dissociation becomes most apparent in the activities and difficulties of the reader (if and when one appears to read the writer's work). The writer's own voice becomes, and must always be read as, a voice from the past (and also from elsewhere too, in many cases). Readers cannot apprehend the writer in the same way that they apprehend anyone who actually speaks to them; and readers are often, perhaps always, inclined to search for the writer in his or her writings. Unthinking assumptions about language underpinning oral communication affect the way we read; we feel that an utterance should issue from an identifiable utterer. Twentieth-century literary theory used to discourage the search for the author in literature as futile and naive; but the search reflects nothing more than the much more basic impulse to connect utterances with utterers—a natural impulse, because they are invariably and inevitably connected in the parallel mode of speech, the influence of which on habits of reading is pervasive.[53] The way that we, as modern readers and critics of the Old English lyrics, seem impelled to explore the texts themselves and every possible historical and literary context in our quest to place the speakers of these poems testifies to our need to know—even, if possible, identify—the writer from his or her writings. The failure of this enterprise, charted earlier in this chapter, is no doubt ultimately attributable to the nature of the lyrics as literary texts: they create an 'absent I' but fail to provide the reader with sufficient information to identify its full individuality.

The possibility that the speakers of the lyrics are fictional offers an escape-route from the impasse created by this strict non-transferability of the first-person writer *in propria persona*; for if the speakers are not to be identified with the poets but are their fictional creations, they are automatically freed from the deictic ties to the circumstances of utterance which bind the writer. There is, of course, a sense in which fictional characters must, like writers, be rooted in a particular time and place; but fictional personae, by virtue of their ontological status as imaginary beings, carry their historical and local environments with them. Fictional characters live within the text and, though dormant, are always available for reactivation by readers, unlike writers who are condemned eternally to straddle the boundary between the linguistic and the extra-linguistic realms whenever they refer to themselves as 'I'. The hypothesis of fictional speakers in the lyrics is therefore a very desirable one; but that does not settle the matter in its favour. To hold that it does would be to assume without argument that the Old English lyrics represent a satisfactory solution to a fundamental problem of deictic reference created by literacy.

The question: fiction or history? has not been entirely passed over by critics of the Old English lyrics, though it has been approached chiefly as a matter of rhetorical forms rather than as a question about the pragmatics of these poems as utterances. Old English writers were exposed to the tradition of Latin rhetoric, though appeal to precedents in a literate tradition in which fiction is an established form will obviously tilt the argument in favour of fictional status for the speakers of the Old English lyrics. Bernard F. Huppé, in an article published

---

[53] See Amodio, *Writing the Oral Tradition*, 10: "An . . . often overlooked fact is that texts in a literate culture are not isolated from orality but are in every way surrounded and influenced by it despite their being produced in a highly intertextual milieu."

as long ago as 1943, tentatively identified the wanderer's speech as an example of ethopoeia, a figure of classical rhetoric defined as "imaginary monologue attributed to a fictitious human character."[54] Huppé's argument drew inspiration from Margaret Schlauch's identification of the speech of the cross in *The Dream of the Rood* as an example of prosopopeia, another rhetorical device, defined as an imaginary monologue attributed to a non-human speaker.[55] Huppé received support in 1955 from E. G. Stanley in a wide-ranging and influential article on Old English verse which gave close attention to both the lyrics and the *Riddles*.[56] Stanley noted that the use of the first-person pronoun, which is the rule in the lyrics, is also fairly typical of the Old English *Riddles*. He found, furthermore, examples in the *Riddles* and others in the lyrics of interchanges of the first and third person singular,[57] and concluded from this that "the convention of the first person could be used without the poet's feeling personal attachment to the first person in his poems"; but Stanley allows that it is "difficult to assess the degree of this personal attachment in individual cases, especially in the 'elegies'."

Discussion of these issues might, however, take a different direction. The pragmatics of the Old English lyrics are not strictly comparable with the pragmatics of the Old English *Riddles*. When a riddle solution describes itself in its own 'voice' and refers to itself as 'I' or 'me', the audience or reader is confronted by what we might call a linguistic impersonation of the solution by the poet, taking 'impersonation' to involve identification with a recognisable, preexisting object—someone or something already known from previous experience, either as a human individual or as a class of objects. There is a distinction to be drawn between impersonation and 'fiction', if 'fiction' is taken (as it usually is) in the sense of an utterance involving the synthesis or creation of imaginary persons or events. Old English poets were clearly capable of impersonating traditional characters or non-human features of the natural world, as when the *Beowulf* poet mimics the words of Beowulf or Hroðgar, or when the *Riddles* poets impersonate the hidden solutions to their puzzles; but the vital point about both these kinds of subject is that they exist prior to their realization in the literary work. They are given to the poets as part of their cultural tradition or as features of the world as they perceive it. The speeches of these subjects are, of course, invented (or recreated), but the subjects themselves are not imaginary creations. The solutions to

---

[54] Bernard F. Huppé, "*The Wanderer*: Theme and Structure," *JEGP* 42 (1943): 516–38 (at 517–18).

[55] See Schlauch, "*The Dream of the Rood* as Prosopopoeia," 30–31, and further below, 245.

[56] E. G. Stanley, "Old English Poetic Diction and the Interpretation of *The Wanderer*, *The Seafarer* and *The Penitent's Prayer*," *Anglia* 73 (1955): 413–66 (at 447–50).

[57] According to James W. Earl, *Thinking about 'Beowulf'* (Stanford: Stanford University Press, 1994), 89–91, the metrical Proem to Alfred's *Metres of Boethius* constitutes another example, though the case seems to me in need of development.

the *Riddles* are, generally speaking, real things; and although there is certainly a large question-mark over the degree of historicity of *Beowulf*, with its monsters and superhuman hero, it is difficult to believe that the hero of the poem was not regarded by poet and contemporary audience as a real (i.e. historical) person. In the broader realm of linguistic expression, the deliberate creation of individual characters and events must belong to fiction alone if the term is to be more than a ragbag to hold all kinds of writing that are not purely factual. I shall use the terms 'fiction' and 'fictional' in that sense from now on.

The identifying characteristics of fiction have themselves been the subject of vigorous scholarly debate. John Searle sees the issues as going beyond the merely linguistic: authorial intention is, in his view, the *sole* factor that we may allow to determine whether a piece of writing is fiction or non-fiction:

> . . . the identifying criterion for whether or not a text is a work of fiction must of necessity lie in the illocutionary intentions of the author. There is no textual property, syntactical or semantic, that will identify a text as a work of fiction. What makes it a work of fiction is, so to speak, the illocutionary stance that the author takes toward it, and that stance is a matter of the complex illocutionary intentions that the author has when he writes or otherwise composes it.[58]

"Illocutionary intention," a term derived from speech-act theory as developed by J. L. Austin,[59] is definable as "an intention to perform an 'illocutionary act', for example, that of asserting, questioning, promising, or warning."[60] According to Lamarque, a writer of fiction

> gives the appearance of performing nonfictional illocutionary acts (like asserting or reporting) but, because of the conventions of storytelling, in fact takes on none of the commitments associated with these illocutionary acts.[61]

But however useful this may be as a starting-point for an analysis of what fiction is, it is obviously of little use as a taxonomic criterion for Old English texts, because the illocutionary intentions of medieval authors are always vague if not inaccessible. If we accept Searle's as the last word on the defining criteria of fictionality, there is a theoretical barrier to proof of a distinction between historical poet and fictional narrator in the Old English lyrics; the speakers could be either.

---

[58] John R. Searle, *Expression and Meaning: Studies in the Theory of Speech Acts* (Cambridge: Cambridge University Press, 1979), 65–66.

[59] J. L. Austin, *How to Do Things with Words: The William James Lectures delivered at Harvard University in 1955*, ed. J. O. Urmson and Marina Sbisà, 2nd ed. (Oxford: Oxford University Press, 1975), 98–120.

[60] Peter Lamarque, *Fictional Points of View* (Ithaca: Cornell University Press, 1996), 27.

[61] Lamarque, *Fictional Points of View*, 27.

It might be objected that this barrier does not exist for modern readers, because they do not decide whether they are reading fact or fiction by reference to the intentions of the author. The nature of modern books as fiction or nonfiction can be proclaimed in all manner of ways: by their titles or subtitles (e.g. "X: a novel"); by their position on labelled shelves in bookshops; or simply by the reputation of the author (as, for example, a novelist or a historian) whose name appears on spine or title-page. In those rare cases where there is genuine uncertainty (as, for example, Christopher Isherwood's purportedly autobiographical writings),[62] readers are compelled to test the content of the work against their sense of natural plausibility: they will judge an utterance to be fiction if they cannot believe that the characters or the events it deals with could exist in the real world. This is, however, an unreliable procedure, particularly for older works. Such judgements as the reader makes will be period- and culture-specific, because ideas of what is naturally plausible change over time. By this criterion, the Old English poem *Beowulf* might well be called fiction by the modern reader because the story, though set in a more or less recognizable world of human beings, also involves 'the supernatural' in the form of monsters and dragons. However, if we accept Searle's view that only the author can answer the question of whether something he or she has written is fact or fiction, we can never know if *Beowulf* is fiction or non-fiction. If we are concerned with the interpretation of texts in their historical context, Searle's point is an awkward one for any medievalist interested in this issue.[63] As I noted earlier, there are no obvious signs that the *Beowulf* poet

---

[62] In Isherwood's *Christopher and his Kind: 1929–1939* (London: Eyre Methuen, 1977), the author describes his book as "as frank and factual as I can make it, especially as far as I myself am concerned" (9), but his general avoidance of the first-person pronoun in what follows in favour of "Christopher" raises a question about who the subject of this apparently autobiographical book really is. Isherwood is, however, evidently making explicit here the separation, implicit in any autobiographical performance, of "the self who is *telling* from the past self or 'selves' who are being *told about*" (Jerome Bruner and Susan Weisser, "The Invention of Self: Autobiography and its Forms," in *Literacy and Orality*, ed. Olson and Torrance, 129–48 [at 132]).

[63] An interesting example of an alternative to Searle's intentionalist theory of fictionality—that the reader's attitude to the relationship between the text he is reading and the real world is irrelevant to the question of whether the text is factual or fictional—is Franz Bäuml's theory, developed (without reference to Searle) to explain certain narratological differences between medieval texts originating in oral tradition and others which are products of literate authors; see Franz H. Bäuml, "Varieties and Consequences of Medieval Literacy and Illiteracy," *Speculum* 55 (1980): 237–65. A basic notion of Bäuml's is that the author or transmitter of a written text (whether he be writer, scribe, reciter, or reader) is released from the kind of "commitment" to its content which the oral poet is necessarily involved in: "form and content of a written narrative can be manipulated by the writing author or scribe and the reciting reader to a much greater extent than a traditional oral poem by a performing oral poet" (250). There is an increased 'distance'

was sceptical about the truth of the story he tells. The test of natural plausibility is of even less value when applied to the Old English lyrics, because they contain no very obvious violations even of the twentieth-century reader's sense of what might possibly happen in real life.

A challenge to the strict intentionalism of Searle is mounted from a narratological standpoint by Dorrit Cohn. Cohn's critique of Searle is founded on an alternative analysis of the following passage from Iris Murdoch's novel *The Red and The Green*, which Searle himself quotes as an exemplification of his theory that "there is no textual property, syntactical or semantic, that will identify a text as a work of fiction":

> Ten more glorious days without horses! So thought Second Lieutenant Andrew Chase-White recently commissioned in the distinguished regiment of King Edward's Horse, as he pottered contentedly in a garden on the outskirts of Dublin on a sunny Sunday afternoon in April nineteen-sixteen.

To Searle, this passage could be a piece of historiography; to Cohn, it can only be fiction:

> What "serious" discourse ever quoted the thoughts of a person other than the speaker's own? Even if the genre-tagged cover page of this novel were removed, we would know from its first sentence that this scene tells of a *fictional* Second Lieutenant—a character known to his narrator as no real person can be known to a real speaker.[64]

Cohn is criticizing Searle for neglecting the narratological dimensions of texts which *do* sometimes enable the reader to decide whether he is faced with historiography or fiction. No "serious" student of Irish history in the early years of

---

between text and content, analogous with the increased distance between author/scribe and text, so that the content of the text can be "subjected to alienating functions." Bäuml cites an example from romance: in Hartmann's *Iwein*, 1029–1044, the narrator professes himself ignorant of the details of a hostile encounter between Iwein and Ascalon "since one is dead and cannot tell about it, the other is far too courtly to boast of his prowess, and no one else was there" (250). In Bäuml's view, "this type of alienation of a traditional narrative element—in this case the traditional battle descriptions in the Arthurian romances—is not likely to occur in the performance of a oral poet" (250–51). Bäuml's theory seems to me to involve a good deal of speculation about the attitudes of oral performers to the subject-matter of their works; and it is in any case of limited value for my purposes because it springs from a primary concern with the transference of traditional material of oral origin into a literary tradition, whereas I am much more concerned here with the formal innovations which literacy involved. I cite it, however, as one illustration of how Searle's intentionalism can be circumvented (though not, perhaps, countered).

[64] Dorrit Cohn, "Signposts of Fictionality: A Narratological Perspective," *Poetics Today* 11 (1990): 775–804 (at 784–85).

the last century would pretend to possess the kind of insight into the mind and emotions of a historical "Second Lieutenant Andrew Chase-White" that the heterodiegetic narrator of Murdoch's novel lays claim to here. As Cohn puts it elsewhere, the fictional domain differs from the real world in being "a world where a speaker *can* tell exactly what another person feels and perceives and remembers and plans without that person ever having told anyone."[65]

Cohn emphasises that this conclusion is relevant only to heterodiegetic third-person narratives—the type exemplified by the passage from Iris Murdoch's novel. Homodiegetic first-person narratives present a quite distinct set of problems. We saw earlier that all of the Old English lyrics, with one possible exception, are homodiegetic first-person narratives. The possible exception is *The Wanderer*, which may or may not contain a heterodiegetic narrator in addition to the main first-person speaker, and may or may not contain speeches by other persons, real or imaginary, reported by the main speaker in lines 1–5 and 92–110. The poem thus contains at least two and possibly three narrative levels. The two main rival analyses of the narrative structure of the poem may be summarized as follows, using Leslie's and Dunning and Bliss's editions to represent one analysis and Richard Hamer's the other:

1. Leslie; Dunning and Bliss:
    a. a heterodiegetic narrator (lines 6–7, 111, and also 88–91 according to Dunning and Bliss) introduces
    b. a first-person speaker, the 'wanderer' (lines 1–5, 8–87, 97–110, 112–15, Leslie also 88–91, Dunning and Bliss also 92–96) who (according to Leslie only) introduces
    c. a lament of a wise man (92–96).

2. Hamer:
    a. a first-person speaker (6–91, 111–15) quotes the words of
    b. an *eardstapa* ('wanderer', 1–5) and a *snottor* ('wise [man]', 92–110).

The main point to notice about these two arrangements is that, in spite of their radical differences, both involve reports (by the narrator in 1, and by the first-person speaker of the poem in 2) of the words or thoughts of another person (the wanderer in 1, the wise man in 2) to which the reporter cannot really have had access. Cohn's remark just quoted on heterodiegetic third-person narrative therefore seems relevant to the question of the ontological status—historical or fictional—of either the wanderer or the wise man, depending on which editorial arrangement one prefers. Earlier I raised the question of how the narrator (if he exists) is supposed

---

[65] Dorrit Cohn, "Fictional *versus* Historical Lives: Borderlines and Borderline Cases," *Journal of Narrative Techniques* 19 (1989): 3–24 (at 8).

to know what the wanderer, silent and apart as he is, is thinking.[66] Cohn's theory seems to supply the answer: if it is only in fiction that narrators can claim to see into the minds of their characters, the fact that either the narrator or the wanderer himself has access to another person's thoughts without being told about them means that either the wanderer or the wise man must be an imaginary, i.e. fictional, being.[67] Just as the narrator in Murdoch's novel can see into the mind of the author's fictional second lieutenant, so one or other of these figures in *The Wanderer* can see into the mind of the isolated individual he describes.

It is perhaps worth pointing out that Cohn's argument is vulnerable to a rather wider perspective on the problem. It discounts the possibility of an unacknowledged passage of information between the person whose thoughts are described and the presenting narrator. To repeat one of Cohn's specific assertions: it is only in the fictional domain that "a speaker *can* tell exactly what another person feels and perceives and remembers and plans without that person ever having told anyone." No doubt this is true; but how can we ever be certain that a person has not revealed his or her innermost thoughts to anyone else? A narrator may report the thoughts of another person in such detail as to suggest that he or she is a mind-reader—or writing fiction; but the narrator might, in theory, have received the information that is being conveyed from a real person through undisclosed channels—private conversations or letters, reports from a third party who became a confidant of the person whose thoughts are being described, and so on. So the test is not absolutely foolproof. The apparently omniscient narrator may be not what he or she seems, but someone with covert access to privileged information. However, it does, admittedly, seem doubtful if in *The Wanderer* the narrator's knowledge of the wanderer's thoughts and feelings, or the wanderer's knowledge of the wise man's thoughts and feelings, result from this kind of contamination. The reflections of both these figures are conveyed directly, as they think. If they were conveyed subsequently to the reporter, why should he conceal the fact?

If Cohn's arguments are, as I believe, relevant to *The Wanderer*, this poem may be cited as a very early—perhaps the earliest—extant example in English of heterodiegetic third-person fiction. Cohn, however, sees texts in this mode as essentially modern, indeed modernist. He cites Dostoevsky's formal analysis of his own story "A Gentle Creature," in which "a man alone in a room with the dead body of his wife recounts the history of his sado-masochistic marriage." Cohn summarizes: ". . . since this tale was neither written down by the teller, nor addressed to an interlocutor, its textual existence presumes the presence in the room of an 'invisible stenographer' who took down everything the man said." The speeches of the wanderer and of the wise man seem to me comparable, formally

---

[66] Above, pp. 194–97.
[67] See further Cohn, "Signposts," 785: "the minds of imaginary figures can be known in ways that those of real persons cannot."

speaking, with that of Dostoevsky's hero: they are alone, so they have no interlocutor and no recording scribe either. Cohn suggests that Dostoevsky's story marks the emancipation of literature from the "mimetic matrix" because there are no conceivable circumstances in the ordinary world under which the words of the hero could have been transmitted.[68] In this sense, Dostoevsky's story heralds the internal-monologue prose narrative as practised by Joyce and other modernist writers of fiction. It would appear, however, that the development in literary form here identified by Cohn should be put back to a much earlier period, and is to be related, not to the rise of modernism, but to the advent of literacy. The potential for fictional writing created by literacy did not, it seems, take twelve centuries to be realized; it is already being developed in the work of a poet writing no later than three hundred years after the first books in English were written.[69]

But if *The Wanderer* offers evidence of an emergent fictionality, the identification of the narrative domain—fiction or historiography—of the other five lyrics is a more difficult problem. Four of them—*The Seafarer, Wulf and Eadwacer, The Wife's Lament,* and *The Husband's Message*—are first-person narratives by unnamed speakers, with no indications of authorship. All four thus represent a subspecies of a type of homodiegetic narrative which the narratologist Philippe Lejeune labels "indéterminé."[70] In an indeterminate text as defined by Lejeune, a nameless 'I' narrates what might seem to be an autobiography; and although the author's name is known, the reader is not given any indication by the author (a "pacte", in Lejeune's terminology) of whether the work is autobiographical or fictional.[71] So the indeterminate text may be defined by the formula: author named; narrator anonymous; no "pacte". Henry Miller's *Tropic of Cancer* is cited by Cohn as a modern instance: Miller objected to a review of his book which took the first-person narrator as a fictional character, whereas Miller wrote the book as autobiography. An indeterminate text, by failing to use fictional names to enable

---

[68] Cohn, "Fictional *versus* Historical Lives," 18.

[69] Chaucer is regarded by some scholars as one of the first English writers to convey his awareness of the fictional nature of his work. Illich and Sanders, in their discussion of *The Canterbury Tales*, point to Chaucer's claim to relate, before he forgets it all, the exact tales told by the pilgrims "in the distinct voice of each of the pilgrims, utilizing their exact metaphor, image, color of language, and idea" (Ivan Illich and Barry Sanders, *ABC: The Alphabetization of the Popular Mind* [Harmonsworth: Penguin, 1988], 89). They find this claim incredible, and reason that ". . . if Chaucer could not possibly have remembered all that he says he has, he must be making it up, embellishing and shaping his initial information. He must be telling a story, inventing a tale. That is, he must be writing fiction" (90–91). Fictionality, according to this view, is a clear (if paradoxical) implication of the form of *The Canterbury Tales*.

[70] Philippe Lejeune, *Le Pacte autobiographique* (Paris: Éditions du Seuil, 1975), 28–29, cited by Cohn, "Fictional *versus* Historical Lives," 15.

[71] "non seulement le personnage n'a pas de nom, mais l'auteur ne conclut aucun pacte" (Lejeune, *Le Pacte*, 29).

the reader to distinguish character from author, "condemns us to vacillate or allows us to oscillate—not only between different modes of fictional readings, but also, more radically, between fictional and referential readings."[72] But the four Old English poems I have cited are even more indeterminate than Miller's *Tropic of Cancer* because we are left ignorant, not only of the names of the speakers but also of the names of the poets (formula: author anonymous; narrator anonymous; no 'pacte'). *Deor* presents a third combination of factors (author anonymous; narrator named; no 'pacte'). In all cases, the onus is placed on the reader to decide whether the text is fact or fiction.[73] These extreme narratological forms are not really accounted for in Lejeune's theory because of its basis in writings of the modern period, where the author's name is almost invariably known to the reader, whereas Old English poetry is usually anonymous.[74]

It would seem, then, that neither Searle's intentionalist theory nor Lejeune's narratological categorizations can help us decide whether any of the six lyrics except *The Wanderer* are historiographical or fictional. It is probably reasonable to exclude *The Husband's Message* from any further consideration here on the grounds that the speaker of the poem is probably not human; but that still leaves four apparently autobiographical poems—*The Seafarer, Wulf and Eadwacer, Deor*, and *The Wife's Lament*—in which the speaker could be either the actual poet or a fictional character. If, of course, the speaker in *Wulf and Eadwacer* is, as Sedgefield suggested, an animal, that poem too could be eliminated on the same grounds as *The Husband's Message*; but as most critics see the speaker as human, it seems safest to continue to regard this poem, provisionally at least, as presenting the same problem as the other three.

If existing theoretical expositions of fictionality fail us here, there are at least two further considerations which might be brought to bear on the question of whether these four lyrics are fictional or not. The first is the explicit claims to autobiography which, as I mentioned earlier in this chapter,[75] are to be found in three of them—*The Seafarer, Deor*, and *The Wife's Lament*. Insofar as these claims testify to the truth of what the speakers are telling us, we can easily imagine them put into the mouths of fictional characters who are telling stories likely to stretch the reader's credulity—tales involving supernatural events, for example, such as Poe's tales—in the service of realism: a speaker telling such a story in the real world is bound to be aware that it will be disbelieved and should therefore show awareness of this in narrating it. However, in our three lyrics, only the Seafarer's claim emphasises truth as such (*The Seafarer* 1–2 *Mæg ic be me sylfum soðgied wrecan, siþas secgan, . . .*, "I can utter a true lay about myself, tell of my experiences . . ."); the other two simply assert the autobiographical nature of the story

---

[72] Cohn, "Fictional *versus* Historical Lives," 15.
[73] "Tout repose alors sur la décision du lecteur" (Lejeune, *Le Pacte*, 33).
[74] See above, 112–15.
[75] Above, 190–91.

6. The Disembodied Speaker

being told (*The Wife's Lament* 1–2a *Ic þis giedd wrece bi me ful geomorre, minre sylfre sið*, "I utter this lay about myself, very sad [as I am], my own experience," and *Deor* 35–6 *Þæt ic bi me sylfum secgan wille, þæt ic hwile wæs. . .*, "I wish to say this about myself, that I was for a time . . ."), perhaps implying that the stories poets tell are more often about other people's lives than about their own. But here we face a difficult problem of interpretation which has to do with realism as a style. In any literary culture it will become more and more difficult, in a tradition of naturalistic fiction, to distinguish fiction from non-fiction if its practitioners go to ever greater lengths to achieve a suspension of disbelief in the reader. A crucial question we are therefore faced with here is whether Old English poets are likely to have achieved as advanced a conception of literary realism as these autobiographical claims in the lyrics would certainly indicate if the speakers were indeed fictional. We do not know the detailed history of realism in literature that a definite answer would require; but if only the very beginnings of fiction are to be glimpsed in Old English literature, it seems likely that the answer is 'no': the autobiographical claims in these three poems should be taken at their face value.

The second factor which seems to me relevant to the question of the fictionality or non-fictionality of the Old English lyrics is the occurrence, within the various first-person speeches, of descriptions in the third person singular of generalized human types. These passages were referred to briefly earlier in this chapter.[76] Here I shall first define and exemplify this particular narrative mode as it manifests itself in the Old English lyrics, then consider its possible bearing on my investigation of fictionality/non-fictionality in these poems.

The following passage from *The Seafarer*, in which the speaker stands back slightly from his own personal predicament and projects it on to a whole class of seafaring persons in situations similar to his own, provides a suitable introduction to this special mode:

```
        Forþon nis þæs modwlonc     mon ofer eorþan,
40      ne his gifena þæs god,       ne in geoguþe to þæs hwæt,
        ne in his dædum to þæs deor, ne him his dryhten to þæs hold,
        þæt he a his sæfore      sorge næbbe,
        to hwon hine dryhten     gedon wille.
        Ne biþ him to hearpan hyge     ne to hringþege,
45      ne to wife wyn      ne to worulde hyht,
        ne ymbe owiht elles,     nefne ymb yða gewealc,
        ac a hafað longunge     se þe on lagu fundað.     (Seafarer 39–47)
```

"Because no man on earth is so proud of heart, nor so generous in his gifts, nor so vigorous in his youth, nor so bold in his deeds, nor has a lord so gracious to him, that he does not always feel anxiety about his sea-voyage, as to what the Lord has in store for him. He has no mind

---

[76] Above, 200–1.

for the harp, nor for the receiving of rings, nor for the happiness of love, nor for worldly ambition, nor for anything else except the rolling of the waves; he who ventures on the sea always suffers yearnings."

Not all third-person utterances by the main speakers of the lyrics are in this mode. On the one hand we must first distinguish it from other third-person passages in which the speakers describe something directly and immediately related to their own circumstances, as for example in *Wulf and Eadwacer* 2 and 7 *willað hy hine aþecgan, gif he on þreat cymeð* (perhaps "Will they feed him if he comes into their midst?"): this is not a generalizing utterance but only a description of an aspect of the speaker's (or rather Wulf's) present material situation. On the other hand, there are other passages in the third person consisting of generalizations just as broad as, if not broader than, the passage from *The Seafarer* just quoted, which do not involve the invocation of a singular, generalized individual of the kind represented by the *Seafarer* passage's restless *mon*. *The Seafarer* also affords an example of this less personalized mode of generalization:

```
80          Dagas sind gewitene,
         ealle onmedlan       eorþan rices;
         næron nu cyningas    ne caseras
         ne goldgiefan        swylce iu wæron,
         þonne hi mæst mid him  mærþa gefremedon
85       and on dryhtlicestum  dome lifdon.
         Gedroren is þeos duguð eal,   dreamas sind gewitene,
         wuniað þa wacran     and þas woruld healdaþ,
         brucað þurh bisgo.              (Seafarer 80b-88)
```

"The days have gone, all the magnificence of the earthly realm. There are not now kings nor emperors nor gold-givers such as there were formerly, when between them they performed the greatest deeds of glory and lived in lordliest renown. This whole company of noble warriors has fallen, the joys have departed, weaker men now live in the world, occupy it with toil and trouble."

The difference between this extract and the preceding one which contributes most to their distinct effects is the difference of grammatical number: in this last passage is described the decline of kings and emperors and warriors simply as an observable historical trend, whereas the first passage, by creating a single figure who embodies so many aspects of the kind of person the seafarer himself has become, has a much more immediate and dramatic impact on the reader, as well as a more intimate connection with the speaker who is (or is presented as being) this figure's creator.

Not all of the four lyrics we are concerned with here contain extensive passages in this mode. One of them, *Wulf and Eadwacer*, has no examples. *The Wife's Lament*'s only clear example comes in the final one-and-a-half lines of the poem:

> Wa bið þam þe sceal
> of langoþe leofes abidan. (*The Wife's Lament* 52b–3)

"Woe is him who must abide in longing for his beloved."

This statement clearly grows out of the speaker's own circumstances and those of her absent lord whose misery she has been imagining in the preceding lines; but it nevertheless represents a synthesis of common human experience which transcends the narrower experience of the speaker and her beloved: it could be, and is meant to be, relevant to the experience of other lovers. *Deor* supplies a more substantial passage of reflection which has a similar relation to the speaker's own predicament as it emerges from the lines (quoted above) which follow it:

>   Siteð sorgcearig, sælum bidæled,
>   on sefan sweorceð, sylfum þinceð
> *30* þæt sy endeleas earfoða dæl.
>   Mæg þonne geþencan, þæt geond þas woruld
>   witig Dryhten wendeþ geneahhe,
>   eorle monegum are gesceawað,
>   wislicne blæd, sumum weana dæl.
> *35* Þæt ic bi me sylfum secgan wille, . . . (*Deor* 28–35)

"The man full of sorrow sits, deprived of joys, his mind grows dark, it seems to him that his share of sorrows is endless. But he is able to reflect that all over the world the wise Lord often brings change, shows mercy, assured prosperity, to many a warrior, and a portion of woes to others. I wish to say this about myself . . ."

This passage is rather similar in both manner and meaning to the opening five lines of *The Wanderer*, quoted earlier:[77] both contain reflections (no doubt meant to be consoling) on the power of God to apportion mercy or misfortune to different individuals. As the choice lies with God, perhaps the implication is that the unhappy individual may hope that God may one day change his mind.

These third-person figures vary considerably from poem to poem in the breadth of generalization they represent. For example, in the first passage quoted from *The Seafarer*, the figure is himself a seafarer who is clearly very similar to the speaker, whereas the extract from *Deor* describes more of an 'everyman'. What all these third-person figures have in common is their ontological status in the

---

[77] Above, 195.

text. It is difficult to label them as fictional characters because they are not fully realized individuals but rather composite types with much in common in terms of traits and experiences. The relationship between the first-person speakers and these third-person figures whom they invoke seems to be of instance to type: the first-person speakers are individual examples of the types represented by the third-person figures. If, however, the first-person speakers are fictional, there is no apparent dynamic or functional relationship between the speakers and the third-person figures: it is difficult to see the point of fitting an imaginary person into a paradigm of generalized human experience—unless we can believe that this is another stroke of realism used by a sophisticated writer of fiction. If, however, the first-person speeches in these poems are truly autobiographical, the social function of the poems may be identified as the validation of the actual experience of individuals by appeal to a recognized pattern. Experience and observation of life leads to a distilled wisdom which individuals may draw upon to reconcile themselves to the unhappier aspects of the human condition. If the first-person speakers were fictional, it would be difficult to escape the conclusion that these were poems which had social integration and man's reconciliation with misfortune as their *themes*; they would be poems about abstract ideas. They do not fit easily into that category because the experience of the first-person speakers seems so particularized; there is nothing universal about the experience of, say, the speakers of *The Wife's Lament*, or *Deor*.[78] This consideration is not, of course, decisive, though it seems to me to support the idea that these are poems about the experience of real individuals, not about the social value of traditional precedents and received wisdom for individuals generally; and if I am right, that makes them essentially non-fictional works.

The first-person speaker in *The Wanderer*—a text which I tentatively identified earlier as a work of fiction on grounds of form and content—also incorporates in his utterances passages in this generalizing third-person mode, for example lines 39–44:

---

[78] Some would disagree with this view. Ursula Schaefer, "From an Aesthetic Point of View . . .: Receptional Aspects of Old English Poetry," in *De Gustibus*, ed. Foley, 494–541, notes in her discussion of the status of the unnamed speakers of the Old English elegies that "what they tell appears to be their own 'personal', 'individual fates'" (530), although "Understanding them as really 'individual' drastically contradicts to [*sic*] all we know of the concept of the individual in the Middle Ages" (530). She continues: "Yet if we take the elegies as 'exemplary', as depictions of what holds for all human beings, then those *personae* appear all the more fictive and their discourses, by the same token, more fictional." This line of thinking reverses my own suggestion here: that it is this very individuality that creates an impression of the speakers as historical persons when they are placed against the background of the general types they describe as a way of contextualizing their own experiences.

	Ðonne sorg ond slæp	somod ætgædre
40	earmne anhogan	oft gebindað,
	þinceð him on mode	þæt he his mondryhten
	clyppe ond cysse,	ond on cneo lecge
	honda ond heafod,	swa he hwilum ær
	in geardagum	giefstolas breac:[79] (*Wanderer* 39–44)

"When sorrow and sleep together often hold fast the wretched solitary man, it seems to him in his imagination that he is embracing and kissing his liege lord, and laying hands and head on his knee, just as he had received gifts from the throne previously from time to time in days gone by:"[80]

The two main rival editorial arrangements of the poem, schematized earlier in this chapter, agree in assigning this passage to the first-person speaker of the poem ('the wanderer', in my terminology), but differ in regarding the wanderer either as a second-level speaker introduced by a first-level heterodiegetic narrator (Leslie, Dunning and Bliss), or as a first-level homodiegetic narrator who quotes, in lines 1–5, the words of an *eardstapa* and, in lines 92–110, the words of a "wise man" (Hamer). This difference of narratological structure has consequences for the interpretation of third-person passages spoken by the wanderer such as the one just quoted. As I argued earlier, the first of these alternative editorial arrangements implies that the wanderer himself is probably to be taken as a fictional figure; whereas the second arrangement (Hamer's) implies that it is only the wise man (111 *snottor*) whose words are quoted in lines 92–110 who is fictional, not the wanderer who quotes the wise man's words. I have just argued that the relationship in the other lyrics between generalizing passages in the third person and the first-person narrators who utter them suggests that that such narrators are autobiographical, not fictional. Hamer's arrangement is thus consistent with my argument (because it does not imply a fictional first-person speaker), and Leslie's and Dunning and Bliss's inconsistent with it. I cannot, of course, insist that Hamer is right only on this basis, though it is, perhaps, a consideration that favours his arrangement of the text.

---

[79] Text from Dunning and Bliss, *The Wanderer*, 111–12.
[80] Dunning and Bliss, *The Wanderer*, 112, note to lines 41–44, discuss various difficulties of interpretation and translation in this passage.

Chapter 7
Conclusions

The aims of this chapter are to consider what light has been shed on the topics and questions raised at the end of Chapter 1 by the intervening discussion; to pursue some of the implications of the conclusions I have reached; and to suggest some other, related lines of inquiry that might modify or supplement the results of my investigation.

§1. Runes versus roman in inscriptions

I begin with the relationship between runic and roman writing in the period. We have seen (Chapter 3) that epigraphical runes, the only form of writing known to the Anglo-Saxons between their arrival in Britain in the fifth century and their conversion to Christianity in the seventh, continued to be used in inscriptions after the conversion, usually as an alternative to roman letters, occasionally alongside or in combination with them. The original and (in the pre-Christian period) exclusive relationship between runes and Old English is generally maintained in the post-conversion period to the extent that runes are very rarely used to represent Latin words or utterances. This almost complete restriction of runes to Old English is no doubt attributable to a strong sense of the traditional link between script and language. It is not difficult to see why runes should have been felt to be a less appropriate representation for Latin than the roman alphabet, within whose province Latin already fell in Christian writings. Of the handful of Latin inscriptions (or parts of inscriptions) that use runes, most are dated early in the post-conversion period. These are the Auzon casket, St. Cuthbert's coffin, and the Ruthwell Cross, none of them older than the eighth century.[1] This occasional encroachment of runes on roman territory is so rare that it is more safely interpreted as a manifestation of the relative popularity of runes for inscriptions in the early centuries following the conversion than as evidence of any general fluidity in the relationship between scripts and languages at this time.

---

[1] A further example is the Whitby comb inscription, not precisely dated. Page (*An Introduction to English Runes*, 164-65) suggests only that it should be placed between the foundation of the *Streoneshalh* monastery in 657 and its destruction in the later ninth century.

This general restriction of runes to the vernacular is not matched by a complementary limitation on the roman alphabet. Roman is used, not only for inscriptions in Latin, but increasingly for Old English inscriptions too as the period progresses. It is probable that the increasing use of roman for Old English inscriptions is nothing more than a symptom of a growing familiarity with the roman alphabet, fostered mainly by its general use in manuscripts. It is difficult to judge whether the final disappearance of runes from inscriptions resulted more from an active preference for the roman alphabet than from a weakening of the runic tradition; either tendency, or a combination of both, would have produced the same effect.

Within the Old English part of the epigraphical corpus there is a marked, though not overwhelming, preference for runes in the presentation of alliterative verse. It is unclear how much significance should be attached to this. These metrical inscriptions are rather few in number, and most of the runic ones are dated fairly early in the post-conversion period (there are no pre-conversion runic inscriptions in verse); so again, as with the few cases of runes for Latin, the apparent preference for runes in verse may be simply a function of their generally commoner use in the early part of the period than in the later. It is of course possible that runes were regarded as a particularly appropriate form of representation for verse because of the parallel continuity between both verse and runes on the one hand and the continental prehistory of the Anglo-Saxons on the other, but the evidence is not really strong enough to prove the point.

§2. Runes versus roman in manuscripts

After the disappearance of runes from inscriptions, the production of inscriptions in roman continued until the end of the Old English period; but the apparently equal status in early post-conversion inscriptions of runic and roman writing is not mirrored in manuscript writings. Here, the roman alphabet (supplemented, as we saw in Chapter 1, by two runic borrowings) dominates from the first—not surprisingly, for the roman alphabet and the medium of parchment came to the Anglo-Saxons as part of the same cultural shipment, so to speak. No surviving Anglo-Saxon manuscripts are written primarily in runes.[2] Chapters 4 and 5 of this book discuss some of the most important examples of Old English poems which, though basically in roman, include runes as part of their texts. The combined evidence of these poems suggests that when used in such contexts, runes had been reduced to a narrow role as a spelling alphabet: they are not used to represent coherent utterances in their own right, only the contextualized letters of particular words which the reader is encouraged to read or reconstruct. The

---

[2] For a detailed account of the use of runes in Anglo-Saxon manuscripts, see René Derolez, *Runica Manuscripta: The English Tradition* (Bruges: De Tempel, 1954).

runes in Cynewulf's signatures, presented in natural order in three of his surviving poems (anagrammatically only in *The Fates of the Apostles*), spell the poet's name, whereas in the *Riddles* the embedded or attached runes, given in most cases either in retrograde order or anagrammatically, pose a greater challenge to the reader's intelligence, as one might expect in verbal puzzles: the runes need to be reordered to spell the word denoting the solution, the identity of which is also artfully suggested by the surrounding discourse in roman. It is obviously possible that Cynewulf's anagram of his name in *The Fates of the Apostles* was inspired by anagrammatic runic riddles. But Cynewulf's method in three of his surviving poems (*Juliana* is the exception) is more ambitious than in the runic *Riddles* in one respect: these three poems show a double use of the runes as both letters to spell 'Cyn(e)wulf' and as logograms for the names of the individual runic characters that are worked into both the grammar and the semantics of the verse. None of the runic *Riddles* attempts the semantic integration of rune-names, and only *Riddles* 24 and 42 achieve satisfactory grammatical integration. The more elaborate technique used in Cynewulf's signatures might well be related to the fact that the poet's name was vulnerable to omission in the course of transmission. The preservation of Cynewulf's identity in relation to his works depended on its thorough integration into the fabric of his verse. As we saw earlier, the chief difficulty he faced in achieving this lay in the area of semantic integration: the archaic and (by Cynewulf's time) obscure frame of reference denoted by the names of the runes of the *fuþorc* made it difficult for him to compose passages that not only incorporated the meanings of the runes spelling his name, but were also sufficiently meaningful and well-integrated into the broader structure of his poems to constitute an indispensable part of them. The runic riddlers did not need to be so concerned with technical integration because the runes were vital clues to the riddle's solution; no doubt the poets themselves realized that any copyist who took it into his head to omit the runic letters would produce unsolvable riddles. Cynewulf's Christian verse-narratives would lose less by the omission of the runic passages. This difference may also help to explain the invariably thorough metrical and alliterative integration of the runic names in Cynewulf's poems, compared with the looser technical integration tolerated by most of the *Riddle* poets. The most conspicuous exception to this generalization is *Riddle* 42, 'Cock and Hen', to which I shall return below.

Although these manuscript texts show runes being used for new and specialized purposes, structural links with their original epigraphical function are not completely lost. They are most obvious in Cynewulf's runic signatures, where (as I suggested in Chapter 4) the metrical, alliterative, and semantic integration of the runic names into the texture of the poem is analogous with the literal act of inscription on a material artifact. The structural and logical relationship between the runic names and the roman text with which they are integrated is comparable, *mutatis mutandis*, with the relationship between an inscription and the artifact into which it is cut.³ In both cases, awareness of the context in which the utterance was formulated and preserved is essential to a grasp of its significance. Cynewulf's name, abstracted from its context, is no more than a linguistic form, of interest to students of onomastics but lacking any communicative force; and the same might be said of epigraphical texts such as (for example) *aldred*, a personal name, presumably of the owner or manufacturer, inscribed in runes on the eighth- or ninth-century Brandon tweezers fragment.⁴ Cynewulf's signatures show runes being used to create a basic form of authorial identity which, in combination with the structural connection with inscriptions, suggests a conception of the composed text as a made thing, just as much an artifact as any manufactured object that includes the inscribed name of its maker as part of its material form. This sense of poetic composition as a craft comparable with the manufacture of material artifacts is no doubt to be related to the materialization of language that writing involves.

The use of runes in the runic *Riddles* is less easily correlated with epigraphical practices than it is in the case of Cynewulf. The relationship between the solution-word spelt by the runes and the descriptive text in roman that encapsulates it has something in common with the link in inscriptions between a caption and a pictorial or plastic representation that it labels, as for example on the eleventh- or twelfth-century Inglesham slab, where a carved figure of the Virgin is marked *Maria*,⁵ though the analogy is, of course, inexact insofar as the enigmatic element, so vital in the *Riddles*, is lacking in such inscriptions. A closer analogy with the mental operations required of the reader by the runic *Riddles* is provided by anagrammatic clues in modern crossword puzzles: here, too, the reader must rearrange a list of given letters to spell a particular word that expresses a concept also hinted at by an enigmatic description. But whereas the crossword-solver is usually left to isolate the sequence of letters that constitutes the anagram within the clue, the job is already done for the reader of the runic *Riddles* because the runes stand out visually from the roman background. Whether this apparently unexacting feature of the runic *Riddles* was compensated for in other ways — for example, by the increasing obscurity of the runic alphabet in the period when the *Riddles* were composed, or the greater challenge presented by spelling games of any kind when literacy was still limited and relatively new — we cannot say; but both kinds of puzzle are clearly and essentially post-literate in conception

---

[3] A connection between material artifacts from the period and poetic form, though in this case in the absence of any linguistic link, is made by John Leyerle, "The Interlace Structure of *Beowulf*," *University of Toronto Quarterly* 37 (1967): 1-17, repr. in *Interpretations of Beowulf: A Critical Anthology*, ed. R. D. Fulk (Bloomington: Indiana University Press, 1991), 146-67.

[4] See above, Chapter 3, category 5(e).

[5] See above, Chapter 3, category 13(a).

and construction. Only literates can spell; indeed, spelling as an activity is itself scarcely conceivable before the advent of literacy.

§3. Concurrent orality and literacy; thinking through form

There is, however, one difference between these modern and medieval puzzles that has important historical implications: crossword-puzzle clues are in prose, but the runic *Riddles* are metrical. It is generally accepted by scholars that the alliterative and metrical character of all the Old English poetry that has survived points, when taken with comparative evidence, to an oral tradition of poetic composition already established among the Anglo-Saxons when they first came to Britain. The adaptation of this alliterative verse-form to Christian subject-matter following the conversion is proved by the survival of numerous poems on Christian themes, some of which have been referred to in various connections in this book. The extent to which a parallel oral poetic tradition continued to flourish after the conversion is more difficult to establish, for the obvious reason that the only direct evidence for the vernacular poetic tradition of the period is in written form;[6] but the runic 'Cock and Hen' *Riddle* 42, discussed in detail in Chapter 5, seems to point to a continuing conception in the literate period of alliterative verse as originally, or even essentially, oral. We saw earlier how this poem embodies a whole bundle of intertwined paradoxes involving ideas of orality versus literacy, speech versus writing, audience versus readers. For instance, the runic letters could be interpreted only by literate readers; but the metrical and grammatical integration of their names in the poem contributes to a speakable quality in them that one would not normally associate with a system of writing. Another paradox resides in the way the text presents itself as an oral poem delivered in a standard 'heroic' environment, even though a narrower appeal to a literate elite is indicated by the address to "runemen" and "those who know books." These and other aspects of the poem suggest a more or less deliberate homology between two oppositions, one between spoken and written poetry, the other between roman and runes. What this homology might be taken to suggest is an idea of the roman alphabet as a means of transcribing originally or formally spoken utterances (such as Old English alliterative verse composed for oral recitation), whereas runes, by contrast, retain their original function as a representation of the 'hand-language' of the writer. *Riddle* 42, by setting up this confrontation between oral and literate traditions in such a way as to emphasise their differences, draws attention to the essentially spoken nature of Old English verse, suggesting that poetry was probably still being composed orally and recited in the traditional way at the time when this poem was written.

---

[6] The indirect evidence is examined by Jeff Opland in *Anglo-Saxon Oral Poetry*.

The 'Cock and Hen' *Riddle* also exemplifies a distinctive mode of poetic thought that is characteristic of other, non-runic *Riddles* in the Exeter Book collection as well: what we might call 'thinking through form'. There is no explicit investigation of abstract conceptions connected with orality and literacy, or with any of the other homologous oppositions that mirror it, in any of these poems. Instead, the oppositions and their often paradoxical implications are left to emerge, chiefly from the form of the poem in the case of the 'Cock and Hen' *Riddle*, but also to some extent from its content, particularly the poet's creation of an oral/aural scene for the poem's reception. Other, non-runic *Riddles* that take the materials and procedures of writing and reading as explicit themes show a more thoroughgoing integration of form with content. In *Riddle* 47, 'Bookmoth', the established vocabulary of speech, most conspicuously OE *word*, is used against the grain of normal usage, as a way of defining the peculiarities of language in its material, written form. The eating of words by the bookmoth larva (assimilation by animal mouth playfully reversing the direction of enunciation by human mouth) pointedly draws attention to the novelty of materialized language, open to actual ingestion by the proto-insect but only to intellectual assimilation by human beings. The 'Bookmoth' *Riddle* thus provokes reflection, not just about orality and literacy, but about language-use and the understanding of language as a distinctively human activity. The caterpillar, none the wiser for its meal, symbolizes the exclusion of the animal world from language. It might be added that the focus of the poem on the concept of the word as a unit of language is something that in itself points to the kind of analytical conceptualizing of language-elements that Olson links with the advent of literacy in any society that acquires it.[7]

In *Riddle* 60, 'Pen', the speaker clearly implies a contrast between writing and speaking in its reference to its own "mouthless" communication with the reader: mouthless communication must be silent; and the silence, and hence the privacy, that only writing can confer on linguistic exchanges is a strong implication of this poem. But its dramatization of writing and reading is accomplished entirely in terms of the standard speech-situation, the 'canonical situation of utterance' that was defined in Chapter 2. The pen's special role as a means of language-production uniquely empowers it to 'speak' directly to the reader as "thee" (14 *þe*). The singular number of the pronoun is a sign, not only of the poet's evocation of 'canonical', oral, one-to-one communication, but also of the poet's individualization of the pen as the particular pen used to write the *Riddle* text into the manuscript in which it is being read—into the Exeter Book itself, for modern readers, for this is our only record of the poem. In this context, the text is 'spoken' by the Exeter Book scribe's own pen as a 'personal' utterance addressed to any individual reader. A situation is thus created which approximates to deictic

---

[7] See Olson, *The World on Paper*, 42, 70-71, 261.

simultaneity (i.e. the co-presence of utterer and receiver in space and time), normally a distinguishing feature of spoken as opposed to written communication. The normal time-lapse involved in written communication is not exactly abolished; but it becomes irrelevant. The poem demonstrates that much of the immediacy, and all the directness, of speech are possible in writing—but only if the 'speaker' is a pen, which of course effectively emphasises its impossibility under normal circumstances. *Riddle* 60 is an excellent example of thinking through form: the ingenious formal and dramatic structure of the poem creates awareness of the strangeness of literacy, and even of some of its limitations, when seen against a background of traditional orality.

The Husband's Message seems to have much in common with *Riddle* 60: both poems elaborately dramatize literate communication in oral terms; both achieve something comparable with the deictic simultaneity that is normally the prerogative of speech; and in both the overall effect, paradoxically enough, is to emphasise the essential differences between the two modes of communication rather than to conflate or confuse them. Texts produced under literacy may function autonomously, without any supporting reference to the human agency of the absent writer, if some level of awareness of themselves as texts can be injected into them. Both these poems create an impression of this kind of self-knowledge. The resemblances between them are so distinctive and closely defined as to suggest that one poet might have composed both. At any rate, their position next to each other in the manuscript can scarcely be accidental.

The intellectual curiosity about the relationship between orality and literacy evinced by the form and content of these poems is likely to be related partly to the newness and (in the case of runic literacy) the rarity of literate practices in the period. To the majority of Anglo-Saxons, writing and reading were no doubt esoteric activities, especially, perhaps, to Old English poets, steeped in a centuries-old tradition of oral poetic composition. It would appear that there is nothing in Old English prose comparable with the kind of probing experimentation with form and ideas that we find in *Riddles* 42, 47, and 60 and *The Husband's Message*; but this is not really surprising. It is to be expected that Old English poets, beneficiaries of a rich oral heritage, would have been more intensely aware than most of the way literacy subverts the directness and immediacy of spoken communication. To them, the new possibilities offered by written communication were perhaps less apparent than its novelty and strangeness; and they might well have been more inclined than other people to see written language as a variant of spoken language. If so, that would help to explain why it often seems as though these poets are pushing written language as far in the direction of speech as it can possibly go. This impression stems, I suggest, not from any desire on their part to reverse the historical development represented by literacy, or even to blur the distinction between written and spoken utterances, but rather from ingrained assumptions about language based on the model of speech which, as poets trained in oral composition, they would have found natural. In this period, it was evidently still difficult for poets, at least, to think about writing in its own terms. Much of the historical value of these poems derives from the distinctive conceptualizations of language that they embody.

§4. Inscriptions and the deictic gap

The adventurous exploration of the implications of written language that takes place in these poems is not matched anywhere among the surviving Anglo-Saxon inscriptions. This is not to be wondered at, for epigraphists obviously wrote with certain specific, practical, and generally non-literary purposes in view: to preserve the identity of craftsmen in relation to their work, for example, or to record ownership, or to ensure that the dead are remembered and to ask for prayers for their souls. Yet it is clear from the way they expressed themselves that they were fully attuned to the implications of literacy. There is scarcely a sign in these inscriptions of any easy, unreflecting transposition into writing of the normal forms of spoken language; on the contrary, as we saw in Chapter 3, the communicative effectiveness of almost every surviving Anglo-Saxon inscription, runic or roman, Old English or Latin, depends on the reader's awareness of the conditions under which it is preserved. The medium is not taken for granted in the way that paper is today; knowledge of the medium's nature and presence is vital to our understanding of the inscribed communication. I have argued (in Chapter 2) that the choice of inscription as a mode of linguistic expression resulted in a confrontation with one of the most basic problems involved in the use of the written word for communication: the 'deictic gap' opened up by literacy. Epigraphists found various ways of bridging the gap, the most distinctive of which was the new, medium-deictic use of the first-person pronoun. Literacy actually creates the "speaking world" of my title; and we should probably conclude that literacy generated its own special forms from the first. The European origins of runic expertise among the Anglo-Saxons' forebears is lost in the centuries preceding the English settlement; but there can be little doubt that the special forms of utterance that literacy promoted were being used and developed in the early, pre-Christian part of our period. It is very doubtful if writing, for these early epigraphists, was ever regarded simply as a means of transcribing oral utterances. As we saw in Chapter 3, some of the earliest surviving inscriptions from the continent (for example, the second-century Norwegian Øvre Stabu spearhead's runic inscription: *raunijaz*, 'tester, prober'), and perhaps one from Anglo-Saxon England too (the Essex silver ring's inscription *dolgbot*, if, as I suggest, this means 'wound-cure'),[8] testify to a special usage of language, magical in its implications, which places it beyond even the broad sphere of interpersonal communication.

---

[8] See Chapter 3, Section 7.

7. Conclusions

These inscriptions reveal a now quite unfamiliar realm of practical word-power; and although evidence for the magical uses and associations of runes in particular during the period of their use is plentiful and well recognized, this magical potential connected with runes was no doubt originally only a manifestation of the general recognition, when literacy was still young, that any act of alphabetic inscription brings this power into being.[9] Only awareness of the essential pragmatics of literacy can satisfactorily explain such inscriptions; and the same goes for the various types of medium-deictic 'speech' that we find much more commonly in the Anglo-Saxon corpus. These utterances cannot have had any precedent or model in orality — except, of course, insofar as they are presented to the reader as written 'speeches'. As we saw in Chapter 2, considerations based on the normal circumstances of oral linguistic communication clearly played a part in the development of their form; but content, form, and pragmatics combine to establish their essential and original nature as writings. I labour this point because of its potential importance for historians of literacy generally. The common-sense assumption that writing is just a channel into which speech, once transformed into visual symbols, can be redirected, is easy to slip into; but evidently we must distinguish, in the English case at least, between the treatment of *langue* and *parole*. No doubt some of the social and cognitive effects of the advent of literacy on societies that acquire it are slow to develop; but it would appear, on present evidence, that the special pragmatics of writing produces novel forms of utterance *from the moment of its adoption*. Perhaps this is the true 'great divide' between orality and literacy.

§5. Inscriptions and manuscript writings: distinctions and intersections

The distinction between inscriptions and manuscript writings was originally closely bound up with the distinction between the runic and roman alphabets: before the conversion, all inscriptions were runic, and manuscripts, produced only after the conversion, are always written primarily in the roman alphabet. After the conversion, as we have seen, the two scripts penetrated each other's domains in a number of ways; but there were other kinds of overlap between the epigraphical and manuscript domains that seem to be independent of the difference

---

[9] Cf. Olson (*The World on Paper*, 75), who claims that the development of syntactic writing (of the sort we find in both the runic and the roman scripts) "spells the death of 'word' magic or more precisely, 'name' magic." This view might seem to be in direct opposition to what I have said here, though the fact that these 'magical' runic inscriptions normally consist of single words rather than phrases or sentences with a syntax might be used as a basis for reconciling his views with mine. Perhaps these inscriptions constitute a bridge between oral and literate mentalities.

of script. The most conspicuous of these lies in the use in manuscript writings of formal and pragmatic conventions similar to those used in inscriptions. The chief general characteristic of Anglo-Saxon inscriptions is the deictic reference most of them make to the medium through which they are preserved, or to their position in space or time. This makes such inscriptions untransferable in the sense that they cannot be taken out of context and still communicate as they were intended to do. However, we saw in Chapter 4 that similar deictic ties link two verse-prefaces, *Thureth* and the *Metrical Preface to Gregory's Dialogues*, to the manuscripts for which they were originally composed. Both these poems exhibit fairly close formal and stylistic resemblances to some of the medium-deictic inscriptions quoted in Chapter 3; and both are technically untransferable, a feature graphically demonstrated in the case of the latter poem by the element of misrepresentation that has resulted from the transfer of the text to a manuscript copied from the one for which it was originally composed. The main difference between these two poems and analogous inscriptions is that deictic reference is made, not to the inscribed medium, but to the copies of the prose texts that these prefaces introduce. The relationship between poem and inscription is thus not dissimilar to that between Cynewulf's runic signature-passages and the kind of maker-inscription that they most resemble. Literate poets, composing directly for manuscripts, developed new forms of deictic reference, basically writing embodied in, and pointing to, other writing; but there is a strong possibility that these poets were inspired in this, at least partly, by epigraphical example.

The relationship between the Ruthwell Cross inscription and *The Dream of the Rood*, considered towards the end of Chapter 4, exemplifies another kind of intersection between the spheres of inscription and manuscript writing. If my argument about the priority of the Ruthwell inscription over the *Dream* is accepted, this is an instance of the direct influence on a literate poet (the poet of the *Dream* must have been literate if he was able to read the Ruthwell inscription for himself) of a particular extant inscription. But what the *Dream* poet took from Ruthwell was not its epigraphical form and pragmatics — the kind of influence exemplified by *Thureth* and *MPD* — but the actual text itself. The form and pragmatics he adapted, by introducing a narrative framework within which the speech of the cross becomes a feature of a dream-vision experienced by a human narrator. Instead of seeing a medium-deictic 'speaker' before us when we read, as at Ruthwell, we are required to imagine a speaking cross when we read the Vercelli Book's poem. Medium-deixis is replaced by literary personification. This obviously represents a much more radical development in literary form than either *Thureth* or *MPD* exemplify, though one of the most startling implications of the speaking cross is undermined by the dream-framework: there is no suggestion here that material objects can somehow speak. As the Ruthwell text suggests, objects can 'speak' only in writing. The 'life' that such 'speaking' objects seem to possess is an illusion created by literacy, though a powerful one.

If, of course, the *Dream* poet had simply transferred the Ruthwell text unchanged to a manuscript, he would have turned it into a 'Cross' riddle. The hypothesis is tantalizing, suggesting a possible source of inspiration for some of the 'Cross' *Riddles* in the Exeter Book collection,[10] and perhaps also for *Riddles* with other kinds of material artifact as their solutions. The general flowering of the riddle genre in early Anglo-Saxon England, described in Chapter 5, might be explained in terms of an aspiration towards textual autonomy in the use of the written word. According to my view of the relationship between the Ruthwell poem and *The Dream of the Rood*, the poet of the latter work has created such an autonomous work, though radical modifications of his source, chiefly in releasing the cross's speech from the requirements of its pragmatics as an inscription, were necessary to achieve it. But in the first-person Exeter Book *Riddles* there is not even a descriptive, scene-setting narrative framework to help us. Only the unmediated words of the hidden 'speaker' are provided; they alone must do all the work of revealing its identity. The *Riddles* illustrate (and exploit) some of the difficulties of knowing the absent utterer from his words. To this extent they seem to represent a kind of experimentation conducted in the course of a general groping towards textual autonomy in writing. It is possible that some of them were composed partly in that spirit.

The relationship between the Ruthwell Cross poem and *The Dream of the Rood* is, as far as I can see, the only possible case of the use of an inscription as a source by the author of a manuscript text. If I am wrong about the direction of the influence, and the Ruthwell poem is an abbreviated version of a full text of *The Dream of the Rood* available to the eighth-century inscriber, the Ruthwell text could be placed alongside other inscriptions that draw on identifiable passages from existing texts, notably the Bible. Some of the clearest cases are assembled in category 16 of my list of types of inscription in Chapter 3. Examples are the various instances of the Greek 'Alpha' and 'Omega' symbols, from Revelation 1:8 and 22:13, and the Driffield gold ring's inscription *Ecce agnus dei*, from John 1:29. Most inscriptions, however, are unique and have no existing source; the utterances they represent are original, obviously formulated to refer in one way or another to the particular artifacts on which they are preserved.

§6. The transcription of oral utterances in the roman alphabet

If most of the Anglo-Saxon runic and roman inscriptions, as well as some manuscript poems that show the influence of epigraphical traditions in script, form, or content, are identifiable as originally literate productions, the question arises

---

[10] *Riddle* 55 is perhaps the most unambiguous example; see Krapp and Dobbie, *The Exeter Book*, 208.

of whether there are any complementary criteria that would enable us to identify written texts transcribed directly from oral tradition. Earlier (§3 above) I suggested, on the basis of my analysis of the different uses to which the roman and runic alphabets were put in manuscript writings, that the former might have come to be thought of as the appropriate form for transcribing originally or formally spoken utterances, while runes continued to be regarded in very much the same way that epigraphical writers had always regarded them: as a way of representing what I call 'hand-language', i.e. utterances of a kind that had no specific oral prehistory and were formally literate productions from the first. From a modern perspective, it would not be particularly surprising if some originally oral poetry had found its way unchanged into inscriptions, with the inscribed medium treated simply as a neutral vehicle for the utterance; but I can find no evidence that this ever happened. All the inscribed Old English poems that survive are medium- or context-dependent for their significance in one way or another, and it may safely be concluded that they were composed for inscription, not for oral recitation.

The very fact that some Old English inscriptions are in alliterative verse shows that inscribers did not think of verse as a rigidly oral form in itself, incapable of meeting the deictic requirements of inscription. It is clear that by the early eighth century at the latest, epigraphists had adapted the form for use in various kinds of medium-deictic inscription, as a new, written form of poetry bridging the deictic gap. But the fact that the gap is never simply ignored indicates that inscribed objects were not in general thought of simply as neutral media for language. Again, the contrast with our modern attitude towards paper (or, indeed, towards digitalized text) is instructive.

As the inscriptions supply no examples of the transcription of pristine orality, we must look to the manuscripts; and in the absence of clear signs of a purely or originally oral tradition of prose composition in the Old English period, attention naturally centres on the verse. Many Old English poems could easily be taken out of their manuscript contexts and recited without any serious loss of meaning or significance. The fact that we may now enjoy electronic recordings of modern scholars reading *Beowulf* suggests that *Beowulf* itself is such a poem; its manuscript is a 'neutral' medium in the sense defined above. The clear influence on the *Beowulf* poet of Christian traditions does not in itself undermine the poem's status as a possibly oral production because (like many of the biblical references in the inscriptions) these traditions could easily have reached the poet in oral form, rather than by his reading of Christian writings. There is, as far as I can see, no conclusive evidence that the *Beowulf* poet ever actually read anything. He does, admittedly, summarize the runic inscription on the giant sword-hilt (1687-99), suggesting a knowledge of historically genuine inscriptions of the 'commissioner formula' type; but he does not quote the inscription.[11] Even if the poet was a reader, he was not necessarily a writer as well. We noted earlier (Chapter 6) that *Beowulf* presents itself in its opening lines as an oral recitation (1-2 *Hwæt, we . . . gefrunon . . .*, "Lo, we have heard . . ."); and there is nothing later in the poem that undermines this sense we get at its very beginning of being addressed by a speaker. In fact, the impression is reinforced by the frequency with which the narrator tells us of what he has 'heard' (e.g. 2172 *Hyrde ic þæt he ðone healsbeah Hygde gesealde*, "I heard that he gave the neck-ring to Hygd"), as well as what he has "not heard" (e.g. 38 *ne hyrde ic cymlicor ceol gegyrwan*, "I have not heard of any vessel more fairly fitted out"), but never what he has read. At the risk of stating the obvious, the fact that we read this speaker's words rather than hear them does not indicate composition by a literate poet; our reception of the poem as a text is a consequence of the way it has been preserved.

But if it is reasonable to speak of *Beowulf* as a formally oral utterance, and of the narrator as a man claiming access only to oral traditions, this does not positively rule out the possibility that the poem was composed by a lettered author who preserved his work in his own hand. There is no reason why a literate poet in contact with a thriving oral tradition should not have sat down and written a new poem so consistently oral in form and style as to conceal its technically literary origins.[12] If we concede this possibility, the question of whether *Beowulf* was composed by an oral or a literate poet seems, not only unanswerable, but much less important than it has been taken to be in the past. The evidence of the poetic inscriptions strongly suggests that literacy and access to poetic tradition could be combined in the same person; and Cynewulf's runic signatures point in the same direction. The chief remaining questions are therefore not whether the *Beowulf* poet had access to vernacular poetic tradition—it seems perfectly clear that he did—but how he acquired his skill as a poet, and what sources he drew upon for his material. I doubt if it can be actually proved that the poet did not derive his knowledge of Beowulf's history from written texts; but there is nothing obvious in the relationship between the style and the content of the poem to suggest that they came separately to the poet. It would certainly seem perverse to insist that the poet's style could have been learnt by extensive reading in manuscript texts of alliterative verse, and that the story itself reached him by some separate route.

---

[11] The poet's report of the inscription's content rather than its actual words might be explained by reference to Olson's observation that oral traditions place less value on verbatim quotation than literate ones: ". . . verbatim memorization seems a uniquely literate activity, assuming as it does, the availability of an original or fixed version against which memory may be checked. Without such a transcript there is greater latitude in what is accepted as exactly what was said. As a result direct and indirect quotation may not be as sharply distinguished in oral contexts and in oral societies more generally" (*The World on Paper*, 101).

[12] Magoun ("Oral-formulaic Character," 212), envisages the composition of the narrative parts of Cynewulf's poems in this way.

There is much to suggest that *Beowulf* is a fairly uncomplicated manifestation of oral poetic tradition — an 'oral-derived' text, in Foley's terms.

§7. Literacy, psychology, and fiction

The point of this digression on *Beowulf* is to draw attention to the fact that although it is sometimes possible to identify unmistakable evidence (of form, pragmatics, script, and content) that an Old English text was composed with readers in mind, and even, in some cases, that its author was himself literate in the sense that he could probably write as well as read, it is much more difficult to prove an oral origin for any text, even one which, like *Beowulf*, proclaims its own nature as an oral utterance in a thoroughly straightforward way. Texts may be 'marked' for literacy in various ways that make it impossible to divert them into the oral channel without loss of significance; but it is difficult to think of any cast-iron criterion for identifying originally oral work. 'Gestural' utterances of the kind exemplified earlier (Chapter 2) by "this big" in the sentence "Meet me here a week from now with a stick about this big" would, of course, indicate an oral original, but there is nothing of that kind in *Beowulf*. Whatever the actual origins of an Old English poem might have been, for the purposes of any practical, modern, pragmatic classification, an 'oral' poem is a traditional poem that might be transferred from the written to the oral channel (or vice-versa) and lose nothing essential in terms of intelligibility by the transfer.

When looked at from this perspective, the Old English lyrics which are the subject of Chapter 6 seem to represent a kind of arbitration between oral poetic tradition and innovative manuscript literacy. The lyrics are all in alliterative verse, a form rooted in orality and no doubt still thriving in the sphere of performance when these poems were composed. All are transferable texts, for their speakers are human beings (if we exclude *The Husband's Message* from the group, as I have done), not artifacts or other texts; nor are any of their speakers animals if we disregard (as most critics do) the puzzling ambiguities of *Wulf and Eadwacer*. All these poems are presented as speeches and use the metalanguage of speech in reporting clauses (*wrecan, secgan, (a)cweðan*). There can be no doubt about the debt owed by these poets to oral poetic tradition and the conventions of speech. On the other hand, we saw earlier how modern critics have failed to contextualize the lyrics' speakers satisfactorily, either by trying to identify them as characters in legendary stories or cycles known from elsewhere, or by relating the speakers and their circumstances to contemporary social conditions, as if their utterances were dramatic monologues of a kind familiar to us today. The critical failure is probably significant: the problems of interpretation presented by the lyrics arise, not from literary decontextualization by medieval transmitters, nor from an insufficiency of characterization *per se*, but from their peculiar position in relation to the development of literate ways of thinking and forms of expression in the period. The essential and most general feature of these poems is their introspective quality; they represent the first attempts we know of to describe the world of mind and feeling in the English language from the inside, so to speak. Psychology begins with them.[13] Their concern with external events is secondary; the focus of interest is on what goes on in people's heads, particularly those reduced by events to living on their own, cut off from all the support, the confirmation of values, companionship, and so on that only social integration can offer. Their poets were not necessarily writers; but the parallel between the position of the writer, who thinks and works alone, sending off his utterances into a temporal and spatial void, and that of the isolated 'speaker' of these poems, the *anhaga* who has no one to address and therefore can only express his own thoughts, suggests that the lyric poets worked in a literate milieu. As I argued earlier, writing is the logical and natural medium of the internal monologue, and there is a case for regarding an awareness of the implications of literacy as a *sine qua non* of this form of composition. If we are prepared to press the point even further, we might even claim that the delay and indirectness that written communication normally involves, and its consequent inhibition of direct, other-orientated utterances, leaves the introspective, first-person utterance as the *only* permissible literary form in which human beings may 'speak' in their own persons. If this seems an extreme position to take up, I only suggest that it might have appeared more reasonable to contemporary, Anglo-Saxon eyes than it does to ours, a thousand years later, now that writing has overcome (or, perhaps, simply elided) the problems of linguistic expression that the basic pragmatics of literacy created in its English childhood.

The difficult question of the ontological status of the speakers of these poems — whether they are historical persons or fictional creations — was also taken up in Chapter 6. It is possible that the lyrics are as much the province of the historian as of the critic, though we seem to see in *The Wanderer* the first hints of those authorially privileged insights into the minds of other persons that are one possible test of fictionality. This development might, in its turn, be related indirectly to the advent of literacy, as the innovations in content represented by the introspective, first-person lyric encouraged poets to extend the analysis of mental processes and emotions to third-person characters, in spite of the implicit claim to know what is logically unknowable that this extension involves.

---

[13] Olson (*The World on Paper*, 234-56) makes (on the basis of observations very different from mine) some tentative links between the development of human subjectivity ("the recognition of one's own and others' mental states as mental states," [234]) and the development of writing and reading. He identifies subjectivity as what "opens the door to introspection" (234).

§8. Other directions

The focus of this book has been on early literacy in England, but more specifically on the impact of literacy on linguistic expression and literary form in Old English.[14] Much of the special interest of the Old English material lies, not only in the variety of perspectives on literacy that it offers, but also on the opportunities it presents for comparing developments related to literacy with preexisting circumstances. Thus the use of runes, an early form of written representation among the Anglo-Saxons, may be compared with the use of the roman alphabet, introduced later; inscriptions, a relatively early mode of writing, are comparable with the later advent of writing in manuscripts with pen and ink; and the adaptation of an originally oral tradition of alliterative verse to the new demands and opportunities presented by literacy may be traced—though not without difficulty in the last case, because we have no *direct* access to pre-Christian, oral poetic traditions. In the first two cases, and perhaps in the third too, the crucial moment of transition coincides with the conversion to Christianity; but conversion also brought a fourth, equally important development: it introduced Latin to the Anglo-Saxons as the language of the Bible and of Christian worship. The possible bearing of Latin's advent on the developments in the vernacular that I have traced in this book obviously cannot be dismissed out of hand, though for the Anglo-Saxons, the perception of Latin as a language will have differed from that of Old English in several ways. Latin had no oral prehistory, so far as they were concerned; and it came to them, not just as a (non-Germanic) foreign language, but also as a fully-fledged language of the book in which a huge literature written in the roman alphabet, much of it on quite unfamiliar topics, had already accumulated. Those who learned to understand and read Latin became heirs to this legacy; but quite apart from the difficulties they might have found in learning the language itself, or in understanding the concerns of Christian writers, their encounters with literacy might have had relatively little in common with those of pre-Christian epigraphists or oral alliterative poets, faced with the problems of committing their mother-tongue to writing for the first time and adapting the forms of their utterances to the new mode. Latin had already achieved such adaptation, so that any early difficulties in getting used to writing and reading Latin that educated Anglo-Saxons might have encountered are likely to be hidden from us: the existing tradition of Latin writing had no doubt already solved these potential problems that beginners might face. We know that the learning, reading, and writing of Latin in Anglo-Saxon England was founded, at least at some stages during the period, on a well-organized educational system.[15] It is, of course, possible that Latin writings provided models for some of the innovations

---

[14] Inscriptions in Latin as well as Old English are, of course, covered in Chapter 3.

[15] See Lapidge, "The Anglo-Latin Background," in *A New Critical History of Old English Literature*, ed. Greenfield and Calder, 5-37.

in vernacular literacy with which this book is chiefly concerned, or alternatively that the vernacular innovations helped to shape similar forms in Latin writings. It remains to be seen how much evidence bearing on this question might be assembled, though we have found here that some forms of inscription are extant in both Old English and Latin, notably the type exemplified by the Pershore censer-cover's roman inscription: *Godric me wvorht*, "Godric made me," exact parallels for which are found in Latin, as for example *Herivvald me fecit*, "Herivvald made me," on the Canterbury VII slab.[16] It is obviously more likely that one form is a translation of the other than that they were invented independently, though it is difficult to judge in which direction the influence is likely to have flowed. As we saw in Chapter 3, inscriptions of this general type (number 1 in my series of categories) are more often in Old English than in Latin, though such crude statistics (which will no doubt be out of date before long, as new inscriptions come to light) obviously cannot be used to settle the question in favour of Old English. The difficulty here could well turn out to be a general one in any broad investigation of formal interrelationships between Anglo-Saxon texts in the two languages with a view to establishing the primary model. Of course, a very large body of scholarly research already exists on the Latin literary sources of particular Old English works in both verse and prose, and questions of genre have not been neglected; but interrelationships at the level of pragmatics and form have not been so intensively studied. Research in this area could scarcely fail to shed fresh light on some of the questions considered in this book, though Kelly's article, summarised briefly in Chapter 1, which draws a line between Latin and vernacular literacy, is a warning against taking contact between the two traditions for granted in considering individual cases. In Chapter 5 I mentioned the research that has been done on relationships between particular Old English *Riddles* and their counterparts in Latin. In cases of close correspondence in wording and solution it is normally assumed that the Latin version is the direct source of the Old English *Riddle*, not the other way round. But the *Riddles* are a very heterogeneous group of texts; they vary considerably in style and subject-matter, and also in the level of their apparent indebtedness to existing Latin sources. The dates of their composition may also be quite diverse. A more open-minded approach to the question of priority and source-use might well result in different or less firm conclusions in some cases.

This difficult question of the independence or interdependence of vernacular and Latin forms and genres is a reminder of other fields of investigation that have scarcely been even touched on here. For example, we saw in Chapter 1 that Goody draws attention to the existence of early Greek inscriptions on personal property of the type "I am X's," which closely parallels the kind of medium-deictic first-person Anglo-Saxon inscription that we find on (for example) the

---

[16] See Chapter 3 under 1(b) in the list of epigraphical forms.

Cuxton silver brooch: *Ælfgivv me ah*, "Ælfgivv owns me."[17] Is this to be taken as evidence of the actual influence, whether direct or indirect, of Greek inscriptions on Anglo-Saxon epigraphists? It seems unlikely, though Greek was known by some Anglo-Saxons.[18] The fact that the same basic form is also found among Scandinavian runic inscriptions raises the same kind of question. Among the Scandinavian examples (of which there are many) are the inscription on the Norum font in Sweden, *suæn kærpe m[ik]*, "Sven made me,"[19] or the long inscription on a door-fitting at Rauland in Norway, which begins: *hake beanar sun a mik suæn osmu(n)dar sun slo mik osofar ræst mik . . .*, "Hake Björnson owns me, Sven Osmundson struck (made) me, Osolv inscribed me . . ."[20] The Scandinavian inscriptions are generally later than the Anglo-Saxon ones; but are we dealing here with the influence of Old English epigraphical forms on Scandinavian inscribers, or with two manifestations of a common continental runic tradition, or with two independent developments, perhaps based on foreign (e.g. Greek) models? A detailed study of Scandinavian epigraphical forms, the dates of the earliest examples of them, and a comparison with the Anglo-Saxon corpus might narrow down the possibilities; but quite apart from questions about possible influence across cultural, national, or linguistic boundaries, the exploitation of the same distinctive linguistic form in similar pragmatic circumstances in three separate language-areas (early Greek, Old English, Old Norse) where literacy was still relatively new may be significant in itself. Even if the forms were borrowed by any of these literate cultures from others where they were already established, the fact that the same choice of form was made suggests that there may indeed be a level of basic, logical response to the phenomenon of literacy, wherever and whenever it takes root. This would not be surprising if, as the linguists tell us, deixis is indeed a universal phenomenon, for the problem of the deictic gap would recur wherever literacy established itself.

The need for focus, and the desire for as much coherence as possible, means that any academic project must be limited in scope, even though different or broader approaches to the chosen topic will often suggest themselves (as they should), both to the researcher in the course of his or her work, and to any reader. It might, for example, have been fruitful to compare here, were I competent to do so, the Old English lyrics discussed in Chapter 6 with other corpora of early

---

[17] Goody, *Interface*, 108 (see Chapter 1 above), and my Chapter 3, under 1 in the categorization of inscriptions. Similar inscriptions are found on other Greek objects, for example tomb-inscriptions that record the name of the dead person in the form "I am the tomb of X"; see Woodhead, *The Study of Greek Inscriptions*, 44.

[18] See Lapidge, "The Anglo-Latin Background," 9, 18.

[19] Sven B. F. Jansson, *Runes in Sweden*, trans. Peter Foote (London: Phoenix House, 1962), 170.

[20] Magnus Olsen, "De Norröne Runeinnskrifter," in *Runorna*, ed. Otto von Friesen (Stockholm: Albert Bonnier, 1933), 83-113 (at 106-7).

medieval lyrics in, for example, Welsh or Irish, to see if the same (or different) problems of personal expression seem to have shaped these other traditions in any way; but only Celticists could do this properly. Similarly, my concentration on inscriptions and related poetry has meant that I have ignored Old English prose writings completely, even though the prose, especially, perhaps, the more or less independently composed prose such as we find among Alfred's writings or in the *Anglo-Saxon Chronicle*, certainly contains much potential material for pragmatics-based research; but again, this work would require a prose specialist and a book of its own.

§9. 'Incipient' literacy?

In Chapter 2 I touched on the modern English vocabulary of orality and literacy in order to indicate some of its shortcomings when it comes to describing the earliest written texts in English. I now turn, finally, to another kind of terminological problem, admittedly partly of my own making, though with important implications for our conception of Anglo-Saxon literacy. Here and there in this book I have used the expression 'incipient literacy' to refer to conditions throughout the whole period. The question of whether or not this usage is appropriate depends on a whole clutch of uncertainties, most of which have to do, in one way or another, with the historical intersection or independence of different spheres of traditional activity and innovation. For example, as the use of runes seems to have been already established among the Anglo-Saxons by the time of the settlement, the characterization of any subsequent signs of literacy as 'incipient' might seem inappropriate; but much depends on the degree of contact between the traditions of runic and roman writing, and also, of course, between the epigraphical tradition generally and the world of books. Literacy may have had many beginnings, even several different kinds of beginning, in the period. I have already mentioned the problem of languages: to what extent did literacy in Latin and in the vernacular go hand-in-hand? Anglo-Latin writing could draw upon an established, sophisticated tradition of literacy; vernacular writing (partly) on an established oral tradition of alliterative poetry. We have seen some evidence in this book of contact between the various domains of literacy; but the overlaps are certainly not enough to justify a designation of Anglo-Saxon society as simply 'literate'. The question of whether 'incipient literacy' is an appropriate characterization of the whole period is not, of course, a very important question in itself; the trouble is that to dispense with it (or some similar expression) opens the way for the image of a full, social, general literacy of the kind that exists in English society today. The tendency to project our modern, socially-based, literate conception of literacy back on to the Anglo-Saxons is, after all, difficult enough to escape even when one is aware of the danger.

It is clear that we need to distinguish the literacy of individuals from any kind of social literacy in this early period. Part of my argument here has been that (in England at least) the logic of written expression generated forms of utterance that would be functionally meaningless if taken out of context and delivered orally in a conventional act of interpersonal communication. For the individual writer, the special pragmatics of writing made certain formal demands which were met in various ways, some of which I have described in this book. Even today, anyone who learns to read and write is subject to constraints when they commit their own utterances to writing, however different their responses to these constraints may be to those of Anglo-Saxon writers. But at what point does the literacy of individuals combine to create a genuine social literacy? For writers, irrespective of when they live and work, we can scarcely speak any longer of 'incipient' literacy once education has instilled in them enough familiarity with existing generic forms of written expression to enable them to express themselves without any conscious and deliberate adaptation to the literary mode. In a literate society, once the activities of reading and writing have nourished each other to the point where such relatively unselfconscious literary expression becomes possible, literacy must be regarded as established, not incipient.

When we try to apply this model of developing literacy to Anglo-Saxon England, however, we run up against the problem of lack of evidence. In how many ecclesiastical or administrative centres in Anglo-Saxon England can we say that literacy was 'established' in this sense? Certainly there was no one, national, general literacy at any one time during the Old English period. The circular letter to his bishops that King Alfred attached to copies of his translation of Gregory's *Pastoral Care* shows that he had a national (if socially restricted) literacy-programme in view; but the king's reminiscences also reveal considerable diversity in literacy in terms of place, time, and language in Anglo-Saxon England. There were certainly some ecclesiastical communities (Canterbury, for example) where the teaching and learning of Latin seems to have been established on a very firm footing; but there must also have been large areas of the country, especially those far from the centres of political or ecclesiastical power, that lagged behind. Again, it seems safest to conclude that literacy began in different places at different times; certainly it is difficult to believe that it developed uniformly in all of them.

Finally, we must always keep in view the oral poetic tradition that provided the basis of one kind of writing that the Anglo-Saxons produced. As the voluminous scholarship of orality has shown, this tradition was not killed off by the advent of literacy, but continued to exercise a powerful influence on the poetic texts that have survived from the period in both inscriptions and manuscripts. There is, of course, room for disagreement over the extent to which the originally oral qualities of this tradition flowed into, or affected, the work of literate authors. We have found some evidence here of 'mixed' forms in which some of the features of orality and literacy are intricately and sometimes deliberately combined; but we

7. Conclusions

still have a great deal to learn about the processes of poetic composition, not only for literate poets but for oral ones as well, in this period, and even more to learn about the impact of literacy on this tradition.

In this book I have done my best to concentrate on identifying a single strand—a basically linguistic, deictic strand—in the skein of Anglo-Saxon incipient literacy from its earliest appearance in our records, and on tracing its continuation and consequences through the period. But the metaphor is perhaps tendentious: throughout my investigation I have been made aware repeatedly of the way this strand becomes entangled with, sometimes scarcely distinguishable from, other strands, whether 'oral' or 'literate'. As research into orality and literacy proceeds, no doubt, more precise definitions and interpretations of these various strands will be achieved, and we will be in a better position to develop a satisfactorily integrated conception of literacy in Anglo-Saxon England.

BIBLIOGRAPHY

Allen, Michael J. B., and Daniel G. Calder. *Sources and Analogues of Old English Poetry: The Major Latin Texts in Translation*. Cambridge: Brewer, 1976.
Amodio, Mark C. "Old-English Oral-Formulaic Tradition and Middle-English Verse." In *De Gustibus: Essays for Alain Renoir*, ed. Foley, 1–20.
———. *Writing the Oral Tradition: Oral Poetics and Literate Culture in Medieval England*. Notre Dame: University of Notre Dame Press, 2004.
———. "Res(is)ting the Singer: Towards a Non-Performative Anglo-Saxon Oral Poetics." In *New Directions in Oral Theory*, ed. idem, 179–208.
———, ed. *New Directions in Oral Theory*. MRTS 287. Tempe: Arizona Center for Medieval and Renaissance Studies, 2005.
Antonsen, Elmer H. *A Concise Grammar of the Older Runic Inscriptions*. Tübingen: Niemeyer, 1975.
Austin, J. L. *How to Do Things with Words: The William James Lectures Delivered at Harvard University in 1955*, ed. J. O. Urmson and Marina Sbisà. 2nd ed. Oxford: Oxford University Press, 1975.
Ball, Sir Christopher. "Inconsistencies in the Main Runic Inscriptions on the Ruthwell Cross." In *Old English Runes and their Continental Background*, ed. Bammesberger, 107–123.
Bammesberger, Alfred, ed. *Old English Runes and their Continental Background*. Anglistische Forschungen 217. Heidelberg: Winter, 1991.
———, and Alfred Wollmann, eds. *Britain 400–600: Language and History*. Anglistische Forschungen 205. Heidelberg: Winter, 1990.
Barley, Nigel. "Structural Aspects of the Anglo-Saxon Riddle." *Semiotica* 10 (1974): 143–75.
Baugh, Albert C., and Thomas Cable. *A History of the English Language*. 3rd ed. London: Routledge & Kegan Paul, 1978.
Bäuml, Franz H. "Varieties and Consequences of Medieval Literacy and Illiteracy." *Speculum* 55 (1980): 237–65.
———. "Medieval Texts and the Two Theories of Oral-Formulaic Composition: A Proposal for a Third Theory." *New Literary History* 16 (1984–1985): 31–49.
Benson, Larry D. "The Literary Character of Anglo-Saxon Formulaic Poetry." *PMLA* 81 (1966): 334–41.
———, ed. *The Riverside Chaucer*. 3rd ed. Oxford: Oxford University Press, 1988.

Benveniste, Emile. *Problems in General Linguistics*, trans. Mary Elizabeth Meet. Miami Linguistics Series 8. Coral Gables: University of Miami Press, 1971.

Binns, J. W., E. C. Norton, and D. M. Palliser. "The Latin Inscription on the Coppergate Helmet." *Antiquity* 64 (1990): 134–39.

Bjork, Robert E., ed. *Cynewulf: Basic Readings*. New York: Garland, 1996.

Blair, John. *The Church in Anglo-Saxon Society*. Oxford: Oxford University Press, 2005.

Bliss, A. J. *The Metre of Beowulf*. 2nd ed. Oxford: Blackwell, 1967.

———. "The Scansion of *Beowulf*," ed. Peter J. Lucas. *Old English Newsletter Subsidia* 22 (1995).

Bloomfield, Morton W. "The Form of *Deor*." In *Old English Literature: Twenty-two Analytical Essays*, ed. Stevens and Mandel, 212–28.

Bonner, Gerald, David Rollason, and Clare Stancliffe, eds. *St. Cuthbert, his Cult and his Community to AD 1200*. Woodbridge: Boydell Press, 1989.

Bosworth, Joseph, and T. Northcote Toller. *An Anglo-Saxon Dictionary*. Oxford: Oxford University Press, 1898.

Bradbury, Nancy Mason. *Writing Aloud: Storytelling in Late Medieval England*. Urbana and Chicago: University of Illinois Press, 1998.

Bradley, S. A. J. *Anglo-Saxon Poetry*. London: Dent, 1982.

Bragg, Lois. *The Lyric Speakers of Old English Poetry*. London: Associated University Presses, 1991.

———. "Runes and Readers: In and Around 'The Husband's Message'." *SN* 71 (1999): 34–50.

Brooks, Kenneth R., ed. *Andreas and The Fates of the Apostles*. Oxford: Oxford University Press, 1961.

Bruner, Jerome, and Susan Weisser. "The Invention of Self: Autobiography and its Forms." In *Literacy and Orality*, ed. Olson and Torrance, 129–48.

Calder, D. G., and M. J. B. Allen. *Sources and Analogues of Old English Poetry: The Major Latin Texts in Translation*. Cambridge: Boydell & Brewer, 1976.

Campbell, A. *Old English Grammar*. Oxford: Clarendon Press, 1959.

Campbell, Jackson J. Review of Williamson, ed., *The Old English Riddles of the Exeter Book*. *MP* 77 (1979–1980): 315–17.

Chafe, Wallace, and Deborah Tannen. "The Relation between Written and Spoken Language." *Annual Review of Anthropology* 16 (1987): 383–407.

Chaytor, H. J. *From Script to Print: An Introduction to Medieval Literature*. Cambridge: Cambridge University Press, 1945.

Cherniss, Michael D. "The Oral-Traditional Opening Theme in the Poems of Cynewulf." In *De Gustibus: Essays for Alain Renoir*, ed. Foley, 40–65.

Clanchy, M. T. *From Memory to Written Record: England 1066–1307*. 2nd ed. Oxford: Blackwell, 1993.

Cohn, Dorrit. "Fictional *versus* Historical Lives: Borderlines and Borderline Cases." *Journal of Narrative Techniques* 19 (1989): 3–24.

———. "Signposts of Fictionality: A Narratological Perspective." *Poetics Today* 11 (1990): 775–804.
Coleman, Joyce. *Public Reading and the Reading Public in Late Medieval England and France*. Cambridge Studies in Medieval Literature 26. Cambridge: Cambridge University Press, 1996.
Colgrave, Bertram, and R. A. B. Mynors, ed. and trans. *Bede's Ecclesiastical History of the English People*. Oxford: Oxford University Press, 1969.
Conner, Patrick. "On Dating Cynewulf." In *Cynewulf: Basic Readings*, ed. Bjork, 23–55.
Cook, A. S. "An Unsuspected Bit of Old English Verse." *MLN* 17 (1902): 7–10.
Derolez, René. *Runica Manuscripta: The English Tradition*. Bruges: De Tempel, 1954.
Desmond, Marilynn. "The Voice of Exile: Feminist Literary History and the Anonymous Anglo-Saxon Elegy." *Critical Inquiry* 16 (1989–1990): 572–90.
Dewa, Roberta J. "The Runic Riddles of the Exeter Book: Language Games and Anglo-Saxon Scholarship." *Nottingham Medieval Studies* 39 (1995): 26–36.
Dickins, Bruce, and Alan S. C. Ross, eds. *The Dream of the Rood*. Repr., with additions and corrections. London: Methuen, 1963.
Doane, A. N., and Carol Braun Pasternack, eds. *Vox Intexta: Orality and Textuality in the Middle Ages*. Madison: University of Wisconsin Press, 1991.
Dobbie, Elliott Van Kirk, ed. *The Anglo-Saxon Minor Poems*. The Anglo-Saxon Poetic Records 6. New York: Columbia University Press, 1942.
Dunning, T. P., and A. J. Bliss, eds. *The Wanderer*. London: Methuen, 1969.
Earl, James W. *Thinking about 'Beowulf'*. Stanford: Stanford University Press, 1994.
Ekwall, Eilert. *The Concise Oxford Dictionary of Place-Names*. 4th ed. Oxford: Clarendon Press, 1960.
Eliason, Norman. "Two Old English Scop Poems." *PMLA* 81 (1966): 185–92.
Elliott, Ralph W. V. "The Runes in *The Husband's Message*." *JEGP* 54 (1955): 1–8.
———. *Runes: An Introduction*. 2nd ed. Manchester: Manchester University Press, 1989.
Fell, Christine E. "Runes and Semantics." In *Old English Runes and their Continental Background*, ed. Bammesberger, 195–229.
———. "Runes and Riddles in Anglo-Saxon England." In *'Lastworda Betst'*, ed. Hough and Lowe, 264–77.
———. "Wax Tablets of Stone." In *'Lastworda Betst'*, ed. Hough and Lowe, 249–63.
———. "Introduction to *Anglo-Saxon Letters and Letter-Writers*." In *'Lastworda Betst'*, ed. Hough and Lowe, 278–87.
Fillmore, Charles J. *Santa Cruz Lectures on Deixis, 1971*. Bloomington: Indiana University Linguistics Club, 1975.
Finnegan, Ruth. "The How of Literature." *Oral Tradition* 20 (2005): 164–87.

Fleischman, Suzanne. "Philology, Linguistics, and the Discourse of the Medieval Text." *Speculum* 65 (1990): 19–37.
Foley, John Miles. *Traditional Oral Epic: The Odyssey, Beowulf, and the Serbo-Croatian Return Song.* Berkeley, Los Angeles, and Oxford: University of California Press, 1990.
———. *Immanent Art: From Structure to Meaning in Traditional Oral Epic.* Bloomington and Indianapolis: Indiana University Press, 1991.
———, ed. *De Gustibus: Essays for Alain Renoir.* New York and London: Garland Publishing, Inc., 1992.
———. "Orality, Textuality, and Interpretation." In *Vox Intexta: Orality and Textuality in the Middle Ages*, ed. Doane and Pasternack, 34–45.
———. *Homer's Traditional Art.* University Park, Pennsylvania: Pennsylvania State University Press, 1999.
Frantzen, Allen J., and John Hines, eds. *Cædmon's Hymn and Material Culture in the World of Bede.* Morgantown: West Virginia University Press, 2007.
von Friesen, Otto, ed. *Runorna.* Stockholm: Albert Bonnier, 1933.
Fulk, R. D., ed. *Interpretations of Beowulf: A Critical Anthology.* Bloomington: Indiana University Press, 1991.
———. *A History of Old English Meter.* Philadelphia: University of Pennsylvania Press, 1992.
———. "Cynewulf: Canon, Dialect, and Date." In *Cynewulf: Basic Readings*, ed. Bjork, 3–21.
Gallagher, Patrick J., and Helen Damico, eds. *Hermeneutics and Medieval Culture.* Albany: State University of New York Press, 1989.
Genette, Gérard. *Narrative Discourse: An Essay in Method*, trans. Jane E. Lewin, intro. Jonathan Culler. Oxford: Blackwell, 1980.
Glorie, Fr., ed. *Collectiones Aenigmatum Merovingicae Aetatis.* Corpus Christianorum, Series Latina 133 and 133A. Turnhout: Brepols, 1968.
Godden, Malcolm, and Michael Lapidge, eds. *The Cambridge Companion to Old English Literature.* Cambridge: Cambridge University Press, 1991.
Goldsmith, Margaret E. "The Enigma of *The Husband's Message.*" In *Anglo-Saxon Poetry: Essays in Appreciation for John C. McGalliard*, ed. Nicholson and Frese, 242–63.
Goody, Jack, ed. *Literacy in Traditional Societies.* Cambridge: Cambridge University Press, 1968.
———. "Introduction" to *Literacy in Traditional Societies*, ed. Goody, 1–26.
———. *The Interface Between the Written and the Oral.* Studies in Literacy, Family, Culture and the State. Cambridge: Cambridge University Press, 1987.
———, and Ian Watt. "The Consequences of Literacy." *Comparative Studies in Society and History* 5 (1963): 304–45. Repr. in *Literacy in Traditional Societies*, ed. idem, 27–68.
Gradon, P. O. E., ed. *Cynewulf's Elene.* London: Methuen, 1958.

Greenfield, Stanley B. "The Formulaic Expression of the Theme of 'Exile' in Anglo-Saxon Poetry." *Speculum* 30 (1955): 200–6.
———. *The Interpretation of Old English Poems*. London: Routledge & Kegan Paul, 1972.
———, and Daniel G. Calder. *A New Critical History of Old English Literature with a Survey of the Anglo-Latin Background by Michael Lapidge*. New York: New York University Press, 1986.
Grein, C. W. M. *Dichtungen der Angelsachsen stabreimend* 2. Göttingen: Wigand, 1859.
Griffiths, Mark. "*Riddle* 19 of the Exeter Book: *snac*, an Old English Acronym." *Notes and Queries* 237, N.S. 39 (1992): 15–16.
Hamer, Richard. *A Choice of Anglo-Saxon Verse*. London: Faber and Faber, 1970.
Hansen, Elaine Tuttle. *The Solomon Complex*. McMaster Old English Studies and Texts 5. Toronto: University of Toronto Press, 1988.
Harris, Roy. *The Origin of Writing*. London: Duckworth, 1986.
Harris, William V. *Ancient Literacy*. Cambridge, MA: Harvard University Press, 1989.
Havelock, Eric A. *Preface to Plato*. Cambridge, MA: Harvard University Press, 1963.
———. "The Oral-Literate Equation: A Formula for the Modern Mind." In *Literacy and Orality*, ed. Olson and Torrance, 11–27.
Hill, Joyce, ed. *Old English Minor Heroic Poems*. Durham Medieval Texts 4. Durham: Durham Medieval Texts, 1983.
Hines, John. "The Runic Inscriptions of Early Anglo-Saxon England." In *Britain 400–600: Language and History*, ed. Bammesberger and Wollmann, 437–55.
———. "Some Observations on the Runic Inscriptions of Early Anglo-Saxon England." In *Old English Runes and their Continental Background*, ed. Bammesberger, 61–83.
Hollowell, Ida Masters. "Was Widsið a Scop?" *Neophilologus* 64 (1980): 583–91.
Holthausen, F. "Kleinere altenglische Dichtungen." *Anglia* 41 (1917): 400–4.
Hough, Carole, and Kathryn A. Lowe, eds. *"Lastworda Betst": Essays in Memory of Christine E. Fell with her Unpublished Writings*, intro. R. I. Page. Donington: Shaun Tyas, 2002.
Houwen, L. A. J. R., and A. A. MacDonald, eds. *Loyal Letters: Studies on Medieval Alliterative Poetry and Prose*. Groningen: Egbert Forsten, 1994.
Huppé, Bernard F. "*The Wanderer*: Theme and Structure." *JEGP* 42 (1943): 516–38.
———. *Doctrine and Poetry: Augustine's Influence on Old English Poetry*. Albany: SUNY Press, 1959.
Illich, Ivan, and Barry Sanders. *ABC: The Alphabetization of the Popular Mind*. Harmondsworth: Penguin, 1988.
Innis, Harold A. *Empire and Communications*. Rev. Mary Q. Innis, intro. Marshall McLuhan. Toronto: University of Toronto Press, 1972.

Irving, Edward B., Jr. *Rereading Beowulf.* Philadelphia: University of Pennsylvania Press, 1989.
Isherwood, Christopher. *Christopher and his Kind: 1929–1939.* London: Eyre Methuen, 1977.
Jahandarie, Khosrow. *Spoken and Written Discourse: A Multi-Disciplinary Perspective.* Contemporary Studies in International Political Communication 1. Stamford, CT: Ablex, 1999.
Jansson, Sven B. F. *The Runes of Sweden*, trans. Peter G. Foote. London: Phoenix House, 1962.
Kahler, Erich. *The Inward Turn of Narrative*, trans. Richard and Clara Winston, intro. Joseph Frank. Bollingen Series 83. Princeton: Princeton University Press, 1973.
Kaske, R. E. "A Poem of the Cross in the Exeter Book: *Riddle 60* and *The Husband's Message.*" *Traditio* 23 (1967): 41–71.
Kelly, Stephen, and John J. Thompson, eds. *Imagining the Book.* Medieval Texts and Cultures of Northern Europe 7. Turnhout: Brepols, 2005.
Kelly, Susan. "Anglo-Saxon Lay Society and the Written Word." In *The Uses of Literacy in Early Medieval Europe*, ed. McKitterick, 36–62.
Ker, N. R. *Catalogue of Manuscripts Containing Anglo-Saxon.* Oxford: Oxford University Press, 1957.
Keynes, Simon. "Royal Government and the Written Word in Late Anglo-Saxon England." In *The Uses of Literacy in Early Medieval Europe*, ed. McKitterick, 226–57.
———, and Michael Lapidge. *Alfred the Great: Asser's Life of King Alfred and Other Contemporary Sources.* Harmondsworth: Penguin, 1983.
Kittay, Jeffrey. "Utterance Unmoored: The Changing Interpretations of the Act of Writing in the European Middle Ages." *Language in Society* 17 (1988): 209–30.
———. "Thinking through Literacies." In *Literacy and Orality*, ed. Olson and Torrance, 165–73.
Klaeber, Fr., ed. *Beowulf and the Fight at Finnsburg.* 3rd ed. Lexington: Heath, 1950.
Klinck, Anne L., ed. *The Old English Elegies: A Critical Edition and Genre Study.* Montreal and Kingston: McGill-Queen's University Press, 1992.
Krapp, George Philip, ed. *The Vercelli Book.* The Anglo-Saxon Poetic Records 2. New York: Columbia University Press, 1932.
———, and Elliott Van Kirk Dobbie, eds. *The Anglo-Saxon Poetic Records: A Collective Edition.* 6 vols. New York: Columbia University Press, 1931–1953.
Krapp, George Philip, and Elliott Van Kirk Dobbie, eds. *The Exeter Book.* The Anglo-Saxon Poetic Records 3. New York: Columbia University Press, 1936.
Lamarque, Peter. *Fictional Points of View.* Ithaca: Cornell University Press, 1996.

Lapidge, Michael. "The Anglo-Latin Background." In *A New Critical History of Old English Literature with a Survey of the Anglo-Latin Background by Michael Lapidge*, ed. Greenfield and Calder, 5–37.
———. "The Career of Aldhelm." *ASE* 36 (2007): 15–69.
———, and J. Rosier, trans. *Aldhelm: The Poetic Works*. Cambridge: Cambridge University Press, 1985.
Lass, Roger. "Cyn(e)wulf Revisited: The Problem of the Runic Signatures." In *An Historic Tongue: Studies in English Linguistics in Memory of Barbara Strang*, ed. Nixon and Honey, 17–30.
Lejeune, Philippe. *Le Pacte autobiographique*. Paris: Éditions du Seuil, 1975.
Lendinara, Patrizia. "The World of Anglo-Saxon Learning." In *The Cambridge Companion to Old English Literature*, ed. Godden and Lapidge, 264–81.
Lerer, Seth. *Literacy and Power in Anglo-Saxon Literature*. Regents Studies in Medieval Culture. Lincoln and London: University of Nebraska Press, 1991.
Leslie, R. F., ed. *Three Old English Elegies*. Manchester: Manchester University Press, 1961.
———, ed. *The Wanderer*. Manchester: Manchester University Press, 1966.
———. "The Integrity of Riddle 60." *JEGP* 67 (1968): 451–57.
Levers, Toby. "The Construction of Subjectivity in the Cædmon Story." *Quaestio Insularis* 6 (2005): 98–119.
Levinson, Stephen C. *Pragmatics*. Cambridge: Cambridge University Press, 1983.
Leyerle, John. "The Interlace Structure of *Beowulf*." *University of Toronto Quarterly* 37 (1967): 1–17. Repr. in *Interpretations of Beowulf: A Critical Anthology*, ed. Fulk, 146–67.
Long, Percy W., ed. *Essays and Studies in Honor of Carleton Brown*. New York: New York University Press, 1940.
Lord, Albert B. *The Singer of Tales*. Harvard Studies in Comparative Literature 24. Cambridge, MA: Harvard University Press, 1960.
———. *The Singer Resumes the Tale*, ed. Mary Louise Lord. Ithaca: Cornell University Press, 1995.
———. "Oral Composition and 'Oral Residue' in the Middle Ages." In *Oral Tradition in the Middle Ages*, ed. Nicolaisen, 7–29.
Lowe, Kathryn A. "Lay Literacy in Anglo-Saxon England and the Development of the Chirograph." In *Anglo-Saxon Manuscripts and their Heritage*, ed. Pulsiano and Treharne, 161–204.
Lucas, Peter J. Review of O'Keeffe, *Visible Song*. *RES* 44 (1993): 401–3.
Lyons, John. *Introduction to Theoretical Linguistics*. Cambridge: Cambridge University Press, 1968.
———. *Semantics*. 2 vols. Cambridge: Cambridge University Press, 1977.
Mackie, W. S. "Notes on the Text of the 'Exeter Book'." *MLR* 28 (1933): 75–78.
McKitterick, Rosamond, ed. *The Uses of Literacy in Early Medieval Europe*. Cambridge: Cambridge University Press, 1990.

McLuhan, Marshall. *The Gutenberg Galaxy: The Making of Typographic Man*. London: Routledge & Kegan Paul, 1962.
Magoun, Francis P., Jr. "The Oral-formulaic Character of Anglo-Saxon Narrative Poetry." *Speculum* 28 (1953): 446–67. Repr. in *An Anthology of Beowulf Criticism*, ed. Nicholson, 189–221.
———. "Bede's Story of Cædmon: The Case History of an Anglo-Saxon Oral Singer." *Speculum* 30 (1955): 49–63.
———. "The Theme of the Beasts of Battle in Anglo-Saxon Poetry." *NM* 56 (1955): 81–90.
Malone, Kemp, ed. *Deor*. Rev. ed. Exeter: University of Exeter, 1977.
———, ed. *Widsith*. London: Methuen, 1936.
———. "The Old English Period (to 1100)." In *The Middle Ages*, ed. Malone and Baugh, 3–108.
———, and Albert C. Baugh. *The Middle Ages*. 2nd ed. A Literary History of England 1. London: Routledge & Kegan Paul, 1967.
Meid, Wolfgang. *Gaulish Inscriptions: Their Interpretation in the Light of Archaeological Evidence and their Value as a Source of Linguistic and Sociological Information*. Archaeolingua, Series Minor 1. Budapest: Archaeological Institute of the Hungarian Academy of Sciences, 1992.
Mitchell, Bruce. "The Narrator of *The Wife's Lament*." *NM* 73 (1972): 222–34.
———. *Old English Syntax*. 2 vols. Oxford: Oxford University Press, 1985.
Mossé, Fernand. *A Handbook of Middle English*, trans. James A. Walker. Baltimore: Johns Hopkins University Press, 1952.
Muir, Bernard J., ed. *The Exeter Anthology of Old English Poetry: An Edition of Exeter Dean and Chapter MS 3501*. 2 vols. Exeter: University of Exeter Press, 1994.
Napier, Arthur S. *Old English Glosses Chiefly Unpublished*. Oxford: Oxford University Press, 1900.
Nelson, Marie. "The Paradox of Silent Speech in the Exeter Book Riddles." *Neophilologus* 62 (1978): 609–15.
Neville, Jennifer. "Joyous Play and Bitter Tears: The *Riddles* and the Elegies." In *'Beowulf' & Other Stories: A New Introduction to Old English, Old Icelandic and Anglo-Norman Literatures*, ed. North and Allard, 130–59.
Nicholson, Lewis E., ed. *An Anthology of Beowulf Criticism*. Notre Dame: University of Notre Dame Press, 1963.
———, and Dolores Warwick Frese, eds. *Anglo-Saxon Poetry: Essays in Appreciation for John C. McGalliard*. Notre Dame: University of Notre Dame Press, 1975.
Nicolaisen, W. F. H., ed. *Oral Tradition in the Middle Ages*. MRTS 112. Binghamton: Center for Medieval and Early Renaissance Studies, State University of New York at Binghamton, 1995.
Niles, John D., ed. *Old English Literature in Context*. Cambridge: D. S. Brewer, 1980.

———. *Homo Narrans: The Poetics and Anthropology of Oral Literature*. Philadelphia: University of Pennsylvania Press, 1999.

———. "The Trick of the Runes in *The Husband's Message*." *ASE* 32 (2003): 189–223.

Nixon, Graham, and John Honey, eds. *An Historic Tongue: Studies in English Linguistics in Memory of Barbara Strang*. London: Routledge, 1988.

North, Richard. "Metre and Meaning in *Wulf and Eadwacer*: Signý Reconsidered." In *Loyal Letters: Studies on Medieval Alliterative Poetry and Prose*, ed. Houwen and MacDonald, 29–54.

———, and Joe Allard, eds. *'Beowulf' & Other Stories: A New Introduction to Old English, Old Icelandic and Anglo-Norman Literatures*. Harlow: Pearson Education, 2007.

Ó Carragáin, Éamonn. *Ritual and the Rood: Liturgical Images and the Old English Poems of the Dream of the Rood Tradition*. London: The British Library and University of Toronto Press, 2005.

Odenstedt, Bengt. "A New Theory of the Origin of the Runic Script: Richard L. Morris's Book *Runic and Mediterranean Epigraphy*." In *Old English Runes and their Continental Background*, ed. Bammesberger, 359–87.

O'Donnell, Daniel Paul. *Cædmon's Hymn: A Multimedia Study, Archive and Edition*. Cambridge: D. S. Brewer, in association with SEENET and The Medieval Academy, 2005.

———. "Material Differences: The Place of Cædmon's Hymn in the History of Anglo-Saxon Vernacular Poetry." In *Cædmon's Hymn and Material Culture in the World of Bede*, ed. Frantzen and Hines, 15–50.

Okasha, Elisabeth. *Hand-List of Anglo-Saxon Non-Runic Inscriptions*. Cambridge: Cambridge University Press, 1971.

———. "A Supplement to *Hand-List of Anglo-Saxon Non-Runic Inscriptions*." *ASE* 11 (1983): 83–118.

———. "A Second Supplement to *Hand-List of Anglo-Saxon Non-Runic Inscriptions*." *ASE* 21 (1992): 37–85.

———. "A Third Supplement to *Hand-List of Anglo-Saxon Non-Runic Inscriptions*." *ASE* 33 (2004): 225–81.

———. "Script-Mixing in Anglo-Saxon Inscriptions." In *Writing and Texts in Anglo-Saxon England*, ed. Rumble, 62–70.

O'Keeffe, Katherine O'Brien. *Visible Song: Transitional Literacy in Old English Verse*. Cambridge Studies in Anglo-Saxon England 4. Cambridge: Cambridge University Press, 1990.

———, and Andy Orchard, eds. *Latin Learning and English Lore: Studies in Anglo-Saxon Literature for Michael Lapidge*. Toronto: University of Toronto Press, 2005.

Olsen, Alexandra Hennessey. "Oral-Formulaic Research in Old English Studies: I." *Oral Tradition* 1 (1986): 548–606.

———. "Oral-Formulaic Research in Old English Studies: II." *Oral Tradition* 3 (1988): 138–90.
Olsen, Magnus. "De Norröne Runeinnskrifter." In *Runorna*, ed. von Friesen, 83–113.
Olson, David R. *The World on Paper: The Conceptual and Cognitive Implications of Writing and Reading*. Cambridge: Cambridge University Press, 1994.
———, and Nancy Torrance, eds. *Literacy and Orality*. Cambridge: Cambridge University Press, 1991.
Ong, Walter J. *Orality and Literacy: The Technologizing of the Word*. London: Methuen, 1982. Repr. London: Routledge, 1988.
———. "Orality, Literacy, and Medieval Textualization." *New Literary History* 16 (1984–1985): 1–12.
Opland, Jeff. *Anglo-Saxon Oral Poetry: A Study of the Traditions*. New Haven: Yale University Press, 1980.
———. "From Horseback to Monastic Cell: The Impact on English Literature of the Introduction of Writing." In *Old English Literature in Context*, ed. Niles, 30–43, 161–63.
Orchard, Andy. *The Poetic Art of Aldhelm*. Cambridge Studies in Anglo-Saxon England 8. Cambridge: Cambridge University Press, 1994.
———. "Enigma Variations: The Anglo-Saxon Riddle-Tradition." In *Latin Learning and English Lore: Studies in Anglo-Saxon Literature for Michael Lapidge*, ed. O'Keeffe and Orchard, 284–304.
Orton, Peter. "The Speaker in *The Husband's Message*." *Leeds Studies in English* N.S. 12 (1981): 43–56.
———. "Cædmon and Christian Poetry." *NM* 84 (1983): 163–70.
———. "An Approach to *Wulf and Eadwacer*." *Proceedings of the Royal Irish Academy* 85C (1985): 223–58.
———. "The Transmission of the West Saxon Versions of *Cædmon's Hymn*: A Reappraisal." *SN* 70 (1998): 153–64.
———. "Anglo-Saxon Attitudes to Kuhn's Laws." *RES* N.S. 50 (1999): 287–303.
———. *The Transmission of Old English Poetry*. Westfield Publications in Medieval and Renaissance Studies 12. Turnhout: Brepols, 2000.
———. "Deixis and the Untransferable Text: Anglo-Saxon Colophons, Verse-Prefaces and Inscriptions." In *Imagining the Book*, ed. Kelly and Thompson, 195–207.
Page, R. I. *Runes and Runic Inscriptions: Collected Essays on Anglo-Saxon and Viking Runes*, ed. David Parsons, bibliography Carl T. Berkhout. Woodbridge: Boydell & Brewer, 1995.
———. "Anglo-Saxon Runes and Magic." *Journal of the British Archaeological Association*, 3rd ser. 27 (1964): 14–31. Repr. with addendum in Page, *Runes and Runic Inscriptions*, ed. Parsons, 105–25.

---. "Roman and Runic on St Cuthbert's Coffin." In *St. Cuthbert, his Cult and his Community to AD 1200*, ed. Bonner et al., 257–65. Repr. with addendum in Page, *Runes and Runic Inscriptions*, ed. Parsons, 315–25.
---. *An Introduction to English Runes*. 2nd ed. Woodbridge: Boydell, 1999.
Parkes, M. B., and Andrew G. Watson, eds. *Medieval Scribes, Manuscripts and Libraries: Essays Presented to N. R. Ker*. London: Scolar Press, 1978.
Parks, Ward. "The Textualization of Orality in Literary Criticism." In *Vox Intexta: Orality and Textuality in the Middle Ages*, ed. Doane and Pasternack, 46–61.
Parry, Adam, ed. *The Making of Homer's Verse: The Collected Papers of Milman Parry*. 1971; repr. Oxford: Oxford University Press, 1987.
Parsons, David N. *Recasting the Runes: The Reform of the Anglo-Saxon Futhorc*. Uppsala: Uppsala Universitet, 1999.
Pinsker, Hans, and Waltraud Ziegler, eds. *Die altenglischen Rätsel des Exeterbuchs*. Heidelberg: Winter, 1985.
Plummer, Charles, ed. *Two of the Saxon Chronicles Parallel*, 2 vols. Oxford: Oxford University Press, 1892–1899. Repr. 1952.
Pope, John C. "Palaeography and Poetry: Some Solved and Unsolved Problems of the Exeter Book." In *Medieval Scribes, Manuscripts and Libraries: Essays Presented to N. R. Ker*, ed. Parkes and Watson, 25–65.
Pulsiano, Phillip, and Elaine M. Treharne, eds. *Anglo-Saxon Manuscripts and their Heritage*. Aldershot: Ashgate, 1998.
Rash, Felicity. *The German Language in Switzerland: Multilingualism, Diglossia and Variation*. German Linguistic and Cultural Studies 3. Bern: Peter Lang, 1998.
Richman, Gerald. "Speaker and Speech Boundaries in *The Wanderer*." *JEGP* 81 (1982): 469–79.
Robinson, Fred C. "Artful Ambiguities in the Old English 'Book-Moth' Riddle." In *Anglo-Saxon Poetry: Essays in Appreciation for John C. McGalliard*, ed. Nicholson and Frese, 355–62.
---. " 'The Rewards of Piety': Two Old English Poems in their Manuscript Context." In *Hermeneutics and Medieval Culture*, ed. Gallagher and Damico, 193–200.
Ronalds, Craig, and Margaret Clunies Ross. "*Thureth*: A Neglected Old English Poem and its History in Anglo-Saxon Scholarship." *Notes and Queries* 246, N.S. 48 (2001): 359–70.
Rumble, Alexander R., ed. *Writing and Texts in Anglo-Saxon England*. Cambridge: D. S. Brewer, 2006.
Saenger, Paul. *Space Between Words: The Origins of Silent Reading*. Stanford: Stanford University Press, 2000.
Sanders, Barry. "Lie It as it Plays." In *Literacy and Orality*, ed. Olson and Torrance, 111–128.
de Saussure, Ferdinand. *Course in General Linguistics*, ed. Charles Bally, Albert Sechehaye, and Albert Riedlinger, trans. Wade Baskin. New York: McGraw-Hill, 1966.

Schaefer, Ursula. "Hearing from Books: The Rise of Fictionality in Old English Poetry." In *Vox Intexta: Orality and Textuality in the Middle Ages*, ed. Doane and Pasternack, 117–136.

———. "From an Aesthetic Point of View ...: Receptional Aspects of Old English Poetry." In *De Gustibus: Essays for Alain Renoir*, ed. Foley, 494–541.

———. *Vokalität: Altenglische Dichtung zwischen Mündlichkeit und Schriftlichkeit*. Scripta Oralia 39. Tübingen: Gunter Narr Verlag, 1992.

Schlauch, M. "*The Dream of the Rood* as Prosopopoeia." In *Essays and Studies in Honor of Carleton Brown*, ed. Long, 23–34.

Schofield, Henry. "Signy's Lament." *PMLA* 17 (1902): 262–95.

Scholes, Robert J., and Brenda J. Willis. "Linguists, Literacy, and the Intensionality of Marshall McLuhan's Western Man." In *Literacy and Orality*, ed. Olson and Torrance, 215–35.

Searle, John R. *Expression and Meaning: Studies in the Theory of Speech Acts*. Cambridge: Cambridge University Press, 1979.

Sedgefield, W. J. "Old English Notes." *MLR* 26 (1931): 74–75.

Shippey, T. A. *Old English Verse*. London: Hutchinson, 1972.

———, ed. *Poems of Wisdom and Learning in Old English*. Cambridge: Brewer, 1976.

Sievers, Eduard. "Zu Cynewulf." *Anglia* 13 (1891): 1–25.

Sisam, Kenneth. "Cynewulf and his Poetry." *Proceedings of the British Academy* 18 (1932): 3–31. Repr. in Sisam, *Studies in the History of Old English Literature*, 1–28.

———. *Studies in the History of Old English Literature*. Oxford: Oxford University Press, 1953. Repr. with corrections, 1962.

Stanley, E. G. "Old English Poetic Diction and the Interpretation of *The Wanderer, The Seafarer* and *The Penitent's Prayer*." *Anglia* 73 (1955): 413–66.

———. "Heroic Aspects of the Exeter Book Riddles." In *Prosody and Poetics in the Early Middle Ages: Essays in Honour of C. B. Hieatt*, ed. Toswell, 197–218.

Stevens, Martin. "The Narrator of *The Wife's Lament*." *NM* 69 (1968): 72–90.

———, and Jerome Mandel, eds. *Old English Literature: Twenty-two Analytical Essays*. Lincoln: University of Nebraska Press, 1968.

Stork, Nancy Porter. *Through a Gloss Darkly: Aldhelm's Riddles in the British Library MS Royal 12.C.xxiii*. Toronto: PIMS, 1990.

Street, Brian V. *Literacy in Theory and Practice*. Cambridge Studies in Oral and Literate Culture 9. Cambridge: Cambridge University Press, 1984. Repr. 1995.

Svenbro, Jesper. *Phrasikleia: An Anthropology of Reading in Ancient Greece*, trans. Janet Lloyd. Ithaca and London: Cornell University Press, 1993.

Swanton, Michael, ed. *The Dream of the Rood*. Manchester: Manchester University Press, 1970.

Toller, T. Northcote. *An Anglo-Saxon Dictionary Supplement*. Oxford: Oxford University Press, 1921. Repr. with revised Addenda by Alistair Campbell, 1972.

Toswell, M. J., ed. *Prosody and Poetics in the Early Middle Ages: Essays in Honour of C. B. Hieatt.* Toronto: University of Toronto Press, 1995.

Tupper, Frederick, Jr., ed. *The Riddles of the Exeter Book.* Boston: Ginn, 1910. Repr. Darmstadt: Wissenschaftliche Buchgesellschaft, 1968.

Webster, Leslie, and Janet Backhouse, eds. *The Making of England: Anglo-Saxon Art and Culture, AD 600–900.* London: British Museum Press, 1991.

Whitbread, L. G. "The Old English Poem *Aldhelm.*" *English Studies* 57 (1976): 193–97.

Whitman, F. J. "Riddle 60 and its Source." *PQ* 50 (1971): 108–15.

Williamson, Craig, ed. *The Old English Riddles of the Exeter Book.* Chapel Hill: University of North Carolina Press, 1977.

Woodhead, A. G. *The Study of Greek Inscriptions.* Cambridge: Cambridge University Press, 1959.

Woolf, Rosemary, ed. *Juliana.* 2nd ed. London: Methuen, 1966.

Wormald, C. P. "The Uses of Literacy in Anglo-Saxon England and its Neighbours." *Transactions of the Royal Historical Society*, 5th ser., 27 (1977): 95–114.

Wyatt, A. J., ed. *Old English Riddles.* Boston: Heath, 1912.

Yerkes, David. "The Full Text of the Metrical Preface to Wærferth's Translation of Gregory." *Speculum* 55 (1980): 505–13.

Zacher, Samantha. "Cynewulf at the Interface of Literacy and Orality: The Evidence of the Puns in *Elene.*" *Oral Tradition* 17 (2002): 346–87.